ACCOUNTING FOR FINANCIAL INSTRUMENTS

Accounting for Financial Instruments is about the accounting and regulatory framework associated with the acquisition and disposal of financial instruments; how to determine their value; how to manage the risk connected with them; and ultimately compile a Business Valuation Report.

Specifically, the book covers the following topics, among others: accounting for investments; bills of exchange; management of financial risks; financial analysis (including the Financial Analysis Report); valuation of a business (including the Business Valuation Report) and money laundering. *Accounting for Financial Instruments* fills a gap in the current literature for a comprehensive text that brings together relevant accounting concepts and valid regulatory frameworks, and related procedures regarding the management of financial instruments (investments), which are applicable in the modern business world.

Understanding financial risk management allows the reader to comprehend the importance of analysing a business concern. This is achieved by presenting an analytical framework to illustrate that an entity's performance is greatly influenced by its external and internal environments. The analysis of the external environment examines factors that impact an entity's operational activities, strategic choices, and influence its opportunities and risks. The analysis of the internal environment applies accounting ratio analysis to an entity's financial statements to examine various elements, including liquidity, profitability, asset utilisation, investment, working capital management and capital structure.

The objective of the book is to provide a fundamental knowledge base for those who are interested in managing financial instruments (investments) or studying banking and finance or those who wish to make financial services, particularly banking and finance, their chosen career. *Accounting for Financial Instruments* is highly applicable to both professional accountants and auditors and students alike.

Emanuel Camilleri was the Director General (Strategy and Operations Support) at the Ministry of Finance, the Economy and Investment, Government of Malta. He has had a long career in the Australian defence industry public sector related to ICT and Operations Research applications, and has managed large projects related to accounting applications and Public Service reforms at the Inland Revenue and VAT Departments in Malta. He is a visiting senior lecturer at the Faculty of Economics, Management and Accountancy, University of Malta. Dr Camilleri is Chairman, Privatisation Unit within Ministry for the Economy, Investment and Small Business (Government of Malta), which has the responsibility to privatise Government assets and issue a wide range of long term concessions related to a diverse spectrum of industries and also Chairman, Foundation for Tomorrow's Schools within Ministry for Education and Employment (Government of Malta), which has the responsibility for the schools building and maintenance programme of Government's Public Education sector with a major aim of introducing reforms related to accounting controls and project management.

Roxanne Camilleri is currently a senior auditor with a leading global accountancy firm, RSM. Previously, she held a position of senior auditor with Grant Thornton. Roxanne has conducted accounting audits of many types and sizes of entities both in the private and public sector in Malta and many other European countries for the last six years. Roxanne has a Bachelor of Science Degree (Honours) in Applied Accounting from Oxford-Brooks University, UK and an Advanced Diploma in Accounting and Business from ACCA. Currently, she is undertaking the final ACCA study unit in Taxation Accounting. Roxanne has completed the full ACCA programme, including the professional modules. She is fluent in four languages; Maltese, English, French and Italian.

ACCOUNTING FOR FINANCIAL INSTRUMENTS

A Guide to Valuation and Risk Management

Emanuel Camilleri
and Roxanne Camilleri

Routledge
Taylor & Francis Group

LONDON AND NEW YORK

First published 2017
by Routledge
2 Park Square, Milton Park, Abingdon, Oxon OX14 4RN

and by Routledge
711 Third Avenue, New York, NY 10017

*Routledge is an imprint of the Taylor & Francis Group,
an informa business*

British Library Cataloguing-in-Publication Data
A catalogue record for this book is available from the British Library

Library of Congress Cataloging-in-Publication Data
A catalogue record for this book has been requested.

ISBN: 978-1-138-23757-5 (hbk)
ISBN: 978-1-138-23759-9 (pbk)
ISBN: 978-1-315-29943-3 (ebk)

Typeset in Bembo
by Florence Production Limited, Stoodleigh, Devon, UK

To Mary Anne, a wonderful wife and mother

CONTENTS

FIGURES

TABLES

FOREWORD

Accounting standards have recently been under review and changes introduced have implications for auditors. This book represents a welcome guide to valuation and risk management as part of accounting for financial instruments. It goes beyond the theory as it is illustrated with a diverse number of practical examples which students and practitioners will find useful when planning and performing auditing procedures related to financial instruments. Originators of financial instruments are continuously developing new products and it is a challenge to provide an exhaustive list of all such instruments. However, the list of examples in this book is to be considered quite exhaustive.

The general principles applicable to auditing financial instruments are applicable to all entities. The guidance in this book is intended to be helpful for auditing of entities with different levels of use of financial instruments. The relevance of each area of guidance may differ considerably between different entities. However, the auditor of an entity with relatively few transactions may also have problems not typically faced in an entity with high levels of trading/use of financial instruments.

This book clearly brings to light that the audit engagement team needs to include members with appropriate competence and capabilities to perform the audit work. The complexity inherent in auditing some financial instruments means that there may be areas of the audit that require particular skills and expertise. At the forefront are valuation and risk management. An understanding of these can help an auditor to identify whether important aspects of a transaction are missing or inaccurately recorded, whether a valuation appears appropriate and whether the risks inherent in them are fully understood and controlled by the entity. Valuations of financial instruments which may be volatile need to be accurate. Large and sudden decreases in value may increase the risk that a loss may exceed the amount recorded on the balance sheet.

This book also provides the auditor with an understanding of the risks to which transacted financial instruments expose an entity. Obtaining an understanding of an entity's use of financial instruments and the related risks assists the auditor in identifying and assessing the risks of material misstatement in the financial statements and designing audit procedures in response to those risks.

Dr Camilleri is to be commended for writing what is clearly a highly recommended exhaustive text on valuations and risk for financial instruments.

Prof J.V. Bannister
Chairman Malta Financial Services Authority

PREFACE AND ACKNOWLEDGEMENTS

This book, entitled *Accounting for Financial Instruments: A Guide to Valuation and Risk Management* is in response to a common criticism about the lack of a holistic text that embraces the fundamental accounting concepts for those commencing their profession in financial services. The term financial services includes a wide spectrum of activities, such as commercial banking, corporate finance, financial planning, hedge funds, insurance, investment banking, money management, private equity and real estate. While these diverse financial services require different skills and talents, they all require a good understanding of accounting and written communication skills.

This book is about the accounting and regulatory framework associated with the acquisition and disposal of financial instruments; how to determine their value; how to manage the risk connected with them; and ultimately compile a business valuation report. Financial instruments are tradable assets that include cash, shares, stock, bonds, ownership of an entity, or a contractual right to receive or deliver cash or another financial instrument. Hence, issues related to money laundering also become notable.

The objective of this book is to provide a fundamental knowledge base for those who are interested in managing financial instruments (investments) or studying banking and finance or those who wish to make financial services, particularly banking and finance, their chosen career.

The book structure leads the reader through different concepts. It commences with a concise explanation of the accounting process by explaining the common business activities, such as operational, financing and investment management, leading to the examination of the accounts maintained by companies and the key components of the financial statements. The diversity of financial instruments requires an accounting and regulatory framework. These are the relevant accounting standards (US GAAP and International Financial Reporting Standards) and the accounting treatment for each category of financial instruments. The focus at this point is on the classification and measurement of financial instruments, such as held-to-maturity, loans and receivables that are both measured at amortised cost; and fair value through profit or loss and available-for-sale both of which are measured at fair value. These concepts are important due to the accounting implications when purchasing and selling financial instruments, particularly when the transaction date is not the maturity date, where complex adjustments are needed.

Once the accounting fundamentals are explained, the book shifts its attention to the business and financial analysis of organisations by first focusing on financial risk management. Risk may stem from events taking place across the globe that have nothing to do with the domestic markets and yet have a significant and immediate effect on domestic events. ICT has caused information to be available instantly, thus becoming a very swift change catalyst, with subsequent financial market reactions occurring rapidly; for example, the immediate financial market reaction in Europe and USA to the Asian financial crisis of 1997–1998 and the financial crisis of 2009–2010. Basically, financial risk management is the identification of what may go wrong and taking the appropriate action to mitigate risks in terms of credit, market, foreign exchange, interest rates and commodity prices, among others that are associated with volatility, liquidity and inflation, where the financial markets' reaction to such changes can swiftly become problematic. Financial risk management focuses on when and how to hedge using financial instruments to manage harmful exposures to risk.

Understanding financial risk management allows the reader to comprehend the importance of analysing a business concern. This is achieved by presenting an analytical framework to illustrate that an entity's performance is greatly influenced by its external and internal environments. The analysis of the external environment examines factors that impact an entity's operational activities, strategic choices, and influence its opportunities and risks. On the other hand, the analysis of the internal environment applies accounting ratio analysis to an entity's financial statements to examine various elements, including liquidity, profitability, asset utilisation, investment, working capital management and capital structure.

Analysing a business concern also provides the basis for assessing an entity's market value. Business valuation is a process employed to approximate the economic value of an owner's interest in a business. Numerous valuation methods are explored that are classified under two main categories, namely non-going concern (an entity that will not remain in business) and going concern. The analysis and valuation of a business concern provides the basis for the Business Valuation Report. The book explains the format and contents of the Business Valuation Report using best practice. It is appropriate for a book regarding financial instruments to also address money laundering issues. The business community, in recent years, has had to face an increasing number of regulations regarding anti- money laundering. There are two important implications, first, the impact of enforceable regulatory measures affects every enterprise, irrespective of size and second, regulatory issues are constantly being reviewed and will have a significant impact on enterprises in the future.

In the recent past, I had the pleasure of lecturing a study unit (Accounting for Bankers) for the third year, University of Malta, BCom (Hon) students in Bank and Finance. To my disappointment there was not a single text which brought together in a structured and systematic manner the various topics within the study unit. The topics were spread through a diverse number of text books. Furthermore, not a single book illustrated how a Financial Analysis Report and Business Valuation Report may be formulated and compiled according to best practice. This book is written in a way that the average reader will find interesting and the more inquisitive reader will find challenging.

Finally, I would like to acknowledge the effort of all the staff at Routledge, namely Kristina Abbotts who provided her invaluable and professional advice regarding the development of the general concept of this book and its specific focus; Emma Redley who assisted me with formatting the book and ensuring that I followed the established Routledge standards; Alice Stoakley who meticulously carried out the corrections and copy editing; Laurence Paul for his valuable assistance in the production process as Project Manager; and the marketing team for the professional way they promoted this book.

Emanuel Camilleri
Roxanne Camilleri

ABBREVIATIONS

AFS	available-for-sale
AICPA	American Institute of Certified Public Accountants
AML	anti-money laundering
ASC	Accounting Standards Codification
AUD	Australian dollar
AVCO	average weighted cost
BCBS	Basel Committee on Banking Supervision
BEPS	base erosion and profit shifting
bp	basis points
BSA	Bank Secrecy Act
CAD	Canadian dollar
CBOT	Chicago Board of Trade
CDD	customer due diligence
CFO	Chief Finance Officer
CFPB	Consumer Financial Protection Bureau
CFT	counter-terrorist financing
CHF	Swiss franc
CLO	collateralised loan obligations
Cr	credit
CRO	Chief Risk Officer
cum-div	cumulative dividend
cum-int	cumulative interest
DNFBP	designated non-financial businesses and professions
Dr	debit
EBIT	earnings before interest and tax
ECB	euro area treasury bills
EDD	enhanced due diligence

EMU	European Monetary Union
EOL	Enron Online
ER	effective interest rate
EU	European Union
Euribor	Euro Interbank Offered Rate
ex-div	excluding dividend
ex-int	excluding interest
FASB	Financial Accounting Standards Board
FATF	Financial Action Task Force
FDIC	Federal Deposit Insurance Corporation
FIFO	first-in-first-out
FinCEN	Financial Crimes Enforcement Network
FIU	Financial Intelligence Unit
FRS	Federal Reserve System
FSA	Financial Services Authority
FSB	Financial Stability Board
FVTPL	fair value through profit or loss
GAAP	US General Accepted Accounting Practices
GBP	pound sterling
GIGO	garbage-in garbage-out
HFT	held for trading
HTM	held-to-maturity
IAS	International Accounting Standards
IAS 19	Employee Benefits
IAS 27	Consolidated and Separate Financial Statements
IAS 28	Investments in Associates
IAS 31	Interests in Joint Ventures
IAS 32	Financial Instruments: Presentation
IAS 39	Financial Instruments: Recognition and Measurement
IASB	International Accounting Standards Board
ICT	Information Communications Technology
IFRS	International Financial Reporting Standards
IFRS 4	Insurance Contracts
IFRS 7	Financial Instruments: Disclosures
IFRS 9	Classification, measurement, de-recognition of financial assets/liabilities
IRR	internal rate of return
IRS	Internal Revenue Service
IVSC	International Valuation Standards Council
L & R	loans and receivables
LIBOR	London Interbank Offer Rate
ML	money laundering
MLCA	Money Laundering Control Act
MLSA	Money Laundering Suppression Act

MOU	Memorandum of Understanding
MVTS	money or value transfer services
NAV	net asset value
NCUA	National Credit Union Administration
NPV	net present value
NYSE	New York Stock Exchange
OCC	Office of the Comptroller of the Currency
OCI	other comprehensive income
OECD	Organisation for Economic Co-operation and Development
OSE	Osaka Stock Exchange
OTC	over-the-counter
P/E	price-earnings ratio
PEP	politically exposed person
PEST	political, economic, social and technological
Pr	probability
PV	present value
RA	Risk Analyst
ROCE	return on capital employed
ROE	return on equity
SAR	Suspicious Activity Report
SBSE	small business and self-employment
SEC	Securities and Exchange Commission
SIMEX	Singapore Money Exchange
SPE	special-purpose entity
SRO	self-regulatory organisation
STR	Suspicious Transaction Report
SWOT	strengths, weaknesses, opportunities and threats
TEGE	tax exempt and government entities
UK	United Kingdom
USA	United States of America
USD	US dollar

PART 1

Accounting fundamentals

The objective of this part is to set the scene and provide the fundamental accounting knowledge that a novice in financial services practice needs to master in the turbulent world of finance. There is an explanation of the accounting principles related to the documentation of business transactions and the classification of business activities, so that voluminous transactions may be presented in a concise and logical manner that enable them to be easily understood by the users of the financial reports.

This part will help the reader to understand the application of three important accounting concepts, namely the accounting process, the double entry bookkeeping method, and the relationship between the accounting financial statements. The accounting process consists of a series of steps that begins with a business transaction and ends with the closing of the accounts and the compilation of the financial statements. Since this process is repeated each reporting period, it is often referred to as the accounting cycle or bookkeeping cycle. The steps in the accounting process adhere to a number of rules and conventions that abide by the accepted accounting standards.

Understanding the relationship between the accounting process and the double-entry bookkeeping framework to obtain a holistic view of the accounting cycle becomes critical, because the financial statements generated by the accounting system provide the underlying information for analysing the financial position of an entity, including credit and equity analysis, and security valuation

1

INTRODUCTION

I never teach my pupils. I only attempt to provide the conditions in which they can learn.

Albert Einstein
Theoretical physicist and philosopher

This book is in response to a common criticism about the lack of a text that embraces the fundamental accounting concepts for those commencing their profession in financial services. The term financial services includes a wide spectrum of activities, such as commercial banking, corporate finance, financial planning, hedge funds, insurance, investment banking, money management, private equity and real estate. While these diverse financial services require different skills and talents, they all require a good understanding of accounting and written communication skills. The level of accounting knowledge does not need to be that of a professional accountant but must be sufficient for one to understand the rationale behind the various accounting entries and to critically analyse accounting numbers.

Book structure and contents

As the book title suggests, the objective of this text is to provide a fundamental knowledge base for those studying banking and finance or those who wish to make financial services, particularly banking and finance, their chosen career. Figure 1.1 illustrates that this book is divided into four related parts, comprising 12 chapters.

Part 1 – Accounting fundamentals

This part of the book consists of three chapters. These three chapters progressively build the readers' knowledge about the fundamental accounting principles. This first

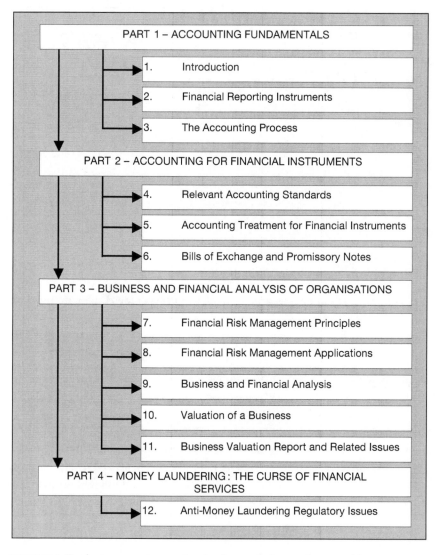

FIGURE 1.1 Book structure: accounting fundamentals for services practitioners

chapter presents a description of the general book structure. Chapter 2 provides a detailed explanation of the financial reporting instruments by presenting the applicable key accounting concepts. It provides a detailed discussion about the common classification of business activities, namely operational, financing and investment management. Chapter 2 also examines the typical accounts maintained by companies and the components of the key financial statements. This includes an explanation of the accounting equations related to the balance sheet, income statement and statement of retained earnings.

Chapter 3, which is the final chapter in Part 1, elaborates further on the accounting principles discussed in Chapter 2. Chapter 3 examines in detail the accounting process, which consists of eight major phases, starting with the initial business transactions and ending with the closing of the accounts and the compilation of the financial statements. The section dealing with the accounting process illustrates the double entry accounting method, which forms an essential basis for posting the accounting transactions into the various company accounts. Finally, Chapter 3 will illustrate the relationship between the financial statements. In other words, it shows how certain balance sheet items are related to the cash flow statement and the statement of owners' equity; and how the resultant net income (loss) from the income statement is related to the retained earnings in the statement of owners' equity. Therefore, these first three chapters provide the reader with a concise explanation of the accounting process and set the scene for the rest of the book. Most importantly, Part 1 provides the fundamental accounting knowledge that a novice in financial services practice needs to master in the turbulent world of finance.

Part 2 – Accounting for financial instruments

This part also consists of three chapters and will specifically focus on the accounting principles related to financial instruments, namely accounting for investments. Each chapter within this part will focus on an explicit accounting aspect. Chapter 4 focuses on the relevant accounting standards related to financial instruments. The International Financial Reporting Standards (IFRS) and US General Accepted Accounting Practices (GAAP) will be examined and discussed in the context of accounting for investments. The four most important IFRS accounting standards that will be closely examined include IAS 32 (Financial Instruments: Presentation); IAS 39 (Financial Instruments: Recognition and Measurement); IFRS 7 (Financial Instruments: Disclosures); and IFRS 9 (classification, measurement and de-recognition of financial assets and liabilities). The GAAP clauses will be discussed in relation to how they compare with the relevant IFRS standards. Chapter 4 identifies the important definitions related to financial instruments and addresses the issues regarding the implications of IAS 32 and IAS 39.

The discussion regarding IAS 32 will focus on a number of key issues, such as the distinction between a financial liability and equity and the determination of how equity shares are accounted for. IAS 39 focuses on the recognition and measurement of financial instruments and specifically addresses the way financial assets are classified and measured, such as, held-to-maturity (HTM) and loans and receivables that are both measured at amortised cost; fair value through profit or loss (FVTPL) and available-for-sale (AFS) both of which are measured at fair value. While FVTPL is measured at fair value through profit or loss, AFS is measured at fair value through equity. IAS 39 also provides a detailed definition of each financial instrument category and other useful definitions, such as fair value and amortisation. IFRS 9 is intended to replace IAS 39. In fact, a number of features related to IFRS 9 have already been implemented, namely the classification and measurement of financial assets and liabilities, and de-recognition of financial assets and liabilities.

Chapter 5 builds on the knowledge of the previous chapter and explicitly addresses the accounting treatment method for each financial instrument category that was identified when discussing the relevant accounting standards. Additionally, the accounting treatment discussion also provides an explanation of the difference in the accounting book entries for each type of financial instrument. Moreover, this chapter provides an explanation of important additional definitions in relation to purchasing and selling of financial instruments, namely, cumulative dividend investments and excluding. dividend investments. Chapter 5 will examine the accounting implications when purchasing and selling financial instruments. Certain issues arise when financial instruments are purchased or sold at a date other than their maturity date.

Cumulative dividend or cumulative interest (cum-div or cum-int) means that a buyer of a security is entitled to receive a dividend or interest that has been declared, but not paid. This means that the security is offered for sale with an entitlement to the next dividend or interest payment attached. This dividend or interest will already have been declared (but not paid) by the company, so the market knows how much it is worth and the share (or bond) price will reflect this. Excluding dividend or excluding interest (ex-div or ex-int) means that the declared dividend or interest will be received by the seller and not the buyer. Hence, stock is given ex-div or ex-int status if an individual or entity has been confirmed by the company to receive the dividend or interest payment. The purchase of shares or bonds without entitlement to recently declared dividends means that the entitlement to receive a dividend or interest remains with the seller of the shares or bonds. Hence, both cum-div and ex-div may require accounting adjustment entries to reflect these specific phenomena. Finally, Chapter 5 will provide a number of practical examples to illustrate the key accounting for investments principles.

The final chapter in Part 2 focuses on bills of exchange and promissory notes. Bills of exchange and promissory notes are a very common variety of financial instruments and have their own particular characteristics. Chapter 6 explains the meaning and implications of bills of exchange and promissory notes and illustrates the particular accounting entries related to them. In addition, this chapter illustrates other important concepts, namely, the computation of the due date related to bills of exchange and promissory notes; and the accounting treatment for the collection and retirement of the bills of exchange and promissory notes.

Part 3 – Business and financial analysis of organisations

Part 3 consists of five chapters and is the nucleus of this book. Chapter 7 provides a very detailed description of financial risk management principles. Basically, financial risk management is the identification of what may go wrong and taking the appropriate action to mitigate the risk. Risk can be mitigated but it is difficult to eliminate completely. Financial risk management endeavours to foresee and deal with uncertainties that jeopardise the financial objectives of an enterprise. It is the practice of using financial instruments to manage the exposure to risk in terms of credit risk, market risk, foreign exchange risk and other risks associated with volatility, liquidity and inflation.

Risk may stem from events taking place across the globe that have nothing to do with the domestic markets and yet have a significant and immediate effect on domestic events. ICT has caused information to be available instantly, thus becoming a very swift change catalyst, with subsequent financial market reactions occurring rapidly. Examples of this are the immediate financial market reaction in Europe and the USA to the Asian financial crisis of 1997–1998 and the financial crisis of 2009–2010.

Financial markets are very sensitive and can be rapidly affected by fluctuations in exchange rates, interest rates and commodity prices. The financial markets' reaction to such changes can swiftly become problematic. Therefore, it is important that financial risks are identified, appraised and continuously managed. Financial risk management is a systematic process to identify, quantify, respond to, and monitor and control all types of financial risk. Furthermore, financial risk management can be qualitative and quantitative. Financial risk management focuses on when and how to hedge using financial instruments to manage harmful exposures to risk.

One should note that regulatory pressures from the Financial Accounting Standards Board (FASB), particularly the International the Financial Reporting Standards (IFRS) are setting in motion measures for better risk management. Under IFRS, entities are required to conduct some basic type of risk measurement in the disclosures section of the financial statements. For instance, both FASB (Section 7a) and IFRS-7 related to 'Quantitative and Qualitative Disclosures' maintain that the financial statements must explicitly state the potential impact of market movements companies are principally exposed to, that is 'Financial Instruments Disclosures: a requirement exists to calculate the potential impact of each market risk variable or conduct a value-at-risk analysis.' Hence, the thrust from the accounting regulatory bodies is compelling entities to find a methodology that is suitable for their resource capability and is supportive to the general risk management policy. In addition, the international banking sector as a rule applies the Basel Accords for tracking, reporting and exposing operational, credit and market risks.

Chapter 8 focuses on financial risk management applications. Therefore, the major issue that will be addressed is when to use financial risk management. Managers of all types of entities are confronted with many opportunities to create value for shareholders using financial risk management. The basic concept is to determine which risks are cheaper for the entity to manage than the shareholders. By and large, market risks that result in unique risks for the entity are the best candidates for financial risk management. An important source of financial risk are those risks arising from an entity's exposure to changes in market prices, such as interest rates, exchange rates and commodity prices. The major concern is to determine when to use financial risk management to mitigate the risks that specifically arise from the changes in interest rates, exchange rates and commodity prices. One should note that financial rates and prices are affected by a number of factors. Hence, it is essential to understand the factors that impact markets because these factors, in turn, impact the potential risk of an entity.

The focus of Chapter 9 is the analysis of the business concern. In the context of this chapter, the 'analysis of the business concern' means the examination and assessment of both the external and internal environment. The basic premise is that an organisation's business and financial performance is influenced by its internal and external environment. Hence, how the organisation responds to these environments (whether reactive or proactive) will determine its business and financial performance.

The analysis of an entity's external environment will look at all outside factors that may affect an organisation. These factors envelop an organisation and have a direct impact on its operational activities, strategic choices, and influence its opportunities and risks. On the other hand, the assessment of an entity's internal environment will principally concentrate on the analysis of the entity's financial statements based on ratio analysis. In other words, the analysis of the internal environment will apply ratio analysis to the financial statements to examine various elements, including liquidity, profitability, asset utilisation, investment, working capital management and capital structure. Chapter 9 presents an analytical framework, which illustrates that an organisation's performance is greatly influenced by the external and internal environments in which it exists.

The focus of Chapter 10 is the valuation of a business. There are many instances when an objective and accurate assessment of a company's value is required. Business valuation is a process and a set of procedures employed to approximate the economic value of an owner's interest in a business. Determining the business worth of an enterprise is not an easy matter. In fact, the correct process to conduct a valuation of a business takes a great deal of effort, planning and reflection. Additionally, it is difficult to determine the value of a business enterprise because there are no precise methods to do this. The term 'business value' means different things to different people. The tendency is for one party to a transaction to increase the value, and for the other to drive the price down.

The determination of the value of a business also depends on the valuation assumptions. For instance, a business owner may assume that a strong linkage between the business and its client base (i.e. goodwill) is worth a great deal. On the other hand, an investor may have the perception that the business value is entirely defined by its historic income stream. Therefore, it all depends on why the valuation is taking place and the circumstances the business is encountering. While there are somewhat straightforward approaches to value particular segments of the business, such as stock and fixed assets (e.g. land, machinery, equipment, etc.), there may be a significant intangible component that is difficult to value. These intangible components include 'goodwill', such as trademarks, a business client base and the reputation of the entity. It is these components that are extremely difficult to value, and in many cases, the value of a business will be based upon the eagerness of a potential buyer to acquire the business in question.

Chapter 10 will be focusing on a number of valuation methods that will be classified under two main categories, namely non-going concern (an entity that will not remain in business) and a going concern (an entity that will remain in business for the foreseeable future). There is only one method under the non-going concern category, namely the asset break-up approach. However, the going concern category contains a number of different valuation methods that are commonly used. These include:

- The asset approach, consisting of three techniques, namely book value, replacement cost, and book value plus goodwill;
- The yield basis, consisting of three techniques, namely earning yield, price-earnings ratio, and dividend yield);
- The economic value, namely the discounted cash flow technique.

Chapter 10 will examine the above valuation methods and explore how other factors may influence the value of a business at any given time. The final chapter within Part 3 is Chapter 11. Chapter 11 specifically addresses the issue of preparing the Business Valuation Report. The application of the analytical information that was the object of a number of previous chapters is the Business Valuation Report. It is therefore appropriate to have a chapter devoted to this aspect to provide the reader with a more comprehensive explanation of the format and contents of the Business Valuation Report using best practice criterion. One must recognise that businesses are being continually transacted, like every other commodity. Therefore, there are numerous situations when an objective and accurate assessment of a business's value is required. Moreover, the previous chapter focused on the procedures to establishing a simple but realistic process by which the value of a business may be determined. This chapter will take the topic of business valuation a step further. It will explain the format and content (i.e. presentation) of the Business Valuation Report based on best practice criterion.

Part 4 – Money laundering: the curse of financial services

Chapter 12 is the final chapter and is specifically about money laundering. As a concluding chapter about the accounting fundamentals for financial services, it is appropriate to focus on the regulatory provisions when dealing with investments. In earlier chapters when discussing accounting practices, certain accounting standards regarding investments were addressed in some detail. The business community in recent years has had to face an increasing number of regulations that require a formalised process that spans a wide spectrum of activities. This final chapter is related to the regulatory provisions when dealing with investments, specifically regarding anti-money laundering.

In this context, Chapter 12 has two important implications. First, the impact of enforceable regulatory measures affects every enterprise, irrespective of size. Second, this chapter examines contemporary regulatory issues, some of which are still under discussion, and will have a significant impact on enterprises in the future, suggesting that the topics covered are relatively new and are still evolving.

Accounting for Financial Instruments: A Guide to Valuation and Risk Management provides a sound knowledge base for those studying banking and finance or those who wish to make financial services, particularly banking and finance, their chosen career.

2

FINANCIAL REPORTING INSTRUMENTS

> Everything that can be counted does not necessarily count; everything that counts cannot necessarily be counted.
>
> Albert Einstein
> Theoretical physicist and philosopher

The key objective of accounting is to provide financial information about any economic entity. This information is utilised by both internal and external stakeholders. Hence, the internal stakeholders, such as management, use the information as an aid to planning and controlling the various business activities of the organisation. Additionally, the external stakeholders, such as owners, investors, creditors and the general public as potential investors, use the information to assess the operating results and financial position of the entity.

A key function of accounting is recording what is taking place within the business enterprise. First, an enterprise needs a system of documenting the various business transactions that are continuously taking place. However, these transactions must be recorded in monetary terms. A business can be visualised as a collection of economic resources with specific objectives, usually defined within the business strategy. Thus, transactions are actually documenting how the economic resources of an organisation are being employed to promote the growth of the business enterprise.

Second, the transactions are usually classified into some logical order, depicting the business activities of the enterprise. Basic business activities include operations, financing and investment activities. Such a classification would help to reduce the voluminous amount of transactions detail into manageable decipherable information that can be understood and used by management. For example, transactions related to a company's financing activities provide information about how the entity is obtaining or repaying its capital.

Third, to be meaningful and helpful to the various stakeholders, the information that has been recorded and classified must be presented in a format that can be easily understood, typically referred to as financial statements. The normal financial statements prepared by companies are: statement of financial position (balance sheet); statement of comprehensive income (profit and loss statement); statement of changes in equity; and statement of cash flows. Additionally, these financial statements are customarily supported by notes to the financial statements; an explanation of financial policies; and management discussion and analysis.

The three stages described above are supported by an accounting process which consists of eight major phases, starting with a transaction and ending with the closing of the accounts and the compilation of the financial statements. Furthermore, as one may appreciate, accounting has evolved over several hundreds of years where rules, conventions and procedures have been documented into accepted accounting standards.

It must be emphasised that accounting is not just limited to generating business data. Accounting transforms business data into information which may be further analysed and interpreted. Thus, accounting embraces the data-information-knowledge-wisdom transformation process. The enterprise commences with the business transactions data. This data must be gathered and organised. The accounting transactions data is processed and transformed to accounting information through summarisation and analysis (that is, compiling of the financial statements and financial ratio analysis). This accounting information is transformed into knowledge by the process of amalgamating data and information for decision making through information interpretation and resultant decisions. Finally, an accumulation of knowledge becomes wisdom, which consists of lessons learnt from previous interpretation and resultant decisions over time. Wisdom deals with the future because it incorporates both vision and design. With wisdom, management can create the future, not just grasp the present and past.

Documenting business transactions

The volume of transactions that a business enterprise encounters in a financial year depends on the size of the entity and the nature of its business. Hence, an entity, such as a bank would handle millions of transactions while in a small business, such as a mechanic, these transactions may still run into the thousands. Whatever the magnitude of the business, the transactions must be carefully documented and recorded. Transactions may include cash deposits; cash and credit sales; procurement activities; staff appointments; staff salaries; adjustments; and many other types of activities that are related to the running of a business enterprise.

Documentation for these transactions normally requires that the records supporting a transaction contain the appropriate approval and authorisation. Moreover, the documentation must support the internal controls that are applicable for the specific transaction type within the organisation. The extent of transaction documentation depends on the accounting system implemented within the organisation.

Minimum documentation is required where the implemented system controls ensure the mitigation of errors. For instance, where transactions are reviewed and approved by someone other than the initiator before it is recorded in the accounting system. Minimum documentation is also required when the accounting system is self-documenting. For instance, a computer accounting systems may be designed to automatically record the transaction description, purpose and the identity of the transaction initiator. Hence, the transaction can be audited from the accounting system itself. However, a higher level of documentation is required for transactions that are of a significantly large value and the transaction is associated with a legally binding contract.

Classification of business activities

One should note that typically business transactions are all given the same accounting treatment. Combined with the fact that a business enterprise may have a huge number of transactions, this makes it difficult to comprehend the holistic accounting transaction information. Therefore, for financial reporting purposes, it is essential that transactions are classified into a small number of transaction categories to depict the business activities of the enterprise. This enables voluminous business transactions to be presented in a concise and logical manner so that they may be easily understood by the users of financial reports.

For financial reporting purposes, business activities may be classified into three key categories, namely operating, investing and financing activities. Operating activities consist of the routine business functions of the organisation. For example, a supermarket's key operational activities are to procure products at wholesale prices and selling these products at retail prices to the various customers; and a hair salon's primary operational activities are to provide the diverse services related to hair care. Investing activities are activities that are concerned with the purchase and sale of fixed assets (or long-term assets), such as property, plant and equipment; and financial instruments such as company shares and securities (bonds and debentures). Financing activities consist of activities associated with securing and paying back capital funding. For example, the issuance of common shares; taking out a bank loan; and issuing bonds.

This type of classification allows the user of financial information to understand how well the company is performing and to determine the profitable and not so profitable business lines. For instance, the generation of the entity's cash flow and resultant profit should mostly be triggered through its operating activities, because an entity's operating activities are viewed as the business's core activities.

Company accounts and key financial statement components

The compilation of financial statements is not the first step in the accounting process, but it is a suitable stage to commence the study of accounting. Financial statements provide a concise depiction of a company's financial position and profitability to management and other relevant stakeholders. In fact, the financial statements are the end product of the accounting process. Having a clear understanding of the financial statements allows one to comprehend the objective and importance of recording and classifying business transactions that were described previously.

Our focus will be limited to four key financial statements, namely the balance sheet (statement of financial position); the income statement; the statement of cash flows; and statement of owners' equity. By and large, the activities of an enterprise that result from the various business transactions are exhibited in a number of generalised categories within the financial statements. These generalised categories within the financial statements include:

- Assets. These represent the different types of economic resources owned or controlled by the business entity. Examples of asset accounts include cash, buildings, inventory, prepaid rent, goodwill, and accounts receivable.
- Liabilities. These correspond to the various types of economic obligations by a business entity, such as accounts payable, bank loan, bonds payable, and accrued interest.
- Owners' equity. This represents the residual equity of a business (after deducting from the assets all the liabilities) including retained earnings and appropriations.
- Revenues. These represent the company's gross earnings. In other words, they reflect the inflows of economic resources to the company. Common examples include sales, service revenue and interest income.
- Expenses. These represent the outflows of economic resources from the company or increases in the liabilities. They reflect the company's expenditures to enable it to operate, such as, electricity and water, rentals, depreciation, doubtful accounts, interest, and insurance.

Under US General Accepted Accounting Practices (GAAP), the financial statement components include assets, liabilities, owners' equity, revenue, expenses, gains and losses. On the other hand, the International Financial Reporting Standards (IFRS) make use of the term 'income' that includes both revenue and gains. For example, the sale of surplus office equipment for more than its cost is referred to as a gain rather than revenue. Similarly, a loss is analogous to an expense but it does not arise from the company's core business activities. For example, if the company sells its surplus office equipment for an amount which is less than its book value, a loss results because selling surplus equipment is not a primary activity for the firm. One should note that gains and losses may be considered part of operations or part of non-operating activities on the income statement. For example, a gain that results from an increase in the value of inventory would be considered as part of operations, whereas, sales of non-trading investments are viewed as non-operating activities.

Generally, business transactions are recorded on the various company accounts, which provide an individual record of any increase or decrease in a particular asset, liability, revenue or expense. The financial statements are compiled by making use of these accounts. It should be noted that there is no standard group of accounts applicable to all companies. The accounts that a particular company uses depends on its specific requirements and the accounting system adopted. The accounts that are used by a company are itemised and described in a chart of accounts. A chart of accounts is a list of the accounts used by a company to define each class of items for which money or the equivalent is spent or received. Hence, a chart of accounts is used to organise the finances of the company and to segregate assets, liabilities, revenue and expenditure so that these accounts may be utilised to compile the financial statements. Furthermore, the structure and headings of accounts should be established to assist in the consistent recording (posting) of transactions on the accounts.

The chart of accounts is typically designed to integrate with the predetermined classification of the financial statements components. Table 2.1 illustrates a simple chart of accounts. All business transactions would be posted to the appropriate account by using the account code. The compilation of the financial statements is made possible by displaying the various accounts within the appropriate account category. This makes it possible for the user of the financial statement to see a concise financial and income position of the entity without having to view the voluminous business transactions that are processed by the organisation.

In the financial statements, assets are divided into three key categories, namely current assets, fixed tangible assets and intangible assets. Current assets include asset items that can be converted to cash fairly quickly, such as inventories; trade and other receivables; and cash and cash equivalents. Inventories consist of products that are held by the entity to be sold to its various customers. Inventories act as a buffer to balance the demand and supply position over a time period. Accounts receivables (also known as trade receivables or debtors) are amounts that are owed to the entity by its customers. These normally result when customers buy from the company on credit or are amounts that may be due from suppliers due to returns of goods. Cash refers to cash in a bank account and cash-on-hand, such as petty cash and cash that have not been deposited in the bank. Cash equivalents are very liquid short-term investments that have a maturity period of 90 days or less.

Fixed tangible assets and intangible assets are designated as non-current assets. These types of assets tend to benefit the entity over a longer period of time, normally more than one year. Examples of fixed tangible assets include property (land and buildings), plant and equipment; while intangible assets include patents, goodwill, trademarks and brand names. Other tangible assets that are classified as non-current assets include investment property; and investments in joint ventures and associates, as well as investments in the securities of other companies.

Some accounts are used to offset other accounts, which are known as 'contra accounts'. A number of balance sheet items have corresponding contra accounts, with negative balances, that offset them. For example, accounts receivable which is an asset account, is used by companies to record the amounts that it is owed

TABLE 2.1 Sample chart of accounts

Account Category	Code	Account Title
Assets	1000	Cash and cash equivalents
	1010	Accounts receivable
	1020	Inventory
	1030	Prepayments
	1040	Property, plant, and equipment
	1050	Investment property
	1060	Intangible assets (patents, trademarks, goodwill)
	1070	Financial assets
	1080	Trading securities
	1090	Investment securities
Liabilities	2000	Accounts payable
	2010	Accrued liabilities
	2020	Financial liabilities
	2030	Current tax liabilities
	2040	Deferred tax liabilities
	2050	Reserves
	2060	Minority interest
	2070	Unearned revenue
	2080	Debt payable
	2090	Bonds payable
Owners' equity	3000	Common stock
	3010	Additional paid-in capital
	3020	Retained earnings
	3030	Other comprehensive income
Revenue	4000	Sales
	4010	Gains
	4020	Grants
	4030	Investment income
Expenses	5000	Cost of goods sold
	5010	Advertising
	5020	Rent
	5030	Utilities
	5040	Salaries
	5050	Payroll tax
	5060	Depreciation
	5070	Amortisation
	5080	Interest expense
	5090	Tax expense
	5095	Losses

by its customers when they purchase their goods and services on credit. Hence, sales made on credit are reflected in accounts receivable. However, a company often assumes that some accounts receivables will be uncollectible (customers will default in making payments for their purchases). Therefore, the company will record an estimate of the amount that may not be collected in an account called 'provision for bad debts'. Since the impact of the 'provision for bad debts' account is to reduce the balance of the company's accounts receivable, it is known as a contra asset account.

Any account that is offset or deducted from another account is called a contra account. Typical contra asset accounts include: (a) accumulated depreciation which is an offset to property, plant and equipment to reflect the amount of the cost of property, plant and equipment that has been allocated to current and preceding accounting periods; (b) sales returns and allowances which is an offset to revenue that reflects the cash refunds, credits on account and discounts from sales prices given to customers who purchased defective or unsatisfactory items; and (c) provision for bad debts which is an offset to accounts receivable for the amount of accounts receivable that are estimated to be uncollectible.

Fundamental accounting equation

The fundamental accounting equation which forms the basis of the balance sheet and the double entry bookkeeping system is: *Assets = Liabilities + Capital*, where capital represents owners' equity. The double entry bookkeeping method will be examined in detail later in this chapter. At this stage, it is sufficient to know that the double entry bookkeeping method is based on the simple concept that for each transaction, the total debits equal the total credits.

As previously explained, the balance sheet reflects the entity's statement of financial position at a specific moment in time. Hence, it shows all the entity's assets and the claims or entitlements on these assets. The claims on the assets refer to the liabilities and equity entitlements. Note that the liabilities are the various economic obligations due by the business entity, whereas equity represents the residual equity of a business (after deducting from the assets all the liabilities) including retained earnings and appropriations.

The concept of the owners' residual claim is reflected by making owners' equity the subject of the accounting equation, that is: *Owners' equity = Assets − Liabilities*. The terminology for owners' equity varies. Owners' equity may be referred to as capital, net worth, net book value, equity, stockholders' equity and shareholders' equity. The term used depends on the entity type. However, the basic equation remains the same. The resulting equation as consequence for making substitutions in the accounting equation is referred to as the expanded accounting equation, because it provides a breakdown of the equity component of the equation. For example, owners' equity consists of capital contributed by owners and earnings retained in the business up to a particular date. Hence, owners' equity is presented by the following equation: *Owners' equity = Contributed capital + Retained earnings*. Therefore, the accounting equation is now: *Assets = Liabilities + Contributed capital + Retained earnings*. Note that contributed capital may also be known as common stock. This formula indicates the fundamental source of owners' equity and manifests the basic principles of accounting. Note that convention depicts the owners' equity segment of a company's balance sheet as also consisting of treasury stock and other comprehensive income. Treasury stock occurs when an entity acquires and holds its own stock. Other comprehensive income includes income that is not reported on the income statement, for example changes in the value of assets or liabilities that are not reflected in the income statement.

Additionally, retained earnings are the net income generated by the entity after distributing the declared dividends. Hence, *Retained earnings = Net income – Dividends*. Therefore, the expanded accounting equation is now: *Assets = Liabilities + Contributed capital + Net income – Dividends*. Moreover, net income may be expressed as the revenue generated by the entity after deducting all the expenses. Hence, *Net income = Revenue – Expenses*. Therefore, the expanded accounting equation becomes: *Assets = Liabilities + Contributed capital + Revenue – Expenses – Dividends*.

The above accounting balance sheet equation provides a link with the income statement. It should be noted that the income statement reflects the entity's performance for a specific period of time, normally a financial year. Hence, the equation applicable in the income statement is: *Net income = Revenue – Expenses*. A negative net income represents a loss. Hence, when an entity's revenue is greater than its expenses, it shows net income; however, when an entity's revenue is less than its expenses, it shows a net loss. As stated previously, revenue and expenses generally arise by the provision of goods or services due to the primary business activities of an entity. Whereas, gains and losses arise due to increases (or decreases) in resources that are not part of the entity's primary business activities. However, for the purposes of the accounting equation, gains are included as part of revenue and losses are included in the expenses.

The link between the balance sheet and income statement may also be illustrated by the retained earnings factor of owners' equity. An entity's retained earnings at the end of the accounting period can be expressed as the retained earnings balance at the beginning of the accounting period (if any), plus net income, minus the dividends distributed to owners (if any). Hence, the basis of equation regarding retained earnings is: *Ending retained earnings = Beginning retained earnings + Net income – Dividends*. By substituting the net income component with: *Revenues – Expenses*, the equation for retained earnings is: *Ending retained earnings = Beginning retained earnings + Revenues – Expenses – Dividends*. Retained earnings are income that is held in reserve by the entity. It is the amount of income that is not distributed as dividends to owners. Therefore, the expanded accounting equation is: *Assets = Liabilities + Contributed capital + Beginning retained earnings + Revenue – Expenses – Dividends*.

To recapitulate, the balance sheet represents an entity's financial position at a specific moment in time, and the income statement reflects an entity's business activity over a period of time, which is normally one year. Figure 2.1 provides a summary of the various expanded accounting equation related to the above discussion.

The next chapter will use the accounting principles discussed above as a basis to describe the three related accounting concepts, namely the accounting process, the double entry bookkeeping method and the relationship between the accounting financial statements.

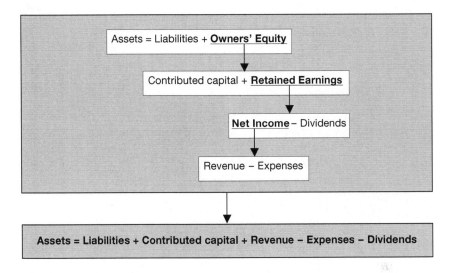

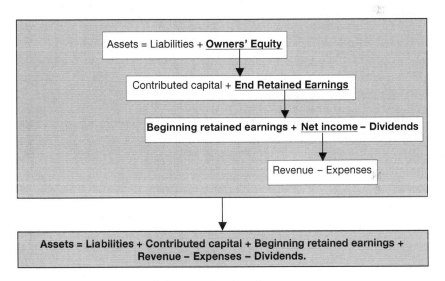

FIGURE 2.1 Summary: expanded accounting equation

Practical problems

1 Objects that represent the different types of economic resources owned or controlled by the business entity are referred to as:

   A   Revenue
   B   Cash inflows
   C   Assets
   D   Equity

2 Objects that represent the outflows of economic resources from the company or increases in the liabilities are referred to as:

A Assets
B Gains
C Appropriations
D Expenses

3 Objects that represent the various types of economic obligations by a business entity are referred to as:

A Losses
B Liabilities
C Cash outflows
D Gains

4 In the table below indicate whether the item is an asset, liability, owners' equity, revenue, or expense:

Accounts payable	
Sales	
Cash	
Prepaid rent	
Consumption of electricity and water	
Accrued interest	
Interest payable	
Interest income	
Accounts receivable	
Depreciation	
Bonds payable	
Buildings	
Goodwill	
Provision of a service	
Doubtful accounts	
Inventory	
Retained earnings	
Insurance payment	
Appropriations	
Rental of building	
Bank loan	

5 Which of the following would probably be classified as a financing activity?

   A   Taking out a bank loan
   B   Sale of food products by a supermarket
   C   Payment of taxes owned to government

6 Which of the following would probably be classified as an operating activity?

   A   Buying common stock in a company
   B   Investing in new machinery for the production goods
   C   Providing a service in the normal course of a business

7 Which of the following would probably be classified as an investment activity?

   A   Issuance of debenture stock
   B   Acquisition of a competitor
   C   Selling of obsolete equipment

8 The financial accountant anticipates that the company will have assets of €25,000 at year-end and liabilities of €18,500. The accountant's forecast of total owners' equity should be about:

   A   €43,500
   B   €6,500
   C   €5,600

9 An accountant has extracted the following information related to the company:

Assets	€150 million
Liabilities	€100 million
Contributed Capital	€45 million

The accountant's estimate of ending retained earnings would be:

   A   €25 million
   B   €95 million
   C   €5 million

10 The accountant has compiled the following information regarding his company:

Assets	€180 million
Liabilities	€110 million
Contributed Capital	€60 million
Net income	€4.5 million

The accountant's estimate of distributed dividends would be:

   A   €5.5 million
   B   €4.5 million
   C   €8.5 million

11 An accountant has collected the following information in advance of his company's year-end earnings declaration:

Estimated net income	€120 million
Beginning retained earnings	€800 million
Estimated distributions to owners	€80 million

The accountant's estimate of ending retained earnings (in millions) would be:

A   €760 million
B   €840 million
C   €1,000 million

12 An accountant has extracted the following information regarding a company of interest:

Liabilities at year-end	€90 million
Contributed capital at year-end	€40 million
Beginning retained earnings	€10 million
Revenue during the year	€25 million
Expenses during the year	€7 million
Distributed dividends to owners	€8 million

The accountant's forecast of total assets at year-end would be:

A   €158 million
B   €250 million
C   €150 million

Solutions

1 C is correct. An asset represents the different types of economic resources owned or controlled by the business entity.
2 D is correct. An expense reflects the outflows of economic resources from the company or increases in the liabilities. They represent the company's expenditures to enable it to operate.
3 B is correct. Liabilities correspond to the various types of economic obligations by a business entity.
4 The table below indicates the correct classification for each item in terms of an asset, liability, owners' equity, revenue, or expense:

Accounts payable	Liability
Sales	Revenue
Cash	Asset
Prepaid rent	Asset
Consumption of electricity and water	Expense
Accrued interest	Liability
Interest payable	Expense
Interest income	Revenue
Accounts receivable	Asset
Depreciation	Expense
Bonds payable	Liability
Buildings	Asset
Goodwill	Asset
Provision of a service	Revenue
Doubtful accounts	Expense
Inventory	Asset
Retained earnings	Owners' equity
Insurance payment	Expense
Appropriations	Owners' equity
Rental of building	Expense
Bank loan	Liability

5   A is correct. Taking out a bank loan would be classified as a financing activity. B and C are incorrect because the sale of food products by a supermarket and the payment of income taxes would be classified as an operating activity.

6   C is correct. Providing a service in the normal course of a business is a primary business activity and would be classified as an operating activity. A and B are incorrect since buying common stock in a company and investing in new machinery for the production goods would be classified as investing activities.

7   B is correct. The acquisition of a competitor is classified as an investing activity. A is incorrect because the issuance of debenture stock is a financing activity. C is also incorrect because selling of obsolete equipment cannot be considered as an investing activity.

8   B is correct. Assets equal to the liabilities plus owners' equity. Hence, €25,000 = €18,500 + Owners' equity. Owners' equity therefore must be €6,500.

9 C is correct. Assets must equal the liabilities plus contributed capital plus retained earnings. Hence, €150 million = €100 million + €45 million + retained earnings. Retained earnings therefore must equal to €5 million.

10 A is correct. Assets must equal the liabilities plus contributed capital plus retained earnings. However, retained earnings are equal to net income minus dividends. Hence, €180 million = €110 million + €60 million + (€4.5 million − dividends). Therefore, dividends must equal to €5.5 million.

11 B is correct. End retained earnings equals beginning retained earnings plus net income minus distributed dividends. Therefore, end retained earnings equals €800 million + €120 million − €80 million. Hence, end retained earnings equal to €840 million.

12 C is correct. Assets = Liabilities plus Contributed capital plus Beginning retained earnings plus Revenues minus Expenses minus Dividend Distributions.

Liabilities €90 million
+ Contributed capital €40 million
+ Beginning retained earnings €10 million
+ Revenues €25 million
− Expenses €7 million
− Dividend distribution €8 million
= Assets €150 million

References

Harrison, Ian. (2006). *Complete A-Z Accounting Handbook*. London: Hodder Arnold.
Wood, F. and Sangster, A. (2007). *Business Accounting*, 10th edn. London: Prentice Hall.

3

THE ACCOUNTING PROCESS

To state the facts frankly is not to despair the future nor indict the past. The prudent heir takes careful inventory of his legacies and gives a faithful accounting to those whom he owes an obligation of trust.

John F. Kennedy, President, United States of America

The accounting process consists of a series of steps that begins with a business transaction and ends with the closing of the accounts and the compilation of the financial statements. Since this process is repeated each reporting period, it is often referred to as the accounting cycle or bookkeeping cycle. The steps in the accounting process adhere to a number of rules and conventions that abide by the accepted accounting standards. The accounting process consists of the following key steps:

- Initiate business transactions.
- Analyse and classify the transactions.
- Post the transactions to the ledger accounts.
- Prepare the trial balance to make sure that debits equal credits.
- Prepare adjusting entries to record accrued, deferred and estimated amounts.
- Prepare closing journal entries.
- Prepare the financial statements.
- Prepare reversing journal entries (optional).

Note that the first three steps are performed throughout the accounting period as the transactions occur. However, the remaining steps are performed at the end of the accounting period. This chapter will build upon the accounting principles discussed in the previous chapter to describe four related accounting concepts, namely the accounting process mechanism; the double entry bookkeeping method;

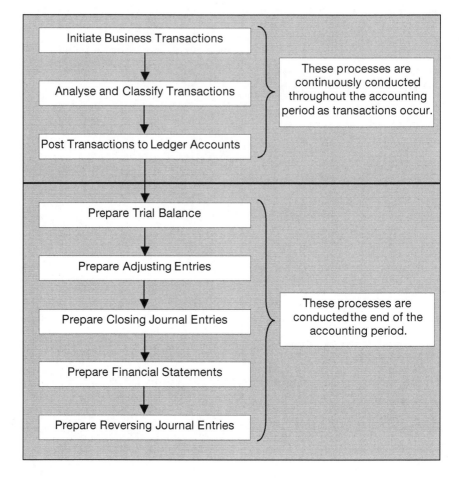

FIGURE 3.1 The accounting process mechanism

the relationship between accounting process and double-entry framework; and the relationship between the accounting financial statements.

The accounting process mechanism

The accounting process is a systematic progression of activities that have the objective of producing the financial statements of a business enterprise and which represent a true and fair view of the financial position of an entity. Figure 3.1 depicts the accounting process mechanism as a series of sequential steps. However, the progression of the process from one step to another cannot take place until a particular step is verified as being correct. Each step in the accounting process is explained below under a separate heading.

Business transactions

A transaction is an economic flow, which denotes the interaction between organisational units by mutual agreement or an action within an organisational unit that is considered advantageous to treat such an action as a transaction. This implies the prior knowledge and consent of the organisational units. However, this does not necessarily mean that all organisational units enter a transaction voluntarily. There are transactions imposed by law, such as, the payment of taxes and the payment of fines and penalties that are not voluntary.

Moreover, business transactions specifically describe the net acquirement of assets or the net initiation of liabilities for the various types of business activities. These types of transactions result from financial and non-financial transactions. Hence, this stage is basically related to the identification of the transaction of a recognisable event (such as purchasing) and the preparation of the transaction source document (such as a purchase order or an invoice).

Analyse and classify transactions (posting transactions to journals)

This stage involves a number of activities. First, the transaction must be quantified and expressed in monetary terms (e.g. dollars, euros). Second, there is the need to identify the accounts that are affected by the transaction. For instance, if the entity is purchasing a vehicle for cash, then the relevant accounts that are affected by the transaction are the 'Bank' account and the asset 'Vehicles' account. Third, it is essential to determine which accounts are credited and debited. For example, the purchasing of a vehicle for cash would require a credit to the 'Bank' account because this asset is being reduced by the amount withdrawn from the account to pay for the asset, and a debt to the 'Vehicles' account since this asset account is being increased by the value of the vehicle which has been purchased. Finally, the transaction is recorded in chronological order in the proper journal as a debit or credit. An entity may have a number of journals that include the subsidiary journals (such as, the sales journal, purchase journal, cash receipts and disbursement journal) and the general journal.

All business transactions are recorded in one of the journals. The journal contains the details of each individual transaction line by line. As noted previously, there are two categories of journals, namely the 'general journal' and the 'subsidiary journals'. The vast majority of the accounting entries will be initiated in the 'subsidiary journals'. However, if the accounting entry is not associated with a subsidiary journal, the entry will be initiated in the 'general journal'. It is important to note that all transactions recorded in the 'subsidiary journals' will end up being recorded in the 'general journal'. Therefore, the 'subsidiary journals' should be viewed as providing a very detailed record of every transaction, while the 'general journal' provides a summary of the transactions.

Post transactions to the ledger accounts

This step consists of recording the transactions in the 'general ledger' from the journals. Therefore, the ledger accounts are a progressive summary of the business transactions. Hence, the subsidiary journals contain the detailed transactions, the general journal is a summarised version of the subsidiary journals, and the general ledger is a further summary of the transactions derived from the general journal. Note that the accounts for the general ledger are defined in the chart of accounts. Every amount listed in the debit or credit column of the journal is posted on the debit or credit side of a ledger account. Hence, this step generally involves copying information from the journal to the ledger accounts.

Prepare the trial balance

The trial balance is prepared to verify that the total of all accounts with debit balances equal the total of all accounts with credit balances. Hence, the trial balance is a listing of all the ledger accounts, with debits in the left column and credits in the right column. The objective is to ensure that the total debits equal the total credits. Note that the actual computed total of each column is not meaningful; however, it is essential that the total value of each column is equal. Nevertheless, having equal columns does not guarantee that there are no errors. For example, columns may still be equal if a transaction is completely omitted or the transaction is recorded to an incorrect account. On the other hand, if the columns are not equal, one may look for posting and arithmetic errors. Posting errors are likely to include posting of an incorrect amount; leaving out a posting; posting in an erroneous column; or posting the same transaction more than once. Therefore, before proceeding to the next step, the preparation of the trial balance must be correctly completed.

Prepare and balance day adjustments

Note that all transactions occurring in an accounting period must be recognised irrespective of whether cash has been received or paid. The key objective of adjusting entries is to make sure that the revenues earned in the accounting period are matched by all the costs incurred for that same accounting period. Otherwise, the end result would be a distorted view of profit because the revenue, expenses, assets, liabilities and equity may be understated or overstated.

This step is required to ensure that the financial statements show a complete and accurate status of the firm's financial performance (earned income) and financial position (net worth). The 'preparation and balancing of day adjustments' stage consists of preparing adjusting entries to record accrued, deferred and estimated amounts; posting the adjusting entries to the ledger accounts; correcting any errors that may be found; and preparing the adjusted trial balance. The preparation of the adjusted trial balance is similar to the preparation of the unadjusted trial balance. The only difference being that the adjusting entries are included.

The accruals adjustments relate to revenue and expense transactions that occur in the current accounting period but the effects of which are not yet recorded and recognised in the accounting period. The deferrals adjustments align recorded revenues and costs with appropriate accounting periods. For example, cash could be received before the goods and services are provided to customers or where cash has been paid in advance for operational costs that relate to future accounting periods. These deferrals are commonly known as unearned revenue (income received in advance) and prepaid expenses (prepayments). The correction of errors is a normal part of this process, since errors may have been made in the recording procedure but their effects were not identified in the trial balance.

The depreciation cost allocation for property, plant and equipment is also viewed as a balance day adjustment. Property, plant and equipment assets are resources that are purchased to aid the business entity generate income. Property, plant and equipment are regarded as long-term fixed assets that are utilised by the entity for more than one accounting period. Hence, the effect of purchasing property, plant and equipment can be viewed as being similar to having a prepaid expenditure. In fact, the cost of holding these types of assets is spread over the economic life (accounting periods) of the assets. This cost allocation to the various accounting periods is known as depreciation. Hence, depreciation estimates are typically conducted at the end of an accounting period and for that reason are viewed as a balance day adjustment.

Prepare closing journal entries

An accounting system typically consists of two types of accounts, namely the permanent (or real) accounts and the temporary (or nominal) accounts. The permanent accounts consist of the assets, liabilities and the owner's capital accounts. The ending balance of these accounts in one accounting period is always the starting balance in the subsequent accounting period. The temporary accounts consist of revenues, expenses, gains, losses and drawing accounts. These accounts are closed to a temporary income summary account, from which the balance is transferred to the retained earnings account (capital) at the end of each fiscal year or, occasionally, at the end of each accounting period. Any dividend or withdrawal accounts also are transferred (closed) to capital. When an account is closed, the account balance returns to zero. Starting the temporary accounts with zero balances each year, makes it easier to track revenues, expenses and withdrawals and to compare them from one year to the next.

There are four closing entries, which transfer all temporary account balances to the owner's capital account. First, income statement accounts with credit balances (commonly revenue accounts) are closed and the balances are carried forward to a temporary income summary account. Second, the income statement accounts with debit balances (normally expense accounts) are closed and the balances are carried forward to the temporary income summary account. When all revenue and expense accounts are closed, the temporary income summary account's balance represents the entity's net income or loss for the period. Third, the temporary income summary account is closed and the balance is carried forward to the owner's capital account or to the retained earnings account. Note that the purpose of the temporary income summary account is merely to keep the permanent owner's capital or retained earnings account orderly. Finally, the owner's drawing account is closed and the balance is carried forward to the owner's capital account. In corporations, this entry closes any dividend accounts to the retained earnings account.

An after-closing trial balance is also prepared to make sure that the debits equal the credits. At this stage, only the permanent accounts are present since all the temporary accounts have been closed. Furthermore, any errors that become evident are corrected.

Prepare financial statements

Four financial statements are commonly prepared once the adjusting accounting entries have been completed. These include the income statement (statement of comprehensive income), statement of retained earnings (statement of changes in equity), balance sheet (statement of financial position), and statement of cash flows. Note that these four financial statements are all inter-related.

The income statement basically reports revenues, expenses and the resultant net income. This statement is prepared by transferring the ledger account balances of the revenue, expenses and capital gains and losses accounts, and any other adjusting entries.

The statement of retained earnings can only be prepared after the income statement has been completed. This statement shows the retained earnings at the beginning and end of the relevant accounting period. The statement of retained earnings is prepared by using the information related to the beginning retained earnings, which is obtained from the previous retained earnings statement; net income from the current income statement; and dividends paid during the current accounting period.

Similarly, the balance sheet can only be prepared after the statement of retained earnings has been completed. The balance sheet discloses the assets, liabilities and shareholder equity of an entity. This financial statement is compiled by utilising the balances of all the asset and liabilities accounts; the capital stock balance; and retained earnings obtained from the current statement of retained earnings.

Finally, the statement of cash flows provides details about the reasons for the changes in the cash balance. This statement shows the sources and uses of cash in the operating, financing and investing activities of the entity. Since the cash flow statement reports on a cash-basis, it cannot be compiled directly from the various ledger account balances if an accrual accounting methodology is used. Hence, it is compiled by converting the accrual information to a cash-basis approach. This conversion process may use the direct or indirect methods. The direct method subtracts cash disbursement from cash receipts and the indirect method adds or subtracts non-cash items from net income. Both methods provide the same result.

Prepare reversing journal entries

Reversing entries are optional. They are recorded in response to accrued assets and accrued liabilities that were created by adjusting entries at the end of a reporting period. The purpose of reversing entries is to simplify an entity's recordkeeping. By reversing the adjusting entry, one avoids double counting the amount when the transaction occurs in the next period. A reversing journal entry is recorded on the first day of the new period.

Double-entry bookkeeping method

Double-entry bookkeeping is a standard accounting method that requires each transaction to be recorded in at least two accounts. Hence, the double-entry method is based on having a transaction that involves equal and opposite entries consisting of debit entries and credit entries. In other words, it results in having a debit to one or more accounts and a credit to one or more accounts. Double-entry accounting provides a quick way of checking accuracy because the summation of all the accounts with debit balances must equal the aggregate of all the credit balance accounts. This provides a built-in error check. This way the only errors that may be undetected automatically are misclassification due to recording a debit or credit in the wrong account or the complete omissions of an accounting transaction entry.

The double-entry bookkeeping method makes use of 'T' accounts to record the accounting transaction entries (refer to Figure 3.2). Notice that the debits (Dr) are placed on the left hand column of the 'T' account and the credits (Cr) are to be found the right hand column. Figure 3.2 illustrates an example where an entity has purchased a vehicle for €18,500 on a cash basis. The double-entry accounting entries would be to credit the bank account (€18,500) to pay for the vehicle and debit the vehicle asset account (€18,500) to recognise that the vehicle is now part of the entity's assets.

Note that the amounts can be split among two or more accounts, but the total amount entered as debit must always equal the total amount entered as credit. For example an entity purchases a vehicle from Zeta Ltd for €18,500. The entity makes a part payment from its bank account for €10,000 and promises to pay the balance of €8,500 to Zeta Ltd in three months' time. Figure 3.3 illustrates the accounting

Bank Account		Asset (Vehicle)	
Debit (Dr)	**Credit (Cr)**	**Debit (Dr)**	**Credit (Cr)**
	€18,500	€18,500	

FIGURE 3.2 Double-entry accounting method 'T' accounts

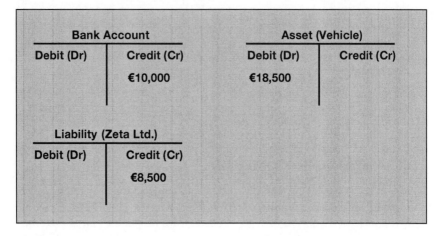

FIGURE 3.3 Example 1: Double-entry accounting method 'T' accounts

entries that are required to record the transactions in the example given. The example shows that the total debits are €18,500 which equals the total credits of €18,500.

General double-entry bookkeeping rules

Basically, an asset is something an entity owns, such as a motor vehicle or the right to receive something in the future, such as a trade debtor who purchases goods from the entity on credit and must pay for these purchases in the future. On the other hand, a liability is where the entity owes something to someone else. For example an entity may borrow money from a bank and needs to pay this amount back (including the interest) or the entity may purchase a service or product on credit and will need to pay for this service or product in the future. As we have seen in the previous chapter, assets and liabilities are 'balance sheet' items that show the net worth of the entity, as opposed to revenue and expenses that are 'profit and loss' items.

The issue is: What are the effects of the business transactions on the 'balance sheet' items and the 'profit and loss' items? Figure 3.4 illustrates that if a transaction increases the value of the assets of an entity or reduces the value of the liabilities then debit the particular asset or liability account. However, if a transaction decreases the value of the assets of an entity or increases the value of the liabilities then credit the particular asset or liability account. Furthermore, if the transaction reduces the profit (expenditure) then debit the particular expenditure account; however if the transaction increases the profit (revenue or income) then credit the account.

To illustrate the application of Figure 3.4, let us consider a simple example. Assume that an entity purchases various goods to be sold to its customers. These goods were purchased for €2,000 and paid in cash (not on credit). Moreover, the

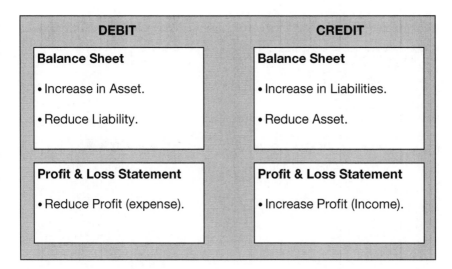

DEBIT	CREDIT
Balance Sheet • Increase in Asset. • Reduce Liability.	**Balance Sheet** • Increase in Liabilities. • Reduce Asset.
Profit & Loss Statement • Reduce Profit (expense).	**Profit & Loss Statement** • Increase Profit (Income).

FIGURE 3.4 Effect of transactions on balance sheet and profit-and-loss items

entity sells goods on cash basis to its customers worth €3,000. The entity also receives a utility (electricity bill) invoice of €400. Additionally, the entity's manager borrows €10,000 from the bank and purchases a delivery van for €9,000 in cash. To simplify matters, assume that all these transaction take place within the same week. Let us now consider the double-entry accounting entries required from these transactions.

Figure 3.5 shows all the relevant accounting entries. The entity purchased stock valued at €2,000 for cash. Hence, applying the rules highlighted in Figure 3.4, the amount paid reduces the cash asset account but increases the stock asset account. Therefore, credit cash account with €2,000 and debit stock account with €2,000. The entity sells goods on cash basis to its customers worth €3,000. This means that the cash asset account increases by €3,000 and the sales (income) account is also increased by €3,000. Hence, applying the rules in Figure 3.4, debit the cash asset account by €3,000 and credit the sales (income) account by €3,000. The entity also receives and pays the utility (electricity bill) invoice of €400. The payment of the electricity invoice results in a decrease of the cash asset account and an increase of the electricity expense account. Hence, once again applying the rules at Figure 3.4, credit the cash asset account by €400 and debit the electricity expense account with the corresponding amount of €400. The entity's manager borrows €10,000 from the bank. This results in an increase of €10,000 in the cash asset account (loan received from bank), but also results in an increase of the entity's liabilities (obligation to repay bank) of €10,000. Hence, debit the cash asset account by €10,000 and credit the liability account by €10,000. Finally, the entity purchases a vehicle for €9,000 in cash. This means that the cash asset account is reduced by €9,000, but the entity has gained a vehicle worth €9,000 resulting in an increase of the vehicles asset account. Hence, applying the rules in Figure 3.4, the cash

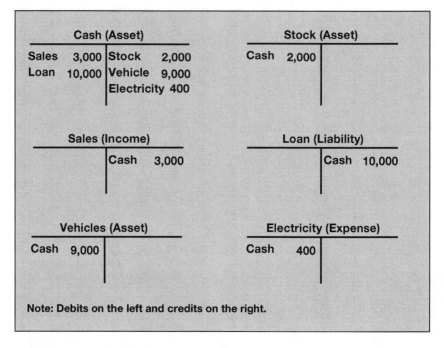

FIGURE 3.5 Transaction entries and their effect on the relevant accounts

Trial Balance			
Cash a/c: Sales	3,000	Cash a/c: Stock	2,000
Cash a/c: Loan	10,000	Cash a/c: Vehicles	9,000
		Cash a/c: Electricity	400
Stock a/c: Purchase	2,000	Sales a/c: Cash Sales	3,000
Vehicle a/c: Asset	9,000	Loan a/c: Liability	10,000
Electricity a/c: Expense	400		
	24,400		24,400

FIGURE 3.6 Trial balance of transaction entries from the relevant accounts

asset account is credited by €9,000 to pay for the vehicle, and the vehicle asset account is debited by €9,000 which represents the value of the van that was purchased and delivered.

It was previously stated that the total of the debits and credits in a double-entry bookkeeping method must be equal. The trial balance shown at Figure 3.6 illustrates that the transactions for the given example results in the debits being equal to the credits, totalling €24,400. Note that the total amount of €24,400 is not of any particular importance or significance. The important issue is that the debits are equal to the credits.

Relationship between accounting process and double-entry framework

In the previous sections of this chapter, the accounting process mechanism and the double-entry bookkeeping method were described. It is now appropriate to discuss the relationship between the accounting process and the double-entry bookkeeping framework to obtain a holistic view of the accounting cycle. Figure 3.7 provides a general view of how the double-entry bookkeeping method is linked to the accounting process.

The cash book (including petty cash) represents the cash at bank and in hand. Hence, the cash book depicts the deposits for cash received and withdrawals for making cash payments. Furthermore, the cash received could be due to cash sales or payments received for credit sales (debtors). Similarly, cash payments may be due to cash purchases or payments made for credit purchases (creditors).

The sales day book itemises all the credit sales details, which are also copied in the subsidiary debtors ledgers for every individual client. When payments are

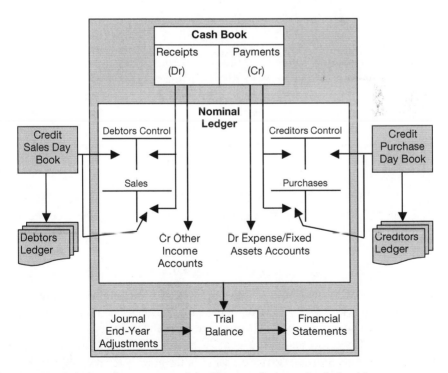

FIGURE 3.7 Accounting process and double-entry framework relationship

received from the debtors, these are also recorded in the client's subsidiary ledger. Likewise, the purchases day book itemises all credit purchases details, which are also copied in the subsidiary creditors ledgers for every individual creditor. When payments are made to the creditors, these are also recorded in the supplier's subsidiary ledger.

The nucleus of the accounting system is the nominal ledger which contains all accounts. For example, two important accounts are the debtors (asset) and creditors (liability) control accounts. These control accounts equal the total of the debtors and creditors subsidiary ledgers. The nominal ledger also contains the sales account which represents income generated through the sales process, while the purchase or stock account (asset) contains all transactions for the procurement of goods that are placed in store as stock before use. The accounts contained within the nominal ledger vary between entities, depending on their individual accounting systems. Hence, the nominal ledger may have a variety of income accounts, expense accounts, fixed asset (land, buildings, machinery and equipment) accounts and liability accounts (short term and long-term loans).

A trial balance is prepared to verify that the total of all accounts with debit balances equal the total of all accounts with credit balances. Furthermore, all transactions occurring in an accounting period must be recognised irrespective of whether cash has been received or paid. The key objective of adjusting entries is to make sure that the revenues earned in the accounting period are matched by all the costs incurred for that same accounting period. Otherwise the end result would be a distorted view of profit because the revenue, expenses, assets, liabilities and equity may be understated or overstated.

When the initial trial balance is satisfactory, the temporary accounts are closed and various journal entries are prepared. The permanent accounts consist of the assets, liabilities and the owner's capital accounts. The temporary accounts consist of revenues, expenses, gains, losses and drawing accounts. An after-closing trial balance is also prepared to make sure that the debits equal the credits after the journal entries are completed. At this stage, only the permanent accounts are present since all the temporary accounts have been closed. Any errors that become evident are corrected.

Once, this procedure is completed the financial statements may be compiled. Four financial statements are usually prepared. These are the income statement, statement of retained earnings, balance sheet, and cash flow statement.

Relationship between the financial statements

All the four financial statements are inter-related, with each individual financial statement focusing on a specific aspect of the entity's financial status. For instance, the income statement presents the revenues, expenses and the resultant net income of the entity. Hence, its focus is the entity's financial performance for a specific accounting period (normally a financial year). On the other hand, the balance sheet presents the entity's resources (assets) and the various claims on these resources

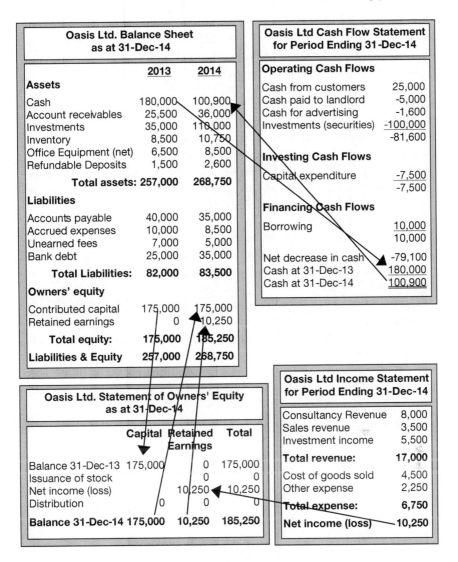

FIGURE 3.8 Relationships between financial statements

(liabilities). In other words, the balance sheet provides information on the net worth of the entity, hence its financial position at a specific point in time. Figure 3.8 illustrates the relationship between the financial statements.

The income statement is prepared from the ledger account balances of the revenue, expenses and capital gains and losses accounts, and any other adjusting entries. The statement of owners' equity is prepared after the income statement has been completed. This statement shows the capital and retained earnings at the beginning and end of the appropriate accounting period. The statement of owners' equity is prepared by using the information from the balance sheet related to 'contributed capital' of the previous financial year adding any additional issuance of capital stock. The resultant ending period capital amount is shown on the balance sheet as the 'contributed capital' for the current period. Furthermore, the net income figure from the income statement is transferred to the statement of owners' equity under the retained earnings, which is then transferred to the balance sheet under the heading 'retained earnings' current period, after adjusting for any distributed dividends during the current accounting period.

As illustrated by Figure 3.8, the balance sheet is prepared after the statement of owners' equity and the cash flow statement have been completed. The balance sheet shows the assets, liabilities and shareholder equity of an entity. The balance sheet is completed by using the balances of all the asset and liabilities accounts; the capital stock balance; retained earnings obtained from the current owners' equity statement; and the current cash balance from the cash flow statement. It should be noted that the cash flow statement itemises the changes in the cash balance of the entity. This statement discloses the sources and uses of cash in the operating, financing and investing activities of the entity. The cash flow statement utilises the cash balance from the balance sheet of the previous financial year and adjusts this figure by including the operating, financing and investing activities of the entity. This provides the current ending cash balance, which must be equal to the balance sheet cash amount for the current financial period. Hence, as Figure 3.8 illustrates, the four accounting statements are closely related to show a clear and accurate picture of the financial position of the entity under consideration.

Accounting adjustments for accruals and valuations

The process of entering business transactions into the accounting system is a straightforward matter that does not normally pose a concern. Moreover, assets and liabilities have a fixed and determinable value that makes the accounting process relatively simple. However, difficulties arise due to a fundamental accounting principle related to the matching concept. Under the matching concept a business is viewed as a continuous affair but its continuity is divided into accounting years for determining its periodic results. Hence, the matching concept requires that expenses should be matched to the revenues of the appropriate accounting period. Therefore, the revenue earned and the expenses incurred to earn these revenues during a particular accounting period must be established. The complexity occurs when a cash receipt or payment occurs in a different period than the related revenue or expense, or when the reportable values of assets differ.

This basically means that under accrual accounting, proceeds and expenses must be recorded when earned or incurred respectively, regardless of when the related cash flow activities take place. Therefore, it is imperative that revenue and expenditure are reported in the correct accounting period otherwise the matching concept would not be adhered to. There are basically four potential circumstances that require accrual entries, these occur when:

- An entity receives cash in advance before earning the revenue (before providing the goods and/or services) known as unearned or deferred revenue.
- An entity earns revenue before receiving cash for providing the goods and/or services but has not yet recognised the revenue at the end of an accounting period, known as unbilled or accrued revenue.
- An entity makes a cash payment prior to recognising an expense, known as a prepaid expense.
- An entity sustains expenses that have not yet been paid as of the end of an accounting period, known as accrued expenses.

The circumstances requiring accrual entries necessitate an originating accounting entry and a minimum of one adjusting accounting entry at a later date. Another fundamental accounting principle that increases the complexity of accounting procedure is the concept of historical cost. According to this concept, an asset is normally recorded at its cost price; in other words, at the price at which it was purchased. Assets recorded in the accounts at cost, with the passage of time are reduced in value due to depreciation or amortisation cost. Additionally, with the passage of time, the market value of assets, such as investments may fluctuate greatly from their original cost. This is the reason why the historical cost concept is contentious and there is growing support for fair market value of assets.

The valuation adjustments to an entity's assets or liabilities are carried out only when stipulated by the accounting standards to ensure that the accounting records reflect the current market value rather than the historical cost. Currently, the accounting standards only oblige entities to record certain assets at current market value. Therefore, some assets are shown at historical cost and others at current market value with the changes in the market value being reported in the income statement (e.g. trading securities that are classified as fair value through profit and loss). However, trading securities classified as available-for-sale are recorded at current market value, but changes in their value are shown in the equity section of the balance sheet, as part of comprehensive income. Moreover, securities that are intended to be held-to-maturity (and are classified as such) are shown at their historical cost. A more detailed discussion of these types of investment assets will be discussed in the appropriate chapter. In circumstances where the valuation adjustment entries are required for assets, the general accounting entries are as follows:

- For increases in assets: The appropriate asset is increased, with the counter entry being a gain on the income statement or an increase in equity section of the balance sheet (other comprehensive income) depending on the classification of the investment asset.
- For decreases in assets: The appropriate asset is decreased, with the counter entry being a loss on the income statement or a decrease in the equity section of the balance sheet (other comprehensive income) depending on the classification of the investment asset.

The accounting system

The accounting system is critical for the proper financial management of an entity. What's more, accounting data provides the essential basis for information because it is an indispensable part of a legal mandatory requirement; is a basis of investor decision making; is historical, therefore factual and verifiable; is defined upon the same common basis, explicitly in monetary terms; and is typically used as a measure of the entity's financial position and performance. Accounting information together with adequate internal control procedures, facilitated by suitable information flow processes provides the fundamental basis for having an accurate presentation of the entity's financial statements. Furthermore, the generated accounting information is normally the basis for management decisions, particularly, budgetary control.

The effectiveness of the accounting system is based upon the scrupulous recording of the detailed transactions of the entity. Figure 3.9 provides an example of the information flow process related with sales order, delivery, and customer

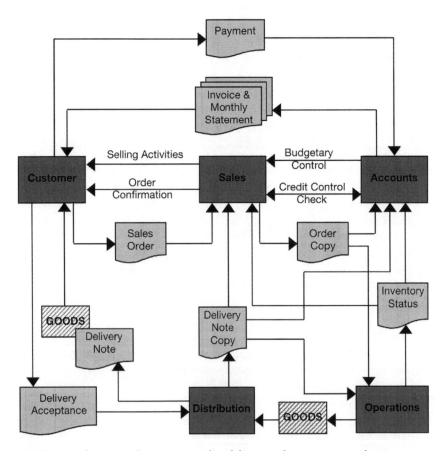

FIGURE 3.9 Information flow process: sales, delivery and payment procedures

payment procedures. This information flow process typically defines the revenue generation capability of an entity and is likely to include data elements regarding the details of the original order quantities; pricing information; and customer details (name and address).

Figure 3.9 also illustrates that from the collected information a number of processes take place, namely, a customer invoice is compiled that will permit the stock control records for goods sold to be updated, thus providing the inventory status; the credit control unit will receive notification of the outstanding debt; and the operations division is notified to assign the goods to the customer and authorise the distribution division to deliver the goods to the customer. Typically, these processes are computerised and allow instant on-line access to accounting information by authorised entity employees; the invoice is transmitted to the customer electronically; likewise the delivery note is confirmed electronically by the customer; and the customer can also make the payment electronically. Hence, no paperwork is necessary since all accounting and other related systems are integrated in an intricate eCommerce best practice.

Additionally, with an eCommerce system, a customer could be a few kilometres down the road or across the globe; it makes no difference except for the distribution method. Moreover, a module of the accounting information system may be designed to permit the entity management to analyse the sales and revenue information by corporate division; product category; geographical area; sales branch or agency; customer or customer group; and salesperson. Hence, such a system will allow the entity to have numerous cascading financial performance measures.

Using financial statements to analyse securities

The financial statements generated by the accounting system provide the underlying information for analysing the financial position of entities, including credit and equity analysis, and security valuation. However, before these financial statements may be applied to analysing an entity, it may be necessary for the user to make adjustments that reflect certain financial aspects that are not disclosed in the financial statements. For example, one may need to examine and evaluate the basis and rationality for various decisions made by management related to accruals, particularly the recognition of revenue and expenditure, and valuations of assets and liabilities.

A difficulty that arises for those making the adjustments to financial statements for evaluation purposes is the lack of access to the internal management decision process (i.e. memorandums and minutes of internal management meetings); individual accounting transactions; and the accounting system in general. It should be noted that judgements and estimates are an essential part of an accounting system, regardless of the intentions of management to accurately or inaccurately disclose the economic position and performance of an entity. Accruals and valuation transactions require significant judgment on the part of management that cause the various limitations of the accounting model.

Hence, in making their evaluations and adjustments, analysts will need to deduce what transactions have taken place and also surmise the backdrop for the various management and accounting policies that the financial statements are based upon. The starting point in evaluating the financial statements should be the detection of the various accruals and valuation transactions. For example, isolate and examine accounting entries related to deferred and unbilled revenue; and prepaid and accrued expenses. These types of accounting entries are usually noted in the accounting policies and estimates section of the entity's annual report under the management discussion and analysis or as part of the notes that complement the financial statements.

Furthermore, examine the depreciation basis of the various assets in terms of the economic useful life, the depreciation rate, and the salvage value. All these variables require judgment on the part of management and directly affect the statement of financial performance (income statement). For instance, an entity that normally operates on an eight-hour-a-day basis may estimate that its primary assets have a useful life of six years and hence the expense for using these assets is spread over a six-year period. However, if in the meantime the entity decides to operate on the three shifts basis (24 hours a day) the useful life of these assets is reduced to below two years. Hence, the expense for using these assets would be higher since the cost of utilising the assets is spread over a lower period and not six years.

Keep in mind that an accounting system may work perfectly, but this does not guarantee that the underlying judgements made by management as the basis for the financial statements are in fact correct. For example, management may intentionally estimate incorrectly the amount of doubtful debts or the amount of warranty claims on products sold. A dishonest manager may post accounting entries that achieve a predetermined result. For example, a manager may have paid for a product but does not want to record it as an expense. Hence, the transaction would be entered in a prepaid asset account instead. A variety of transactions related to cash payments and revenue may be recorded in a similar manner by fictitiously creating liability (accounts payable) or asset (accounts receivable) accounts.

It should be noted that for every transaction entry there is a counter entry; this is the basis of the double entry accounting method. This is the primary means to detecting improper accounting entries because typically a dishonest manager in the process of 'fixing' one account will need to adjust another account with an amount that may not always make sense. For instance, entering fabricated revenue will probably result in an increase in debtors (accounts receivable) with a consequence that collecting the certain debtors will be doubtful. Hence, in the medium term such transactions will be difficult to conceal. Applying the accounting equation together with ratio analysis will help to reveal insistent or fraudulent accounting.

When examining financial statements, always look for sudden increases or decreases in accounts receivable and accounts payable, or other accounting elements that influence generated income. Furthermore, compare the entity's financial statements elements (as a percentage of total assets or total revenue) with the industry average or with a key competitor. Again examine the differences and obtain an explanation for these differences. A more detailed discussion on these and other analytical issues will be covered in Chapter 9.

Practical problems

1   Carry out the activities as required below.

   a   Enter the following transactions in the general journal of Oscar Ltd.
       On 2 April, Ms. R. Kramer established an entity 'Oscar Ltd' with a cash investment of €260,000. On the 3 April, the established company purchased land for its office site for €77,000. Oscar Ltd also purchased a prefabricated building for the office site on 5 April for €144,000.
       On 15 April, the management of Oscar Ltd sold part of its office site land to Smite Fast Foods plc for €30,000 to be paid within three months. Oscar Ltd purchased office furniture from Delta Furniture Ltd on 17 April for €18,000 and computer equipment from Ascot-It Ltd for €7,650 on 18 April. Both these transactions were purchased on credit.
       On 22 April, Smite Fast Foods made a part payment of €5,500 for land purchased from Oscar Ltd. On 24 April, Oscar Ltd made a part payment of €9,000 to Delta Furniture Ltd for the office furniture and on 26 April, made a part payment of €4,000 to Ascot-It Ltd for the computer equipment.
   b   Post the above journal entries to the proper ledger accounts.
   c   Take a trial balance of the transactions posted to the ledger accounts.
   d   Show the financial position of Oscar Ltd.

2   This problem is a continuation of Problem 1 and therefore the information obtained from answering Problem 1 will also be used in this problem.
   Carry out the activities as required below.

   a   Enter the following transactions in the general journal of Oscar Ltd.
       On 3 May, Oscar Ltd paid €1,800 for advertising on the local media. On 8 May, the company was paid €9,750 for selling goods on a sales commission basis. Oscar Ltd received an electricity bill on 14 May to be paid in 30 days for €900.
       On 22 May, Oscar Ltd invoiced one of its clients for selling goods on commission for €11,300 to be paid in 30 days. On 24 May the company received a telephone bill for €480 to be paid by the end of May.
       On 31 May the company paid the workers their wages totalling €8,400 and Ms R Kramer withdrew cash from the company for €6,600.
   b   Post the above journal entries to the proper ledger accounts (using where appropriate the accounts and balances from Problem 1).
   c   Take a trial balance of the transactions posted to the ledger accounts of Oscar Ltd.

    d   Record the depreciation for the end of May accounting period in the general journal and ledger accounts using the following data:

        i   The building has a useful life of 25 years with no salvage value. A straight-line depreciation method is used by the company.

        ii The office furniture has a useful life of 10 years with no salvage value. A straight-line depreciation method is also used.

        iii The computer equipment has a useful life of 5 years with salvage value of €30. A straight-line depreciation method is also used.

    e   Take an adjusted trial balance of the transactions posted to the ledger accounts of Oscar Ltd.

    f   Prepare the following financial statements:

        i   Income statement for period ending 31 May 20xx.

        ii Statement of changes to owner's equity as at 31 May 20xx.

        iii Statement of cash flows for period ending 31 May 20xx.

        iv Statement of financial position as at 31 May 20xx.

Solutions

1   The required activities are as follows.

    a   The journal entries of Oscar Ltd for the month of April are shown below. First establish a chart of accounts for the established company as shown at Table 3.1.

       The general journal entries for Oscar Ltd's transactions are shown at Table 3.2.

    b   The transactions posted from the journal entries to the ledger accounts are as shown in Figure 3.10.

    c   The trial balance for the transactions posted to the ledger accounts is shown at Table 3.3.

    d   The financial position of Oscar Ltd is shown at Table 3.4.

2   The required activities are as follows.

    a   The journal entries of Oscar Ltd for the month of May are shown below. First update the chart of accounts for the company as shown at Table 3.5. The general journal entries for Oscar Ltd's transactions are shown at Table 3.6.

    b   The transactions posted from the journal entries to the ledger accounts are as follows (using where appropriate the accounts and balances from Problem 1):

    c   The trial balance for the transactions posted to the ledger accounts is shown at Table 3.7.

    d   The recorded depreciation for the end of May accounting period in the general journal and ledger accounts are shown below.

The depreciation charge for the month of May needs to be calculated before it can be recorded in the general journal and ledger accounts. The data regarding the depreciation charge for the relevant assets is as follows:

- The building has a useful life of 25 years with no salvage value. A straight-line depreciation method is used by the company.
- The office furniture has a useful life of 10 years with no salvage value. A straight-line depreciation method is also used.
- The computer equipment has a useful life of 5 years with salvage value of €30. A straight-line depreciation method is also used.

The depreciation for the month of May is calculated by the equation:

Depreciation = (Asset Value − Salvage Value) ÷ Useful Life in months

The depreciation computations for the relevant assets are shown at Table 3.8.

The chart of accounts with the additional accounts is shown at Table 3.9. The general journal entries for the transactions related to depreciation are shown at Table 3.10.

The ledger accounts for the transactions related to depreciation are shown at Figure 3.12.

e   The adjusted trial balance with the depreciation transactions included is shown at Table 3.11.

f   The financial statements are shown below as follows:

    i   Income statement for period ending 31 May 20xx (Table 3.12).

    ii   Statement of changes to owner's equity as at 31 May 20xx (Table 3.13).

    iii   Statement of cash flows for period ending 31 May 20xx (Table 3.14).

    iv   Statement of financial position as at 31 May 20xx (Table 3.15).

TABLE 3.1 Chart of accounts for Oscar Ltd

Account Category	Code	Account Title
Assets	1	Bank
	5	Accounts Receivable
	25	Land
	26	Building
	30	Office Furniture
	32	Computer Equipment
Liabilities	40	Accounts Payable
Owners' equity	60	Ms. R. Kramer, capital

TABLE 3.2 General journal for Oscar Ltd

Date	Accounts Titles and Particulars	L.F	Debit (€)	Credit (€)
1 April	Bank	1	260,000	
	Ms. R. Kramer, capital	60		260,000
	Set-up an entity 'Oscar Ltd' with a cash investment.			
3 April	Land	25	77,000	
	Bank	1		77,000
	Oscar Ltd purchased land for office site.			
5 April	Building	26	144,000	
	Bank	1		144,000
	Purchased prefabricated building from K-Builders Ltd.			
15 April	Accounts Receivable	5	30,000	
	Land	25		30,000
	Sold part of land to Smite Fast Foods Plc to be paid within 90 days.			
17 April	Office Furniture	30	18,000	
	Accounts Payable	40		18,000
	Purchased furniture from Delta Furniture Ltd on credit.			
18 April	Computer Equipment	32	7,650	
	Accounts Payable	40		7,650
	Purchased computer equipment from Ascot-It on credit.			
22 April	Bank	1	5,500	
	Accounts Receivable	5		5,500
	Smite Fast Foods made a part payment for land.			
24 April	Accounts Payable	40	9,000	
	Bank	1		9,000
	Part payment to Delta Furniture Ltd for furniture.			
26 April	Accounts Payable	40	4,000	
	Bank	1		4,000
	Part payment to Ascot-It Ltd for computer equipment.			
	Total:		**555,150**	**555,150**

Bank		A/c no. 01			**Accounts Receivable**		A/c no. 05	
01-Apr	260,000				15-Apr	30,000		
		03-Apr	77,000					
		05-Apr	144,000				22-Apr	5,500
22-Apr	5,500							
		24-Apr	9,000					
		26-Apr	4,000					

Land		A/c no. 25			**Building**		A/c no. 26	
03-Apr	77,000				05-Apr	144,000		
		15-Apr	30,000					

Office Furniture		A/c no. 30			**Computer Equipment**		A/c no. 32	
17-Apr	18,000				18-Apr	7,650		

Accounts Payable		A/c no. 40			**Ms. R. Kramer, capital**		A/c no. 60	
		17-Apr	18,000				01-Apr	260,000
		18-Apr	7,650					
24-Apr	9,000							
26-Apr	4,000							

FIGURE 3.10 Ledger accounts for Oscar Ltd

TABLE 3.3 Oscar Ltd trial balance 30 April 20xx

Bank	1	€ 31,500	
Accounts Receivable	5	€ 24,500	
Land	25	€ 47,000	
Building	26	€ 144,000	
Office Furniture	30	€ 18,000	
Computer Equipment	32	€ 7,650	
Accounts Payable	40		€ 12,650
Ms. R. Kramer, capital	60		€ 260,000
		€ 272,650	**€ 272,650**

TABLE 3.4 Oscar Ltd balance sheet as at 30 April 20xx

Assets:

Bank	€ 31,500
Accounts Receivable	€ 24,500
Land	€ 47,000
Building	€ 144,000
Office Furniture	€ 18,000
Computer Equipment	€ 7,650
Total Assets:	**€ 272,650**

Liabilities

Accounts Payable	€ 12,650

Owner's Equity

Ms. R. Kramer, capital	€ 260,000
Total Liabilities and Owner's Equity:	**€ 272,650**

TABLE 3.5 Updated chart of accounts for Oscar Ltd

Account Category	Code	Account Title
Assets	1	Bank
	5	Accounts Receivable
	25	Land
	26	Building
	30	Office Furniture
	32	Computer Equipment
Liabilities	40	Accounts Payable
Owners' equity	60	Ms. R. Kramer, Capital
	61	Ms. R. Kramer, Drawings
Revenue	71	Sales Commissions
Expenses	80	Advertising Expense
	82	Wages Expense
	84	Telephone Expense
	85	Electricity Expense

TABLE 3.6 Updated general journal for Oscar Ltd

Date	Accounts Titles and Particulars	L.F	Debit (€)	Credit (€)
3 May	Advertising Expense	80	1,800	
	Bank	1		1,800
	Oscar Ltd paid for advertising on the local media.			
8 May	Bank	1	9,750	
	Sales commissions	71		9,750
	Company was paid for selling goods on a sales commission basis.			
14 May	Electricity Expense	85	900	
	Accounts Payable	40		900
	Received electricity bill to be paid in 30 days.			
22 May	Accounts Receivable	5	11,300	
	Sales commissions	71		11,300
	Invoiced client for selling goods on commission to be paid in 30 days.			
24 May	Telephone Expense	84	480	
	Accounts Payable	40		480
	Received a telephone bill to be paid by the end of May.			
31 May	Wages Expense	82	8,400	
	Bank	1		8,400
	Paid the workers their wages.			
31 May	Ms. R. Kramer, Drawings	61	6,600	
	Bank	1		6,600
	Ms Kramer withdrew cash from the company for €600.			
	Total:		39,230	39,230

Bank		A/c no. 01			**Accounts Receivable**		A/c no. 05	
01-Apr	260,000				15-Apr	30,000		
		03-Apr	77,000				22-Apr	5,500
		05-Apr	144,000					
22-Apr	5,500				22-May	11,300		
		24-Apr	9,000					
		26-Apr	4,000					
		03-May	1,800					
08-May	9,750							
		31-May	8,400					
		31-May	6,600					

Land		A/c no. 25			**Building**		A/c no. 26	
03-Apr	77,000				05-Apr	144,000		
		15-Apr	30,000					

Office Furniture		A/c no. 30			**Computer Equipment**		A/c no. 32	
17-Apr	18,000				18-Apr	7,650		

Accounts Payable		A/c no. 40			**Ms. R. Kramer, capital**		A/c no. 60	
		17-Apr	18,000				01-Apr	260,000
		18-Apr	7,650					
24-Apr	9,000							
26-Apr	4,000							
		14-May	900					
		24-May	480					

Ms. R. Kramer, Drawings		A/c no. 61			**Sales Commissions**		A/c no. 71	
31-May	6,600						08-May	9,750
							08-May	11,300

Advertising Expense		A/c no. 80			**Wages Expense**		A/c no. 82	
03-May	1,800				31-May	8,400		

Telephone Expense		A/c no. 84			**Electricity Expense**		A/c no. 85	
24-May	480				31-May	900		

FIGURE 3.11 Updated ledger accounts for Oscar Ltd

TABLE 3.7 Oscar Ltd trial balance 31 May 20xx

Bank	1	€ 24,450	
Accounts Receivable	5	€ 35,800	
Land	25	€ 47,000	
Building	26	€ 144,000	
Office Furniture	30	€ 18,000	
Computer Equipment	32	€ 7,650	
Accounts Payable	40		€ 14,030
Ms. R. Kramer, Capital	60		€ 260,000
Ms. R. Kramer, Drawings	61	€ 6,600	
Sales Commissions	71		€ 21,050
Advertising Expense	80	€ 1,800	
Wages Expense	82	€ 8,400	
Telephone Expense	84	€ 480	
Electricity Expense	85	€ 900	
		€ 295,080	**€ 295,080**

TABLE 3.8 Depreciation computations for relevant assets

Building	
Asset Value:	€ 144,000
Less Salvage Value:	€0
Value for depreciation purposes:	€ 144,000
Depreciation for month of May = €144,000 ÷ 300 months	**= €480**
Office Furniture	
Asset Value:	€ 18,000
Less Salvage Value:	€0
Value for depreciation purposes:	€ 18,000
Depreciation for month of May = €18,000 ÷ 120 months	**= € 150**
Computer Equipment	
Asset Value:	€ 7,650
Less Salvage Value:	€30
Value for depreciation purposes:	€ 7,620
Depreciation for month of May = € 7,620 ÷ 60 months	**= € 127**

Summary of Depreciation Transactions

31 May	Depreciation for:	Building	€ 480
31 May	Depreciation for:	Office Furniture	€ 150
31 May	Depreciation for:	Computer Equipment	€ 127

TABLE 3.9 Updated chart of accounts

Account Category	Code	Account Title
Assets	27	Provision for Depreciation: Building
	31	Provision for Depreciation: Office Furniture
	33	Provision for Depreciation: Computer Equipment
Expenses	86	Depreciation Expenses: Building
	87	Depreciation Expenses: Office Furniture
	88	Depreciation Expenses: Computer Equipment

TABLE 3.10 General journal entries for depreciation transactions

Date	Accounts Titles and Particulars	L.F	Debit (€)	Credit (€)
31 May	Depreciation Expenses: Building	86	480	
	Provision for Depreciation: Building	27		480
	Depreciation for Building			
31 May	Depreciation Expenses: Office Furniture	87	150	
	Provision for Depreciation: Office Furniture	31		150
	Depreciation for Office Furniture			
31 May	Depreciation Expenses: Computer Equipment	88	127	
	Provision for Depreciation: Computer Equipment	33		127
	Depreciation for Computer Equipment			
	Total:		€ 757	€ 757

Provision for Depreciation: Building	A/c no. 27		
		31-May	480

Provision for Depreciation: Office Furniture	A/c no. 31		
		31-May	150

Provision for Depreciation: Computer Equipment	A/c no. 33		
		31-May	127

Depreciation Expenses: Building	A/c no. 86		
31-May	480		

Depreciation Expenses: Office Furniture	A/c no. 87		
31-May	150		

Depreciation Expenses: Computer Equipment	A/c no. 88		
31-May	127		

FIGURE 3.12 Updated ledger accounts for depreciation transactions

TABLE 3.11 Oscar Ltd trial balance 31 May 20xx

	Before Adjustments		After Adjustments	
Bank	24,450		24,450	
Accounts Receivable	35,800		35,800	
Land	47,000		47,000	
Building	144,000		144,000	
Provision for Depreciation: Building				480
Office Furniture	18,000		18,000	
Provision for Depreciation: Office Furniture				150
Computer Equipment	7,650		7,650	
Provision for Dep.: Computer Equipment				127
Accounts Payable		14,030		14,030
Ms. R. Kramer, Capital		260,000		260,000
Ms. R. Kramer, Drawings	6,600		6,600	
Sales Commissions		21,050		21,050
Advertising Expense	1,800		1,800	
Wages Expense	8,400		8,400	
Telephone Expense	480		480	
Electricity Expense	900		900	
Depreciation Expenses: Building			480	
Depreciation Expenses: Office Furniture			150	
Depreciation Expenses: Computer Equipment			127	
	295,080	295,080	295,837	295,837

TABLE 3.12 Income statement for period ending 31 May 20xx

Sales Commissions		€ 21,050
Expenses:		
Advertising Expense	€ 1,800	
Wages Expense	€ 8,400	
Telephone Expense	€ 480	
Electricity Expense	€ 900	
Depreciation Expenses: Building	€ 480	
Depreciation Expenses: Office Furniture	€ 150	
Depreciation Expenses: Computer Equipment	€ 127	€ 12,337
Net Income:		€ 8,713

TABLE 3.13 Statement of changes to owner's equity as at 31 May 20xx

Ms. R. Kramer, Capital 30 April 20xx	€ 260,000
Investment during the month	€ 0
Net income (loss)	€ 8,713
	€ 268,713
Ms. R. Kramer, Drawings	€ 6,600
Ms. R. Kramer, Capital 31 May 20xx	**€ 262,113**

TABLE 3.14 Statement of cash flows for period ending 31 May 20xx

Operating Cash Flows	
Sales Commissions	€ 9,750
Advertising Expense	-€ 1,800
Wages Expense	-€ 8,400
Investing Cash Flows	
Capital Expenditure	€ 0
Ms. R. Kramer, Drawings	-€ 6,600
Financing Cash Flows	
Borrowing	€ 0
Net Increase/Decrease in Cash	-€ 7,050
Cash at Beginning of Period (1 May 20xx)	€ 31,500
Cash at End of Period (31 May 20xx)	**€ 24,450**

TABLE 3.15 Statement of financial position as at 31 May 20xx

Assets

Bank		€24,450
Accounts Receivable		€35,800
Land		€47,000
Building	€144,000	
Less: Provision for Depreciation: Building	€480	€143,520
Office Furniture	€18,000	
Less: Provision for Depreciation: Office Furniture	€150	€17,850
Computer Equipment	€7,650	
Less: Provision for Depreciation: Computer Equipment	€127	€7,523
Total Assets:		**€276,143**

Liabilities

Accounts Payable		€14,030

Owner's Equity

Ms. R. Kramer, Capital		€260,000
Net Income (loss)	€8,713	
Less: Ms. R. Kramer, Drawings	€6,600	€2,113
Total Liabilities and Owner's Equity:		**€276,143**

References

Harrison, Ian. (2006). *Complete A-Z Accounting Handbook*. London: Hodder Arnold.
Wood, F. and Sangster, A. (2007). *Business Accounting*, 10th edn. London: Prentice Hall.

PART 2

Accounting for financial instruments

The focus of this part is on three important aspects in relation to financial instruments, namely, the relevant accounting standards that impact directly designated financial instruments; the accounting treatment method that is applicable to each category of financial instrument as defined by the accounting standards; and a focused analysis of bills of exchange and promissory notes, since they are a very common and popular type of financial instrument.

The relevant IFRS and GAAP accounting standards form the basis of the study regarding accounting for investments. Accounting standards that directly impact financial instruments are essential because they provide a consistent definition of the various categories of financial instruments, particularly how they are measured, namely amortised cost or fair value depending on the financial instrument category. Moreover, the standards also address the issue related to the information that should be disclosed about each category of financial instruments within the financial statements.

The accounting treatment of financial instruments depends on the specific investment category, namely, held-to-maturity, and loans and receivables, both of which are measured at amortised cost; and fair value through profit or loss and available-for-sale both of which are measured at fair value. The accounting treatment is particularly important when purchasing and selling financial instruments at a date other than their maturity date. In this regard, two additional concepts are provided in relation to purchasing and selling of financial instruments, namely, cumulative dividend investments and excluding dividend investments.

Cumulative dividend or cumulative interest (cum-div or cum-int) means that a buyer of a security is entitled to receive a dividend or interest that has been declared, but not paid. This means that the security is offered for sale with an entitlement to the next dividend or interest payment attached. Excluding dividend or excluding interest (ex-div or ex-int) means that the declared dividend or interest will be received by the seller and not the buyer. Hence, stock is given ex-div or ex-int status if an individual or entity has been confirmed by the company to receive the dividend or interest payment. The purchase of shares or bonds without entitlement to recently declared dividends means that the entitlement to receive a dividend or interest remains with the seller of the shares or bonds. Hence, both cum div and ex div may require accounting adjustment entries to reflect these specific phenomena.

Bills of exchange and promissory notes are specifically included in Part 2 because they are classified as financial assets because of two principal attributes, namely they are highly liquid and have distinct legal characteristics. Moreover, bills of exchange and promissory notes are important financial instruments because they represent conventional everyday accounting entries and may be categorised as held-to-maturity; loans and receivables; fair value through profit or loss; and available-for-sale depending upon their financial nature. However, a number of issues in relation to bills of exchange and promissory notes need to be addressed, particularly the accounting treatment for their collection and retirement. The above demonstrates that the chapters in Part 2 provide a comprehensive accounting treatment for financial instruments that forms the theoretical basis of the book in general.

4

RELEVANT ACCOUNTING STANDARDS

> Mandatory reporting must remain focused on the ultimate objectives of disclosure requirements for both companies and governments: good tax governance, accountability and transparency.
>
> Fox Business (2013)

Currently, the greatest difficulty with accounting for financial instruments is the imprecise or ill-defined nature of this accounting segment. The major reasons for this state of affairs are basically two, the convergence between the standards established by the US Financial Accounting Standards Board (FASB) and the International Accounting Standards Board (IASB); and the transition process from the International Accounting Standards (IAS) to the International Financial Reporting Standards (IFRS) undertaken by the IASB. The amount of accounting standards writing currently taking place is very dynamic and intricate, with standards being revised and in many cases completely rewritten.

This chapter will discuss some key accounting standards aspects in relation to financial instruments, namely the relevant IFRS/IAS accounting standards and the comparison between IFRS/IAS and US GAAP.

Relevant IFRS and IAS accounting standards for financial instruments

Before discussing the individual IFRS/IAS standards that are relevant to financial instruments, it is best to consider the implication of the IFRS/IAS in general. IFRS/IAS is a response to the need to have a common global set of rules that allows the accounts of entities to be more meaningful, comprehendible and comparable across international boundaries. They are an essential consequence of globalisation and have replaced the various national accounting standards. Initially, these accounting standards were known as the International Accounting Standards (IAS) that had been issued between 1973 and 2001. However, after 2001, earnest discussions commenced between IASB and FASB with the objective of establishing a framework for updating and converging these dominant accounting standards.

IFRS are used in over 100 countries, with the number growing every year. The benefit to users of financial statements from the worldwide acceptance of IFRS is related to better decision making due to the increasing quality and reliability of financial information, particularly the cost savings of preparing comparative statements for deciding between alternative investments. The relevant IASB accounting standards related to accounting for financial instruments include:

- IAS 32 Financial Instruments: Presentation;
- IAS 39 Financial Instruments: Recognition and Measurement;
- IFRS 7 Financial Instruments: Disclosures;
- IFRS 9 Financial Instruments.

IAS 32 Financial Instruments: Presentation

IAS 32 has two key objectives, namely to establish the principles for presenting financial instruments as liabilities or equity and for offsetting financial assets and financial liabilities; and to improve the understanding for those using the financial statements of the implication and importance of the financial instruments to an entity's financial position, performance and cash flows.

IAS 32 takes the perspective of the issuer of the financial instrument. IAS 32 is applicable to the classification of financial instruments into financial assets, financial liabilities and equity instruments; the classification of related interest, dividends, losses and gains; and the circumstances in which financial assets and financial liabilities should be offset. The principles in IAS 32 are designed to work in close association with the principles for the recognition and measuring of financial assets and financial liabilities in IAS 39 (Financial Instruments: Recognition and Measurement), and for disclosing information about financial assets and financial liabilities in IFRS 7 (Financial Instruments: Disclosures).

Generally, IAS 32 applies to all entities for every type of financial instrument. More specifically, IAS 32 applies to all contracts for buying or selling a non-financial item that can be settled net in cash or another financial instrument, or by exchanging financial instruments, as if the contracts were financial instruments. The exception to this rule are contracts that were entered into and continue to be held for the purpose of the receipt or delivery of a non-financial item in accordance with the entity's expected purchase, sale, or usage requirements.

Additionally, IAS 32 applies to all entities, except where it specifically refers to another standard and/or a different accounting treatment. For example, IAS 32 does not apply to interests in subsidiaries, associates, or joint ventures, whose accounting treatment are dealt with by IAS 27 (Consolidated and Separate Financial Statements), IAS 28 (Investments in Associates) or IAS 31 (Interests in Joint

Ventures), respectively. Similarly, IAS 32 does not apply to employers' rights and obligations under employee benefit plans, since these are provided for by IAS 19 (Employee Benefits), nor does it apply to insurance contracts as defined in IFRS 4 (Insurance Contracts).

However, the standard applies to derivatives that are embedded in insurance contracts, particularly when IAS 39 requires the entity to account for them separately. Moreover, an issuer of a financial instrument must apply IAS 32 to financial guarantee contracts when the issuer applies IAS 39 in recognising and measuring the contracts, unless the issuer elects, in accordance with paragraph 4(d) of IFRS 4, to apply IFRS 4 in recognising and measuring them. IAS 32 also does not apply to financial instruments, contracts and obligations under share-based payment transactions except for limited exceptions that are catered within the scope of IAS 32, since these are covered by IFRS 2 (Share-based Payment).

Before going further with the explanation of IAS 32, it is best to establish the definitions for the key terms. These definitions are found in Table 4.1. It should be noted that there is a link between the financial instruments standards. Hence, IAS 32 provides the key definitions as to what constitutes a financial instrument, but the standard also refers the reader to IAS 39 for other definitions, noting that the terms defined in IAS 39 are used in IAS 32 with the meaning specific to IAS 39.

The essential issue with IAS 32 is presentation. The issuer of a financial instrument shall classify the instrument, or its component parts, on initial recognition as a financial liability, a financial asset or an equity instrument in accordance with the substance of the contractual arrangement and the definitions of a financial liability, a financial asset and an equity instrument. A key issue is how to distinguish between a financial liability and equity. Traditionally, preference shares were classified as equity. However, according to IAS 32, preference shares with a fixed rate of dividend and mandatory redemption date are considered as a financial liability. But preference shares with no fixed interest rate and no mandatory redemption period are defined as equity. Some financial instruments, such as convertible debt, may combine features associated with both equity instruments and financial liabilities. Hence, the issuer of a non-derivative financial instrument should assess the terms of the financial instrument to ascertain if the financial instrument has both a liability and an equity component. Depending on this assessment, the identified components must be classified according to their attribute (financial liabilities, financial assets, or equity instruments).

With some exceptions related to puttable instruments, an important characteristic in differentiating a financial liability from an equity instrument is the existence of a contractual obligation of one party to the financial instrument to either deliver cash or another financial asset to the other party, or an obligation to exchange financial assets or financial liabilities with the holder under conditions that are potentially unfavourable to the issuer. In essence, the equity instrument owner has no authority to oblige an issuer to make such distributions because the issuer has no contractual obligation to deliver cash or another financial asset to the equity

TABLE 4.1 Key definitions of the terms used in IAS 32

Financial Instrument. A financial instrument is any contract that gives rise to a financial asset of one entity and a financial liability or equity instrument of another entity.
Financial Asset. A financial asset is any asset that is: • Cash; • An equity instrument of another entity; • A contractual right to receive cash or another financial asset from another entity or to exchange financial assets or financial liabilities with another entity under conditions that are potentially favourable to the entity; • A contract that will or may be settled in the entity's own equity instruments and is a non-derivative for which the entity is or may be obliged to receive a variable number of the entity's own equity instruments; or a derivative that will or may be settled other than by the exchange of a fixed amount of cash or another financial asset for a fixed number of the entity's own equity instruments.
Financial Liability. A financial liability is any liability that is: • A contractual obligation to deliver cash or another financial asset to another entity; or to exchange financial assets or financial liabilities with another entity under conditions that are potentially unfavourable to the entity; • A contract that will or may be settled in the entity's own equity instruments and is a non-derivative for which the entity is or may be obliged to deliver a variable number of the entity's own equity instruments; or a derivative that will or may be settled other than by the exchange of a fixed amount of cash or another financial asset for a fixed number of the entity's own equity instruments.
Equity Instrument. An equity instrument is any contract that evidences a residual interest in the assets of an entity after deducting all of its liabilities.
Fair Value. Fair value is the amount for which an asset could be exchanged, or a liability settled, between knowledgeable, willing parties in an arm's length transaction.
Puttable Instrument. A puttable instrument is a financial instrument that gives the holder the right to put the instrument back to the issuer for cash or another financial asset or is automatically put back to the issuer on the occurrence of an uncertain future event or the death or retirement of the instrument holder.

instrument holder. Moreover, dividends do not make an equity instrument a financial liability because dividends are not mandatory, even though some preferred shares contain a cumulative stipulation. On the other hand, an obligation meets the definition of a financial liability when an entity lacks an unconditional right to avoid delivering cash or another financial asset to settle a contractual obligation. The exceptions to this rule are those related to puttable instruments.

Thus, puttable instruments are handled in a different way from other financial instruments. A puttable instrument is a financial instrument that gives the holder the right to put the instrument back to the issuer for cash or another financial asset or is automatically put back to the issuer on the occurrence of an uncertain future event or the death or retirement of the instrument holder. For example, units of a mutual fund would be considered puttable financial instruments since the holder has the right to redeem or convert the unit for cash at any time.

IAS 39 Financial Instruments: Recognition and Measurement

Generally, IAS 39 provides the requirements for the recognition and measurement of financial assets, financial liabilities and various contracts to buy or sell non-financial items. Financial instruments are initially recognised when an entity becomes a party to the contractual provisions of the instrument, and are classified into various categories depending upon the type of instrument. The measurement of the instrument (typically amortised cost or fair value) is determined once the instrument type is established. However, particular rules apply to embedded derivatives and hedging instruments.

The IASB has decided to replace IAS 39 over a period of time by IFRS 9. The first phase was issued as IFRS 9 Financial Instruments in November 2009, which dealt with classification and measurement of financial assets. The second phase came into effect in October 2010. This added to IFRS 9, the requirements for classification and measurement of financial liabilities and de-recognition of financial assets and liabilities. As a consequence, parts of IAS 39 are being superseded and will become obsolete for annual periods beginning on or after 1 January 2013 – earlier application was permitted in 2010. The remaining requirements of IAS 39 continue in effect until superseded by the implementation of future phases of IFRS 9. Hence, IAS 39 will be replaced in its entirety. Table 4.2 provides details of the financial instruments that are excluded from IAS 39, while Table 4.3 contains the financial instruments that are covered by IAS 39.

As stated previously, IAS 39 incorporates various definitions from IAS32 (Financial Instruments: Presentation). These include the definitions of financial instrument; financial asset; financial liability; and equity instrument. Moreover, when an entity applies IFRS 9 (Financial Instruments) before the mandatory application date of 1 January 2015, the definitions of de-recognition, derivative, fair value, financial guarantee contract are incorporated from IFRS 9. Table 4.4 provides other definitions that are found in IAS 39.

While IAS 39 addresses accounting for financial liabilities, it does not deal with accounting for equity instruments issued by the reporting enterprise. As already explained this issue is addressed by IAS 32 (Financial Instruments: Presentation). Figure 4.1 illustrates that IAS 39 identifies two categories of financial liabilities, namely financial liabilities at fair value through profit or loss and other financial liabilities measured at amortised cost using the effective interest method. The former category is divided further into two subclasses, namely designated and held for trading. Designated is a financial liability that is categorised by the entity as a liability at fair value through profit or loss upon initial recognition. Whereas, held for trading is a financial liability which the entity holds for trading, such as an obligation for securities borrowed in a short sale that has to be returned in the future.

TABLE 4.2 Financial instruments excluded from IAS 39

Particulars	Standard Applicable
Interests in subsidiaries, associates, and joint ventures.	For periods beginning on or after 01 Jan 2013. • IFRS 10 Consolidated Financial Statements • IAS 27 Separate Financial Statements • IAS 28 Investments in Associates and Joint Ventures
Employers' rights and obligations under employee benefit plans.	• IAS 19 Employee Benefits
Forward contracts between an acquirer and selling shareholder to buy or sell an acquiree that will result in a business combination at a future acquisition date.	
Rights and obligations under insurance contracts.	• IAS 39 applies to financial instruments that take the form of an insurance (or reinsurance) contract but that mainly involve the transfer of financial risks and derivatives rooted in insurance contracts.
Financial instruments that meet the definition of own equity.	• IAS 32 Financial Instruments: Presentation
Financial instruments, contracts and obligations under share-based payment transactions.	• IFRS 2 Share-based Payment
Rights to reimbursement payments.	• IAS 37 Provisions, Contingent Liabilities and Contingent Assets

Figure 4.2 demonstrates that IAS 39 classifies financial assets in one of four categories, that is, financial assets at fair value through profit or loss; available-for-sale financial assets; loans and receivables; and held-to-maturity investments. The specific classification of the particular financial assets determines how they are recognised and measured in the financial statements.

Financial assets classified as fair value through profit or loss has two subcategories similar to financial liabilities. These two subcategories are designated and held for trading. Designated refers to any financial asset that is categorised on initial recognition as one to be measured at fair value with fair value changes in profit or loss. On the other hand, held for trading consists of all derivatives (except those designated hedging instruments) and financial assets acquired or held for the purpose of selling in the short-term or for which there is a recent pattern of short-term profit generation.

Available for sale (AFS) assets are measured at fair value in the balance sheet. AFS assets with fair value changes are recognised directly in equity, through the

TABLE 4.3 Financial instruments covered by IAS 39

Particulars
Leases:
• Lease receivables with respect to de-recognition and impairment provisions.
• Lease payables with respect to the de-recognition provisions.
• Derivatives embedded in leases.
Financial guarantees:
Financial guarantee contracts issued.
IAS 39 or IFRS 4 apply if the financial guarantees were treated as insurance contracts.
Loan commitments:
Loan commitments are outside the scope of IAS 39 if they cannot be settled net in cash or another financial instrument; they are not designated as financial liabilities at fair value through profit or loss; and the entity does not have a past practice of selling the loans that resulted from the commitment shortly after origination.
Contracts to buy or sell financial items:
Contracts to buy or sell financial items are covered by IAS 39, unless one of the other exceptions applies.
Contracts to buy or sell non-financial items:
Contracts to buy or sell non-financial items are covered by IAS 39:
• If they can be settled net in cash or another financial asset and are not entered into and held for the purpose of the receipt or delivery of a non-financial item in accordance with the entity's expected purchase, sale, or usage requirements.
• If net settlement occurs. Net settlement is deemed to occur if the terms of the contract permit either counterparty to settle net; there is a past practice of net settling similar contracts; there is a past practice, for similar contracts, of taking delivery of the underlying and selling it within a short period after delivery to generate a profit from short (term fluctuations in price, or from a dealer's margin); or the non-financial item is readily convertible to cash.
Weather derivatives:
Contracts requiring payment based on climatic, geological or other physical variable are covered by IAS 39 unless they are covered by IFRS 4.

statement of changes in equity. The exceptions to this rule are interest on AFS assets, which is recognised as income on an effective yield basis; impairment losses; and foreign exchange gains or losses that are generated for interest-bearing AFS debt instruments. However, the cumulative gain or loss that was recognised in equity is recorded in profit or loss when an available-for-sale financial asset is derecognised.

Loans and receivables are non-derivative financial assets that are not quoted in an active market and generate fixed or determinable payments and in which the holding entity does not intend to trade. Hence, this means that their value is not derived from the expected future price movements of an underlying asset as in the case of derivatives. However, loans and receivables should be classified as available-

TABLE 4.4 Definitions of terms found in IAS 39

Financial Instrument. A financial instrument is any contract that gives rise to a financial asset of one entity and a financial liability or equity instrument of another entity. Examples of a financial instrument:

- Cash; demand and time deposits; and commercial paper;

- Accounts, notes, and loans receivable and payable;

- Debt and equity securities. These include investments in subsidiaries, associates, and joint ventures;

- Asset backed securities such as collateralised mortgage obligations, repurchase agreements, and securitised packages of receivables;

- Derivatives, including options, rights, warrants, futures contracts, forward contracts, and swaps.

Derivative. A derivative is a financial instrument whose value changes in response to the change in an underlying variable such as an interest rate, commodity or security price, or index; that requires no initial investment, or one that is smaller than would be required for a contract with similar response to changes in market factors; and that is settled at a future date. Examples of derivatives:

- Forwards: Contracts to purchase or sell a specific quantity of a financial instrument, a commodity, or a foreign currency at a specified price determined at the outset, with delivery or settlement at a specified future date. Settlement is at maturity by actual delivery of the item specified in the contract, or by a net cash settlement.

- Interest rate swaps and forward rate agreements: Contracts to exchange cash flows as of a specified date or a series of specified dates based on a notional amount and fixed and floating rates.

- Futures: Contracts similar to forwards but have the following differences. Futures are generic exchange-traded, whereas forwards are individually tailored. Futures are generally settled through an offsetting (reversing) trade, whereas forwards are generally settled by delivery of the underlying item or cash settlement.

- Options: Contracts that give the purchaser the right, but not the obligation, to buy (call option) or sell (put option) a specified quantity of a particular financial instrument, commodity, or foreign currency, at a specified price (strike price), during or at a specified period of time. These can be individually written or exchange traded. The purchaser of the option pays the seller (writer) of the option a fee (premium) to compensate the seller for the risk of payments under the option.

- Caps and floors: These are at times referred to as interest rate options. An interest rate cap will compensate the purchaser of the cap if interest rates rise above a predetermined rate (strike rate) while an interest rate floor will compensate the purchaser if rates fall below a predetermined rate.

---

for-sale if the holder does not substantially recover all of the initial investment (unless this is due to credit deterioration).

Generally, loans and receivables are measured at amortised cost using the effective interest rate method. This means that the actual interest rate in an accounting period is based on the book value of the financial instrument at the beginning of that accounting period. For example, if the book value decreases the amount of interest due also decreases and vice-versa. This method is more accurate on a period-to-period basis than the straight-line method but it requires

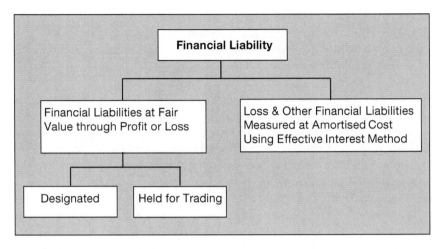

FIGURE 4.1 Recognition of financial liabilities under IAS 39

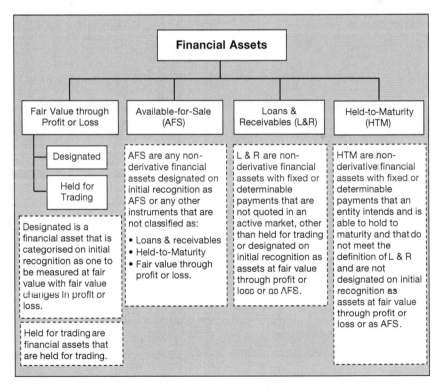

FIGURE 4.2 Classification of financial assets under IAS 39

a more difficult computational process since it needs to be recalculated every month. In practice, the effective interest rate discounts the expected future cash inflows and outflows expected over the life of a financial instrument thus the interest earnings or expense recognised in an accounting period is the effective interest rate multiplied by the carrying amount of a financial instrument.

Loans and receivables are normally included in current assets except for the portion falling due beyond 12 months from the end of the reporting period and therefore classified as non-current. The gains and losses are recognised in the consolidated statement of income when the loans and receivables are derecognised or impaired, in addition to the amortisation process. Interest earned or incurred is recorded in 'Interest Income' in the consolidated statement of income. The above may be illustrated by some practical examples.

Example 1: Assume that Novice Ltd has some access cash and has invested this cash by issuing a loan to Ajax Ltd for a principal value of €2,500 which will mature in five years at a fixed interest rate of 10 per cent per annum. The loan terms and conditions are: principal amount for €2,500 at 1.1×5 to Ajax Ltd for five years at 10 per cent interest rate. In other words, Novice Ltd derives an effective interest rate of 9.10 per cent (i.e. $1/1.1 = 9.09$ per cent). Table 4.5 provides the computations and resulting accounting entries regarding the example related to 'Loans and Receivables' at amortised cost.

The accounting entries involve four accounts. The amortisation values per annum and interest income are posted as a credit to the 'Loan Account' and 'Interest Income Account' respectively. The balances of these two accounts equal to the balance of the 'Cash Account' (i.e. €1,250).

Example 2: Assume that Capricorn Ltd is lending an entity a principal amount of €2.5 million that will mature over a 10-year duration at an interest rate of 10 per cent per annum. The original effective interest rate is 9.89 per cent with an initial carrying value of €2,517,500. Furthermore, the original fee charged to the borrowing entity is €17,500 and the origination costs incurred by Capricorn Ltd are €35,000. Table 4.6 provides the amortisation computations and Table 4.7 shows the resulting accounting entries regarding the example related to 'Loans and Receivables' at amortised cost.

The 'Interest Income' column at Table 4.6 is equal to the 'Ending Amortised Cost' of the previous row times the 'Effective Interest Rate' (ER). For example, €2,517,500 × ER (where ER is approximately 9.886632 per cent) = €248,896 and so on.

Held-to-maturity investments are also measured at amortised cost. If an entity sells a held-to-maturity investment other than in insignificant amounts or as a consequence of a non-recurring, isolated event beyond its control that could not be reasonably anticipated, all of its other held-to-maturity investments must be reclassified as available-for-sale for the current and next two financial reporting years.

Financial assets and liabilities need to be measured following their initial recognition and classification into their respective category. All financial assets and liabilities including derivatives should be measured at fair value. Fair value is the

TABLE 4.5 Example 1: 'Loans and receivables' at amortised cost

Principal Amount: €2,500			Interest Rate:	10%	
			Effective Interest Rate:	9.09%	

Year	Beginning Amortised Cost	Cash Inflows	Interest Income	Amortisation Of Net Fees	Ending Amortised Cost
1	€2,500	€250	€227	€23	€2,477
2	€2,477	€250	€225	€25	€2,452
3	€2,452	€250	€223	€27	€2,425
4	€2,425	€250	€220	€30	€2,396
5	€2,396	€2,750	€218	€32	€2,364
		€3,750	€1,113	€137	€2,500

Accounting Entries

Cash Account

		Start Loan €2,500
Year-1[b]	€250	
Year-2[b]	€250	
Year-3[b]	€250	
Year-4[b]	€250	
Year-5[b]	€250	
Maturity	€2,500	
Balance	**€1,250**	

Loan Account

Start Loan €2,500		
	Year-1[a]	€23
	Year-2[a]	€25
	Year-3[a]	€27
	Year-4[a]	€30
	Year-5[a]	€32
	Maturity	€2,500
	Balance	**€137**

Debtors Account

Year-1[a]	€250	Year-1[b]	€250
Year-2[a]	€250	Year-2[b]	€250
Year-3[a]	€250	Year-3[b]	€250
Year-4[a]	€250	Year-4[b]	€250
Year-5[a]	€250	Year-5[b]	€250
		Balance	**Nil**

Interest Income Account

	Year-1[a]	€227
	Year-2[a]	€225
	Year-3[a]	€223
	Year-4[a]	€220
	Year-5[a]	€218
	Balance	**€1,113**

Notes:

a. Contractual interest accrued at the due date.
b. Receipt of Interest payment.

amount for which an asset could be exchanged, or a liability settled, between knowledgeable, willing parties in an arm's length transaction. However, there are some exceptions to this rule. Loans and receivables, held-to-maturity investments and non-derivative financial liabilities must be measured at amortised cost using the effective interest method. The effective interest method computes the actual interest rate in a period based on the amount of a financial instrument's book value at the beginning of the accounting period. Hence, if the book value increases, so

TABLE 4.6 Example 2: 'Loans and receivables' computations

Principal Amount (p): €2,500,000		Interest Rate (IR): 10%	
		Effective Interest Rate (ER): 9.89%	
Year	(A) Cash Inflows (P x IR)	(B) Interest Income (D x ER)	(C) Amortisation Of Net Fees (A – B)	(D) Ending Amortised Cost
		Starting from	>>>>>>>>>	€2,517,500
1	€250,000	€248,896	€1,104	€2,516,396
2	€250,000	€248,787	€1,213	€2,515,183
3	€250,000	€248,667	€1,333	€2,513,850
4	€250,000	€248,535	€1,465	€2,512,385
5	€250,000	€248,390	€1,610	€2,510,775
6	€250,000	€248,231	€1,769	€2,509,006
7	€250,000	€248,056	€1,944	€2,507,062
8	€250,000	€247,864	€2,136	€2,504,926
9	€250,000	€247,653	€2,347	€2,502,579
10	€250,000	€247,421	€2,579	€2,500,000
	€2,500,000	**€2,482,500**	**€17,500**	**€2,500,000**

too will the amount of related interest and vice versa. This approach is used to accurately account for bond premiums and discounts. Therefore, by amortising the discount at the market interest rate, an entity's accounting statements reflect more closely the economic reality of the bond issue and the entity's actual cost of debt. Furthermore, investments in equity instruments with no reliable fair value measurement must be measured at cost. It should be noted that financial assets and liabilities that are designated as a hedged item or hedging instrument are subject to measurement under the hedge accounting requirements of the IAS 39.

Figure 4.3 illustrates how a financial instrument's fair value is determined under different circumstances. Quoted market prices in an active market are the best verification of fair value, and when available should be used. However, if the financial instrument is not part of an active market, reliable estimates may be used. An acceptable valuation approach would include all the elements that market participants would take into consideration in establishing a price and is consistent with accepted economic principles for pricing financial instruments. However, if reliable estimates are not available then an entity must measure the financial instrument at cost less impairment.

The phasing out of IAS 39 has the objective of resolving some major lingering concerns. The key concerns are related to fair value accounting and having a uniform hedging accounting criteria for all derivatives. These concerns result in the volatility of the financial statements, particularly the income statement. This section will now focus on two aspects of IAS 39, namely (a) impairment and uncollectibility of financial assets measured at amortised cost; and (b) hedging.

TABLE 4.7 Example 2: 'Loans and receivables' accounting entries

Cash Account				Loan Account		
		Start Loan €2,500,000	Start Loan €2,500,000			
		Year-0^c €35,000	Year-0^c €35,000			
Year-0^d	€17,500				Year-0^d	€17,500
Year-1^b	€250,000				Year-1^a	€1,104
Year-2^b	€250,000				Year-2^a	€1,213
Year-3^b	€250,000				Year-3^a	€1,333
Year-4^b	€250,000				Year-4^a	€1,465
Year-5^b	€250,000				Year-5^a	€1,610
Year-6^b	€250,000				Year-6^a	€1,769
Year-7^b	€250,000				Year-7^a	€1,944
Year-8^b	€250,000				Year-8^a	€2,136
Year-9^b	€250,000				Year-9^a	€2,347
Yr-10^b	€250,000				Yr-10^a	€2,579
Maturity	€2,500,000				Maturity	€2,500,000
Balance €2,482,500			**Balance**	**Nil**		

Debtors Account				Interest Income Account	
Year-1^a €250,000	Year-1^b	€250,000		Year-1^a	€248,896
Year-2^a €250,000	Year-2^b	€250,000		Year-2^a	€248,787
Year-3^a €250,000	Year-3^b	€250,000		Year-3^a	€248,667
Year-4^a €250,000	Year-4^b	€250,000		Year-4^a	€248,535
Year-5^a €250,000	Year-5^b	€250,000		Year-5^a	€248,390
Year-6^a €250,000	Year-6^b	€250,000		Year-6^a	€248,231
Year-7^a €250,000	Year-7^b	€250,000		Year-7^a	€248,056
Year-8^a €250,000	Year-8^b	€250,000		Year-8^a	€247,864
Year-9^a €250,000	Year-9^b	€250,000		Year-9^a	€247,653
Year-10^a €250,000	Year-10^b	€250,000		Year-10^a	€247,421
	Balance	**Nil**		**Balance**	**€2,482,500**

Notes:

a. Contractual interest accrued at the due date.
b. Receipt of interest payment.
c. Origination costs incurred by lender.
d. Origination fee charged to borrower.

According to IAS 39 an entity shall assess at the end of each reporting period whether there is any objective evidence that a financial asset or group of financial assets measured at amortised cost is impaired. However, if the expected life of a financial asset cannot be reliably established, then the contractual life is used. If there is objective evidence that an impairment loss on financial assets measured at amortised cost has been incurred, the amount of the loss is measured as the difference between the asset's carrying amount and the present value of estimated future cash flows (excluding future credit losses that have not been incurred) discounted at the financial asset's original effective interest rate, that is the effective interest rate computed at initial recognition. The carrying amount of the asset shall be reduced either directly or through the use of an allowance account. The amount of the loss shall be recognised in profit or loss.

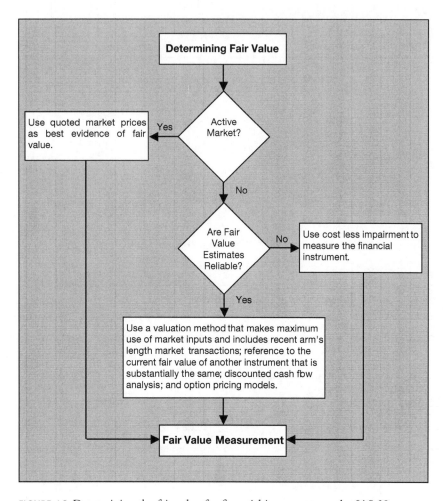

FIGURE 4.3 Determining the fair value for financial instruments under IAS 39

The remaining issue to be considered under IAS 39 is hedging. Figure 4.4 illustrates the types of hedging relationships. A hedging relationship qualifies for hedge accounting only when all the conditions itemised below are met:

a   At the inception of the hedge there is formal designation and documentation of the hedging relationship and the entity's risk management objective and strategy for undertaking the hedge. The documentation shall include identification of the hedging instrument; the hedged item or transaction; the nature of the risk being hedged; and how the entity will assess the hedging instrument's effectiveness in offsetting the exposure to changes in the hedged item's fair value or cash flows attributable to the hedged risk.

b   The hedge is expected to be highly effective in achieving offsetting changes in fair value or cash flows attributable to the hedged risk, consistently with

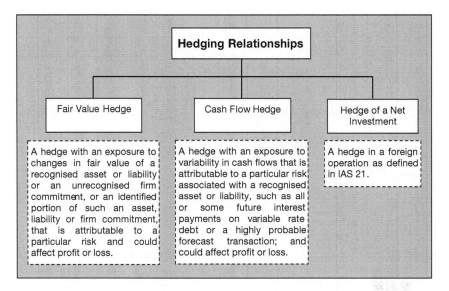

FIGURE 4.4 Types of hedging relationships under IAS 39

the originally documented risk management strategy for that particular hedging relationship.

c   For cash flow hedges, a forecast transaction that is the subject of the hedge must be highly probable and must present an exposure to variations in cash flows that could ultimately affect profit or loss.

d   The effectiveness of the hedge can be reliably measured. In other words, the fair value or cash flows of the hedged item that are attributable to the hedged risk and the fair value of the hedging instrument can be reliably measured.

e   The hedge is assessed on an ongoing basis and determined actually to have been highly effective throughout the financial reporting periods for which the hedge was designated.

The accounting treatment for a hedge depends on its relationship type. For a fair value hedge, the gain or loss from re-measuring the hedging instrument at fair value is recognised in profit or loss. This is also applicable to the gain or loss from the foreign currency component of its carrying amount measured in accordance with IAS 21 (for a non-derivative hedging instrument). Furthermore, the gain or loss on the hedged item as a result of a hedged risk shall adjust the carrying amount of the hedged item and be recognised in profit or loss assuming the hedged item is not measured at cost. This also applies if the hedged item is an available-for-sale financial asset.

For a cash flow hedge, the share of the gain or loss on the hedging instrument that is due to an effective hedge is to be recognised in other comprehensive income and the ineffective segment is to be recognised in profit or loss. A similar treatment is applied for hedges of a net investment in a foreign operation. The part of the gain or loss on the hedging instrument that is due to an effective hedge is recognised in other comprehensive income and the ineffective segment is recognised in profit or loss.

IFRS 7 Financial Instruments: Disclosures

The objective of IFRS 7 is to define the disclosures that entities are to provide in their financial statements. These disclosures will enable users to evaluate the significance of financial instruments for the entity's financial position and performance; and the nature and extent of the risks arising from financial instruments to which the entity is exposed during the period and at the end of the reporting period, and how the entity manages those risks. This standard implies that there are qualitative and quantitative disclosures. The qualitative disclosures are related to management's objectives, policies and processes for managing risks. On the other hand, the quantitative disclosures present information about the extent of the entity's exposure to risk, derived from internally generated information that is available to the entity's senior management team. Hence, collectively these disclosures present a reasonable indication of the risk exposures that financial instruments generate; and how well management are exploiting the entity's financial instruments.

IFRS 7 is applicable to all entities, irrespective of whether an entity has extensive or a few financial instruments. For example, a bank's assets and liabilities are mainly financial instruments, whereas a retailer's financial instruments would likely to consist of accounts receivable and accounts payable.

All financial instruments measured at fair value must be classified into three levels that indicate how fair value has been established. These three levels include:

- Level 1. Fair value is based on quoted prices in active markets.
- Level 2. Fair value is based on observable market data since quoted prices in active market are not available.
- Level 3. Fair value is limited since quoted prices in active markets and observable market data are both not available. Further disclosures are required for this category, namely reconciliation between opening and closing balances, incorporating gains/losses, purchases/sales/settlements, transfers; and if changing one or more inputs to a reasonably possible alternative that would result in a significant change in fair value.

A financial instrument must be classified based on the lowest level of any one of the inputs used for its valuation. Additionally, the following must also be disclosed: significant transfers of financial instruments between classes and the reasons for this transfer; and amount of gains and losses, including where these are presented in profit and loss.

IFRS 7 specifically defines the quantitative disclosure of financial instruments by classifying them into three risk types, namely:

- Liquidity risk: This is the risk that an entity will encounter difficulty in meeting obligations associated with financial liabilities.
- Credit risk: This is the risk that one party to a financial instrument will cause a financial loss for the other party by failing to discharge an obligation.
- Market risk: This is the risk that the fair value or future cash flows of a financial instrument will fluctuate due to changes in market prices. Market risk consists of currency risk, interest rate risk and other price risk.

The principles in IFRS 7 complement the principles for recognising, measuring and presenting financial assets and financial liabilities in IAS 32 (Financial Instruments: Presentation) and IFRS 9 (Financial Instruments).

IFRS 9 Financial Instruments

As previously stated, the IASB is phasing out IAS 39 in stages and replacing this standard with IFRS 9. Hence, IFRS 9 is replacing the multiple classification and measurement models in IAS 39 for financial assets and liabilities with a single model that has only two measurement categories, namely amortised cost and fair value. Therefore, classification under IFRS 9 will be based by an entity's business model for managing the financial assets, including their contractual attributes. Furthermore, IFRS 9 does not require embedded derivatives within a financial asset to be reported separately, thus the complete contract is classified as either amortised cost or fair value. However, the separation of embedded derivatives within financial liabilities has been retained.

This addresses the key concern with IAS 39 regarding the establishment of a uniform hedge accounting criteria for all derivatives, which aims to decrease the volatility of an entity's financial statements, particularly the income statement.

Initially, when an entity enters into a contractual agreement regarding financial assets, these financial instruments are recognised on the statement of financial position at fair value. Fair value may also include any costs that are directly attributable in conducting the transaction, if the financial assets are not classified at fair value through profit or loss. The direct attributable transaction costs are incremental costs that are specifically due to the acquisition, issue or disposal of a financial asset or financial liability. The subsequent classification and measurement of the financial assets shall be at either amortised cost or fair value on the basis of both the entity's business model for managing the financial assets and the contractual cash flow attributes of the financial asset.

Business model assessment is based on whether the financial assets are held for the collection of contractual cash flows. Hence, the assessment is not based on the instrument itself but on the overall business model of the entity as determined by the senior management team. The concern with this approach is that an entity may have several business models that may result in different categories of financial assets. Additionally, even though the central thrust is the collection of contractual cash flows, it is not mandatory to hold all of the assets until maturity. Hence, financial assets may be sold without jeopardise their status as being held for the collection of contractual cash flows.

On the other hand, the assessment of the contractual terms for cash flows is conducted on a case by case basis. Hence, financial assets with cash flows that are exclusively payments of principal and interest on the principal amount outstanding, are classified at amortised cost. The interest on the principal amount outstanding consists of two elements, one being the consideration for the time value of money and the other for the credit risk associated with the principal amount outstanding during a particular period. Moreover, the assessment of financial assets designated in foreign currency is based on the currency in which the financial asset is denominated.

As stated above, the financial asset may be measured as amortised cost using the effective interest method and fair value. For the financial instrument to be measured as amortised cost, it must abide by two conditions. The financial asset must be held within a business model with the aim of holding assets in order to collect contractual cash flows; and the contractual terms of the financial asset give rise on specified dates to cash flows that are exclusively payments of principal and interest on the principal amount outstanding.

The financial asset may be measured at fair value but there are two options. It may be valued at fair value through other comprehensive income (OCI) or fair value through profit and loss. Fair value through OCI may be applied for investments in equity instruments that are not held for trading. However, this is an irreversible option and changes in fair value are not subsequently recycled to profit and loss but dividends that are considered as return on investment are recognised in profit or loss. Financial assets that do not meet the criteria to be held at amortised cost are classified as at fair value through profit or loss and measured at fair value, with all gains and losses being recognised in profit or loss.

Financial liabilities are recognised on the statement of financial position the moment the entity becomes party to the contractual provisions of the instrument. All financial liabilities are initially measured at fair value less any transaction costs that are directly due to the transaction (if the financial liability is not classified at fair value through profit or loss). Financial liabilities are classified and subsequently measured at amortised cost using the effective interest method. However, there are a number of exceptions to this rule as shown in Table 4.8.

Derecognition of Financial Assets and Financial Liabilities (IFRS 9)

The final issue to be considered under IFRS 9 is derecognition of financial assets and financial liabilities. According to KPMG (2014) IFRS 9 retains, largely unchanged, the requirements of IAS 39 relating to scope and the recognition and derecognition of financial instruments. Generally, the derecognition of financial assets may take place if the rights to the cash flows from the financial asset have ended or the rights to receive cash flows from the financial asset have been transferred by the entity and the entity has transferred considerably all risks and rewards.

TABLE 4.8 Exceptions to the amortised cost rule

Fair Value Through Profit and Loss (FVTPL):
• Financial liability is held for trading or is a derivative liability.
• The entity on initial recognition has chosen the option to irreversibly designate the financial liability at FVTPL when:
An entire hybrid contract where the embedded derivative does not significantly modify cash flows or where separation would be permitted in a similar hybrid instrument;
It removes or mitigates a measurement or recognition inconsistency from measuring assets or liabilities or recognising the gains and losses on them on different bases;
A group of financial instruments are evaluated on a fair value basis, consistent with documented risk management or investment strategy, and in line with information provided to the entity's senior management personnel.
• Financial liability is shown in the statement of comprehensive income and profit or loss where the amount of fair value change that is due to changes in credit risk is disclosed in OCI and the remaining amount of change in the fair value is disclosed in profit or loss.
Transfer of a financial asset that does not qualify for de-recognition:
• If the transferred asset is measured at amortised cost, the amortised cost of the rights and obligations are retained by the entity.
• If the transferred asset is measured at fair value, the fair value of the rights and obligations retained by the entity are measured on a case by case basis.
Financial guarantee contracts and/or commitments to provide a below-market interest rate:
• Subsequent to initial recognition, the resulting liability is measured at the higher of the amount established in accordance with IAS 37 or the amount initially recognised less (if applicable) the cumulative amortisation realised in accordance with IAS 18.

If these two conditions have not been met the entity must continue to recognise the financial asset. Hence, the focus is on the existence of control, which differs from IAS 39, in that IAS 39 is primarily concerned with 'risks and rewards' and control being a secondary test. According to the IFRS Staff Paper (2015), two specific aspects require particular attention.

The first aspect is that entities should consider whether the contractual rights to the cash flows from the asset expire (paragraph 3.2.3(a) of IFRS 9 and paragraph 17 of IAS 39) and if so, the asset should be derecognised. The second aspect considered by IFRS Staff Paper (2015) is related to the contractual rights to the cash flows that have not expired (paragraphs 3.2.3(b)-3.2.5 of IFRS 9 and paragraphs 17(b)-19 of IAS 39). If the contractual rights to the cash flows have not expired, entities should evaluate the extent to which it retains the risks and rewards of ownership of the financial asset. Therefore, if the entity transfers substantially all the risks and rewards of ownership of the financial asset, the entity should derecognise the financial asset and recognise separately as assets or liabilities any rights and obligations created or retained in the transfer (paragraph 3.2.6(a) of IFRS 9 and paragraph 20(a) of IAS 39). However, if the entity retains substantially all the risks and rewards of ownership of the financial asset, the entity shall continue to recognise the financial asset. Figure 4.5 is a procedural flowchart of financial assets derecognition that has been adapted from IFRS Staff Paper (2015). The flowchart illustrates the evaluation procedure of whether and to what extent a financial asset is derecognised.

IFRS Staff Paper (2015) notes that there is no specific direction in IFRS 9 or IAS 39 regarding whether financial assets that are modified or exchanged should be derecognised. This is dissimilar to the derecognition requirements for financial liabilities. On derecognition of a financial asset, a number of accounting entries are required in the books of the transferor and transferee, depending on the circumstances.

For example, consider a situation where a sale of a financial asset takes place for cash flows that have been explicitly identified. Let us assume that in this example Melita Investments Ltd holds a portfolio of AAA-rated fixed-rate corporate euro-bonds that are traded in a highly liquid market. These euro-bonds are classified as 'available-for-sale' and will mature in about four years' time. Since Melita Investments Ltd purchased the bonds, interest rates have decreased and as a consequence the value of the bonds has increased from €150 million, which was the original purchase price, to its current value of €165 million. The Board of Directors of Melita Investments Ltd decided to transfer the rights to 80 per cent of the principal payments on the bonds to Grand Trust Ltd for a cash payment of €120 million. However, Melita Investments Ltd will keep on receiving all the interest payments on the whole portfolio and 20 per cent of the principal payments on the condition that when the bonds mature, Melita Investments Ltd will convey to Grand Trust Ltd 80 per cent of the principal amount that is reimbursed. On the other hand, Grand Trust Ltd will accept the credit risk on any defaults of its newly acquired 80 per cent of the principal amount. It is noted that the fair value of the fixed-rate corporate euro-bonds portfolio at the date of transfer was €165 million and the fair value of the interest segment at the date of transfer was €50 million. Furthermore, the gain in fair value of €15 million was previously recognised in equity.

To determine the accounting entries, the procedure at Figure 4.5 is applied. Consolidation of subsidiaries is not an issue in this example. However, we need to establish whether the principles regarding derecognition should be applied to part of a financial asset (or a group of similar financial assets) or a financial asset (or a group of similar financial assets) in its totality. To this end, it is known that the financial instruments included in Melita Investments Ltd's debt securities portfolio have similar features, in that they have the same security type (corporate eurobonds); currency (euro); credit rating (AAA); fixed interest rate; and maturity period (approximately four years). Therefore, they should be assessed as a group of similar financial assets. Moreover, the transaction is related to 80 per cent fully

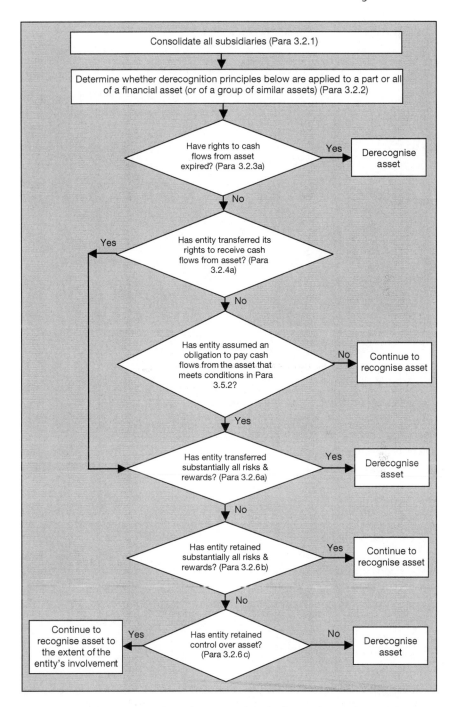

FIGURE 4.5 Evaluation procedure: derecognition of a financial asset

proportionate share of cash flows, which are specifically identified from the portfolio (i.e. the principal repayments). Therefore, the derecognition principles are to be applied to that part of the portfolio.

Next, we need to decide on the issue of the expiry of rights to cash flow. We know that the bonds have not yet matured so the rights to the cash flows still exist. We now also need to determine whether Melita Investments Ltd has transferred its rights to receive cash flows from financial asset. We know from the data that Melita Investments Ltd has transferred 80 per cent of the principal cash flows related to these debt securities to Grand Trust Ltd. Hence, this meets the criteria of a transfer, even though Melita Investments Ltd continues to operate as a collection agent. However, Melita Investments Ltd has no further rights regarding the 80 per cent principal even though it is able to put up for sale the remaining 20 per cent principal portion and the interest segment.

Finally, we need to assess the associated risks and rewards. We know that Melita Investments Ltd has assigned the credit and late payment risks related to the transfer of the financial asset (i.e. 80 per cent of the principal cash flows). There is no expected variability in the cash flows from the variation of interest rates, since the transferred financial asset is of a fixed amount and does not vary with interest rate fluctuations. In addition, the variation of the fair value of the financial asset from interest rates fluctuations has been assigned to Grand Trust Ltd. It may be concluded that Melita Investments Ltd has substantially transferred all the risks and rewards in relation to the 80 per cent portion of the transferred financial asset and should therefore derecognise this portion.

The above give rise to a number of accounting entries on both the transferors' (the entity making the transfer of the financial asset) and transferees' (the entity who receives the financial asset) accounts. The accounting computations from the transferors' side are as follows:

1 On the transfer date: In a situation where a partial sale of the financial asset is made, the preceding carry forward amount of the larger portion of the financial asset is allocated between the segment that continues to be recognised and the segment that is derecognised, based on the relative fair values of those portions on the date of transfer. Table 4.9 shows the various computations leading to the calculation of the 'gain recycled on derecognition'.

2 Accounting entries on transfer date: The accounting entries required on the date of the transfer of the financial asset are shown at Table 4.10. The accounting entries basically recognise the cash received for the sale of the 80 per cent of the financial asset and to recycle the gain on derecognition of €8.36m related to the sale of that segment. Note that afterwards, Melita Investments Ltd's 20 per cent principal segment and its entire interest portion will continue to be measured at fair value through equity conditional on the recognition of interest using the effective interest rate method and normal impairment testing.

TABLE 4.9 Computations leading to gain recycled on derecognition

Fair value of the principal value only (Fv): $Fv = Fp - Fi$ Where: (a) Fp = 'Fair value of the entire portfolio' (b) Fi = 'Fair value of the interest only segment' $Fv = €165m - €50m = €115m$ Fair value of 80% of principal only (Fx) = 80% transferred of Fv = 0.80 x €115m = €92m
Cumulative gain or loss allocated to asset on the basis of relative fair values that had been recognised directly in equity (Ce): $Ce = (Fp - Fo) \times (Fx \div Fp)$ Where: (a) Fp = 'Fair value of the entire portfolio' (b) Fo = original value of 'Fair value of the entire portfolio' (c) Fx = 'Fair value of 80% of principal only' $Ce = (€165m - 150m) \times (92m \div 165m) = 8.364m$
Gain or loss on sale (Sr): $Sr = (Sv + Ce) - Cf$ Where: (a) Sv = consideration received for the part derecognised (b) Ce = cumulative gain or loss allocated to it (on the basis of relative fair values) that had been recognised directly in equity (c) Cf = carry forward amount allocated to the part derecognised $Sr = (€92m + €8.364m) - €92m = €8.364m$
Gain recycled on derecognition (Gd): $Gd = Sv - Cf + Ce = €92m - €92m + €8.364 = €8.364m$

TABLE 4.10 Accounting entries for transferor on transfer date (financial asset)

(In € millions)	Dr	Cr
Cash	92	
Debt Securities		92
Available-for-Sale Reserve Equity	8.364	
Gain on Derecognition (Profit or Loss)		8.364

The accounting computation from the transferees' side is as follows:

1 On the transfer date: Since Melita Investments Ltd derecognised 80 per cent of the principal of its financial asset because it sold the bonds to Grand Trust Ltd, Grand Trust Ltd will need to recognise the 80 per cent of the principal of the bonds it has purchased and derecognise the cash outflow it paid for them. Table 4.11 shows the accounting entry required by the transferee (i.e. Grand Trust Ltd). The accounting entry basically recognises the purchase of the 80 per cent stake of the financial asset (i.e. principal of the bonds) in its eurobonds portfolio. Note that later the accounting method used will depend on how Grand Trust Ltd classifies its financial asset under IAS 39. In other words, whether Grand Trust Ltd will classify the financial asset purchased as fair value through profit or loss, available-for-sale or held to maturity.

Let us now consider derecognition of a financial liability. Generally, derecognition of a financial liability is a straightforward matter. Paragraph 3.3.1 of IFRS 9 (paragraph 39 of IAS 39) maintains that an entity should derecognise a financial liability (or part of it) when and only when it is extinguished. In other words, derecognition of a financial liability (or part of it) may only occur if the obligation specified in the contract is fulfilled, annulled or expires. Therefore, an entity may only stop recognising (derecognise) a financial liability when the obligation is discharged, cancelled or expired, or when the debtor is legally released from the liability by law or by the creditor agreeing to such a release.

Furthermore, paragraph 3.3.2 of IFRS 9 (paragraph 40 of IAS 39) is specific when dealing with modifications and exchanges of financial liabilities with the same lender. A swap between an existing borrower and lender of debt instruments with significantly different terms or extensive modification of the terms of an existing financial liability of part thereof is accounted for as an extinguishment. In addition, paragraph B3.3.6 of IFRS 9 (paragraph AG62 of IAS 39) establishes the concept of a quantitative '10 per cent test'. This concept states that for the purpose of paragraph 3.3.2, the terms are considered substantially different if the discounted present value of the cash flows under the new terms, including any fees paid net of any fees received and discounted using the original effective interest rate, is at least 10 per cent different from the discounted present value of the remaining cash flows of the original financial liability.

TABLE 4.11 Accounting entries for transferee on transfer date (financial asset)

(In € millions)	Dr	Cr
Debt Securities	92	
Cash		92

IFRS Staff Paper (2015) notes that the guidance on the derecognition of financial liabilities in IFRS 9 and IAS 39 already introduces the concept that both an exchange between an existing borrower and lender of debt instruments with substantially different terms and a substantial modification of the terms of an existing financial liability should be accounted for as an extinguishment of the original financial liability and the recognition of a new financial liability. However, IFRS Staff Paper (2015) argues that 'linking' a new derivative with an existing financial asset for derecognition and, by implication, treating the two as one for subsequent accounting purposes, could have significant consequences.

IFRS Staff Paper (2015) contends that if new guidance is developed for derecognition of modified financial assets, there may be a need to consider the potential implications for derecognition of financial liabilities. However, it argues that this may depend upon the view as to how much symmetry there should be between the issuer and holder of an instrument on derecognition of the instrument. Moreover, IFRS Staff Paper (2015) claims that it would be necessary to consider whether any specific guidance on derecognition of modified financial assets (including any definition of 'modification') would apply to derecognition of modified financial liabilities either by analogy or directly (through a revision of the existing requirements). IFRS Staff Paper (2015) cites a situation where a specific qualitative test is introduced to determine whether modified financial assets are derecognised; they question whether this test should similarly be explicitly introduced for derecognition of modified financial liabilities. On derecognition the accounting entry for a financial liability would appear in the profit or loss for the amount equal to the book value of financial liability extinguished or transferred minus the consideration paid.

Comparison of IFRS and US GAAPs

The US GAAP is organised under the Accounting Standards Codification (ASC). It should be noted that accounting standards are conceived as a guide for the accounting treatment of various transactions. Hence, the US GAAP guidance for financial instruments is spread over ten ASC Topics, while the IFRS guidance for financial instruments is limited to four issues. Table 4.12 provides the US GAAP and IFRS standards that specifically address financial instruments.

At first glance, Table 4.12 illustrates that IFRS specifically addresses the issue of financial instruments, whereas US GAAP is organised on a different basis. However, when one examines the standards in detail it becomes evident that both US GAAP and IFRS oblige users to classify financial instruments into distinct categories so that their measurement may be determined. Furthermore, both standards explain the conditions under which financial instruments are to be recognised or derecognised. Moreover, both standards allow hedge accounting and the use of a fair value option. Additionally, both standards compel users to include all derivatives on the statement of financial position and in particular require that all financial instruments presented on the financial statements are to be accompanied by detailed disclosures in the notes to these financial statements.

TABLE 4.12 US GAAP and IFRS financial instruments standards

US GAAP Topics and Standards	IFRS Financial Instruments Standards
ASC 300 Assets • ASC 310-10-35: Receivables – Overall – Subsequent Measurement • ASC 320: Investments – Debt and Equity Securities **ASC 400 Liabilities** • ASC 470: Debt • ASC 480: Distinguishing Liabilities from Equity **ASC 800 Broad Transactions** • ASC 815: Derivatives and Hedging • ASC 820: Fair Value Measurement • ASC 825-10-25: Financial Instruments – Overall – Recognition • ASC 825-10-50: Financial Instruments – Overall – Disclosures • ASC 860: Transfers and Servicing **ASC 900 Industry** • ASC 948: Financial Services – Mortgage Banking	• IAS 32: Financial Instruments – Presentation • IAS 39: Financial Instruments – Recognition and Measurement • IFRS 7: Financial Instruments – Disclosures • IFRS 9: Financial Instruments

However, there are significant differences between US GAAP and IFRS regarding the issue of financial instruments. These major differences are explained in the following sections.

Distinction between debt and equity

The first major difference is regarding the distinction between debt and equity. Under US GAAP, certain financial instruments that are identified with attributes of both debt and equity must be classified as liabilities. However, under IFRS the focus when particular financial instruments have attributes pertaining to both debt and equity is on the contractual obligation to hand over cash, assets or an entity's own shares. A contractual obligation is an agreement with specific terms between two or more parties or entities in which there is a promise to do something in return for a valuable benefit known as consideration. Hence, having a desire to generate cash or other financial resources does not amount to a contractual obligation.

Additionally, US GAAP stipulates that contracts which are indexed to an entity's own stock and which have the possibility of being defrayed by an entity's own stock may be classified as equity if they: (a) require physical or net-share defrayal or (b) assign the issuer the option of net-cash payment or settlement in its own shares. IFRS is less flexible, with contracts being classified as equity if they are indexed to an entity's own stock and which have the possibility of being defrayed by an entity's own stock and they are settled by delivering a fixed number of shares for a fixed amount of cash.

Compound financial instruments also referred to as hybrid financial instruments, such as convertible bonds, are not divided into debt and equity unless particular circumstances are adhered to, but they may be divided into debt and derivative components, with the derivative segment adhering to fair value accounting. IFRS requires that hybrid financial instruments are divided into a debt, equity and derivative portion if applicable. The derivative segment may need to adhere to fair value accounting treatment.

Impairment recognition and measurement

When discussing impairment recognition and measurement issues it is essential to bear in mind that there are three distinct types of financial instruments. These are available-for-sale (AFS) debt instruments; available-for-sale (AFS) equity instruments; and held-to-maturity (HTM) debt instruments. These three types of financial instruments are treated differently by the IFRS and US GAAP accounting standards.

There are key differences between IFRS and US GAAP when dealing with impairment recognition for AFS debt instruments. Normally, under IFRS, the only indication that a credit default has occurred, is when impairment is recognised in the income statement for an AFS debt instrument. This impairment loss is measured as the difference between the debt instrument's amortised cost and its fair value. However, under IFRS impairment losses for AFS debt instruments may be reversed through the income statement if the fair value of the instrument increases in a subsequent period and the increase can be objectively related to an event occurring after the impairment loss was recognised.

Under US GAAP, dealing with impairment recognition for AFS debt instruments is slightly more complex than IFRS. For instance, decreases in fair value below cost may result in an impairment loss being recognised in the income statement on an AFS debt instrument due to a change in interest rates, whether risk-free or otherwise. This will occur if an entity has the intent to sell the debt instrument or there is the likelihood that it will be required to sell the debt instrument before its anticipated recovery. In this case, the impairment loss is measured as the difference between the debt instrument's amortised cost and its fair value similar to IFRS. However, when a credit loss occurs, but the entity does not intend to sell the debt instrument, or there is the likelihood that the entity will be required to sell the debt instrument before the recovery of the remaining cost, the impairment is segmented into the amount representing the credit loss and the amount related to all other factors. Moreover, the amount of the total impairment related to the credit loss is recognised in the income statement and the amount related to all other factors is recognised in other comprehensive income, net of applicable taxes. Impairment losses recognised in the income statement cannot be reversed for any future recoveries. Additionally, once an impairment loss is recognised in the income statement, a new cost basis in the instrument is recognised that is equal to the previous cost less the impairment recognised in the earnings.

There are only slight differences between IFRS and US GAAP regarding the treatment of impairment recognition for AFS equity instruments. Under US GAAP, impairment of an AFS equity instrument is acknowledged in the income statement only if the equity instrument's fair value is not expected to recover sufficiently in the near future to allow a full recovery of the entity's cost basis. However, to do this, an entity must have the intention and ability to hold an impaired equity instrument until such near future recovery is possible, otherwise an impairment loss must be shown in the income statement. On the other hand, under IFRS an impairment of an AFS equity instrument is shown in the income statement only when there is objective confirmation that the AFS equity instrument is impaired and the cost of the investment in the equity instrument may not be recovered. In addition, a significant or protracted decline in the fair value of an equity instrument below its cost is considered proof of impairment.

The differences between IFRS and US GAAP regarding impairment loss of an HTM instrument are significant. Under IFRS, the impairment loss of an HTM instrument is measured as the difference between the carrying amount of the instrument and the present value of estimated future cash flows discounted at the instrument's original effective interest rate. Thus, the carrying amount of the HTM instrument is diminished either directly or through the use of an allowance account. Moreover, under IFRS the amount of impairment loss is recognised in the income statement. On the other hand, under US GAAP the impairment loss of an HTM instrument is measured as the difference between its fair value and amortised cost basis. However, US GAAP requires that the total impairment amount related to the credit loss is shown in the income statement, and the amount related to all other factors is presented in other comprehensive income. Furthermore, under US GAAP, the carrying amount of an HTM investment after the recognition of impairment is determined as the fair value of the debt instrument at the date of the impairment. Hence, the new cost basis of the debt instrument is equal to the previous cost basis less the impairment recognised in the income statement. In addition, the impairment shown in other comprehensive income is added to the carrying amount of the HTM instrument through other comprehensive income over its remaining life.

Derivatives and hedging

Generally, to be recognised as a derivative under US GAAP, a financial instrument must have one or more objects such as an asset, index, or interest rate, one or more notional amounts or payment provisions or both, must require no initial net investment, as defined, and must be able to be settled net, as defined. However, the definition of a derivative under IFRS does not require that a notional amount be indicated, nor net settlement.

Hedging a risk component of a financial instrument is more flexible under IFRS. US GAAP explicitly defines the risk components that may be hedged, with no further flexibility. However, IFRS allows risks associated with only a portion of the instrument's cash flows or fair value provided that effectiveness can be measured. In other words, as long as the portion can be distinctly identifiable and is discretely measurable the risk components may be hedged.

There is a major difference between US GAAP and IFRS when considering hedge effectiveness. Under US GAAP, the shortcut method for interest rate swaps hedging is permitted for recognised debt instruments, but this is not permitted under IFRS. Moreover, the long-haul method of assessing and measuring hedge effectiveness for a fair value hedge of the benchmark interest rate component of a fixed rate debt instrument necessitates that all contractual cash flows be considered in calculating the change in the hedged item's fair value even though only a component of the contractual coupon payment is the designated hedged item. On the other hand, under IFRS, assessment and measurement of hedge effectiveness considers only the change in fair value of the designated hedged portion of the instrument's cash flows, as long as the portion is identifiable and individually measurable. Additionally, the inclusion of an option's time value is permitted under US GAAP but not permitted under IFRS.

Derecognition

Under US GAAP, derecognition of financial assets occurs when effective control over the financial asset has been surrendered. In practice, this means that the transferred financial assets are legally inaccessible from the transferor; that each transferee has the right to pledge or exchange the transferred financial assets (or beneficial interests); and the transferor does not maintain effective control over the transferred financial assets or beneficial interests.

On the other hand, derecognition of financial assets under IFRS is based on a mixed model that considers both transfer of risks and rewards and control. Transfer of control is considered only when the transfer of risks and rewards assessment is not conclusive. If the transferor has neither retained nor transferred substantially all of the risks and rewards, there is then an evaluation of the transfer of control. Control is considered to be surrendered if the transferee has the practical ability to unilaterally sell the transferred asset to a third party without restrictions. In this case there is no legal isolation test.

Both US GAAP and IFRS permit the derecognition provisions to be applied to a portion of a financial asset. However, under US GAAP this is permitted only if the financial asset mirrors the characteristics of the original entire financial asset. Whereas, under IFRS it is permitted if the cash flows are specifically identified or represent a pro rata share of the financial asset or specifically identified cash flows.

Loans and receivables

US GAAP obliges that interest for amortised cost-based assets is calculated using the catch-up approach, retrospective method or prospective method, depending on the type of instrument. In contrast, IFRS stipulates that the original effective interest rate is used throughout the life of the instrument for all financial assets and liabilities. However, for certain reclassified financial assets, the effect of increases in cash flows are recognised as prospective adjustments to the effective interest rate.

Differences also exist between US GAAP and IFRS regarding the measurement of loans and receivables. Under US GAAP, unless the fair value option is chosen, loans and receivables are classified as either held for investment, which are measured at amortised cost, or held for sale, which are measured at the lower of cost or fair value. On the other hand, under IFRS loans and receivables are carried at amortised cost unless classified as fair value through profit or loss or available-for-sale, in which case they are carried at fair value on the balance sheet.

Fair value

There is no uniform definition of fair value. Under US GAAP, with limited exceptions, there is only one measurement model that is used for defining fair value. According to US GAAP, fair value is the price that would be received to sell an asset or paid to transfer a liability in an orderly transaction between market participants at the measurement date. Hence, fair value is an exit price, which may differ from the transaction price at inception. In contrast, various IFRS standards use slightly different wording to define fair value. The most common definition of fair value is as prescribed by IAS 39. Fair value is defined as the amount for which an asset could be exchanged, or a liability settled, between knowledgeable, willing parties in an arm's length transaction. Hence, contrary to US GAAP, under IFRS, fair value is the price of the transaction at inception.

Under IFRS, day one gains and losses are recognised only when all inputs to the measurement model are observable. However, according to US GAAP, entities are not prevented from acknowledging day one gains and losses related to financial instruments reported at fair value even when all inputs to the measurement model are not observable. According to US GAAP, fair value may be measured by using the price within the bid-ask spread that is the most representative of fair value in the circumstances. However, entities are not prevented from using mid-market pricing as a practical measure of fair value. Conversely, under IFRS, the fair value of assets held (or liabilities to be issued) is typically established by using the current bid price, while liabilities held (or assets to be acquired) are calculated using the current ask price. Furthermore, an entity that has assets and liabilities with offsetting market risks may use mid-market prices to determine the fair value of an offsetting positions, and apply the bid or ask price (as appropriate) to the net open position.

Originate-and-hold and originate-and-distribute banking strategies

The banking industry without doubt remains the largest dealer of financial instruments. Therefore, it is appropriate at this stage to provide a brief explanation of the two primary banking strategies that directly affect the major categories of financial assets, namely held-to-maturity and held-for-trading (available for sale).

The concept of held-to-maturity and held-for-trading (available for sale) in terms of loans is part of the banking strategies related to originate-and-hold and originate-and-distribute. It is to be noted that policy-makers and supervisors in many countries in the Asia–Pacific geographic region appear to encourage banks to adopt a business model that predominantly leans towards the 'buy-and-hold' approach rather than the 'originate-to-distribute' model that is preferred by various western banks prior to the financial crisis.

The traditional 'buy-and-hold' model requires banks to extend credit up to their regulatory or economic limits and then hold on to them until maturity. Research shows that a buy-and-hold strategy works provided that a long enough timeline is in place. In other words, long-term investment strategies have a time horizon of decades with the buy-and-hold approach working as long as the investor has a decade or two available to sustain the investment policy. Otherwise, market fluctuations, such as inflation, bears and overall downturns, will cause investors to dispose of their investments within a relatively short duration (within two to five years). For clarity, a bear is an investor who perceives that a particular value of a security is moving downward and will endeavour to make a profit from the decline in prices. Therefore, with a buy-and-hold strategy there will be times when the investor will lose money in a particular fiscal year; however by holding on to the investment, the outcome will be an increase in the return on the investment. This type of strategy is applicable to those who do not have pressures to dispose of their investment due to liquidity demands.

On the other hand, the originate-to-distribute approach is the emerging alternative model being used by banks. Berndt and Gupta (2009) posit that over the last two decades, bank credit has evolved from the traditional relationship banking model to an originate-to-distribute model where banks can originate loans, earn their fee, and then sell them off to investors who desire such exposures. Berndt and Gupta's (2009) research findings suggest that the borrowers whose loans are sold in the secondary market under-perform other bank borrowers by between 8 per cent and 14 per cent per year on a risk-adjusted basis over the three-year period following the sale of their loan. Furthermore, Berndt and Gupta (2009) found that borrowers whose loans are sold in the secondary market suffer a value destruction of about 15 per cent compared to their peers over the same period. Their findings suggest that this effect is more severe for small, high leverage, speculative grade borrowers. Berndt and Gupta (2009) offer two alternative explanations for this underperformance:

(a) Either the banks are originating and selling bad loans based on unobservable private information, similar to the events in the current subprime mortgage crisis; and/or

(b) The severance of the bank-borrower relationship allows the borrowers to undertake suboptimal investment and operating decisions, in the absence of the discipline of bank monitoring.

Their results indicate that borrowers whose loans are not sold in the secondary market do not underperform their peers; reinforcing the inference that bank loan financing is indeed 'special', except for borrowers whose loans are sold. Hence, they conclude that in light of these moral hazard and adverse selection problems, the originate-to-distribute model of bank credit may not entirely be 'socially desirable'. Berndt and Gupta (2009) propose regulatory restrictions on loan sales, increased disclosure, and a loan trading exchange with a clearing house as mechanisms to alleviate these problems.

The research findings of Bord and Santos (2012) generally confirm those of Berndt and Gupta (2009). These researchers argue that the originate-to-distribute model has reduced the exposure of banks to the credits they originated over the past two decades. Bord and Santos (2012) findings suggest a number of important implications for the banking industry. First, they argue that the banks' increasing use of the originate-to-distribute model in their term-lending business will lead to a transfer of important portions of credit risk out of the banking system and thus as a consequence will contribute to the growth of financial intermediation outside the banking system, including a larger role for unregulated 'shadow banking' institutions. They posit that this will also, over time, make the credit kept by banks on their balance sheets less representative of the still essential role they perform in financial intermediation.

Second, Bord and Santos (2012) suggest that the banks' increasing use of the originate-to-distribute model could lead to some weakening of lending standards. They cite that according to several theories, including those of Ramakrishnan and Thakor (1984), Diamond (1984) and Holmström and Tirole (1993), banks add value because of their comparative advantage in monitoring borrowers. Thus they argue that to carry out this task properly, banks must hold the loans they originate until maturity; otherwise if they instead anticipate keeping only a small portion of a loan, their incentives to screen loan applicants properly and to design the terms of the loan contract will diminish.

Third, Bord and Santos (2012) maintain that banks will also have less incentive to monitor borrowers during the life of the loan. Bord and Santos (2012) argue that the growth of the collateralised loan obligations (CLO) business has likely exacerbated these risks because CLO investors invest in new securities that depend on the performance of the 'reference portfolio,' which is made up of many loans, often originated by different banks.

Fourth, Bord and Santos (2012) assert that the banks' adoption of the originate-to-distribute model may also hinder the ability of corporate borrowers to renegotiate their loans after they have been issued. This difficulty may arise not only because the borrower will have to renegotiate with more investors but also because the universe of investors acquiring corporate loans is more heterogeneous (Bord and Santos, 2012). Finally, Bord and Santos (2012) provide evidence to suggest that banks continue to use the traditional originate-to-hold model in the provision of credit lines, which supports the argument that banks retain a unique ability to provide liquidity to corporations, possibly because of their access to deposit funding.

The above research suggests that the originate-to-distribute model needs to be viewed with caution. The results from Berndt and Gupta (2009) strongly imply that banks are either originating and selling loans of lower quality borrowers based on unobservable private information (adverse selection), and/or loan sales lead to diminished bank monitoring that affects borrowers negatively (moral hazard). Hence, their recommendations that propose regulatory restrictions on loan sales, increased disclosure, and a loan trading exchange/clearing house as mechanisms to alleviate these problems should be supported by regulatory authorities.

Conclusion

Both IFRS and US GAAP are designed to be a common language for business affairs so that company accounts are understandable and comparable across international boundaries. Accounting standards are the rules to be followed by accountants to maintain the books of accounts that are comparable, understandable, reliable and relevant for the varying type of internal and external users. However, US GAAP is designed to cater for the United States business entities, whereas the IFRS is designed as a global accounting standard. Furthermore, the convergence process which commenced more than a decade ago is continuing, with the goal of having one dominant global accounting standard.

The convergence of the accounting standards is a consequence of growing international shareholding and trade, and its outcome is particularly important for entities that have business connections in various countries. IFRS is increasingly replacing the numerous national accounting standards. What began as an attempt to harmonise accounting across the European Union, the IFRS has enabled various national accounting bodies to recognise the value of harmonisation and has rapidly developed into a global concept.

Practical problems

1   Amortisation is specifically associated with:

    A   Debt instruments
    B   Equity instruments
    C   Discounted value of equity instruments
    D   Equity and debt instruments

2   When reference is made to amortised cost, what exactly is being amortised?

    A   Asset value
    B   Appropriations
    C   A discount or premium
    D   Cost of the liability

3   How do you treat transaction costs that are associated to amortised cost?

    A   Cash outflows
    B   Expensed
    C   Added to the liabilities
    D   Added to the value of the financial instrument

4   Which method should be applied to avoid accounting mismatches?

    A   No preferable method
    B   Amortised cost method
    C   A combination of methods
    D   Fair value method

5   How is transaction costs that are associated to Fair Value treated?

    A   Cash outflows
    B   Expensed
    C   Added to the liabilities
    D   Added to the value of the financial instrument

6   Under which method are a majority of derivatives accounted for?

    A   Fair Value through Profit and Loss
    B   Fair Value through Equity
    C   Amortised cost

7   Where are gains and losses due to investments in equity instruments shown?

    A   Under other comprehensive income
    B   Other comprehensive income if the instrument is not held for trading
    C   Under profit and loss

8   Allied Ltd purchases a financial asset for €85 with associated legal costs of €8. At the end of the accounting financial period the market value of the financial asset increased to €110. Due to market conditions the value of the financial asset decreased significantly to €78. However, the interest received on this financial asset was €7. The market conditions for the financial asset improved substantially and thus the market value of the asset was estimated to be €115. Following the revaluation of the financial asset the company decided to sell the asset for €123. Show the accounting entries for the above financial activities.

9   The Board of Directors of Lindersberg Ltd authorised the company to issue
      a five-year loan at 5 per cent interest rate, with the interest being paid at
      the end of each year. A client, Global Ltd lends Lindersberg Ltd €150,000,
      which includes a commission of €10,000 that was paid on day one for t
      he loan. Hence, Lindersberg Ltd receives only €140,000 in cash, with the
      commission of €10,000 representing a discount. Furthermore, the effective
      interest rate includes the commission value and has an effective rate of 6.1 per
      cent. Thus the discount of €10,000 is amortised in Lindersberg Ltd's books
      over the period of the loan, using the effective interest rate of 6.1 per cent.
      You are required to:

   a   Show the computations for the amortisation of the discount;
   b   Provide all the accounting entries for the five-year loan period in Global
       Ltd's books.

Solutions

1   A is correct. Amortisation is the paying off of debt with a fixed repayment
      schedule in regular instalments over a period of time.
2   B is correct. For example, an amortised bond is considered to be an asset, with
      the discount amount being amortised to interest expense over the life of the
      bond.
3   D is correct. Transaction costs incurred due to the amortisation process are
      added to the value of the financial instrument.
4   D is correct. Designating a financial instrument at fair value eliminates or signi-
      ficantly reduces a measurement or recognition inconsistency (an 'accounting
      mismatch') that would otherwise arise from measuring assets or liabilities or
      recognising the gains and losses on them on different bases.
5   B is correct. Transaction costs directly attributable to the acquisition of
      financial assets or financial liabilities at FVTPL are recognised as expenses as
      incurred.
6   A is correct. An entity should recognise all derivatives as either assets or liabili-
      ties in the statement of financial position and measure those instruments
      at fair value.
7   B is correct. If an equity investment is not held for trading, an entity can make
      an irrevocable election at initial recognition to measure it at Fair Value
      through Other Comprehensive Income with only dividend income recognised
      in profit or loss. [IFRS 9, paragraph 5.7.5].
8   This example is illustrating the concept of financial assets at fair value through
      profit and loss. Revaluation of a financial asset results when the value of that
      asset increases. However, the term impairment usually occurs when the market
      value of the asset has decreased significantly. For example, if the undiscounted
      future cash flows from the asset (including the sale amount) are less than the
      asset's carrying amount (current book value), an impairment loss is reported.

TABLE 4.13 Solution to Problem 8: financial assets at FVTPL

Cash Account

Interest	€7	Purchase Asset	€85
Sold Financial Asset	€123	Transaction Cost	€8
Balance	**€37**		

Financial Asset

Purchase Asset	€85	Revaluation Expense	€32
Revaluation	€25	Sold Financial Asset	€115
Revaluation	€37		
Balance	**Nil**		

Revaluation Income

	Revaluation	€25
	Revaluation	€37
	Balance	**€62**

Transaction Costs

Transaction Cost	€8	
Balance	**€8**	

Revaluation Expense

Revaluation Expense	€32	
Balance	**€32**	

Interest Received

	Interest Received	€7
	Balance	**€7**

Profit on Sale of Financial Asset

	Gain on Sale	€8
	Balance	**€8**

If the impairment loss is reported, the amount of the impairment loss is measured by subtracting the asset's fair value from its carrying value. The accounting entries are shown at Table 4.13.

9   This example is similar to the example regarding 'loans and receivables' at amortised cost that was illustrated by Table 4.5. One should note that the accounting entries are the same for loans and receivables or held to maturity under IAS29.

TABLE 4.14 Solution to Problem 9: amortised cost

Cash Account

Interest[b]	€7,500	Upon Lending	€140,000
Interest[c]	€7,500		
Interest[d]	€7,500		
Interest[e]	€7,500		
Interest[f]	€7,500		
At maturity[f]	€150,000		
Balance:	**€47,500**		

Financial Asset (Loan A/c Global Ltd)

Upon Lending	€150,000	At maturity[f]	€150,000
Balance	**€0**		

Deferred Commission

Commission[b]	€1,753	Commission[a]	€10,000
Commission[c]	€1,868		
Commission[d]	€1,992		
Commission[e]	€2,124		
Commission[f]	€2,264		
Balance:	**€0**		

Interest Receivable

		Interest[b]	€7,500
		Interest[c]	€7,500
		Interest[d]	€7,500
		Interest[e]	€7,500
		Interest[f]	€7,500
		Balance:	**€37,500**

Commission

		Commission[b]	€1,753
		Commission[c]	€1,868
		Commission[d]	€1,992
		Commission[e]	€2,124
		Commission[f]	€2,264
		Balance:	**€10,000**

Note:

a. Deferred Commission recorded upon lending on day-1
b. End of Year-1   c. End of Year-2   d. End of Year-3
e. End of Year-4   f. End of Year-5

References

Berndt, A. and Gupta, A. (2009). Moral hazard and adverse selection in the originate-to-distribute model of bank credit. *Journal of Monetary Economics*, 56(5), 725–743.

Bord, V.M. and Santos, A.C. (2012). The rise of the originate-to-distribute model and the role of banks in financial intermediation. *FRBNY Economic Policy Review*, July, 21.

Diamond, D.W. (1984). Financial intermediation and delegated monitoring. *Review of Economic Studies*, 51(3), 393–414.

Ernst & Young. (2011). *US GAAP versus IFRS: The Basics*. Ernst & Young, International Financial Reporting Standards Group.

Ernst & Young. (2011). *IFRS 7 Financial Instruments: Disclosures: Impending Changes Effective for 2011 and 2012*. Ernst & Young, International Financial Reporting Standards Group.

Ernst & Young. (2012). *IFRS 9: New Mandatory Effective Date and Transition Disclosures*. Ernst & Young, International Financial Reporting Standards Group.

Holmström, B.R. and Tirole, J. (1993). Market liquidity and performance monitoring. *Journal of Political Economy*, 101(4), 678–709.

IFRS Staff Paper. (2015). *IFRS 9 Financial Instruments/IAS 39 Financial Instruments: Recognition and Measurement: Derecognition of Modified Financial Assets*. IFRS Interpretations Committee Meeting, IFRS.

KPMG. (2014). *First Impressions: IFRS 9 Financial Instruments*. KPMG, International Standards Group, KPMG IFRG.

PricewaterhouseCoopers. (2008). *IAS 39 – Derecognition of Financial Assets in Practice*. PricewaterhouseCoopers International.

PricewaterhouseCoopers. (2010). *A Practical Guide to IFRS 7: For Investment Managers and Investment, Private Equity and Real Estate Funds*. PricewaterhouseCoopers International.

Ramakrishnan, R.T.S. and Thakor, A.V. (1984). Information reliability and a theory of financial intermediation. *Review of Economic Studies*, 51(3), 415–432.

5

ACCOUNTING TREATMENT FOR FINANCIAL INSTRUMENTS

One can't say that figures lie. But figures, as used in financial arguments, seem to have the bad habit of expressing a small part of the truth forcibly, and neglecting the other part, as do some people we know.

Fred Schwed (1901–1966), US author

This chapter will discuss and illustrate the accounting treatment, including the accounting entries and adjustments for each key category of financial instruments. The main issue that this chapter addresses is: What is the difference in the accounting entries for the various financial instruments? The answer to this question is related to the accounting standards that were discussed in the previous chapter. In other words, the recognition and measurement of the respective financial instrument type as contemplated by IAS 39 and IFRS 9. Hence, the way financial instruments are measured determines their accounting treatment.

Accounting treatment of financial instruments

This section will demonstrate the accounting treatment for each key category of financial instruments, namely:

- held-to-maturity (HTM);
- loans and receivables (L & R);
- fair value through profit and loss (FVTPL);
- available for sale (AFS).

Accounting treatment: held-to-maturity (HTM) financial instruments

As stated previously the accounting treatment for a particular financial instrument depends on how the financial instrument is measured. HTM are measured through amortised cost. The accounting treatment of HTM can best be illustrated by an example.

Let us assume that Zeta Ltd purchased 1,000 government bonds on 1 January, for the amount of €104 each, with the investment maturing in two years' time, where Zeta Ltd will receive €100 per bond. The interest rate applicable is 5 per cent per annum with interest being paid on 31 December. Furthermore, the opening balance of the bank account when the purchase of the bonds was made stood at €150,000. The accounting transactions for this example during the life cycle of the financial instrument are shown at Table 5.1, with the transaction postings being illustrated at Figure 5.1.

Table 5.1 and Figure 5.1 illustrate that four general ledger accounts are affected by the resultant accounting transactions. The Investment Account reflects the procurement of the financial instrument (i.e. government bonds initially shown as €104,000) and its subsequent amortisation over a period of two years (i.e. €2,000 per year causing the value of the bonds to €100,000). The Investment Account has a zero balance when the bonds mature, with the owner of the bonds receiving €100,000 representing the value of the bonds. Furthermore, the Bank Account reflects the initial purchase of the financial instrument (cash outflow of €104,000) and interest received during the two-year period until the financial asset's maturity. The Bank Account also shows a cash-inflow of €100,000 which represents the amount received by the company when the financial instrument (bonds) matured after the duration of two years.

Additionally, the Interest Earned Account basically reflects the interest earned by the government bonds, which were later transferred to the Profit and Loss Account. One should note that the Profit and Loss Account reflects the gains and losses from the various transactions. For instance, the amortised value is shown as debit in the Profit and Loss Account reflecting the decrease in the value of the government bonds as they move towards maturity. On the other hand, the interest received from the Government Bonds reflects the earnings that are generated by the government bonds until maturity.

Accounting treatment: loans and receivables (L & R) financial instruments

Accounting wise, loans and receivables (L & R) are treated in a similar manner as HTM financial instruments, and as such are measured through amortised cost. It should be noted that L & R are non-derivative financial assets with fixed or determinable payments that are not quoted in an active market, except for those:

• that the company intends to sell immediately or in the near term, which shall be classified as held for trading (HFT), and those that the company upon initial recognition designates as at fair value through profit or loss (FVTPL);
• that the company upon initial recognition designates as AFS; or
• for which the holder may not recover substantially all of its initial investment, other than because of credit deterioration, which shall be classified as AFS.

TABLE 5.1 Accounting transactions – Zeta Ltd.

Bank A/c:	Dr.	Cr.
Bank opening balance: Year-1	€150,000	
1st January Year-1: Purchase Bonds		€104,000
31st December Year-1: Interest Received	€5,000	
31st December Year-2: Interest Received	€5,000	
31st December Year-2: Maturity of Bonds	€100,000	
Total:	**€260,000**	**€104,000**
Bank Balance:	**€156,000**	

Investment A/c:		
1st January Year-1: Purchase Bonds	€104,000	
31st December Year-1: Amortisation		€2,000
31st December Year-2: Amortisation		€2,000
31st December Year-2: Maturity of Bonds		€100,000
Total:	**€104,000**	**€104,000**
Investment A/c Balance:	**€0**	

Interest Earned A/c:		
31st December Year-1: Interest Received		€5,000
31st December Year-1: T/F to P & L A/c	€5,000	
31st December Year-2: Interest Received		€5,000
31st December Year-2: T/F to P & L A/c	€5,000	
Total:	**€10,000**	**€10,000**
Interest Earned A/c Balance:	**€0**	

Profit and Loss A/c:		
31st December Year-1: Interest Earned		€5,000
31st December Year-1: Amortisation	€2,000	
31st December Year-2: Interest Earned		€5,000
31st December Year-2: Amortisation	€2,000	
Total:	**€4,000**	**€10,000**
Profit and Loss A/c Balance:		**€6,000**

For instance, a variation in interest rates may result in a possibility that an entity will not recuperate the amount it paid for a financial asset. Hence, even though such an asset meets the definition of loans and receivables, it should be classified as AFS, since the holder may not recover substantially all of its initial investment. Examples of assets that are typically classified as loans and receivables include loans to other entities, bank deposits, trade debtors and bank accounts.

Dr.	**Investment A/c**		Cr.
1-Jan/Yr1	104,000	31-Dec/Yr1	2,000
Balance Yr1	102,000		
		31-Dec/Yr2	2,000
		31-Dec/Yr2	100,000
Balance Yr2	0		

Dr.	**Bank A/c**		Cr.
Balance Yr0	150,000		
31-Dec/Yr1	5,000	1-Jan/Yr1	104,000
Balance Yr1	51,000		
31-Dec/Yr2	5,000		
31-Dec/Yr2	100,000		
Balance Yr2	156,000		

Dr.	**Interest Earned A/c**		Cr.
		31-Dec/Yr1	5,000
T/F P&L A/c	5,000		
		31-Dec/Yr2	5,000
T/F P&L A/c	5,000		

Dr.	**Profit & Loss A/c**		Cr.
31-Dec/Yr1	2,000	31-Dec/Yr1	5,000
		Balance Yr1	3,000
31-Dec/Yr2	2,000	31-Dec/Yr2	5,000
		Balance Yr2	6,000

FIGURE 5.1 HTM financial instrument – accounting transactions postings

The accounting treatment of L & R can best be illustrated by an example. The example below illustrates the amortisation of the discount on a note receivable (with equal annuity payments) using the Effective Interest Method. Assume that Cohen Ltd received a note receivable from a customer for the exchange of services that was provided to the customer at the beginning of Year 1. Let us assume the services provided amounted to €10,000 and that the note receivable is to be paid over five yearly instalments, being end of Year 1 thru Year 5 to pay for the services provided. Hence, the payment per year will amount to €2,000. Let us further assume that the fair rate of return is 10 per cent.

First we need to calculate the present value (PV) of the annuity. The PV amounts to €7,582 (use EXCEL function: PV(x, y, -z) where x = 10 per cent interest rate; y = 5 instalments, z = €2,000 being the value of each instalment). Therefore, we now know that the amortised interest over the five-year period at 10 per cent interest rate is €2,418 (i.e. €10,000–€7,582). Now we need to amortise (allocate) the interest revenue earned on the note receivable to the income statement over the five-year period. Table 5.2 illustrates the amortisation discount of the note receivable using the Effective Interest Method. It shows the note receivable (annuity) discounted back five years at 10 per cent fair rate of return.

The accounting transactions for this example during the life cycle of the financial instrument are shown at Table 5.3, with the transaction postings being illustrated at Figure 5.2.

Table 5.3 and Figure 5.2 illustrate that four general ledger accounts are affected by the resulting accounting transactions. The Bank Account transactions of €2,000 each reflect the payments being received from the Notes Receivables, while the

TABLE 5.2 Cohen Ltd: note receivable discounted back 5 years @ 10 per cent

Year	(A) Opening Balance	(B) Interest (10%) (A x B)	(C) Payment	(D) Closing Balance [A – (C – B)]
1	€7,582	€758	€2,000	€6,340
2	€6,340	€634	€2,000	€4,974
3	€4,974	€497	€2,000	€3,471
4	€3,471	€347	€2,000	€1,818
5	€1,818	€182	€2,000	€0

transactions in the Notes Receivable Account reflect the reduction in this account for each payment being received from the debtor.

However, one should note that the note receivable (annuity) is being discounted back for five years at 10 per cent fair rate of return. This aspect of the transaction is reflected in the Discount Note Receivable Account and the Service Revenue (i.e. Profit and Loss Account).

Let us consider another example that illustrates how to amortise and record a loan with annuity type loan payments (equal payments), calculate the interest revenue on the loan for the duration of the loan, then amortise the interest revenue and recognise the revenue on the income statement. hofstein plc received a note receivable from a Kruger Ltd for exchange of services valued at €25,000 that was provided at the beginning of Year-1. The note receivable is to be paid in five equal instalments of €5,000 at a fair rate of return of 8 per cent per annum. The following steps are required:

1 Discount the loan back to the issue date using the interest rate on the loan;
2 Establish the debt amortisation schedule and amortise the interest revenue over the duration of the loan; and
3 Record on balance sheet and income statement the loan receivable, discount loan receivable (contra account) and interest revenue, detailed calculations for accounting and recording the loan receivable.

Step 1: Calculate the present value (PV) of the annuity. The PV amounts to €19,964 (use EXCEL function: PV(x, y, -z) where x = 8 per cent interest rate; y = 5 instalments, z = €5,000 being the value of each instalment). Therefore, we now know that the amortised interest over the five-year period at 8 per cent interest rate is €5,036 (i.e. €25,000–€19,964).

Step 2: Amortise (allocate) the interest revenue earned on the note receivable to the income statement over the five-year period. Table 5.4 shows the amortisation discount of the note receivable (annuity) using the Effective Interest Method discounted back five years at 8 per cent fair rate of return.

TABLE 5.3 Accounting transactions – Cohen Ltd

Bank A/c:		Dr.	Cr.
Payment received Year-1		€2,000	
Payment received Year-2		€2,000	
Payment received Year-3		€2,000	
Payment received Year-4		€2,000	
Payment received Year-5		€2,000	
	Total:	**€10,000**	**€0**

Notes Receivable (Services Provided) A/c:			
1st January Year-1: When services provided		€10,000	
Payment received Year-1			€2,000
Payment received Year-2			€2,000
Payment received Year-3			€2,000
Payment received Year-4			€2,000
Payment received Year-5			€2,000
	Total:	**€10,000**	**€10,000**

Discount Note Receivable A/c: (Services Provided)			
1st January Year-1: When services provided			€2,418
Discount Note Receivable Year-1		€758	
Discount Note Receivable Year-2		€634	
Discount Note Receivable Year-3		€497	
Discount Note Receivable Year-4		€347	
Discount Note Receivable Year-5		€182	
	Total:	**€2,418**	**€2,418**

Service Revenue (P & L) A/c: (Interest on Note Receivable)			
1st January Year-1: When services provided			€7,582
Interest Revenue recognised Year-1			€758
Interest Revenue recognised Year-2			€634
Interest Revenue recognised Year-3			€497
Interest Revenue recognised Year-4			€347
Interest Revenue recognised Year-5			€182
	Total:	**€0**	**€10,000**

Step 3: Record the accounting transactions for the life cycle of the financial instrument as shown at Table 5.5, with the transaction postings being illustrated at Figure 5.3.

The accounting mechanics in this example is similar to the previous one in that as illustrated in Table 5.5 and Figure 5.3, four general ledger accounts are affected by the resulting accounting transactions. The Bank Account transactions of €5,000 each reflect the payments being received from the Notes Receivables, while the

Dr.	**Bank A/c**	Cr.	Dr.	**Notes Receivable A/c:**	Cr.
31-Dec/Yr1	2,000		01-Jan/Yr1	10,000	
31-Dec/Yr2	2,000			31-Dec/Yr1	2,000
31-Dec/Yr3	2,000			31-Dec/Yr2	2,000
31-Dec/Yr4	2,000			31-Dec/Yr3	2,000
31-Dec/Yr5	2,000			31-Dec/Yr4	2,000
				31-Dec/Yr5	2,000
Balance Yr5	10,000		Balance Yr5	0	

Dr.	**Discount Note Receivable A/c**	Cr.	Dr.	**Service Revenue (P & L) A/c**	Cr.
		01-Jan/Yr1 2,418		01-Jan/Yr1	7,582
31-Dec/Yr1	758			31-Dec/Yr1	758
31-Dec/Yr2	634			31-Dec/Yr2	634
31-Dec/Yr3	497			31-Dec/Yr3	497
31-Dec/Yr4	347			31-Dec/Yr4	347
31-Dec/Yr5	182			31-Dec/Yr5	182
Balance Yr5	0			Balance Yr5	10,000

FIGURE 5.2 Cohen Ltd: L & R financial instrument – transactions postings

TABLE 5.4 Hofstein plc: note receivable discounted back 5 years @ 8 per cent

Year	(A) Opening Balance	(B) Interest (8%) (A x B)	(C) Payment	(D) Closing Balance [A – (C – B)]
1	€19,964	€1,597	€5,000	€16,561
2	€16,561	€1,325	€5,000	€12,885
3	€12,885	€1,031	€5,000	€ 8,916
4	€ 8,916	€ 713	€5,000	€ 4,630
5	€ 4,630	€ 370	€5,000	€ 0

transactions in the Notes Receivable Account reflect the reduction in this account for each payment being received from the debtor.

Once again, one should note that the note receivable (annuity) is being discounted back for five years at 8 per cent fair rate of return. This aspect of the transaction is reflected in the Discount Note Receivable Account and the Service Revenue (i.e. Profit and Loss Account).

Accounting treatment: fair value through profit and loss (FVTPL)

Financial assets at FVTPL are subdivided into two categories, namely financial assets designated on initial recognition at FVTPL and held for trading (HFT) financial

TABLE 5.5 Accounting transactions – Hofstein plc

Bank A/c:		Dr.	Cr.
Payment received Year-1		€5,000	
Payment received Year-2		€5,000	
Payment received Year-3		€5,000	
Payment received Year-4		€5,000	
Payment received Year-5		€5,000	
	Total:	**€25,000**	**€0**

Notes Receivable (Services Provided) A/c:			
1st January Year-1: When services provided		€25,000	
Payment received Year-1			€5,000
Payment received Year-2			€5,000
Payment received Year-3			€5,000
Payment received Year-4			€5,000
Payment received Year-5			€5,000
	Total:	**€25,000**	**€25,000**

Discount Note Receivable A/c: (Services Provided)			
1st January Year-1: When services provided			€5,036
Discount Note Receivable Year-1		€1,597	
Discount Note Receivable Year-2		€1,325	
Discount Note Receivable Year-3		€1,031	
Discount Note Receivable Year-4		€713	
Discount Note Receivable Year-5		€370	
	Total:	**€5,036**	**€5,036**

Service Revenue (P & L) A/c: (Interest on Note Receivable)			
1st January Year-1: When services provided			€19,964
Interest Revenue recognised Year-1			€1,597
Interest Revenue recognised Year-2			€1,325
Interest Revenue recognised Year-3			€1,031
Interest Revenue recognised Year-4			€713
Interest Revenue recognised Year-5			€370
	Total:	**€0**	**€25,000**

assets. There are a number of reasons that may motivate an entity to designate financial assets at FVTPL. For instance, an entity may desire to eliminate or significantly reduce an accounting mismatch, particularly when recognition or measurement inconsistency occurs with respect to a transaction that gives rise to both a financial asset and liability, which may result in these being classified differently.

The concern arises because the classification of financial assets influences its measurement. Therefore, the financial statements would present more relevant

Dr.	Bank A/c		Cr.		Dr.	Notes Receivable A/c:		Cr.
31-Dec/Yr1	5,000				01-Jan/Yr1	25,000		
31-Dec/Yr2	5,000						31-Dec/Yr1	5,000
31-Dec/Yr3	5,000						31-Dec/Yr2	5,000
31-Dec/Yr4	5,000						31-Dec/Yr3	5,000
31-Dec/Yr5	5,000						31-Dec/Yr4	5,000
							31-Dec/Yr5	5,000
Balance Yr5	25,000				Balance Yr5	0		

Dr.	Discount Note Receivable A/c		Cr.		Dr.	Service Revenue (P & L) A/c		Cr.
		01-Jan/Yr1	5,036				01-Jan/Yr1	19,964
31-Dec/Yr1	1,597						31-Dec/Yr1	1,597
31-Dec/Yr2	1,325						31-Dec/Yr2	1,325
31-Dec/Yr3	1,031						31-Dec/Yr3	1,031
31-Dec/Yr4	713						31-Dec/Yr4	713
31-Dec/Yr5	370						31-Dec/Yr5	370
Balance Yr5	0						Balance Yr5	25,000

FIGURE 5.3 Hofstein plc: L & R financial instrument – transactions postings

information if both asset and liability were designated at FVTPL since this would achieve consistency in the measurement of both financial asset and liability. Another reason for the FVTPL designation is to mitigate the compliance process that hedge accounting requires, since these tend to be cumbersome. Therefore, designating the financial assets at FVTPL achieves the hedge accounting objective at a lower compliance cost.

An entity classifies financial assets as HFT (refer to IAS 39.9) when it is acquired predominantly for the purpose of resale in the short-term and/or the financial asset is a derivative. It may also be designated as HFT when on initial recognition it forms part of a portfolio of acknowledged financial instruments that are jointly managed and for which there is verification of recent short-term profit making transaction activity. Let us consider an example of FVTPL designation.

Gregory Enterprises Ltd holds an investment of 5,500 shares in HSBC. The investment was purchased for a price of €2.50 per share on 1 December. The com pany's opening balance of the bank account when the purchase of the shares was made stood at €150,000. Currently, the company is in the process of preparing its financial statements for year ending 31 December. Furthermore, the fair value of the HSBC's shares on 31 December was €2.65 per share. We now need to establish how the above transactions are reflected in the accounting books of Gregory Enterprises Ltd.

First, fair value movement is the difference between the purchase price of the share and its fair value on 31 December, showing a gain of €0.15 per share (i.e. €2.65–€2.50). Hence, the total gain is €825 (i.e. €0.15 × 5,500 shares). The accounting transactions for this example during the life cycle of the financial instrument are shown at Table 5.6, with the transaction postings being illustrated at Figure 5.4. Hence, FVTPL financial assets are measured at fair value and fair value changes are recognised as profit or loss (and recorded in the Profit/Loss Account).

In this example Table 5.6 and Figure 5.4 show that four general ledger accounts are affected by the accounting transactions. The Bank Account and the Investment Account are both asset accounts and reflect the procurement of the HSBC shares on 1 December. The cash withdrawn from the Bank Account is utilised to purchase the shares. The Net Unrealised Profit (AFS Assets) Account reflects the fair market value of the shares, which is also reflected in the Investment Account since the asset (shares) gained a value of €0.15 per share. The net gain due to fair market value is shown in the Profit and Loss Account as an increase in income for the company.

TABLE 5.6 Accounting transactions – Gregory Enterprises Ltd

Bank A/c:	Dr.	Cr.
Bank opening balance: Year-1	€150,000	
1st December Year-1: Purchase Shares		€13,750
Total:	€150,000	€13,750
Bank Balance:	€136,250	
HSBC Investment A/c:		
1st December Year-1: Purchase Shares	€13,750	
31st December Year-1: Fair Value Gain/Loss	€825	
Total:	€14,575	€0
HSBC Investment A/c Balance:	€14,575	
Fair Value Gain/Loss A/c:		
31st December Year-1: Fair Value Gain		€825
31st December Year-1: Fair Value Gain	€825	
Total:	€825	€825
Fair Value Gain/Loss A/c Balance:		€0
Profit and Loss A/c:		
31st December Year-1: Fair Value Gain		€825
Total:	€0	€825
Profit and Loss A/c Balance:		€825

Dr.	**HSBC Investment A/c**	Cr.
1-Dec/Yr1	13,750	
31-Dec/Yr1	825	

Dr.	**Bank A/c**		Cr.
Balance Yr1	150,000		
		1-Dec/Yr1	13,750

Dr. **Net Unrealised Profit: AFS Assets**		Cr.
	31-Dec/Yr1	825
31-Dec/Yr1	825	

Dr.	**Profit & Loss A/c**		Cr.
		31-Dec/Yr1	825

FIGURE 5.4 Fair value through profit & loss – accounting transactions

Accounting treatment: available for sale (AFS)

Available for sale financial assets (AFS) are a residual category for non-derivative financial assets. In other words, they do not fall into any of the previous three categories. An asset may be designated as AFS on initial recognition. However, the reason why AFS financial assets are acquired is normally not for trading purposes. But should an entity wish to sell the AFS financial assets, it will be able to do so. Furthermore, AFS financial assets are measured by fair value through equity. Hence, the accounting treatment for AFS is also different from the other categories.

Two important factors are taken into account when deciding to classify a financial asset as AFS, namely liquidity and the failure to establish a fair value. Maintaining optimal liquidity is an important aspect to most entities. Therefore, these entities are constrained to classify some of their financial instruments as AFS, particularly when the entity's liquidity status declines significantly. Hence, the entity may sell its financial assets to support its liquidity position.

Fair value is easily established when the financial asset is quoted on the stock market. However, an entity can categorise the financial asset as AFS when the asset is not quoted and fair value cannot be established using normal valuation practices, due to the scarcity of accurate and consistent records. These types of financial assets are recorded at cost and subjected to an impairment test where appropriate. Hence, unlike the financial assets that are classified as FVTPL, fair value changes resulting from measurement of AFS financial assets affect other comprehensive income (i.e. equity).

Let us consider an example for a financial asset designated as AFS. Moreover, assume the same numerical data as the previous example using the FVTPL designation. This will enable us to examine the accounting treatment differences between AFS and FVTPL designations and will also demonstrate the impact of each respective designation on the financial statements (statement of financial position and statement of financial performance).

Pearson Investments Ltd holds an investment of 5,500 shares in HSBC. The investment was purchased for a price of €2.50 per share on 1 December. The company's opening balance of the bank account when the purchase of the shares was made stood at €150,000. Furthermore, the fair value of the HSBC's shares on 31 December was €2.65 per share. Currently, the company is in the process of preparing its financial statements for year ending 31 December. It is now necessary to establish how the above transactions are reflected in the accounting books of Pearson Investments Ltd.

Similar to the previous example, the fair value movement is the difference between the purchase price of the share on 1 December and its fair value on the 31 December, showing a gain of €0.15 per share (i.e. €2.65–€2.50) resulting in a total gain of €825 (i.e. €0.15 × 5,500 shares). The accounting transactions for this example during the life cycle of the financial instrument are shown at Table 5.7, with the transaction postings being illustrated at Figure 5.5. Table 5.7 and Figure 5.5 illustrate that the AFS financial assets are measured at fair value. However, the fair value changes are recognised in equity account of the company and not Profit/Loss Account.

Table 5.7 and Figure 5.5 illustrate that three general ledger accounts are affected by the transactions. The Bank Account reflects the procurement transaction at the

TABLE 5.7 Accounting transactions – Pearson Investments Ltd

Bank A/c:		**Dr.**	**Cr.**
Bank opening balance: Yr-1		€150,000	
1st December Yr-1: Purchase Shares			€13,750
	Total:	**€150,000**	**€13,750**
	Bank Balance:	**€136,250**	

HSBC Investment A/c:			
1st December Yr-1: Purchase Shares		€13,750	
31st December Yr-1: Net unrealised profit on AFS assets		€825	
	Total:	**€14,575**	**€0**
	HSBC Investment A/c Balance:	**€14,575**	

Accumulated Other Comprehensive Income A/c			
31st December Yr-1: Net unrealised profit on AFS assets			€825
	Total:	**€0**	**€825**
Acc. Other Comprehensive Income A/c Balance:			**€825**

Dr.	**HSBC Investment A/c**	Cr.		Dr.	**Bank A/c**		Cr.
1-Dec/Yr1	13,750			Balance Yr1	150,000		
31-Dec/Yr1	825					1-Dec/Yr1	13,750

Dr.	**Accumulated Other Comprehensive Income A/c**	Cr.
		31-Dec/Yr1 825

FIGURE 5.5 Available for sale (AFS) – accounting transactions

time the shares were purchased. The Investment Account reflects the initial value of the shares at the time of purchase. However, the Investment Account also reflects the fair market value of the shares at the end of the financial year by increasing the value of the shares by €825 (i.e. gain in value of €0.15 per share). Furthermore, the gain in the value of the shares is reflected in Accumulated Other Comprehensive Income Account. It should be noted that this account is not an income account (i.e. it is not part of the statement of financial performance) but it is a balance sheet account reflecting the equity (owners' capital) side of the statement of financial position.

The above illustrate how the accounting transactions are reflected in accounts of Pearson Investments Ltd. However, on closer examination there is a conceptual difference between the impact of FVTPL and AFS on the presentation of the financial statements (statement of financial position and statement of financial performance). In other words, Gregory Enterprises Ltd (the example preceding Pearson Investment Ltd) due to the FVTPL designation of the financial asset will have registered a gain in the statement of financial performance of €825. On the other hand, due to the AFS designation of the financial asset, no effect is registered on the statement of financial performance of Pearson Investments Ltd. The reason for this is that the gain is recorded directly in the statement of financial position (equity). One may ask: what difference does this make?

Consider the recent financial crisis. Let us assume that instead of a gain on the share price there was a loss. Furthermore, let us further assume that the number of shares involved was much higher, hence the net loss would be more substantial. In this scenario, Gregory Enterprises Ltd would likely have registered a substantial loss in the statement of financial performance, whereas Pearson Investments Ltd's statement of financial performance would not have been affected. Admittedly, Pearson Investments Ltd's equity (owners' capital) would be negatively affected, but the company's performance in terms of profitability would not be. Furthermore, the dividend policy of both companies would be influenced by this situation, but it is likely Pearson Investments Ltd would be in a better position in terms of declaring a dividend.

Accounting implications when purchasing and selling financial instruments

This section will examine the accounting implications when purchasing and selling financial instruments. Certain issues arise when financial instruments are purchased or sold at a date other than their maturity date. However, before these issues can be examined in detail, it is important to introduce two important terms related to the purchasing and selling of financial instruments, namely: (a) cumulative dividend investments; and (b) excluding dividend investments.

Significance of cumulative dividend or cumulative interest investments

Cumulative dividend or cumulative interest (cum-div or cum-int) means that a buyer of a security is entitled to receive a dividend or interest that has been declared, but not paid. This means that the security is offered for sale with an entitlement to the next dividend or interest payment attached. This dividend or interest will already have been declared (but not paid) by the company, so the market knows how much it is worth and the share (or bond) price will reflect this. It is a requirement with cumulative dividend that preference stock dividends are paid in full before any common dividend payment is made.

A simple example will illustrate the meaning of 'cumulative dividend/interest' investments. Let us assume that a company normally declares a dividend for its shares twice a year, namely 30 June and 31 December. This means that a dividend declared for 30 June covers the period for 1 January to 30 June. It also means that the dividend declared for 31 December covers the period for 1 July to 31 December. Let us assume that we buy the shares from the company on the 1 October. This means that on 31 December, we will receive the dividend for the period 1 July to 31 December. However, the portion of the dividend from 1 July to 30 September does not belong to us since we purchased the shares on 1 October. Hence, we are only entitled for the portion of the dividend from 1 October to 31st December. We must refund the portion of the dividend from 1st July to 30 September to the seller of the shares.

Significance of excluding dividend or excluding interest investments

Excluding dividend or excluding interest (ex-div or ex-int) means that the declared dividend or interest will be received by the seller and not the buyer. Hence, a stock is given ex-div or ex-int status if an individual or entity has been confirmed by the company to receive the dividend or interest payment. The purchase of shares or bonds without entitlement to recently declared dividends means that the entitlement to receive a dividend or interest remains with the seller of the shares or bonds.

Let us consider a similar example to the cum-div/cum-int situation to illustrate the meaning of 'Excluding Dividend/Interest' investments. Let us assume that a company normally declares a dividend for its shares twice a year, namely 30 June and 31 December. This means that a dividend declared for 30 June covers the period for 1 January to 30 June. It also means that the dividend declared for 31 December covers the period for 1 July to 31 December. Let us assume that we buy the shares from the company on 1 October. Under the ex-div or ex-int situation, this means that on 31 December, the seller of the shares will receive the dividend for the period 1 July to 31 December. However, the seller is only entitled to the portion of the dividend from 1 July to 30 September. Therefore, the seller of the shares must refund us the portion of the dividend from 1 October to 31 December. Generally, the stock price falls the day the ex-div period starts, since the buyer will not receive the benefit of a dividend payout until the next dividend date.

Accounting adjustments when purchasing and selling financial instruments

The above sections regarding the significance of cum-div (cum-int) and ex-div (ex-int) financial instruments highlight the need for accounting adjustments when purchasing and selling financial instruments. As stated previously, the need for accounting adjustments arises when financial instruments are purchased or sold at a date other than their maturity date.

It should be noted that normally all investments are assumed to be cum-div or cum-int unless otherwise stated to be specifically ex-div or ex-int. Furthermore, brokerage charges and applicable stamp duties (if any) are part of the capital cost associated with the purchase of the investment. Brokerage charges on the sale of the investment are deducted from the capital cost, and as such the capital proceeds are the net amount after the deduction of all expenses associated with the sales transaction. Hence, there is no need for a further adjustment regarding to the fixed interest or fixed dividend. Moreover, the accounting adjustment procedure for the purchasing and selling of financial instruments occurs only once. It occurs at the time of the first dividend or interest due after the sale or purchase of the financial instrument takes place, and only if the financial instruments are purchased or sold at a date other than their maturity date.

Accounting adjustments for cum-div and cum-int financial instruments

Cum-div and cum-int financial instrument purchase means that the buyer receives the whole of the next payment of the dividend or interest without having held the financial instrument for the whole of the period to which that payment relates.

In other words, the buyer of the financial instrument receives a dividend or interest payment that is not entirely due to him. Hence, under cum-div and cum-int the purchase price of the financial instrument is increased by (or includes) the accrued dividend or interest. This results in the buyer of the financial instrument refunding the amount that is not due to purchaser.

This may be depicted diagrammatically (refer to Figure 5.6) by the following example. Let us assume that an investment was purchased as cum-div on 1 October and the entity normally pays the dividend twice annually that is, 30 June and 31 December. Therefore, as Figure 5.6 illustrates, under cum-div the seller is entitled to receive the dividend from 1 July to 30 September, however, the buyer will actually receive the entire dividend payment on 31 December, covering the period 1 July to 31 December.

Hence, to compensate the seller for not receiving the dividend from 1 July to 30 September, the purchase price is inclusive of the dividend due from 1 July to 30 September. The net effect is that the buyer receives only the portion of the dividend from 1 October to 31 December.

Let us consider an example. Assume that Mr J Cohen has a bank balance of €200,000 and buys a financial instrument for €100,000 as cum-int on 1 October. The interest related to this investment is paid twice yearly on 30 June and 31 December. The financial instrument earns 5 per cent per annum. Therefore, the seller of the financial instrument is entitled to receive the interest from 1 July to 30 September (three months). In other words, the interest earned by the financial instrument between 1 July and 31 December is €2,500 (i.e. €100,000 × 0.05 ÷ 2 = €2,500) which is to be equally divided between the buyer and the seller (i.e. €1,250 interest each, being their share of the three months' interest earned). However, under the cum-int rule, the buyer will receive the entire interest payment of €2,500 on 31 December, covering the interest period from 1 July to 31 December. Hence, to compensate the seller of the financial investment for not receiving the interest due from 1 July to 30 September, the purchase price of the financial instrument is inclusive of the interest due from 1 July to 30 September, that is, €101,250 (i.e. €100,000 + (€2,500 ÷ 2)). The net effect is that the buyer receives only what is due, that is, the interest from 1 October to 31 December (i.e. €1,250).

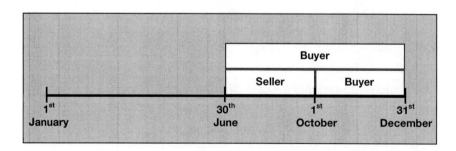

FIGURE 5.6 Cum-div (and cum-int) financial instruments purchase

The remaining issue to be addressed is the accounting entries to represent the above transaction from the buyer's point of view. First, we need to show the value of the financial instrument, which is the financial asset, separate from the interest payment. Therefore, we must show the value of the financial asset (€100,000) and its respective interest earnings (€1,250). The accounting entries representing the transaction are as shown in Figure 5.7.

Figure 5.7 illustrates that on 1 October the buyer of the financial instrument pays the seller €101,250 (i.e. credit Bank Account by €101,250 and debit Investment Account). This payment includes the purchase price of the financial instrument that amounts to €100,000 and the seller's interest entitlement of €1,250 for the period 1 July to 30 September. The interest amount of €1,250 paid to the seller is viewed as a payment in advance; hence the reason why the 'Investment Account' is credited by €1,250 and the 'Interest Received Account' is debited by €1,250.

On 31 December under the cum-div rule, the buyer of the financial instrument receives the full interest payment of €2,500 for the period 1 July to 31 December. Since the seller was compensated by the amount of €1,250 on 1 of October, the entire amount of €2,500 is kept by the buyer. This is why the 'Bank Account' is debited by €2,500 and the 'Interest Received Account' is credited by €2,500. The end result is a balance of €100,000 in the 'Investment Account' and the transfer

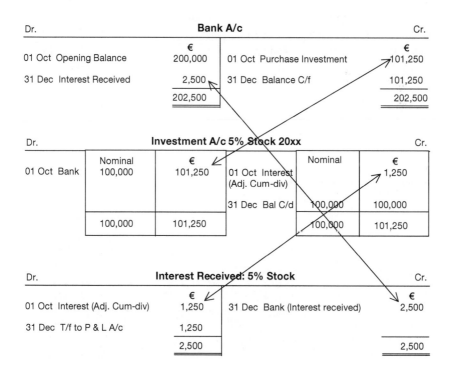

FIGURE 5.7 Cum-div (and cum-int) accounting entries

of €1,250 from the 'Interest Receivable Account' to the 'Profit and Loss Account' for year ending 31 December.

Accounting adjustments for ex-div and ex-int financial instruments

Generally, the accounting procedure for the ex-div (ex-int) financial instruments is opposite to the cum-div (cum-int) process. With ex-div or ex-int financial instruments the buyer does not physically receive the next dividend or interest payment even though the buyer is rightfully entitled to the dividend or interest payment. Hence, the purchase price is reduced by the dividend or interest due to reflect the dividend or interest entitlement.

Once again, this may be depicted diagrammatically (refer to Figure 5.8) by the following example. Let us assume that an investment was purchased as cum-div on 1 December and the entity normally pays the dividend twice annually that is, 30 June and 31 December. Therefore, as Figure 5.8 illustrates, under ex-div the seller is entitled to receive the dividend from 1 July to 30 November and the buyer is entitled to receive the dividend from 1 December to 31 December. However, under the ex-div or ex-int rule, the seller will actually physically receive the entire dividend or interest payment on 31 December, covering the period 1 July to 31 December.

Hence, to compensate the buyer for not receiving the dividend from 1 December to 31 December, the purchase price is reduced by the dividend or interest due from 1 December to 31 December. The net effect is that the seller receives only the portion of the dividend or interest that the seller is entitled to, that is, from 1 July to 30 November. Therefore, the net effect is that the seller receives the dividend or interest from 1 July to 30 November and the buyer receives the dividend or interest from 1 December to 31 December.

Let us consider an example. Assume that Ms R. Borg has a bank balance of €120,000 and buys a financial instrument for €100,000 as ex-int on 1 December. The interest related to this investment is paid twice yearly on 30 June and 31 December. The financial instrument earns 4.8 per cent per annum. Hence, the interest earned per month is €400 (i.e. €100,000 × 0.048 ÷ 12). Therefore, the seller of the financial instrument is entitled to receive the interest from 1 July to 30 November (five months). In other words, the interest earned

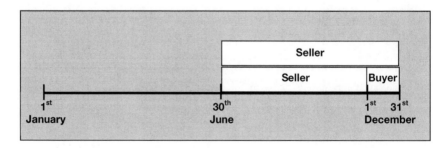

FIGURE 5.8 Ex-div (and ex-int) financial instruments purchase

by the financial instrument between 1 July and 31 December is €2,400 (i.e. €100,000 × 0.048 ÷ 2 = €2,400) of which five months of the interest belongs to the seller and one month of interest belong to the buyer (i.e. €2000 interest belongs to the seller and €400 belongs to the buyer). However, under the ex-int rule, the seller will physically receive the entire interest payment of €2,400 on 31 December, covering the interest period from 1 July to 31 December. Hence, to compensate the buyer of the financial investment for not receiving the interest due from 1 December to 31 December, the purchase price of the financial instrument is reduced by the interest due from 1 December to 31 December, that is, €99,600 (i.e. €100,000 − €400). The net effect is that the seller receives only what is due, that is, the interest from 1 July to 30 November (€2,000). Keep in mind that this situation occurs only for the first interest period of the investment after the sale or purchase takes place.

The remaining issue to be addressed is the accounting entries to represent the above transaction from the buyer's point of view. First, we need to show the value of the financial instrument, which is the financial asset, separate from the interest payment. Therefore, we must show the value of the financial asset (€100,000) and its respective interest earnings (€400) that is due to the buyer. The accounting entries representing the transaction are as shown in Figure 5.9.

Figure 5.9 illustrates that on 1 December the buyer of the financial instrument pays the seller €99,600 (i.e. credit 'Bank Account' and debit 'Investment Account'

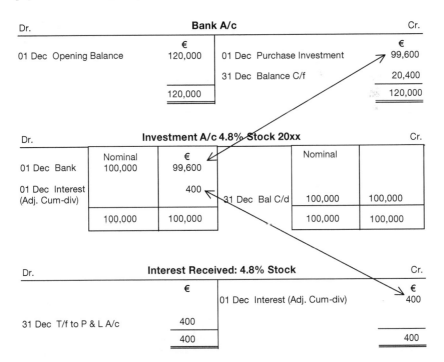

FIGURE 5.9 Ex-div (and ex-int) accounting entries

by €99,600). This payment includes the purchase price of the financial instrument that amounts to €100,000 less the buyer's interest entitlement of €400 for the period 1 December to 31 December (€99,600). However, an adjusting accounting entry is required to show that the buyer in fact purchased the financial instrument for under €100,000 and that the €400 was the interest due from this investment for the period 1 December to 31 December. This is why the 'Investment Account' is debited by €400 and the 'Interest Received Account' is credited by €400. The end result is a balance of €100,000 in the 'Investment Account' and the transfer of €400 from the 'Interest Received Account' to the 'Profit and Loss Account' for year ending 31 December. Therefore, the accounting entries show that the value of the financial instrument is €100,000. However, the physical cash flow exchanged between the buyer and seller was €99,600.

Accounting adjustments for taxation

The practical application of the taxation adjustments is beyond the scope of this text. However, some basic concepts are being provided. The terms 'Tax at Source' and 'Withholding Tax' have basically the same impact. In this text 'Tax at Source' is defined as tax which is deducted by the entity that is paying dividend or interest. However, 'Withholding Tax' is defined as the tax that is deducted by the payer of the dividend or interest through a third party (e.g. stockbroker or bank).

With 'Tax at Source' the dividend or interest is usually received net of tax. Therefore, the recipient of the dividend or interest would need to gross up the amount received in the 'Profit and Loss Account'. In other words, there is a need to convert the net amount received into its equivalent amount before the tax was deducted. Moreover, the tax at source amount is recognised as a tax credit in the tax return.

Similarly, with 'Withholding Tax' the investment income is normally received net of final withholding tax. This would also need to be grossed up with the amount received in the 'Profit and Loss Account'. Hence, converting the net amount received into its equivalent amount before the tax was deducted, with the tax at source amount being recognised as a tax credit in the tax return.

Let us assume that Mr G. Tysen receives a dividend cheque dated 31 December, amounting to €850 after the deduction of 'Tax at Source' of €150. Further assume that Mr Tysen's bank balance is €1,500 at the time when the dividend cheque is received. The accounting entries for this example are shown at Figure 5.10.

First, the amount received of €850 must be grossed up to include the amount of tax, which is €150. Therefore, the amount of the dividend received in a practical sense is recognised as being €1,000 (i.e. €850 + €150). Hence, the amount of €1,000 is debited to the 'Bank Account' and credited to the 'Profit and Loss Account' (as dividend received). Second, the amount of €150, which represents the tax at source, is recognised as a tax credit. Hence, €150 tax at source is debited

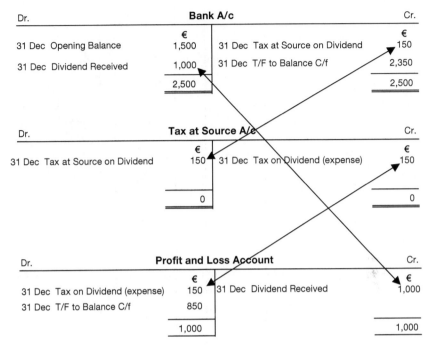

Dr.   **Bank A/c**   Cr.

	€		€
31 Dec Opening Balance	1,500	31 Dec Tax at Source on Dividend	150
31 Dec Dividend Received	1,000	31 Dec T/F to Balance C/f	2,350
	2,500		2,500

Dr.   **Tax at Source A/c**   Cr.

	€		€
31 Dec Tax at Source on Dividend	150	31 Dec Tax on Dividend (expense)	150
	0		0

Dr.   **Profit and Loss Account**   Cr.

	€		€
31 Dec Tax on Dividend (expense)	150	31 Dec Dividend Received	1,000
31 Dec T/F to Balance C/f	850		
	1,000		1,000

FIGURE 5.10 Accounting adjustments for taxation

to the 'Profit and Loss Account' and credited to the 'Tax at Source Account'. Finally, the €150 tax at source is debited to the 'Tax at Source Account' since it represents a decrease in a liability and credited to the 'Bank Account' as a decrease in the cash asset (i.e. recognised as a payment to the tax authorities).

The same transactions would be recorded for the withholding tax scenario. However, in this case the 'Tax at Source Account' would be titled 'Withholding Tax Account'.

Maintaining (format) investment accounts

Typically, there are two options available for the maintenance (formatting) of investment accounts. The first option has two main accounts maintained for each financial instrument (security). One account would represent the investment or the financial instrument which is an asset appearing in the statement of financial position (balance sheet). This shows the movement or fluctuation in the value of the capital. The other account would be the income account which appears in the in the statement of comprehensive income. This shows the gain or loss on the capital. Hence, under the first option, the basis of the accounts is the 'T' account which is similar to the example provided previously (refer to Figures 5.7, 5.9 and 5.10).

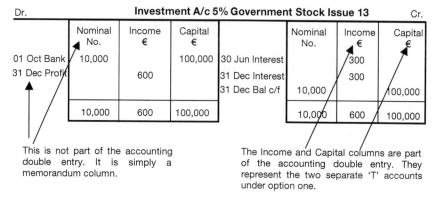

Dr.   **Investment A/c 5% Government Stock Issue 13**   Cr.

	Nominal No.	Income €	Capital €			Nominal No.	Income €	Capital €
01 Oct Bank	10,000		100,000	30 Jun Interest			300	
31 Dec Profit		600		31 Dec Interest			300	
				31 Dec Bal c/f		10,000		100,000
	10,000	600	100,000			10,000	600	100,000

This is not part of the accounting double entry. It is simply a memorandum column.

The Income and Capital columns are part of the accounting double entry. They represent the two separate 'T' accounts under option one.

FIGURE 5.11 Example of a combined format investment account

The second option entails combining the asset and income accounts into a single format. Good practice requires that income is kept separate from the capital cost of the investment therefore each investment account has a column for income and a column for capital. In addition, a column is used to show the nominal value of the stock which is used for convenience and does not form a part of the double accounting entry method. Figure 5.11 illustrates that a particular investment account has the following columns on each side of the account:

- *Column 1*: A date column to show when the transaction was undertaken and a general comment;
- *Column 2*: A memorandum column in which is recorded the nominal value of each transaction in either value or quantitative terms (i.e. €100,000 or 1,000 shares) and does not form part of the accounting entry;
- *Column 3*: An income column to record the investment income transactions (part of the double accounting entry);
- *Column 4*: A capital column to record the investment capital transactions (part of the double accounting entry).

Example regarding the accounting treatment of financial instruments

The following example applies option two which is the combined format for the investment account. Osprey Investment Ltd has its financial year ending on the 31 December 20xx. The company had the following transactions:

- On 31 March 20xx Osprey Investment Ltd acquires 10,000 shares in Eagle Insurance plc for €20,000. These shares are classified as Available-for-Sale (AFS).
- On 30 June 20xx Eagle Insurance plc declares and pays a dividend of five cents per share.

- On 31 December 20xx the fair value of Eagle Insurance plc shares was €2.20 each.
- On 15 January 20x1 Osprey Investment Ltd sells its entire shareholding in Eagle Insurance plc for €2.50 per share.

Record the accounting entries in the investment account for Osprey Investment Ltd using the combined format for the investment account. One should note that according to IAS 39 accounting standards, financial instruments declared as AFS are initially measured at the purchase value then they are revalued at fair market value. The information also highlights that a dividend was declared and paid for Eagle Insurance plc in June but no such dividend was declared (nor paid) in December.

The full solution to this example is found at Figure 5.12. This example is best explained by working out the entries, a transaction at a time, as follows:

- *Transaction One*: On 31 March 20xx Osprey Investment Ltd acquires 10,000 shares in Eagle Insurance plc for €20,000. Therefore, the share price is €2.00 per share (i.e. €20,000 ÷ 10,000 shares = €2.00 per share). Furthermore, these shares are classified as AFS; therefore the investment is measured at purchase value. The accounting entry in the Investment Account is:

  1   Nominal: 10,000 (memorandum only).
  2   Debit Capital A/c: €20,000 (i.e. debit transaction because it represents an increase in the asset investments).
  3   Credit Bank A/c: €20,000 (i.e. credit transaction because it represents a decrease in the asset cash at bank).

- *Transaction Two*: On 30 June 20xx Eagle Insurance plc declares and pays a dividend of five cents per share. Therefore, the total dividend received is €500 (i.e. €0.05 × 10,000 shares = €500). The accounting entry in the Investment Account is:

  1   Credit Income A/c: €500 (i.e. credit transaction because it represents an increase in income to the company).
  2   Debit Bank A/c: €500 (i.e. debit transaction because it represents an increase in the asset cash at bank)

- *Transaction Three*: On 31 December 20xx the fair value of Eagle Insurance plc shares was €2.20 each. Therefore, the increase in share value through revaluation of the shares is €2,000 (i.e. 10,000 shares × (€2.20 − €2.00) = €2,000). The accounting entry in the Investment Account is:

  1   Debit Capital A/c: €2,000 (i.e. debit transaction because it represents an increase in asset investments).
  2   Credit Equity A/c: €2,000 (i.e. credit transaction because it represents an increase in the equity).

Dr.   **Investment A/c 5% Government Stock Issue 13**   Cr.

	Nominal No.	Income €	Capital €		Nominal No.	Income €	Capital €
31-Mar Bank	10,000		20,000	30-Jun Dividend		500	
31-Dec Revaluation			2,000	31-Dec Bal c/f	10,000		22,000
31-Dec Income		500					
	10,000	500	22,000		10,000	500	22,000
31-Dec Bal C/f	10,000		22,000	15-Jan Bank	10,000		25,000
15-Jan Profit on disposal			3,000				
	10,000	0	25,000		10,000	0	25,000

Dr.   **Bank A/c**   Cr.

	€		€
30-Jun Dividend from Shares	500	31-Mar Purchase Shares	20,000
15-Jan Disposal of shares	25,000		

Dr.   **Equity A/c**   Cr.

			€
		31-Dec Revaluation of Shares	2,000
		31-Dec Profit on Disposal of Shares	3,000

Dr.   **P & L A/c**   Cr.

			€
		31-Dec Income from dividend	500

FIGURE 5.12 Example: Osprey Investment Ltd investment account entries

- *Close Books (End of Year)*: 31 December 20xx is the end of the financial year hence we need to close the accounts. The general remarks regarding the Investment Account are:

  1 The nominal number of shares remains the same.
  2 The fair value of the shares is now €22,000 (Purchase price + increase in value due to revaluation = €20,000 + €2,000 = €22,000).
  3 Income from the declared and paid dividend is €500 which is transferred to the Profit and Loss A/c.

- *Transaction Four*: On 15 January 20x1 Osprey Investment Ltd sells its entire shareholding in Eagle Insurance plc for €2.50 per share. Therefore, the profit on disposal of shares is €3,000 (i.e. 10,000 shares × (€2.50 − €2.20) = €3,000). The accounting entry in the Investment Account is:

1   Credit Capital A/c: €25,000 (i.e. credit transaction because it represents a decrease in asset investments).
2   Debit Bank A/c: €25,000 (i.e. debit transaction because it represents an increase in asset cash at bank).
3   Debit Capital A/c: €3,000 (i.e. debit transaction because it represents an increase asset capital).
4   Credit Equity A/c: €3,000 (i.e. credit transaction because it represents an increase in the equity).

Valuation of financial instruments (investments)

Typically, individual investors and investment firms would hold a variety of financial instruments that have been purchased on different terms and/or at different dates. Hence, an important issue that needs to be addressed by these investors is to valuate a portfolio of financial instruments (investments). There are basically two main methods for the valuation of investments, these include: (a) average cost and (b) first-in-first-out (FIFO). The average cost method takes the weighted average of the different cost of the investment acquired at different prices, while the FIFO method takes the cost of the investment on the cost of first-in-first-out basis.

Let us consider an example. Schneider Investments plc had the following transactions regarding interest-bearing securities related to Government Stocks Issue 2025 at 7 per cent interest paid twice yearly on 30 June and 31st December:

- *Transaction One*: On 1 March the company purchased €40,000 worth of stock (nominal value of €100 each) at 96 cum-int.
- *Transaction Two*: On 1 May the company purchased €60,000 worth of stock (nominal value of €100 each) at 99 cum-int.
- *Transaction Three*: On 31 October the company disposed of €50,000 worth of stock (nominal value of €100 each) at 97 cum-int.

The objective is to construct the investment account in the accounting books of Schneider Investments plc using both the weighted average cost and FIFO methods. To construct the investment account the following workings need to be calculated:

- *Transaction One (see Figure 5.8)*: On 1 March the company purchased €40,000 worth of stock (nominal value of €100 each) at 96 cum-int. Hence, 400 stocks of €100 each were procured. However, under the purchase terms of 96 cum-int the price paid for these government stocks is €38,400 (i.e. 400 stocks × €96 = €38,400). The accounting entries in the Investment Account are:

1   Nominal: 400 (memorandum only).
2   Debit Capital A/c: €38,400 (i.e. debit transaction because it represents an increase in the asset investments).

3   Credit Bank A/c: €38,400 (i.e. credit transaction because it represents a decrease in the asset cash at bank).

We also need to calculate the cum-int adjustment. The last interest paid was 31 December hence the next interest period would be 30 June. Therefore, the purchase price includes two months (January and February) accrued interest that must be reimbursed to the seller. The amount of reimbursement is €467 (i.e. €40,000 @ 7 per cent ÷ 12 × 2). The accounting entries in the Investment Account for the cum-int adjustment are:

1   Debit Income A/c: €467 (i.e. debit transaction because it represents a decrease in the income account).
2   Credit Capital A/c: €467 (i.e. credit transaction because it represents a decrease in the asset investment account).

• *Transaction Two (see Figure 5.9)*: On 1 May the company purchased €60,000 worth of stock (nominal value of €100 each) at 99 cum-int. Hence, 600 stocks of €100 each were procured. However, under the purchase terms of 99 cum-int the price paid for these government stocks is €59,400 (i.e. 600 stocks × €99 = €59,400). The accounting entries in the Investment Account are:

1   Nominal: 600 (memorandum only).
2   Debit Capital A/c: €59,400 (i.e. debit transaction because it represents an increase in the asset investments).
3   Credit Bank A/c: €59,400 (i.e. credit transaction because it represents a decrease in the asset cash at bank).

Additionally, we also need to calculate the cum-int adjustment. The last interest paid was 31 December hence the next interest period would be 30 June. Therefore, the purchase price includes four months (January to April) accrued interest that must be reimbursed to the seller (i.e. the other party). The amount of reimbursement is €1,400 (i.e. €60,000 @ 7 per cent ÷ 12 × 4). The accounting entries in the Investment Account for the cum-int adjustment are:

1   Debit Income A/c: €1,400 (i.e. debit transaction because it represents a decrease in the income account).

TABLE 5.8 Example: Schneider Investments plc – Transaction 1

No	Transaction Details	Dr.	Cr.
	Transaction One:		
01	1st March: Capital A/c (buy €40,000 stock @ 96 cum-int)	€38,400	
01	1st March: Bank (pay for purchased stock)		€38,400
02	1st March: Income A/c (Cum-int Adjustment - 2 months)	€467	
02	1st March: Capital A/c (Cum-int Adjustment - 2 months)		€467

TABLE 5.9 Example: Schneider Investments plc – Transaction 2

No	Transaction Details	Dr.	Cr.
	Transaction Two:		
03	1ˢᵗ May: Capital A/c (buy €60,000 stock @ 99 cum-int)	€59,400	
03	1ˢᵗ May: Bank (pay for purchased stock)		€59,400
04	1ˢᵗ May: Income A/c (Cum-int Adjustment - 4 months)	€1,400	
04	1ˢᵗ May: Capital A/c (Cum-int Adjustment - 4 months)		€1,400

2   Credit Capital A/c: €1,400 (i.e. credit transaction because it represents a decrease in the asset investment account).

• *Transaction Three (see Figure 5.10):* On 31 October the company disposed of €50,000 worth of stock (nominal value of €100 each) at 97 cum-int. Hence, 500 stocks of €100 each were sold. However, under the selling terms of 97 cum-int the amount received for these government stocks is €48,500 (i.e. 500 stocks × €97 = €48,500). The accounting entries in the Investment Account are:

1   Nominal: 500 (memorandum only).
2   Credit Capital A/c: €48,500 (i.e. credit transaction because it represents a decrease in the asset investment account).
3   Debit Bank A/c: €48,500 (i.e. debit transaction because it represents an increase in the asset cash in bank).

There is also the need to calculate the cum-int adjustment. The last interest paid was 30 June hence the next interest period would be 31 December. Therefore, the selling price includes four months (July to October) accrued interest that must be reimbursed to the seller (Schneider Investments plc). The amount of reimbursement is €1,167 (i.e. €50,000 @ 7 per cent ÷ 12 × 4). The accounting entries in the Investment Account for the cum-int adjustment are:

1   Debit Capital A/c: €1,167 (i.e. debit transaction because it represents an increase in the asset investment A/c).

TABLE 5.10 Example: Schneider Investments plc – Transaction 3

No	Transaction Details	Dr.	Cr.
	Transaction Three:		
05	31ˢᵗ October: Capital A/c (sold €50,000 stock @ 97 cum-int)		€48,500
05	31ˢᵗ October: Bank A/c (sold €50,000 stock @ 97 cum-int)	€48,500	
06	31ˢᵗ October: Income A/c (Cum-int Adjustment - 4 months)		€1,167
06	31ˢᵗ October: Capital A/c (Cum-int Adjustment - 4 months)	€1,167	

2 Credit Income A/c: €1,167 (i.e. credit transaction because it represents an increase in the income account).

- *Calculate the Interest Received from the Investments (see Figure 5.11)*: Interest is received twice yearly for the investment holding, that is 30 June and 31 December. The interest calculations taking into consideration the various purchase and selling dates of the investments are as follows:

  1 On 30 June the company was holding €100,000 worth of investments which consist of €40,000 purchased on 1 March and €60,000 purchased on 1 May. Hence, the interest that is received due to the cum-int rule would be for the whole six months and would amount to €3,500 (i.e. €100,000 @ 7 per cent ÷ 12 × 6).
  2 On 31 December the company was holding €50,000 worth of investments because it had sold €50,000 worth of investments on 31 October. However, the interest that is received due to the cum-int rule would be for the whole six months and would amount to €1,750 (i.e. €50,000 @ 7 per cent ÷ 12 × 6).
  3 Therefore, the total interest income received for the financial year ending 31st December is €5,250 (i.e. 30 June €3,500 + 31 December €1,750).
  4 However, due to the cum-int rule:

     a The amount of €467 in interest which represents two months' interest (January and February) that does not belong to Schneider Investments plc (refer to Transaction One, adjustment for cum-int transaction) must be deducted from the total interest income.
     b The amount of €1,400 in interest which represents four months' interest (January to April) that does not belong to Schneider Investments plc (refer to Transaction Two, adjustment for cum-int transaction) must also be deducted from the total interest income.
     c The amount of €1,167 in interest which represents four months' interest (July to October) that belongs to Schneider Investments plc (refer to Transaction Three, adjustment for cum-int transaction) must now be added to the total interest income.

  5 Therefore, the actual interest earned by Schneider Investments plc is €4,550 (i.e. €5,250 − €467 − €1,400 + €1,167 = €4,550). The accounting entries in the Investment Account for the interest received are:

     a Debit Income A/c: €4,550 (i.e. debit transaction because it represents a decrease in income A/c).
     b Credit P & L A/c: €4,550 (i.e. credit transaction because it represents an increase in income).

- *Average Weighted Cost Method Calculation (AVCO) (see Figure 5.12)*: The issue now is to compute the average cost of the investments. In other words, the average cost of stock sold and the average cost of stock in hand. First we need

TABLE 5.11 Example: Schneider Investments plc – interest received

No	Transaction Details	Dr.	Cr.
	Interest Received on Investments:		
07	30th June: €100,000 @ 7% for 6 months: €3,500		€3,500
08	31st December: €50,000 @ 7% for 6 months: €1,750		€1,750
09	30th Jun/31st Dec: Total Interest Income (Bank): €5,250	€5,250	
	Less cum-int adjustment on stock purchased 1st Mar: €467		
	Less cum-int adjustment on stock purchased 1st May:€1,400		
	€3,383		
	Add cum-int adjustment on stock sold 31st October: €1,167		
	Transfer to P & L A/c: €4,550		
10	31st December: Income A/c (Interest Earned by Investments)	€4,550	
10	31st December: P & L A/c (Interest Earned by Investments)		€4,550

to compute the value of the investment, which is the purchase price minus the cum-int adjustment(s). The calculation is as follows:

1 *1 March*: Purchase price for 400 stock at 96 cum-int less cum-int adjustment: €38,400 – €467 = €37,933.

2 *1 May*: Purchase price for 600 stock at 99 cum-int less cum-int adjustment: €59,400 – €1,400 = €58,000.

The following are the computations required:

a The total value for 1000 stocks = €37,933 + €58,000 = €95,933. Hence, the value of the stock in hand after the company sold €50,000 worth of stock on the 31 October at 97 cum-int is computed by a simple ratio calculation: If 1000 stocks = €95,933, how much would 500 stock be? Answer: (500 ÷ 1,000) × €95,933 = €47,967.

b Now we need to compute the value of the investment sold, which is the sales proceeds from the sale of 500 stocks @ 97 cum-int on the 31 October minus the cum-int adjustment(s), that is: €48,500 – €1,167 = €47,333. Third, we need to calculate the gain or loss from the sale, which is the difference between the proceeds received for the stock minus the value of the stock, that is: €47,333 – €47,967 = €634 (loss in value). The accounting transactions are:

1 Credit Capital A/c: €633 (i.e. credit transaction because it represents a decrease in the value of the asset investment A/c).

2 Debit Equity A/c: €633 (i.e. debit transaction because it represents a decrease in equity as a liability).

• *First-in-first-out cost method calculation (FIFO) (see Figure 5.13)*: The goal now is to compute the value of the investments using the FIFO method. Hence, the issue is to calculate the cost of stock sold and the value of stock in hand using the FIFO approach. First we need to compute the cost of sales of the 500 stock

TABLE 5.12 Example: Schneider Investments plc – AVCO

No	Transaction Details	Dr.	Cr.
	AVCO: Revaluation of Stock (gain or loss):		
11	31st December: Capital A/c (decrease in investment value)		€633
11	31st December: Equity A/c (decrease in investment value)	€633	

(€50,000) sold on 31 October. The value of the investment is the purchase price minus the cum-int adjustment(s). The calculations are as follows:

1   *1 March*: Purchase of stock: Nominal 400 stocks at €37,933 (i.e. purchase price of €38,400 – cum-int adjustment of €467 = €37,933).

2   *1 May*: Purchase of stock: Nominal 600 stocks at €58,000 (i.e. purchase price of €59,400 – cum-int adjustment of €1,400 = €58,000).

The following are the computations required:

a   We need to remember that the amount of stocks sold was 500 at a nominal value of €50,000. Hence, under the FIFO method the 400 stocks purchased on 1 March are disposed of first (valued at €37,933), followed by 100 stocks from those purchased on 1 May. The value of the 100 stocks purchased on 1 May is calculated by a simple ratio computation: 600 stocks are valued at €58,000, how much are 100 stocks valued? Hence, the value of 100 stocks purchased on 1 May = (100 ÷ 600) × €58,000 = €9,667. Therefore, the value of the 500 stock sold equals €37,933 + €9,667 which is €47,600.

b   However, on 31 October, the amount the company received for selling 500 stock was €47,333 (i.e. 500 stock at cum 97 minus the cum-int adjustment of €1,167 = €48,500 – €1,167 = €47,333). This means that under the FIFO method the company made a loss from the disposal of 500 stock of €267 (i.e. proceeds received €47,333 – value of the stock €47,600). Furthermore, the cost of the remaining stock on hand (500) is calculated by a simple ratio computation: 600 stocks are valued at €58,000, how much are 500 stocks valued? Hence, the value of 500 stocks remaining on hand = (500 ÷ 600) × €58,000 = €48,333. The accounting transactions are:

1   Credit Capital A/c: €267 (i.e. credit transaction because it represents a decrease in the value of the asset investment A/c).

2   Debit Equity A/c: €267 (i.e. debit transaction because it represents a decrease in equity as a liability).

All the investment account postings using the combined option for the AVCO and FIFO methods regarding the Schneider Investments plc example are shown at Figure 5.13 and Figure 5.14.

TABLE 5.13 Example: Schneider Investments plc – FIFO

No	Transaction Details	Dr.	Cr.
	FIFO: Revaluation of Stock (gain or loss):		
12	31st December: Capital A/c (decrease in investment value)		€267
12	31st December: Equity A/c (decrease in investment value)	€267	

Dr.   **Investment A/c Government Stocks Issue 2025 at 7%**   Cr.

		Nominal No.	Income €	Capital €			Nominal No.	Income €	Capital €
01-Mar Bank	01	400		38,400	10-Mar Cum-int	02			467
01-Mar Cum-int	02		467						
01-May Bank	03	600		59,400	01-May Cum-int	04			1,400
01-May Cum-int	04		1,400						
					30-Jun Interest	07		3,500	
					31-Oct Sale	05	500		48,500
31-Oct Cum-int	06			1,167	31-Oct Cum-int	06		1,167	
					30-Jun Interest	08		1,750	
31-Dec P & L	10		4,550		31-Dec Equity	11			633
					31-Dec Bal C/f		500		47,967
		1,000	6,417	98,967			1,000	6,417	98,967

Dr.   **Bank A/c**   Cr.

		€				€
			01-Mar Purchase Stock	01	38,400	
			01-May Purchase Stock	01	59,400	
30-Jun Interest	09	3,500				
31-Oct Sell Stock	05	48,500				
31-Dec Interest	09	1,750				

Dr.   **Equity A/c**   Cr.

		€	
31-Dec Loss from sale of stock	11	633	

Dr.   **P & L A/c**   Cr.

			€
	31-Dec Income from interest	10	4,550

FIGURE 5.13 Example: Schneider Investments plc accounting entries (AVCO)

Dr.   **Investment A/c Government Stocks Issue 2025 at 7%**   Cr.

		Nominal No.	Income €	Capital €			Nominal No.	Income €	Capital €
01-Mar Bank	01	400		38,400	10-Mar Cum-int	02			467
01-Mar Cum-int	02		467		01-May Cum-int	04			1,400
01-May Bank	03	600		59,400	30-Jun Interest	07		3,500	
01-May Cum-int	04		1,400		31-Oct Sale	05	500		48,500
					31-Oct Cum-int	06		1,167	
31-Oct Cum-int	06			1,167	30-Jun Interest	08		1,750	
					31-Dec Equity	11			267
31-Dec P & L	10		4,550		31-Dec Bal C/f		500		48,333
		1,000	6,417	98,967			1,000	6,417	98,967

Dr.   **Bank A/c**   Cr.

		€			€
			01-Mar Purchase Stock	01	38,400
			01-May Purchase Stock	01	59,400
30-Jun Interest	09	3,500			
31-Oct Sell Stock	05	48,500			
31-Dec Interest	09	1,750			

Dr.   **Equity A/c**   Cr.

	€	
31-Dec Loss from sale of stock 11	267	

Dr.   **P & L A/c**   Cr.

		€
	31-Dec Income from interest	10 4,550

FIGURE 5.14 Example: Schneider Investments plc accounting entries (FIFO)

Conclusion

This chapter has discussed and illustrated the accounting treatment for each key category of financial instruments, including the accounting entries and necessary accounting adjustments. It has been shown that the accounting treatment for each key category of financial instruments varies according to the accounting standards, particularly, the recognition and measurement of the respective financial instrument type as contemplated by IAS 39 and IFRS 9.

Additionally, this chapter has also examined in detail the accounting implications when purchasing and selling financial instruments. This section examined the accounting implications when purchasing and selling financial instruments. A concern arises when financial instruments are purchased or sold at a date other than their maturity date and whether the financial instruments were purchased (or sold) as cum-div (or cum-int) investments or ex-div (ex-int) investments. As we have seen, cum-div or cum-int means that a buyer of a security is entitled to receive a dividend or interest that has been declared, but not paid. This means that the security is offered for sale with an entitlement to the next dividend or interest payment attached. Ex-div or ex-int means that the declared dividend or interest will be received by the seller and not the buyer. Hence, a stock is given ex-div or ex-int status if an individual or entity has been confirmed by the company to receive the dividend or interest payment. The purchase of shares or bonds without entitlement to recently declared dividends means that the entitlement to receive a dividend or interest remains with the seller of the shares or bonds. The chapter also illustrated that purchasing (or selling) financial instruments as cum-div/int or ex-div/int requires an accounting adjusting entry to compensate the buyer or seller for not receiving a portion of the dividend or interest payments as a consequence of the cum-div/int and ex-div/int rule.

The chapter also illustrated the presentation format of investment accounts and how these accounts are maintained. Two options were discussed; the first option was related to the use of normal accounting 'T' accounts in presenting the double accounting entry system. The second option presented a combined income/capital investment account. This entailed combining the asset and income accounts into a single format to make it easier for the user to comprehend and maintain the investment account with the various accounting transactions.

Finally, the chapter provides a simple way of valuating a portfolio of investments that belong to the same investment issue but are purchased and/or sold at under different conditions and at different dates. Basically, two investment valuation methods were shown, these were the weighted average cost approach (AVCO) and the first-in-first-out method. These methods were illustrated through a comprehensive example. Hence, this chapter provided a comprehensive explanation of the accounting treatment for different categories of financial instruments. Below a further practical problem is provided to allow the reader to become more proficient this topic.

Practical problem

Oasis Investment Ltd has it financial ending on 31 December and during its financial year conducted a number of transactions with respect to Omega plc €1 Ordinary Shares. Omega plc normally declares and pays a dividend quarterly, with the first quarterly period ending 31 March. The transactions with respect to Omega plc included the following:

a   5 March: Acquired 10,000 shares at €3 cum-div (classified as AFS).
b   31 March: Omega plc declared and paid a dividend of €0.075 per share.
c   30 June: Acquired a further 5,000 shares at €3.50.
d   30 June: Omega plc did not declare a dividend.
e   30 September: Omega plc declared and paid dividend of €0.05 per share.
f   30 November: Oasis Investment Ltd sold 5,000 shares for €20,000.

g   31 December: Omega plc shares have a market price of €4.20.
h   31 December: Omega plc did not declare a dividend.

Write up the investment account (combined capital and interest account) showing all calculations to the nearest euro, for the year ending 31 December in the books of Oasis Investment Ltd using both the average cost method (AVCO) and first-in-first-out cost method (FIFO). Assume that the financial year in question is not a leap year.

Solution

The objective is to construct the investment account in the accounting books of Oasis Investment Ltd using both the weighted average cost and FIFO methods. To construct the investment account the following workings need to be calculated:

*   *Transaction One (see Figure 5.14):* On 5 March the company acquired 10,000 shares at €3 cum-div (classified as AFS). Hence, the company paid €30,000 (i.e. 10,000 shares × €3 = €30,000). The accounting entries in the Investment Account are:

    1   Nominal: 10,000 (memorandum only).
    2   Debit Capital A/c: €30,000 (i.e. debit transaction because it represents an increase in the asset investments).
    3   Credit Bank A/c: €30,000 (i.e. credit transaction because it represents a decrease in the asset cash at bank).

*   *Transaction Two (see Figure 5.15):* On 31 March Omega plc declared and paid a dividend of €0.075 per share. We also need to calculate the cum-div adjustment. The last dividend paid was 31 December hence the dividend period is 90 days (January 31 days + February 28 days + March 31 days = 90 days). Therefore, this means that the buyer (Oasis Investment Ltd) is only entitled to 26 days (from 5 March to 31 March) of the dividend. In other words, the buyer is entitled to 28.89 per cent of the dividend (26 days out of 90 days) and the seller is entitled to 71.11 per cent (64 days out of 90 days). The dividend paid is €750 (10,000 shares × €0.075 = €750) of which €217 belongs to Oasis Investment Ltd and €533 belongs to the seller. Therefore, €533 (dividend) must be reimbursed to the seller. The accounting entries in the Investment Account for the cum-div adjustment are:

TABLE 5.14 Solution: Oasis Investment Ltd – Transaction 1

No	Transaction Details	Dr.	Cr.
	Transaction One:		
01	5th March: Capital A/c (buy 10,000 shares @ €3 cum-div)	€30,000	
01	5th March: Bank (pay for purchased shares)		€30,000

1   Debit Bank A/c: €750 (i.e. debit transaction because it represents an increase in the bank asset account).
2   Credit Income A/c: €750 (i.e. credit transaction because it represents an increase in the income account).
3   Credit Bank A/c: €533 (i.e. reimbursement to seller)
4   Debit Income A/c: €533 (i.e. decrease to income a/c due to reimbursement to seller).

• *Transaction Three (see Figure 5.16)*: On 30 June, Oasis Investment Ltd acquired a further 5,000 shares at €3.50. Hence, the company paid €17,500 (i.e. 5,000 shares × €3.50 = €17,500). The accounting entries in the Investment Account are:

1   Nominal: 5,000 (memorandum only).
2   Debit Capital A/c: €17,500 (i.e. debit transaction because it represents an increase in the asset investments).
3   Credit Bank A/c: €17,500 (i.e. credit transaction because it represents a decrease in the asset cash at bank).

Note that Omega plc did not declare a dividend on 30 June. Therefore, there is no need for cum-div accounting adjustments.

• *Transaction Four (see Table 5.17)*: On 30 September, Omega plc declared and paid dividend of €0.05 per share. Hence, a dividend amount of €750 was received (i.e. 10,000 shares purchased on 5 March + 5,000 shares purchased on 30 June = 15,000 shares × €0.05 = €750). The dividend payment all belongs to Oasis Investment Ltd. The accounting entries in the Investment Account are:

TABLE 5.15 Solution: Oasis Investment Ltd – Transaction 2

No	Transaction Details	Dr.	Cr.
	Transaction Two:		
02	31st March: Bank A/c (Dividend received)	€750	
02	31st March: Income A/c (Dividend earnings		€750
03	31st March: Income A/c (Reimbursement to seller)	€533	
03	31st March: Bank A/c (Reimbursement to seller)		€533

TABLE 5.16 Solution: Oasis Investment Ltd – Transaction 3

No	Transaction Details	Dr.	Cr.
	Transaction Three:		
04	30th June: Capital A/c (buy 5,000 shares @ €3.50 cum-div)	€17,500	
04	30th June: Bank (pay for purchased shares)		€17,500

1 Debit Bank A/c: €750 (i.e. debit transaction because it represents an increase in the bank asset account, dividend received).
2 Credit Income A/c: €750 (i.e. credit transaction because it represents an increase in the income account, dividend received).

- *Transaction Five (see Table 5.18):* On 30 November, Oasis Investment Ltd disposed of 5,000 shares for €20,000. The accounting entries in the Investment Account are:

1 Nominal: 5,000 (memorandum only).
2 Credit Capital A/c: €20,000 (i.e. credit transaction because it represents a decrease in the asset investment account).
3 Debit Bank A/c: €20,000 (i.e. debit transaction because it represents an increase in the asset cash in bank).

Note that Omega plc did not declare a dividend on the 31 December. Therefore, there is no need for cum-div accounting adjustments for the period October and November.

- *Average Weighted Cost Method Calculation (AVCO) (see Table 5.19):* The issue now is to compute the average cost of the investments. In other words, the average cost of the shares sold and the average cost of shares in hand. First we need to compute the value of the investment. The calculation is as follows:

i 5 March: Cost of 10,000 shares at € 3.00 = €30,000
ii 30 June: Cost of 5,000 shares at € 3.50 = €17,500

The total number of shares held is 15,000 at a total value of € 47,500. Thus, using a simple ratio computation, calculate the cost of the 5,000 shares that were sold. Hence, 15,000 shares cost € 47,500. What is the cost of 5,000 shares?

TABLE 5.17 Solution: Oasis Investment Ltd – Transaction 4

No	Transaction Details	Dr.	Cr.
	Transaction Four:		
05	30th September: Bank A/c (Dividend received)	€750	
05	30th September: Income A/c (Dividend received)		€750

TABLE 5.18 Solution: Oasis Investment Ltd – Transaction 5

No	Transaction Details	Dr.	Cr.
	Transaction Five:		
06	30th November: Capital A/c (sold 5,000 shares)		€20,000
06	30th November: Bank A/c (earnings: sale of 5,000 shares)	€20,000	

The cost for 5,000 shares = $(5,000 \div 15,000) \times €47,500 = €15,833$. However, the proceeds from sale of 5,000 shares on 30 November are €20,000. Therefore, the profit/(loss) on disposal is €4,167 (i.e. €20,000 − €15,833 = €4,167). Furthermore, the fair value of the shares held in hand is €42,000 (i.e. 10,000 shares × the market share price as at 31st December of €4.20 = $10,000 \times €4.20 = €42,000$).

Therefore, the gain/(loss) on fair value is the difference between the cost of shares held and the market share value which is €10,333. That is, the cost of shares held is €31,667 (i.e. $10,000 \div 15,000) \times €47,500 = €31,667$) and the market share value is €42,000 (i.e. 10,000 shares × the market share price as at 31 December of €4.20 = $10,000 \times €4.20 = €42,000$). The difference between the cost of shares held and the market share value is €42,000 minus €31,667 which equals €10,333. Therefore, the profit from fair valuation is €10,333. The accounting transactions are:

1 Debit Capital A/c: €4,167 (i.e. debit transaction because it represents an increase in the value of the asset investment A/c).
2 Credit Equity A/c: €4,167 (i.e. credit transaction because it represents an increase in equity as a liability).
3 Debit Capital A/c: €10,333 (i.e. debit transaction because it represents an increase in the value of the asset investment A/c).
4 Credit Equity A/c: €10,333 (i.e. credit transaction because it represents an increase in equity as a liability).

• *First-In-First-Out Cost Method Calculation (FIFO) (see Table 5.20)*: The goal now is to compute the value of the investments using the FIFO method. Hence, the issue is to calculate the cost of stock sold and the value of stock in hand using the FIFO approach. First, the fair value calculation of the 10,000 shares currently held is €42,000 (i.e. 10,000 shares × €4.20 per share = €42,000). Second, we need to compute the profit/loss on the sale of 5,000 shares sold on 30 November and third, the gain on fair market value on 31 December. The calculations are as follows:

1 *Compute the profit/loss on the sale of 30 November*: Oasis Investment Ltd acquired 10,000 shares at €3 on 5 March and a further 5,000 shares were acquired on 30 June at €3.50. Using the FIFO basis, the 5,000 shares

TABLE 5.19 Solution: Oasis Investment Ltd accounting entries (AVCO)

No	Transaction Details	Dr.	Cr.
	AVCO: Revaluation of Stock (gain or loss):		
07	30th November: Capital A/c (gain on disposal AVCO)	€4,167	
07	30th November: Equity A/c (gain on disposal AVCO)		€4,167
08	31st December: Capital A/c (gain on fair value AVCO)	€10,333	
08	31th December: Equity A/c (gain on fair value AVCO)		€10,333

sold on 30 November were from the first purchased batch of the 10,000 shares. Hence, the cost of the 5,000 shares sold is €15,000 (i.e. 5,000 shares × €3.00 per share = €15,000). The proceeds from the 5,000 shares sold on 30 November was €20,000. Therefore, the profit from the sale of 5,000 shares is €5,000 (i.e. €20,000 − €15,000 = €5,000).

2   *Compute the gain on fair market value on 31 December:* We are now interested in the cost of the shares that are currently held by Oasis Investment Ltd after the disposal of the 5,000 shares on 30 November based on the FIFO approach. As stated previously, the Oasis Investment Ltd acquired 10,000 shares at €3 on 5 March and a further 5,000 shares were acquired on 30 June at €3.50. Using the FIFO basis, the 5,000 shares sold on 30 November were from the first purchased batch of the 10,000 shares. Hence, the company has on hand 5,000 shares from the first batch (purchased 5 March at €3 each) and 5,000 shares from the second batch (purchased 30 June at €3.50 each). Therefore, the cost of the shares currently held by Oasis Investment Ltd is €32,500 (i.e. 5,000 shares × €3 per share + 5,000 shares × €3.50 per share = €15,000 + €17,500 = €32,500). Furthermore, the fair market of 10,000 shares currently held by Oasis Investment Ltd is €42,000 (i.e. 10,000 shares × €4.20 per share = €42,000). Therefore, the gain from the fair market value (revaluation of 10,000 shares) is equal to the fair market of 10,000 shares currently held by Oasis Investment Ltd (€42,0000) minus the cost of the shares currently held (€32,500) which is €9,500 (i.e. €42,000 − €32,500 = €9,500).

The accounting transactions are:

1   Debit Capital A/c: €5,000 (i.e. debit transaction because it represents an increase in the value of the asset investment A/c).
2   Credit Equity A/c: €5,000 (i.e. credit transaction because it represents an increase in equity as a liability).
3   Debit Capital A/c: €9,500 (i.e. debit transaction because it represents an increase in the value of the asset investment A/c).4 Credit Equity A/c: €9,500 (i.e. credit transaction because it represents an increase in equity as a liability).

All the investment account postings using the combined option for the AVCO and FIFO methods regarding the Oasis Investment Ltd example are shown at Figure 5.15 and Figure 5.16.

References

Ernst & Young. (2011). *US GAAP Versus IFRS: The Basics.* Ernst & Young, International Financial Reporting Standards Group.

Ernst & Young. (2011). *IFRS 7 Financial Instruments: Disclosures: Impending Changes Effective for 2011 and 2012.* Ernst & Young, International Financial Reporting Standards Group.

TABLE 5.20 Solution: Oasis Investment Ltd accounting entries (FIFO)

No	Transaction Details	Dr.	Cr.
	FIFO: Revaluation of Stock (gain or loss):		
07	30th November: Capital A/c (gain on disposal FIFO)	€5,000	
07	30th November: Equity A/c (gain on disposal FIFO)		€5,000
08	31st December: Capital A/c (gain on fair value FIFO)	€9,500	
08	31th December: Equity A/c (gain on fair value FIFO)		€9,500

Dr.   **Investment A/c: Shares in Omega plc**   Cr.

		Nominal No.	Income €	Capital €			Nominal No.	Income €	Capital €
05-Mar Bank	01	10,000		30,000	31-Mar Dividend	02		750	
31-Mar Cum-div	03		533						
30-Jun Bank	04	5,000		17,500					
					30-Sep Dividend	05		750	
30-Nov Gain/Loss	07			4,167	30-Nov Shares	06	5000		20,000
31-Dec Gain/Loss	08			10,333					
31-Dec P & L	11		967		31-Dec Bal C/f	11	10,000		42,000
		15,000	1,500	62,000			15,000	1,500	62,000

Dr.   **Bank A/c**   Cr.

		€				€
			05-Mar Purchase Shares	01		30,000
31-Mar Dividend	02	750	31-Mar Cum-div	03		533
			30-Jun Purchase Shares	04		17,500
30-Sep Dividend	05	750				
30-Nov Sale of Shares	06	20,000				

Dr.   **Equity A/c**   Cr.

			€
	30-Nov Gain - sale of shares	07	4,167
	31-Dec Gain - sale of shares	08	10,333

Dr.   **P & L A/c**   Cr.

			€
	31-Dec Income from interest	11	967

FIGURE 5.15 Solution: Oasis Investment Ltd accounting entries (AVCO)

Dr.   **Investment A/c: Shares in Omega plc**   Cr.

		Nominal No.	Income €	Capital €			Nominal No.	Income €	Capital €
05-Mar Bank	01	10,000		30,000	31-Mar Dividend	02		750	
31-Mar Cum-div	03		533						
30-Jun Bank	04	5,000		17,500					
					30-Sep Dividend	05		750	
30-Nov Gain/Loss	07			5,000	30-Nov Shares	06	5000		20,000
31-Dec Gain/Loss	08			9,500					
31-Dec P & L	11		967		31-Dec Bal C/f	11	10,000		42,000
		15,000	1,500	62,000			15,000	1,500	62,000

Dr.   **Bank A/c**   Cr.

		€			€
			05-Mar Purchase Shares	01	30,000
31-Mar Dividend	02	750	31-Mar Cum-div	03	533
			30-Jun Purchase Shares	04	17,500
30-Sep Dividend	05	750			
30-Nov Sale of Shares	06	20,000			

Dr.   **Equity A/c**   Cr.

		€
30-Nov Gain - sale of shares	07	5,000
31-Dec Gain - sale of shares	08	9,500

Dr.   **P & L A/c**   Cr.

		€
31-Dec Income from interest	11	967

FIGURE 5.16 Solution: Oasis Investment Ltd accounting entries (FIFO)

Ernst & Young. (2012). *IFRS 9: New Mandatory Effective Date and Transition Disclosures*. Ernst & Young, International Financial Reporting Standards Group.

Morris, James E. (2004). *Accounting for M&A, Equity, and Credit Analysts*. New York: McGraw-Hill.

PricewaterhouseCoopers. (2010). *A Practical Guide to IFRS 7: For Investment Managers and Investment, Private Equity and Real Estate Funds*. PricewaterhouseCoopers International.

Rosenfield, Paul and Rubin, Steven. (1985). *Consolidation, Translation, and the Equity Method: Concepts and Procedures*. New York: John Wiley & Sons.

6

BILLS OF EXCHANGE AND PROMISSORY NOTES

> When money realises that it is in good hands, it wants to stay and multiply in those hands.
>
> Idowu Koyenikan, African author

Bills of exchange and promissory notes are considered to be important financial instruments because they are a common vehicle for conducting many routine business transactions. They are also considered important because as financial instruments, they are highly liquid and have distinct legal characteristics depending upon their financial nature. The objective of this topic is to enable the reader to understand the meaning of bills of exchange and promissory notes, and to be aware of their underlying features. This chapter will enable the reader to comprehend the accounting treatments relating to the issuance, acceptance, discounting, maturity and endorsement of bills of exchange and promissory notes in the accounts of both the drawer and drawee.

This chapter will also illustrate the accounting technique related to the accommodation bills and the special treatment needed in case of insolvency, as well as early retirement of a bill of exchange and promissory note. Additionally, this chapter will provide a logical link between the accounting approach for financial instruments and financial risk management.

The significance of bills of exchange

Basically, bills of exchange are financial documents that require the individual or business that is addressed in the document to pay a specified amount of money on a date that is cited within the text of the document. It is important to recognise that bills of exchange are considered to be a negotiable instrument, with the date for the demand to pay generally ranging from the current date to a date within the next six calendar months (although it could be for a longer duration).

A bill of exchange will also require the authorised signature of the debtor in order to be considered legal and binding. The following essential points should be noted regarding a bill of exchange:

- It must be in writing and properly dated;
- It must contain an order to pay a certain sum of money;
- The money must be payable to a definite person or to his order to the bearer;
- The draft must be accepted for payment by the party to whom the order is made;
- It must have an authorised signature of the debtor.

The above suggests that a bill of exchange is a negotiable financial instrument that requires the authorised signature of the debtor in order for it to be legal and binding. As an unconditional order to pay a fixed sum of money to a creditor, the bill of exchange may take a number of formats, the most common being a bank cheque. Figure 6.1 provides an example of a bill of exchange having the common form of a bank cheque. This example illustrates that a bank cheque specifies who is to receive the funds, with the order to pay the face value of the cheque to the order of the creditor and it specifies the exact amount of the payment. The date shown on a bank cheque is often the issue date for the cheque, but it may also be the date that the bank is to honour the payment. This procedure is often referred to as post-dating a bank cheque because the creditor will physically receive the cheque at some time before it will be honoured.

A bank draft is also an example of a bill of exchange. Similar to a bank cheque, bank drafts are usually written with a fixed sum of payment, and with specific instructions of when to issue the payment to the creditor. Due to the different formats a bill of exchange can take, a bill of exchange can be a very simplistic document or one that is very detailed. In many countries, the use of a bill of exchange is a customary way of conducting business. There is a possibility that a

National West Bank 231-467-50

Gillbourne, University of Ballarat Branch
University of Ballarat, Gillbourne, Ballarat 3025

Date: 15 October 2015

Pay: *Gillbourne University Bookshop* $150.00

One hundred and fifty dollars only E. R. MAHONY

Cheque No. Sort Code Account No.

||01911|| 44|890 || 0483412380711 *E.R. Mahony*

FIGURE 6.1 Example of a bill of exchange in the form of a bank cheque

bill of exchange is not honoured. In such a situation, the holder of the financial instrument is at liberty to take legal action against the debtor according to local laws, or to sell the bill of exchange to a collector at a discounted rate of exchange. The possibility that a bill of exchange is not honoured is a primary reason why electronic payments instead of using cheques are increasing in popularity in conducting business transactions. However, as stated previously, not all bills of exchange take the form of a bank cheque.

The significance of a promissory note

A promissory note is similar to a bill of exchange. However, a promissory note is normally used when taking out a loan. It provides the specific details on the amount of the original loan (the principal) showing the repayment schedule and any applicable interest rate. It is not uncommon for a promissory note to also contain details such as grace periods or penalties for defaulting. A grace period is a provision that permits a payment on a loan to be received for a certain period of time after the actual due date. Hence, during the grace period no late fees will be charged, and the late payment will not result in default or cancellation of the loan. A grace period on a loan is typically 15 days. Additionally, a grace period is normally the only attribute of a loan on which interest is calculated monthly, if interest is applicable. The majority of loan contracts have interest compounding during the grace period. However, a loan contract may contain a clause that exempts interest for any outstanding payments during a grace period. Hence, one needs to examine the loan contract carefully for the details on any grace periods applicable.

It should be noted that once the relevant parties sign a promissory note, the precise terms of that contract are the ones that will be enforced during any future legal proceedings. It is also important to be aware that a promissory note is not the same as an informal IOU. A personal IOU may acknowledge that a debt exists, but the precise repayment details may be excluded. It is for this reason that most mercantile lending companies frequently request borrowers to read and sign a very detailed promissory note before a loan can be processed and subsequently deposited. It is essential that the borrower retains the promissory note until the loan maturity period because it contains crucial information related to interest rates and the amount of the principal to be repaid.

Having a suitably worded and signed promissory note is generally sufficient to prevail in any legal proceeding against the borrower. However, there are some exceptions:

- A promissory note cannot be signed under excessive coercion from the lender. An arbitrator or judge may declare the promissory note null and void if excessive coercion is proven.
- The borrower must sign and initial the complete document, not simply placing a signature at the bottom of a blank page.

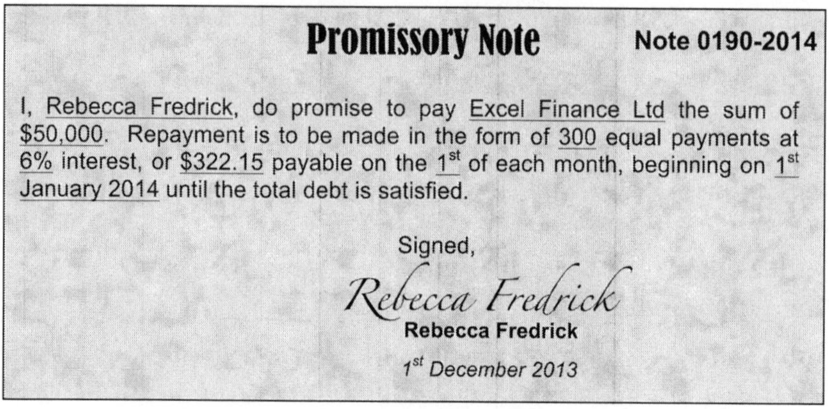

Promissory Note   Note 0190-2014

I, <u>Rebecca Fredrick</u>, do promise to pay <u>Excel Finance Ltd</u> the sum of $50,000. Repayment is to be made in the form of <u>300</u> equal payments at 6% interest, or $322.15 payable on the 1st of each month, beginning on 1st January 2014 until the total debt is satisfied.

Signed,

Rebecca Fredrick

Rebecca Fredrick

1st December 2013

FIGURE 6.2 Example of a promissory note illustrating the terms and conditions

- A promissory note must not have provisions that would be regarded as illegal elsewhere. For example, an unfeasibly high interest rate or supplementary penalties not defined in writing.

Therefore, a promissory note has conditions of payment terms and interest due, whereas bills of exchange have the payment amount and the maturity date (payment due date). Figure 6.2 provides an example of a typical promissory note that stipulates the principal, the repayment terms and the interest rate applicable.

The characteristics of a promissory note

A promissory note has a number of attributes that distinguishes it from a bill of exchange. These attributes include:

- It must be formalised in a written document.
- It must contain a clear promise to pay. A mere acknowledgement of a debt is not a promissory note.
- The promise to pay must be unconditional. For example: 'I promise to pay $1,500 as soon as I can' is not an unconditional promise to pay.
- The party making the promise (i.e. maker) must sign the promissory note.
- The maker must be a specific person.
- The payee (the person to whom the payment is promised) must also be a specific party (person or entity).
- The sum payable in the promissory note must be explicit. For example: 'I promise to pay $1,500 plus all the applicable fines' is not explicit.
- The payment must be in the legal currency of the country the promissory note is applicable in.
- It should not be made payable to the bearer of the promissory note.
- It should be properly stamped.

Advantages of bills of exchange and promissory notes

Bills of exchange and promissory notes share some common advantages. Both are financial instruments that are legally binding. The major advantage of the promissory note is that it is a legal contract where the borrower is obliged to repay the money according to the law with interest. In case of default the lender can take the borrower to court. In the promissory note, the loaned amount has to be repaid fully within the date specified or can be divided into several monthly instalments. However, the main disadvantage of a promissory note is that the lender must know the whereabouts of the borrower to receive the repayment. If the borrower travels interstate or disappears, then the lender will not be able to receive the money owed by the borrower. In case of default, the lender will need to institute a court case against the borrower for repayment. This could prove to be costly and time consuming.

On the other hand, bills of exchange are used in the settlement of debts and are a proven method of providing fixed-rate financing for international transactions. Hence, bills of exchange are more extensive than promissory notes. Similar to promissory notes, bills of exchange fix the date of payment and provide a written and signed acknowledgement of the debt. Furthermore, a debtor enjoys the full period of credit until the bill of exchange is due. However, the prime advantage of a bill of exchange over a promissory note is that a drawer can easily convert the bill into cash by getting it discounted with the bank. Hence, bills of exchange are considered to be negotiable financial instruments, while promissory notes are not.

Parties involved in bills of exchange

Promissory notes are relatively simple in operation because they are not negotiable financial instruments. Therefore, with a promissory note you have two specific parties, namely the lender and the borrower. As stated previously, a promissory note cannot be made payable to the bearer of the promissory note.

On the other hand, bills of exchange are negotiable financial instruments. In other words, they may be traded. Hence, the parties involved in bills of exchange can be more complex in that they may involve parties that were not originally implicated when the bill of exchange was originally drawn up. This implies that with a bill of exchange four parties may be involved:

- Drawer: The drawer is the person who writes the bill of exchange. The drawer must be the seller or creditor to whom the money is owing.
- Drawee: The drawee is the person on whom the bill is drawn, that is the purchaser or debtor who is ordered by the drawer to pay the amount.
- Payee: The payee is the person who has the right to receive the amount specified on the bill of exchange. The payee may be a third person or the drawer.
- Acceptor: The acceptor is the debtor who has agreed to pay the bill.

If the bill of exchange was not a negotiable financial instrument only two parties would be involved, namely the drawer and drawee. However, because a bill of exchange may be traded (bought and sold) the type of parties involved is extended to the four parties indicated above.

The operation of bills of exchange

The operation of bills of exchange depends on the circumstances of the parties involved and whether the bill is being traded. Let us take a situation where a retail trader wants to purchase goods from a manufacturer but does not have the cash to do so. This retail trader may agree to accept a bill of exchange drawn upon him/her at some future date for the value of the goods he/she wants to purchase. Furthermore, let us assume that the manufacturer agrees to sell the goods for a 90 days credit period and the goods are worth €10,000. Figure 6.3 illustrates how a bill of exchange operates in this circumstance.

Figure 6.3 illustrates the following steps:

1   The Retail Trader expresses the request to buy on credit.
2   The drawer (Manufacturer) concurs to the request and draws a bill of exchange for €10,000 on the customer.
3   The drawee (Retail Trader) accepts the bill of exchange (thus becoming the acceptor of the bill) and returns it to the drawer.
4   The drawer delivers the furniture and has a 90 days bill of exchange for €10,000.

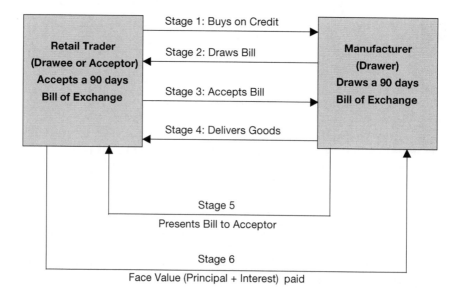

FIGURE 6.3 Procedure for a normal bill of exchange

5   The drawer (Manufacturer) keeps the bill of exchange till the due date and presents it to the drawee on the due date for payment.
6   The drawee (the acceptor) acknowledges the obligation in the bill of exchange and honours the bill (pays amount due) on the due date.

If the drawee is a reputable entity, the bill of exchange is as good as cash and a bank may pay its face value at a discount rate, similar to factoring. There are special types of banks that provide a 'discount of bill of exchange' service, called discount houses. Discount houses cash the bill of exchange by giving the drawer the present value of the bill of exchange. In this case, the present value of the bill of exchange is the face value of the bill minus the interest at an agreed rate for the number of days the discount house (bank) has to wait for payment. Therefore, the drawer who makes use of this banking service will receive an amount that is less than the face value of the bill of exchange.

Figure 6.4 illustrates such an example. On the due date it is the discount house (bank) that will present the bill to the acceptor. The acceptor has the obligation to honour the bill of exchange by paying the full value. Hence, the bank will earn the amount of interest that it deducted when it discounted the bill of exchange.

Figure 6.4 illustrates the following steps:

1   The Retail Trader expresses the request to buy on credit.
2   The drawer (Manufacturer) concurs to the request and draws a bill of exchange for €10,000 on the customer.
3   The drawee (Retail Trader) accepts the bill of exchange (thus becoming the acceptor of the bill) and returns it to the drawer.
4   The drawer delivers the furniture and has a 90 days bill of exchange for €10,000.
5   The drawer (Manufacturer) may require cash and therefore endorses the bill of exchange in favour of a discount house (bank) in return for the face value of the bill minus the interest at an agreed rate for the number of days the discount house (bank) has to wait for payment.
6   The discount house that will keep the bill of exchange till the due date must present it to the drawee on the due date for payment.
7   The drawee (the acceptor) acknowledges the obligation in the bill of exchange and honours the bill (pays amount due) on the due date.

Note that there is nothing to prevent the discount house from trading (endorsing) the bill of exchange with another party with this process being repeated. However, at maturity the entity that has the physical possession of the bill of exchange will present it to the drawee on the due date for payment. Therefore, you may have a situation where Step 5 is repeated a number of times. However, a discount house that keeps the bill of exchange till the due date must present it to the drawee on the due date for payment.

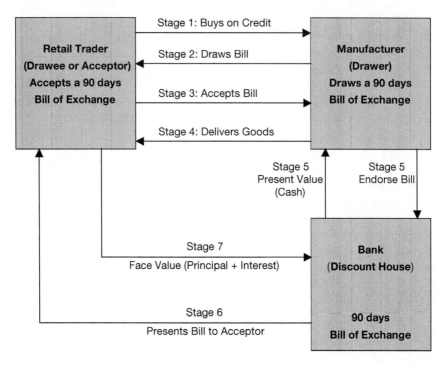

FIGURE 6.4 Operation of bills of exchange: discount house (bank)

What happens if the drawer (in the example the Manufacturer) endorses the bill of exchange not with a discount house (bank) but with another trader? As stated previously, bills of exchange are tradable financial instruments. Therefore, they may be liberally traded with anyone who is willing to accept the risk of the debt. Hence, in the case where the drawer (Manufacturer) endorses the bill in favour of a trade creditor (most probably to clear a debt) the drawer (manufacturer) would receive the face value of the bill of exchange. The face value will include the principal and interest (or other remuneration conditions) defined in the bill of exchange. In this case there may be no discounting, although discounting cannot be ruled out. It all depends on the agreement when the endorsement is made. At the end of 90 days (maturity) the trade creditor would present the bill of exchange for payment. Moreover, as stated before, a bill of exchange can be endorsed on many occasions until it is due. However, the endorser (in this case the Manufacturer) would be liable for the bill of exchange. The liability for the bill of exchange (in case of default) can be traced back to the drawee. Figure 6.5 illustrates the above situation. One should note the difference in how a bill of exchange is treated when a discount house is involved as compared with the involvement of a trade creditor as the party to whom the bill of exchange is endorsed to.

Accounting entries for bills of exchange and promissory notes

Let us now examine the accounting entries for bills of exchange and promissory notes. One should note that both a bill of exchange and a promissory note have the same accounting treatment. First, let us establish some basic principles. The bill of exchange after it is accepted is referred to as the bill receivable to the drawer and bill payable to the acceptor. Hence, the accepter is liable for a bill of exchange or promissory note to the drawer (obviously if the drawer retains them). When the bill of exchange is negotiated and endorsed to a payee, the drawer becomes liable on the bill of exchange as well as the acceptor. Let us now consider the accounting entries at every stage of the bill of exchange process.

Accounting transactions for a bill of exchange and promissory note occur at three stages as follows and affect both the drawee's and drawer's accounts:

- On acceptance of the bill of exchange (i.e. Stage 3 in Figure 6.4 and Figure 6.5).
- Period before the presentation of the bill of exchange (i.e. Stage 5 in Figure 6.4 and Figure 6.5).
- Maturity of the bill of exchange (i.e. Stage 6 and Stage 7 in Figure 6.4 and Figure 6.5).

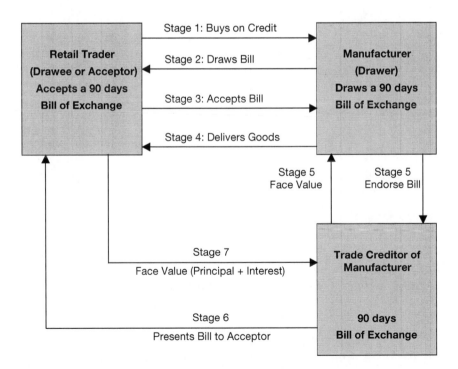

FIGURE 6.5 Operation of bills of exchange: trade creditor of manufacturer

Let us examine the accounting entries for each stage.

On acceptance of the bill (Stage 3 in Figure 6.4 and Figure 6.5)

Let us first consider the accounting entries in the drawee's books. In other words, the accounting entries in the accounting books of the borrower on the acceptance of a bill of exchange (e.g. a retailer):

1   Debit (Dr): Manufacturer's A/c (purchase).
2   Credit (Cr): Bill Payable A/c (liability).

Now, let us consider the accounting entries in the drawer's books. In other words, the accounting entries in the accounting books of the lender when the bill of exchange is accepted, for example by a retailer:

1   Debit (Dr): Bills Receivable A/c (increase in current asset).
2   Credit (Cr): Retailer A/c (sales).

Period before presentation of bill (i.e. Stage 5 in Figure 6.4 and Figure 6.5)

This stage only affects the drawer. At this point, the holder of the bill of exchange (drawer) has three options:

1   Hold on to the bill of exchange until maturity. Therefore, there are no accounting entries until the maturity of the bill.
2   The bill of exchange can be endorsed in favour of a third party (e.g. a trade creditor). In this case, the accounting entries are:

   a   Debit (Dr): Party who now owns the bill (decrease in liability, that is, the bill is being used to pay the creditor).
   b   Credit (Cr): Bills Receivable A/c (decrease in asset).

3   The bill of exchange can be discounted with a bank (discount house). In this case, the accounting entries are:

   a   Debit (Dr): Bank A/c (asset increased with the money actually received).
   b   Debit (Dr): Discount A/c (decrease income with amount deducted by bank).
   c   Credit (Cr): Bills Receivable A/c (decrease in current asset).

Maturity of bill (i.e. Stage 6 and Stage 7 in Figure 6.4 and Figure 6.5)

On the date of maturity there are two possibilities. The bill of exchange may be:

1   Honoured. In this case, there are also two possibilities. If the bill of exchange was endorsed in favour of a third party or discounted with a bank, no accounting

entries are required in the books of the originator of the bill of exchange because the money for the bill at maturity would be received by someone else. However, if the bill of exchange was kept by the holder the accounting entries would be:

a   Books of drawee: debit (Dr) bills payable (decrease in liability) and credit (Cr) bank a/c (decrease in asset since the bill is paid).

b   Books of the drawer: debit (Dr) bank a/c (increase in asset with the money actually received when the bill of exchange is presented) and credit (Cr) bills receivable a/c (decrease in asset since bill has been honoured).

2   Dishonoured. In this case, the party accepting the bill of exchange is liable to pay the amount of the bill and any expenses incurred to collect the bill. The accounting entries would only be applicable to the drawer. In this situation there are three possibilities:

a   If the bill of exchange was kept until maturity: debit (Dr) party giving the bill (decrease in income – non-payment) and credit (Cr) bills receivable a/c (decrease in current asset).

b   If the bill of exchange was endorsed in favour of a creditor: debit (Dr) party giving the bill (decrease in income – non-payment) and credit (Cr) creditor a/c (increase in current liability).

c   If the bill of exchange was discounted with a bank: debit (Dr) party giving the bill (decrease in income – non-payment) and credit (Cr) bank a/c (decrease in current asset).

The accounting entries illustrate that in the case of a dishonoured bill of exchange (or promissory note), where the acceptor does not pay the amount due at presentation, the situation may develop into a complex one, particularly if the bill has been endorsed several times. The party which issued and gave the bill must be debited because it has become liable to pay the amount upon presenting the bill of exchange. However, the credit entry would have three possibilities:

1   If the bill was retained the credit entry would be to the Bills Receivable Account.
2   If the bill was endorsed to a creditor, it would be to the Creditor A/c (increase in liability).
3   If the bill was discounted with a bank, it would be to the Bank Account (increase in liability).

Calculating the bill of exchange (or promissory note) due date

An important issue with bills of exchange and promissory notes is the due date. Normally, if the due date is made payable on a specific date, then that will be the due date. However, it all depends on the circumstances.

When the bill or promissory note is made payable at a stated number of month(s) after date it is issued, the date on which the term of the bill shall expire shall be the due date. In other words, the bill or promissory note shall mature on that day of the month which corresponds with the day on which the bill or promissory note is dated. For example, if a bill of exchange is dated 3 March and is due after three months, the due date would correspond to 3 June. However, if the month in which the maturity period has no corresponding day, the due date shall be deemed to be the last day of such a month. For example, if the bill of exchange is dated simply as March (but with no day specified) and is due after three months, the due date would correspond to 30 June.

If a situation arises where the corresponding day is the 31st day of the month, however, if the expiry month is February, and since February does not have a 31st day, the maturity day would be either 28 or 29 February, depending on whether February is a leap year.

When the bill or promissory note is made payable at a stated number of days after date of issuance, the due date is calculated by adding the stated number of days to the date of issuance. For example, if the issuance date of a bill of exchange is 4 March due after 10 days, the due date of the bill would be 14 March.

As stated previously, the due date of a bill of exchange or promissory note depends on the circumstances. For instance, when the due date is a public holiday, the preceding business day will be the due date. Furthermore, when the due date is declared by government as an emergency or unforeseen holiday, the following day will be the due date of the bill of exchange or promissory note.

One needs to pay particular attention to the terminology applied. The term of a bill of exchange or promissory note '*after sight*' commences from the date of acceptance. The term of a bill of exchange or promissory note '*after date of drawing a bill*' commences from the date of drawing of the bill of exchange or promissory note.

The global market place of commerce

Having a suitable payment method is an essential factor for succeeding in today's global marketplace. Exporters need to provide their customers with attractive sales terms and conditions supported by an effective payment approach to be able to compete successfully. The primary goal is to get paid in full in a timely manner for each export sale. Therefore, the payment method selected needs to mitigate the payment risk while also facilitating the needs of the buyer.

Bills of exchange and promissory notes are traditional methods for conducting business transactions dating back to the second century BC, when the Romans used them as a means of payment. However, it was not until the Geneva Convention of 7 June 1930 that bills of exchange were standardised in the laws of many European countries. Nonetheless, their role as an instrument of payment and credit has been until recently diminishing. According to Keefer (2010) the current economic climate has seen resurgence in their application, particularly in international trade finance and as alternative hedging instruments.

It is a well-known fact that international trade poses a wide range of risk that manifests itself as a major cause of uncertainty over the timing of payments between the exporter (seller) and importer (foreign buyer). To mitigate their risk, exporters want to receive payment, preferably as soon as an order is placed or before the goods are sent to the importer. On the other hand, importers want to delay payment as long as possible, preferably until after the goods are resold to generate enough income to pay the exporter. Hence, the payment method that is used has a significant effect on the financing that is required and the level of risk exposure.

Typical payment methods

An open account payment method normally has a credit term of 30 days and commences when the goods and invoice are sent out to the overseas customer. With this payment method all the risk of offering credit is with the exporter, who also needs to secure the finance to support the whole of the transaction. One should note that this payment method is normally applied for exports within the same geographical region (e.g. within the EU) and there is an established robust relationship between the parties involved in the transaction.

A bill of exchange is a traditional payment method and permits the exporter (seller) to keep control of the goods and raise additional finance. For instance, an overseas bank, acting on the exporter bank's behalf, will release the required documents to the importer (purchaser) so that the importer may take possession of the goods only when they formally accept the terms of the bill. However, with this method there is the risk that the bill of exchange will not be accepted by the importer, which means that the exporter has ownership and control of the goods, but in the importer's country. Furthermore, unless the bill of exchange has been guaranteed by the bank, there is the risk that the exporter will not receive payment. This method is usually used for exports outside the EU and where there is an established robust relationship with the customer.

Documentary credits (or 'letters of credit') are the most secure method of payment (other than payment in advance) and are very similar to bills of exchange. The importer instructs its bank to issue a letter of credit, which pays a correspondent bank when all the necessary documentation is submitted. This method carries with it very little credit risk. As long as the relevant documents are accurate, the issuing bank guarantees to pay the exporter within the stipulated time. By confirming the letter of credit, the importer's bank agrees to pay the exporter if the issuing bank defaults. Moreover, the exporter's bank will charge a commission based on how creditworthy the issuing bank is. The letter of credit stipulates the credit period the exporter is offering. However, a 'term' credit, where the payment is effected after the established credit term, will require the exporter to finance the duration between the delivery of the goods and payment for the goods. One should note that the exporter can use a valid, current letter of credit to secure additional finance in a similar way to using a bill of exchange. This method of payment is normally christmasused for new customers (first time buyers) and for importers and countries that present particular credit risks.

Use of bills of exchange in foreign trade

It is appropriate at this stage to discuss bills of exchange and promissory notes in the context of foreign trade. According to Keefer (2010) in an international context: (a) a bill of exchange is established by the exporter for the importer, who then duly accepts the draft by signing it; and (b) a third party may be designated by the drawer as the payment recipient in connection with the acceptance (payment order). Keefer (2010) argues that at the time of drafting, the creditor is usually unaware of who the ultimate beneficiary of the acceptance shall be, in which case the creditor then endorses with his or her signature and name with an appropriate written statement such as 'Drawn to me' or 'to own order'.

Furthermore, Keefer (2010) observes that unlike bills of exchange, promissory notes are drafted by the borrower/payer himself, who in the document undertakes to pay a specific amount to the creditor/payee, thus the name of the drawee as required in a formal bill of exchange is redundant because the drafter of the note is the payer. Risk is mitigated by bills of exchange when the payment of the face value of the bill of exchange is fully or partially secured by a guarantor. Having a bill of exchange fully guaranteed minimises the risk involved. Thus, the party guaranteeing the bill of exchange appends a declaration 'per aval (for the drawee)' with its signature thus taking on the responsibility to meet the payment obligation specified by the bill of exchange as a consequence of the payer being unable to pay the amount in question. Keefer (2010) argues that when such 'aval' is provided by a prime commercial bank, forfeiting of the acceptance/promissory note is an attractive liquidity option for the payee/beneficiary.

Normally commercial law provides a remedy to the drawer, any endorsers and other guarantors if the drawee fails to pay on the due date. Keefer (2010) maintains that in the international trade context it is often recommend that the exporter as payee/creditor requests a promissory note from the importer client (the payer) in order to exclude this risk. Keefer (2010) argues that bills of exchange have almost faded into obscurity, but when no other hedging/financing instrument is suitable, bills of exchange may be a sensible alternative. Keefer (2010) maintains that bills of exchange and promissory notes can be applied in a variety of ways, namely as a:

1 Method of payment. For example a bill of exchange may be sanctioned in favour of a third party. This method is widespread in the Asian trade finance industry.
2 Credit instrument. In this case the bill of exchange is designated to be paid on an explicit future date, thus the drawer (exporter) provides a credit facility for the relevant period to the drawee (importer).
3 Collateral (Guarantee). This method takes advantage of the legal formality related to bills of exchange. To protect a loan (suppliers' credit) an exporter

may agree to be given a promissory note for each due date loan payment. Should the importer pay without delay the amounts owed on the due dates, the exporter does not submit the bills of exchange to the designated payment bank on the promissory note but returns each promissory note after payment to the importer. However, should the amount due not be paid, the exporter may acquire the amount owed by presenting the bill of exchange to the designated bank for payment.

4   Form of Liquidity. Bills of exchange can be negotiated with a bank before the due date.

The above demonstrates that bills of exchange and promissory notes still have a role to play within the commercial community. Furthermore, they are a common method of conducting business transactions.

Practical problems

In this section a number of practical examples will be presented regarding accounting entries, bills of exchange for collection and the retirement of bills of exchange.

Example one: renewal of bill of exchange before maturity

Galaxy plc sold goods to Goldstep plc on 1 September 2015 for €4,000. Goldstep plc immediately accepted a three months bill of exchange. On the due date, Goldstep plc requested that the bill be renewed for a fresh period of two months. Galaxy agrees to this request, subject to the condition that Goldstep plc pays 9 per cent interest immediately in cash. Goldstep plc agrees to this condition. The second bill was met on due date. Provide the journal entries in the books of Galaxy plc.

This example is best illustrated in stages, with each stage representing a transaction towards the progression of the bill of exchange towards its maturity:

1   Stage-01: Galaxy plc sold goods to Goldstep pcl on 1 September, 2015 for €4,000. The accounting entries for this transaction are shown at Figure 6.6.
2   Stage-02: Goldstep plc immediately accepted a three months bill of exchange. On the due date Goldstep plc requested that the bill be renewed for a fresh period of two months. Galaxy plc agrees to this request provided that interest at 9 per cent was paid immediately in cash by Goldstep plc. Goldstep plc agrees to this condition. The accounting entries for this transaction are shown at Figure 6.7.
3   Stage-03: Goldstep plc accepted the renewal of the bill of exchange for two more months. On the due date of the second (renewed) bill of exchange, Goldstep plc paid the amount due. The accounting entries for this transaction are shown at Figure 6.8.

2015	**Books of Galaxy Plc** **Journal**		**Dr** **€**	**Cr** **€**
01-Sep	Goldstep Plc	Dr.	4,000	
	To Sales Account (sales to Goldstep as per invoice)			4,000
	Bill Receivable Account	Dr.	4,000	
	To Goldstep			4,000

Explanation

(a) Debit: Goldstep Plc €4,000 Dr. (Subsidiary ledger)

    Credit: Sales Account €4,000 Cr. Increase in Income General Ledger A/c

(b) Debit: Bill Receivable A/c €4,000 Dr. Increase in Asset General Ledger A/c

    Credit: Goldstep Plc A/c €4,000 Cr. (Subsidiary ledger)

FIGURE 6.6 Stage-01: Accounting entries – sale of goods

2015	**Books of Galaxy Plc** **Journal**		**Dr** **€**	**Cr** **€**
04-Dec	Goldstep Plc	Dr.	4,000	
	To Bill Receivable Account			4,000
	Goldstep Plc	Dr.	60	
	To Interest A/c			60

Explanation

(a) Debit: Goldstep Plc €4,000 Dr. (Subsidiary ledger)

    (3 months acceptance received from Goldstep for the amount due.)

    Credit: To Bill Receivable A/c €4,000 Cr. Decrease in Asset General Ledger A/c

    (Goldstep's acceptance cancelled due to renewal)

(b) Debit: Goldstep Plc A/c €60 Dr. (Subsidiary ledger)

    Credit: To Interest A/c €60 Cr. Increase in Income General Ledger A/c

    (Interest at 9% on €4,000 due from Goldstep for 2 months because of renewal.

FIGURE 6.7 Stage-02: Accounting entries – acceptance of bill of exchange

2015	**Books of Galaxy Plc** **Journal**		Dr €	Cr €
04-Dec	Bill Receivable A/c	Dr.	4,000	
	Cash A/c	Dr.	60	
	To Goldstep Plc			4,060
2016 07-Feb	Cash A/c	Dr.	4,000	
	To Bill Receivable A/c			4,000

Explanation		
(a) Debit: Bill Receivable	€4,000 Dr.	Increase in Asset General Ledger A/c
Debit: Cash A/c	€60 Dr.	Increase in Asset General Ledger A/c
Credit: To Goldstep A/c	€4,060 Cr.	(Subsidiary Ledger)
(Renewal for 2 months for €4,000 and cash for interest received from Goldstep)		
(b) Debit: Cash A/c	€4,000 Dr.	Increase in Asset General Ledger A/c
(Cash received against Goldstep's second acceptance of the bill of exchange.)		
Credit: To Bill Receivable A/c	€4,000 Cr.	Decrease in Asset General Ledger A/c

FIGURE 6.8 Stage-03: Accounting entries – maturity of bill of exchange

Example two: discounting of bill of exchange

Roland Ltd borrowed €1,500 from Spectre Ltd. On 1 October 2015, Roland Ltd accepted a bill of exchange drawn by Spectre Ltd for the amount borrowed at three months. However, before the maturity of the bill of exchange, Spectre Ltd discounted the bill with its bank for €1,350 on 3 October 2015. On 28 December 2015 before the due date of the bill of exchange, Roland Ltd approached Spectre Ltd to request a renewal of the bill of exchange. Spectre Ltd agreed to renew the bill of exchange on a number of conditions, namely, that €750 be paid immediately, that interest would be paid on the remaining amount at 10 per cent per annum for three months and for the balance, Roland Ltd should accept a new bill of exchange at three months. These arrangements were carried out. However, on 31 January 2016, Roland Ltd became insolvent and only 40 per cent of the amount could be recovered from its assets. Show the journal entries with narration that would be required in the accounting books of Spectre Ltd.

Below are the stages that this particular bill of exchange will go through until it reaches maturity. Each stage shown below represents the transaction that would be processed towards the progression of the bill of exchange towards its maturity:

1 Stage-01: Roland Ltd borrowed €1,500 from Spectre Ltd. On 1 October 2015, Roland Ltd accepted a bill of exchange drawn by Spectre Ltd for the amount borrowed at three months. However, before the maturity of the bill of exchange, Spectre Ltd discounted the bill with its bank for €1,350 on 3 October 2015. The accounting entries for this transaction are shown at Figure 6.9.

2 Stage-02: On 28 December, 2015 before the due date of the bill of exchange, Roland Ltd approached Spectre Ltd to request a renewal of the bill of exchange. Spectre Ltd agreed to renew the bill of exchange on a number of conditions, namely, that €750 be paid immediately, that interest would be paid on the remaining amount at 10 per cent per annum for three months and for the balance, Roland Ltd should accept a new bill of exchange at three months. These arrangements were carried out commencing 1 January 2016. The accounting entries for this transaction are shown at Figure 6.10.

2015	Books of Spector Ltd Journal		Dr €	Cr €
01-Oct	Bill Receivable A/c	Dr.	1,500	
	To Roland Ltd			1,500
03-Oct	Bank A/c	Dr.	1,350	
	Discount A/c	Dr.	150	
	To Bill Receivable A/c			1,500

Explanation

(a) Debit: Bill Receivable   €1,500 Dr. Increase in Asset General Ledger A/c

Credit: To Roland Ltd A/c   €1,500 Cr. (Subsidiary ledger)

(Being 3 month's bill of exchange drawn on Roland Ltd for the amount due)

(b) Debit: Bank A/c   €1,350 Dr. Increase in Asset General Ledger A/c

Debit: Discount A/c   €150 Dr. Decrease in Income General Ledger A/c

Credit: Bill Receivable A/c   €1,500 Cr. Decrease in Asset General Ledger A/c

(Being the bill of exchange discounted.)

FIGURE 6.9 Stage-01: Accounting entries – acceptance and discounting of bill

2016	**Books of Spector Ltd** **Journal**		**Dr** **€**	**Cr** **€**
01-Jan	Roland Ltd A/c	Dr.	1,500	
	To Bank A/c			1,500
01-Jan	Roland Ltd A/c	Dr.	18.75	
	To Interest A/c			18.75
01-Jan	Bank A/c	Dr.	768.75	
	To Roland Ltd A/c			768.75

Explanation

(a) Debit: Roland Ltd A/c   €1,500 Dr. (Subsidiary ledger)

    Credit: To Bank A/c   €1,500 Cr. Decrease in Asset
                                                          General Ledger A/c

(Being the bill cancelled due to Roland Ltd's inability to pay it.)

(b) Debit: Roland Ltd A/c   €18.75 Dr. (Subsidiary ledger)

    Credit: To Interest A/c   €18.75 Cr. Increase in Income
                                                          General Ledger A/c

(Being the interest due on €750 @ 10% for 3 months.)

(c) Debit: Bank A/c   €768.75 Dr. Increase in Asset
                                                           General Ledger A/c

    Credit: To Roland Ltd A/c   €768.75 Cr. (Subsidiary ledger)

(Being the receipt of a portion of the amount due on the bill of exchange together with interest.)

FIGURE 6.10 Stage-02: Accounting entries – cancellation of bill and interest paid

3   Stage-03: On 31 January 2016, Roland Ltd became insolvent and only 40 per cent of the amount could be recovered from its assets. The accounting entries for this transaction are shown at Figure 6.11.

Example three: issuance of two concurrent bills of exchange

Degwood Ltd sells merchandise to various distributors. It has supplied Topline Ltd with goods for two separate orders, amounting to €5,000 and €12,000 respectively. Topline Ltd does not have the cash to pay for the goods and requests Degwood Ltd to provide it with credit. Degwood Ltd accepts this request and draws two bills of exchange on 1 January 2015; one for €5,000 for two months and the other for €12,000 for three months. Both bills of exchange are accepted by Topline Ltd. On 4 March 2015, Topline Ltd asks Degwood Ltd to renew the first bill of exchange. Degwood Ltd agrees to this request but would charge Topline Ltd

2016	Books of Spector Ltd Journal		Dr €	Cr €
01-Jan	To Bills Receivable A/c	Dr.	750	
	Roland Ltd A/c			750
01-Feb	Roland Ltd A/c	Dr.	750	
	To Bills Receivable A/c			750
01-Feb	Bank A/c	Dr.	300	
	Bad Debts A/c	Dr.	450	
	To Roland Ltd A/c	Cr.		750

Explanation

(a) Debit: To Bills Receivable A/c   €750 Dr.   Increase in Asset General Ledger A/c

     Credit: Roland Ltd A/c   €750 Cr. (Subsidiary ledger)

     (Being the new bill of exchange drawn for the balance due.)

(b) Debit: Roland Ltd A/c   €750 Dr. (Subsidiary ledger)

     Credit: To Bills Receivable A/c   €750 Cr.   Decrease in Asset General Ledger A/c

     (Being the dishonour of the bill of exchange due to Roland Ltd's insolvency.)

(c) Debit: Bank A/c   €300 Dr.   Increase in Asset General Ledger A/c

     (Received 40% of the amount due from Roland Ltd's assets.)

     Debit: Bad Debts A/c   €450 Dr. Decrease in Income General Ledger A/c

     (Being the amount which is uncollectable due to Roland Ltd's insolvency.)

     Credit: To Roland Ltd A/c   €750 Cr. (Subsidiary ledger)

     (Being the receipt of 40% of the amount due on the bill of exchange from Roland's Assets and the amount of Bad Debts due to its insolvency.)

FIGURE 6.11 Stage-03: Accounting entries – insolvency of drawee

an interest rate of 12 per cent per annum for a period of two months. On 20 March 2015, Topline Ltd retires the acceptance for €12,000, with an interest rebate of €120 (being equivalent to a 10 per cent discount). However, before the due date of the renewed bill (€5,000), Topline Ltd becomes insolvent and only 40 per cent could be recovered after liquidation by Degwood Ltd. Provide the journal entries in the books of Degwood Ltd. Similar to the other examples, this example is best illustrated in stages, with each stage representing a transaction towards the progression of the bill of exchange towards its maturity:

2015	Books of Degwood Ltd Journal		Dr €	Cr €
01-Jan	Bill Receivable A/c (01)	Dr.	5,000	
	Bill Receivable A/c (02)	Dr.	12,000	
	To Topline Ltd. A/c			17,000

Explanation

(a) Debit: Bill Receivable A/c (01) €5,000 Dr. Increase in Asset General Ledger A/c

Debit: Bill Receivable A/c (02) €12,000 Dr. Increase in Asset General Ledger A/c

Credit: To Topline Ltd. A/c €17,000 Cr. (Subsidiary ledger)

(Being drawings of Bill Receivable A/c 01 with a maturity date of 4 Mar 2015 and Bill Receivable A/c 02 with a maturity date of 4 April 2015.)

FIGURE 6.12 Stage-01: Accounting entries – drawing and acceptance of bill

1 Stage-01: Degwood Ltd draws two bills of exchange on 1 January 2015; one for €5,000 for two months and the other for €12,000 for three months. Both bills of exchange are accepted by Topline Ltd. The accounting entries for this transaction are shown at Figure 6.12.
2 Stage-02: On 4 March 2015, Topline Ltd asks Degwood Ltd to renew the first bill of exchange. Degwood Ltd agrees to this request but would charge Topline Ltd an interest rate of 12 per cent per annum for a period of two months. The accounting entries for this transaction are shown at Figure 6.13.
3 Stage-03: On 20 March 2015, Topline Ltd retires the acceptance for €12,000, with an interest rebate of €120 (being equivalent to a 10 per cent discount). However, before the due date of the renewed bill (€5,000), Topline Ltd becomes insolvent. The accounting entries for this transaction are shown at Figure 6.14.
4 Stage-04: Topline Ltd becomes insolvent and only 40 per cent could be recovered after liquidation by Degwood Ltd. The accounting entries for this transaction are shown at Figure 6.15.

Example four: bills of exchange for collection

A company that obtains a bill of exchange may choose to collect the total amount owing by keeping the bill until its due date (maturity). However, for security reasons the company may convey the bill of exchange to a bank with the instructions that the bill of exchange is to be retained and realised only when due. Hence, the company is not trading the bill of exchange with the bank (i.e. discounting)

2015	**Books of Degwood Ltd** **Journal**		**Dr** €	**Cr** €
04-Mar	Topline Ltd A/c	Dr.	5,000	
	To Bills Receivable A/c (01)			5,000
04-Mar	Bills Receivable A/c (03)	Dr.	5,100	
	To Interest A/c			100
	To Topline Ltd A/c			5,000

Explanation

(a) Debit: Topline Ltd A/c   €5,000 Dr. (Subsidiary ledger)

   Credit: To Bills Receivables A/c (01)   €5,000 Cr. Decrease in Asset
                                                         General Ledger A/c
   (Being reversal accounting entry for bill of exchange (01) on agreed renewal.)

(b) Debit: Bills Receivable A/c (03)   €5,100 Dr. Increase in Asset
                                                         General Ledger A/c

   Credit: To Interest A/c   €100 Cr. Increase in Income
                                                         General Ledger A/c

   Credit: To Topline Ltd A/c   €5,000 Cr. (Subsidiary ledger)

   (Being the drawing of bill of exchange (03) due for maturity on 7 May 2015 together with the interest at 12% per annum for two months in lieu of the original acceptance of Topline Ltd.)

FIGURE 6.13 Stage-02: Accounting entries – renewal of 1st bill with interest

but merely issuing instructions to the bank when payment is to take place. Furthermore, the bank will not credit the company with the amount due until that amount is actually received. This type of transaction is referred to as 'Bill sent for collection'. However, in this case the transaction is still recorded in accounting books to denote the objective of the transaction. Let us consider an example to illustrate a 'bill sent for collection' transaction.

Trident Ltd holds two bills of exchange dated 1 January 2015 made out to Nexus plc for €7,500 and €5,000 respectively which are due on 15 April 2015. Trident Ltd conveys the bills of exchange to a bank with the instructions that the bills of exchange are to be retained and realised only when due. On 15 April 2015, Nexus plc honours the first bill (€7,500) but defaults on the second bill (€5,000). Provide the journal entries in the books of Trident Ltd. Like the other examples, this example is best illustrated in stages, with each stage representing a transaction towards the progression of the bill of exchange towards its maturity:

1   Stage-01: Trident Ltd holds two bills of exchange dated 1 January 2015 made out to Nexus plc for €7,500 and €5,000 respectively which are due on 15 April 2015. Trident Ltd conveys the bills of exchange to a bank with the instructions

2015	Books of Degwood Ltd Journal		Dr €	Cr €
20-Mar	Bank A/c	Dr.	11,880	
	Discount A/c	Dr.	120	
	To Bills Receivable A/c (02)			12,000
07-May	Topline Ltd A/c	Dr.	5,150	
	To Bills Receivable A/c 03			5,150

Explanation

(a) Debit: Bank A/c   €11,880 Dr.   Increase in Asset
                                                        General Ledger A/c

   Debit: Discount A/c (01)   €120 Dr.   Decrease in Income
                                                     General Ledger A/c

   Credit: To Bills Receivable A/c (02)   €12,000 Cr.   Decrease in Asset
                                                        General Ledger A/c

(Being the amount received on the retirement of bill of exchange (02) before the due date.)

(b) Debit: Topline Ltd A/c   €5,150 Dr. (Subsidiary ledger)

   Credit: To Bills Receivable A/c (03)   €5,150 Cr.   Decrease in Asset
                                                       General Ledger A/c

(Being the amount due from Topline Ltd on the dishonour of its acceptance on the presentation of the bill on the due date i.e. includes 12% interest for 3 months)

FIGURE 6.14 Stage-03: Accounting entries – retirement of 2nd bill with interest

that the bills of exchange are to be retained and realised only when due. The accounting entries for this transaction are shown at Figure 6.16.

2   Stage-02: On 15 April 2015, Nexus plc honours the first bill (€7,500) but defaults on the second bill (€5,000). Provide the journal entries in the books of Trident Ltd. The accounting entries for this transaction are shown at Figure 6.17.

Example five: retirement of a bill of exchange

An option available to a person or entity that does not have the finances to settle the bill of exchange on the due date is to request the renewal of the bill of exchange with an appropriate due date. However, the opposite situation may develop. That is, the acceptor (drawee) may have excess funds and be in a position to settle the bill of exchange before it is due. In this case, the drawee may request the drawer to accept payment before the maturity date. However, in such a situation the drawee will seek a discount for paying the bill of exchange before the due date.

2015	Books of Degwood Ltd Journal		Dr €	Cr €
07-May	Bank A/c	Dr.	2,575	
	To Topline Ltd A/c			2,575
07-May	Bad Debts A/c	Dr.	2,575	
	To Topline Ltd A/c			2,575

Explanation

(a) Debit: Bank A/c €2,575 Dr. Increase in Asset General Ledger A/c

Credit: To Topline Ltd A/c €2,575 Dr. (Subsidiary ledger)

(Note: €5,150 was the amount due from Topline Ltd on the dishonour of its acceptance on presentation of the bill of exchange on the due date (see Figure 6.14).)

The transaction above is the amount received from official assignee of Topline Ltd at €0.50 per €1 against the dishonoured bill. i.e. 50% of €5,150)

(b) Debit: Bad Debts A/c €2,575 Dr. Decrease in Income General Ledger A/c

Credit: To Topline Ltd A/c €2,575 Cr. (Subsidiary ledger)

(Being the balance due from Topline Ltd (50%) arising out of the dishonoured bill of exchange that is written off as bad debts.)

FIGURE 6.15 Stage-04: Accounting entries – insolvency of Topline Ltd

Hence, as consideration for the premature payment of the bill of exchange the acceptor will receive interest (i.e. income) and the holder of the bill of exchange (payee) will incur an expense equivalent to the income received by the acceptor. The advantage to the payee (drawer) is twofold: (a) the risk of default by the acceptor is eliminated and (b) receiving the funds earlier provides an opportunity for reinvesting the funds received. Let us consider a practical example.

On 1 April 2015, Vodacom plc draws a bill of exchange on Evergreen plc for €20,000 which is due for payment after four months. The Board of Directors of Evergreen plc approve and accept this bill of exchange. However, after a Board of Director's resolution, of 4 June 2015, Evergreen plc retires the bill of exchange at a discount of 15 per cent per annum. Provide the journal entries in the accounting books of Vodacom plc. This example has only one stage, with this stage representing a transaction towards the progression of the bill of exchange towards its maturity:

1   Stage-01: On 1 April 2015, Vodacom plc draws a bill of exchange on Evergreen plc for €20,000 which is due for payment after four months. The Board

2015	**Books of Trident Ltd** **Journal**		**Dr** **€**	**Cr** **€**
01-Jan	Bills for Collection A/c (01)	Dr.	7,500	
	Bills for Collection A/c (02)	Dr.	5,000	
	To Bills Receivable A/c (01)			7,500
	To Bills Receivable A/c (02)			5,000

Explanation

(a) Debit: Bills for Collection A/c (01)   €7,500 Dr.   Increase in Asset General Ledger A/c

Debit: Bills for Collection A/c (02)   €5,000 Dr.   Increase in Asset General Ledger A/c

Credit: To Bills Receivable A/c (01)   €7,500 Cr.   Decrease in Asset General Ledger A/c

Credit: To Bills Receivable A/c (02)   €5,000 Cr.   Decrease in Asset General Ledger A/c

(Being the amount due from Nexus Plc and sent to the Bank with instructions that the bills of exchange are to be retained and realised only when due.)

FIGURE 6.16 Stage-01: Accounting entries – bill sent for collection

2015	**Books of Trident Ltd** **Journal**		**Dr** **€**	**Cr** **€**
15-Apr	Bank A/c	Dr.	7,500	
	To Bills for Collection A/c (01)			7,500
	Nexus A/c	Dr.	5,000	
	To Bills for Collection A/c (02)			5,000

Explanation

(a) Debit: Bank A/c   €7,500 Dr.   Increase in Asset General Ledger A/c

Credit: Bills for Collection A/c (01)   €7,500 Cr.   Decrease in Asset General Ledger A/c

(Being the amount paid to Trident Ltd by Nexus Plc for the first bill of exchange due on 15 April 2015.)

(b) Debit: Nexus A/c   €5,000 Dr.   (Subsidiary Ledger)

Credit: Bills for Collection A/c (02)   €5,000 Cr.   Decrease in Asset General Ledger A/c

(Being the amountdue to Trident Ltd but dishonoured by Nexus Plc for the second bill of exchange due on 15 April 2015.)

FIGURE 6.17 Stage-02: Accounting entries – bill sent for collection (maturity)

2015	**Books of Evergreen Plc** **Journal**		**Dr** **€**	**Cr** **€**
01-Apr	Vodacom Plc A/c	Dr.	20,000	
	To Bills Payable A/c			20,000
04-Jun	Bills Payable A/c	Dr.	20,000	
	To Bank A/c			19,500
	To Interest A/c (Discount)			500

Explanation

(a) Debit: Vodacom Plc A/c   €20,000 Dr. (Subsidiary Ledger)

   Credit: To Bills Payable A/c   €20,000 Cr. Increase in Liability General Ledger A/c

(Being the amount of the bill of exchange drawn by Vodacom Plc and accepted by Evergreen Plc due on 1 July 2015.)

(b) Debit: Bills Payable A/c   €20,000 Dr. Decrease in Liability General Ledger A/c

   Credit: To Bank A/c   €19,500 Cr. Decrease in Asset General Ledger A/c

   Credit: To Interest A/c (Discount)   €500 Cr. Increase in Income General Ledger A/c

(Being the retirement of thebill of exchange two months before the due date with an allowable interest rate of 15%.)

FIGURE 6.18 Stage-01: Accounting entries – retirement of a bill of exchange

of Directors of Evergreen plc approve and accept this bill of exchange. However, after a Board of Director's resolution, of 4 June, 2015, Evergreen plc retires the bill of exchange at a discount of 15 per cent per annum. The accounting entries for this transaction are shown at Figure 6.18.

Additional practical problem

On 1 March 201X, BeCare plc bought goods valued €75,000 from Ajax plc. BeCare plc did not have adequate cash to cover the purchase value. However, Ajax plc agreed to draw a bill of exchange on BeCare plc for four months settlement, commencing on the purchase date for the outstanding amount of €40,000. BeCare plc accepted this bill of exchange. Unfortunately, Ajax plc required cash urgently and on 30 March 201X decided to discount the bill of exchange accepted by BeCare plc with the bank at 8 per cent per annum. Furthermore, on the bill of exchange due date, BeCare plc did not meet the amount due. The holder of the bill of exchange (bank) instituted recourse against Ajax plc. To settle matters, on 1 July 201X, Ajax plc drew a new bill of exchange on BeCare plc at three months for €40,000 which was the original value of the bill plus 15 per cent interest. The new bill of exchange was accepted by BeCare plc. Required: Provide the ledger accounts in the accounting books of BeCare plc.

Solution

The accounting entries for this problem are shown at Figure 6.19.

201X	Books of BeCare Plc Bills Payable Account	Dr €	Cr €
01-Mar	Ajax Plc A/c (Bill accepted: Original)		40,000
30-Jun	Ajax Plc A/c (Bills dishonoured)	40,000	
01-Jul	Ajax Plc A/c (New Bill accepted: Face Value + 15% for 3 months)		41,500

201X	Books of BeCare Plc Ajax Plc Account	Dr €	Cr €
01-Mar	Bills Payable A/c (Bill accepted: Original)	40,000	
01-Mar	Outstanding Purchases		40,000
30-Jun	Bills Payable A/c (Bills dishonoured)		40,000
01-Jul	Bills Payable A/c (Face Value €40,000 + Interest charged)	41,500	
01-Jul	Interest Payable A/c (€40,000 @ 15% for 3 months)		1,500

201X	Books of BeCare Plc Interest Payable Account	Dr €	Cr €
01-Jul	Ajax Plc A/c (Interest charged: €40,000 + 15% for 3 months)	1,500	

Explanatory Note:

(a) On maturity of the original bill of exchange, the bank (discount house) will present the bill to BeCare Plc.

(b) Because BeCare Plc defaults on the payment (dishonoured bill), the bank will give back the bill to Ajax Plc and will debit Ajax's bank account with the face value of the bill (€40,000).

(c) However, in the accounting book of Ajax Plc, the amount owing is debited back to BeCare's account to show that BeCare Plc is still in debt.

FIGURE 6.19 Ledger accounts in the accounting books of BeCare plc.

References

Fan, Jianhong and Tao, Yang. (2007). Negotiable instruments, in particular bills of exchange in Macau, China. *Journal of International Commercial Law and Technology*, 2(2), 83–93.

Keefer, Jacqueline. (2010). The renaissance of bills of exchange in foreign trade. *Trade & Export Finance – Insight*, Spring 2010 edition, UBS Switzerland.

Mengenli, Ozge Akin. (2007). Has the 'United Nations Convention on International Bills of Exchange and International Promissory Notes' achieved its objectives? *Ankara Law Review*, Winter, 199–212.

Szasz, Paul C. (1989). *United Nations Convention on International Bills of Exchange and International Promissory Notes*. New York: United Nations.

Voica, Ileana. (2011). Bills of exchange and promissory notes – comparative perspective. *Juridical Tribune*, 1(2), 107–117.

PART 3

Business and financial analysis of organisations

This part is the focus of this book, consisting of five dynamic chapters that explore a spectrum of inter-related topics. These topics range from:

- Financial risk management principles;
- Financial risk management application;
- Business and financial analysis;
- Business valuation methods; and
- Business Valuation Report.

To begin with, a very detailed description of financial risk management principles provides the theoretical framework in relation to how risk may be mitigated. It is possible to mitigate risk but it is extremely difficult to eliminate it completely. Hence, the financial risk management theoretical framework discussed in Chapter 7 endeavours to foresee and deal with uncertainties that make vulnerable the achievement of the financial objectives of an enterprise.

Financial risk management is the practice of using financial instruments to manage the exposure to risk in terms of various financial transactions that reflect credit, market, foreign exchange and others risks associated with volatility, liquidity and inflation. Contemporary technological advancement, particularly in relation to data communications, has caused the immediate availability of information, thus becoming a very swift change catalyst, with subsequent financial market reactions occurring rapidly. Therefore, risk may take place from events that occur across the globe, which have nothing to do with the domestic markets and yet have a significant and immediate effect on domestic events. Financial risk management in this context takes a particular dimension. It focuses on when and how to use hedging to manage harmful exposures to risk, related specifically to financial instruments.

Financial risk management is also influenced by regulatory pressures, particularly the accounting standards, which have implemented measures that aim for better financial risk management. The driving force from the accounting regulatory bodies, including the Basel Accords are compelling entities to find a methodology that is suitable for their resource capability and is supportive to the general risk management policy.

While Chapter 7 deals with the theoretical aspects of financial risk management, Chapter 8 focuses on its applications, particularly when to use financial risk management. As a rule, market risks that result in unique risks for the entity are the best candidates for financial risk management. The major concern that is addressed by this chapter is to determine when to use financial risk management to mitigate the risks that specifically arise from the changes in interest rates, exchange rates and commodity prices. An understanding of the factors that impact financial markets is important because these factors, in turn, impact the potential risk of an entity.

Chapter 9 provides an analytical framework for the analysis of a business concern through the assessment of both the external and internal environment. The appraisal of the external environment highlights those factors that directly impact an entity's operational activities and strategic choices that influence its opportunities and risks. On the other hand, the evaluation of an entity's internal environment will apply ratio analysis to the financial statements to examine various fiscal elements, including liquidity, profitability, asset utilisation, investment, working capital and capital structure.

The focus of Chapter 10 is the business valuation of an entity. This chapter is a continuation of the theme related to the analysis of a business concern and has the objective of providing a methodology for assessing an approximate economic value of an owner's interest in a business. The valuation methods are classified under two main categories, namely non-going concern (an entity that will not remain in business) and a going concern (an entity that will remain in business for the foreseeable future). This chapter will examine a number of valuation methods and explore how other factors may influence the value of a business at any one given time.

Chapter 11 is the final chapter within Part 3. This chapter specifically addresses the issue of preparing the Business Valuation Report. The application of the analytical information that was the object of a number of previous chapters cumulates into the Business Valuation Report. It is therefore appropriate to have a chapter devoted on this aspect to provide the reader with a more comprehensive explanation of the format and contents of the business valuation report using best practice criterion. One must recognise that businesses are being continually transacted, like every other commodity. Therefore, there are numerous situations when an objective and accurate assessment of a business's value is required. Moreover, the previous chapter focused on the procedures to establishing a simple but realistic process by which the value of a business may be determined. This chapter will take the topic of business valuation a step further. It will explain the format and content (i.e. presentation) of the business valuation report based on best practice criterion.

7

FINANCIAL RISK
MANAGEMENT PRINCIPLES

Living at risk is jumping off the cliff and building your wings on the way down.

Ray Bradbury, Author

All undertakings carry a certain magnitude of risk. However, frequent and thorough risk analysis and risk management techniques can help to resolve concerns before they arise or become serious. A risk is an event that may happen and if it occurs may have an unfavourable effect on an enterprise's financial activity, such as financial loss on investments. Hence, risk has a probability attached to it and the consequence of it happening may have an adverse effect on the economic activity of an entity.

Basically, financial risk management is the identification of what may go wrong and taking the appropriate action to mitigate the risk. Risk can be mitigated but it is difficult to eliminate completely. Financial risk management endeavours to foresee and deal with uncertainties that jeopardise the financial objectives of an enterprise. It is the practice of using financial instruments to manage the exposure to risk in terms of credit risk, market risk, foreign exchange risk and others risks associated with volatility, liquidity and inflation.

One should note that while financial risk has increased significantly in recent years, risk and risk management are not contemporary issues. They are not something new. However, one may ask: What has increased financial risk in recent years? The answer to this question is relatively simple. The growth of global financial markets and the globalisation of trade, together with the vast advances in information communications technology (ICT), have significantly increased financial risk. Risk may stem from events taking place across the globe that have nothing to do with the domestic markets and yet have a significant and immediate effect on domestic events. ICT has caused information to be available instantly, thus becoming a very swift change catalyst, with subsequent financial market reactions occurring rapidly. Examples of this are the immediate financial market reaction in Europe and the USA to the Asian financial crisis of 1997–1998 and the financial crisis of 2009–2010.

Financial markets are very sensitive and can be rapidly affected by fluctuations in exchange rates, interest rates and commodity prices. The financial markets' reaction to such changes can swiftly become problematic. Therefore, it is important that financial risks are identified, appraised and continuously managed. Financial risk management is a systematic process to identify, quantify, respond to, and monitor and control all types of financial risk. Furthermore, financial risk management can be qualitative and quantitative. Financial risk management focuses on when and how to hedge using financial instruments to manage harmful exposures to risk.

One should note that regulatory pressures from Financial Accounting Standards Board (FASB), particularly the International Financial Reporting Standards (IFRS) are setting in motion measures for better risk management. Under IFRS, entities are required to conduct some basic type of risk measurement in the disclosures section of the financial statements. For instance, both FASB (Section 7a) and IFRS-7 related to 'Quantitative and Qualitative Disclosures' maintain that the financial statements must explicitly state the potential impact of market movements companies are principally exposed to, that is 'Financial Instruments Disclosures: a requirement exists to calculate the potential impact of each market risk variable or conduct a value-at-risk analysis.' Hence, the thrust from the accounting regulatory bodies is compelling entities to find a methodology that is suitable for their resource capability and is supportive to the general risk management policy. In addition, the international banking sector as a rule apply the Basel Accords for tracking, reporting and exposing operational, credit and market risks.

A very important point to remember is that risk is not always bad; there are both opportunities and threats. The opportunities represent the beneficial risks, whereas the threats are the adverse risks. Therefore, financial risk management consists of processes, tools, and methods that will aid the financial analyst to increase the likelihood and impact of positive events and to decrease the probability and impact of negative events. Furthermore, financial risk management is a continuous process to be conducted during the entire operational cycle of an enterprise.

Meaning of risk

Risk provides the basis for an opportunity to make a gain; usually the higher the risk the higher the gain. However, the converse is also applicable. Terminology is important when discussing risk. For instance, the terms exposure and risk are dissimilar in their meaning even though they are often used interchangeably. Exposure is normally used as a general term, to convey the possibility of loss or gain, whereas risk specifically refers to the probability of a loss or gain. Thus, risk is expressed as a numerical number, for example a probability of 0.50 (or 50 per cent), which in this case means that there is an equal chance of an event occurring. Therefore, it may be concluded that risk arises as a result of exposure.

It should be noted that exposure to financial markets has a direct or indirect impact on most entities. Financial market exposure may provide strategic or competitive benefits. For example, if an exchange rate of a particular country is devalued, that country will be able to export more of its goods because they will be cheaper than before the currency was devalued. Additionally, imports will be more expensive, therefore commodities produced domestically may be promoted further. The strategic impact emanating from the currency devaluation may be a change in the pricing policies of entities that market imported goods, with the competitive benefits being that the domestic products would compete better (on price) with their imported equivalents.

Risk is the likelihood (probability) of a loss or gain resulting from events such as changes in market prices. Events may have a low probability of occurring, but their impact may be great, resulting in a high loss. Moreover, events may become problematic because they are often not anticipated. As stated previously, risk may be viewed as a threat or opportunity, therefore it is not desirable (or/and possible) to eliminate risk. As a general principle, the first step in determining how risk is to be managed is to understand it. In other words, identifying risk exposures and risks shape the basis for an appropriate financial risk management strategy.

From the above, we conclude that all undertakings carry a certain magnitude of risk. A risk is an event that may happen and if it occurs may have an unfavourable (or favourable) effect; so not all risk is bad. Hence, risk consists of three major elements: the event, the probability that the event will occur and the consequences should the event occurs. Examples of the unfavourable (or favourable) impact that may result from risk include a weakening (or strengthening) in the exchange rate of a particular currency thus affecting the price of goods or an increase (or decrease) in interest rates thus affecting inflows and outflows of capital in a particular country. However, the consequence of the impact is financial loss (or gain). For instance, a decrease in interest rates means that a business enterprise may borrow at a lower cost, but an investor who has substantial deposits in a financial institution will receive a lower interest return on its investments.

Therefore, we may conclude that the aim of risk management is an endeavour to foresee and deal with uncertainties that jeopardise the objectives of an undertaking. Hence, an entity needs to take a proactive stand and not take a wait and see attitude (reactive). As we have seen, a risk is an event that is uncertain and has a negative or positive impact on some task. However, it should be emphasised that in finance risk relates to speculative risk rather than pure risk, which can exist in other areas. With pure risk there are only two possible outcomes, either something bad happening or nothing is happening, thus it is insurable. The outcomes of pure risk are predicted by using the law of large numbers, a priori data or empirical data. An example of pure risk is the risk of having sustained damages to a car as a result of a car accident. Pure risk is constrained to the risk of loss without the possibility of gain and hence the reason why it is the only type of risk that can be insured.

Speculative Risk involves three possible outcomes, namely loss, gain or no change. For example, trading on the stock market may result in either making a profit or loss or no change in the investment value. This is the reason why speculative risk cannot be insured using the traditional insurance market but other methods, such as hedging speculative risk through diversification and derivatives may be used.

Let us consider an example using an insurance company to illustrate the difference in meaning of the terms 'risk' and 'risk analysis'. For example, an insurance company specialises in vehicle accident insurance. To this insurance company a risk is the event of an accident of any of its policyholders. The insurance company is not in a position to know which of its policyholders will be involved in an accident in a given period (uncertainty) nor does it know the costs the company will pay out for repairing the damaged vehicle (negative impact on profitability). This is what constitutes a risk for the insurance company. On the other hand, risk analysis is the process of appraising the risks. Risk analysis requires an accumulation of historical data which will allow the insurance company to estimate both the uncertainty of the risk (probability) and its impact (outcome). Hence, by using the historical database of its policyholders and the various insurance claims made, the car accident insurance company may estimate the number of accidents in a specific duration and the estimated value they will have to pay out during the period in question.

Therefore, risk may be viewed as a combination of the uncertainty of an event happening (probability) and the consequences if the event happens (outcome). Risk is measured by the probability of an event happening. For example, the car accident insurance company may estimate the probability of an accident happening for a specific period of time by simply dividing the number of accidents by the total number of policyholders (i.e. probability of an accident = number of accidents ÷ number of policyholders). Note that if an event is anticipated but has an insignificant impact, it may not represent a risk, since it has no impact or influence. Additionally, an unlikely event with a significant impact (consequence) may also not represent a risk either. Therefore, it is the blend of the likelihood (probability) and consequence (impact) of an event that provides the possibility of loss or gain (exposure). Hence, risk may be expressed as the summation of the probabilities multiplied by the consequences of all the events.

Occurrence of financial risk

An important issue that must be addressed is how financial risk arises. Financial risk occurs through an entity's financial transactions, it is considered to be speculative risk involving three possible outcomes, namely loss, gain or no change. These financial transactions occur daily as the entity conducts its business and include dealings related to sales, purchases, investments, loans and numerous other business activities. An entity's business activities embrace a host of events, such as conducting normal legal transactions, debt financing, being involved in company mergers or acquisitions, undertaking new projects and a variety of other dealings on a local and international level that involve different exchange and interest rates.

For instance, a wholesaler sells products to a retailer on credit but the retailer may honour or default on payment. A company enters into a contract for the supply and installation of an ICT network which is essential for carrying out its business, but the supplier may file for bankruptcy during the delivery process. An investor purchases shares in a company but the share price declines (or increases). An entity borrows at a rate of interest but a week later interest rates decline or increase. Hence, the risk occurs when the transaction takes place.

In other words, when financial rates and prices change significantly, these may result in an escalation of costs, a reduction of cash inflows with a resultant decrease in income and profitability. Financial fluctuations in rates and prices make it more difficult for entities to allocate capital, establish a pricing and service policy, and to plan and define the entity's budget. For instance, these financial fluctuations may arise through civil unrest, for example the effect on business in the southern Mediterranean region due to the unrest in Libya, Tunisia and Egypt during the so-called Arab Spring. They may also arise through a shortage of certain commodities, such as steel, leather, cereals, crude oil and many others.

The above examples illustrate that basically there are three main sources of financial risk:

- Those resulting from internal activities or failure on the part of the entity particularly related to decisions regarding individuals, processes and systems. For example, liquidity concerns; making bad or erroneous management decisions; production capacity concerns; failure of computer systems resulting in significant loss of production time; and failure of system controls resulting in fraud.
- Those arising from the activities and transactions with other entities such as, suppliers, customers and counterparties in derivatives transactions. For example, default in making payments by debtors; non-delivery of goods from suppliers; and the financial failure of key strategic partners.
- Those arising from an entity's exposure to fluctuations in market prices, such as interest rates, exchange rates and commodity prices.

The above discussion clearly illustrates that financial risk occurs through many sources particularly through an entity's financial transactions.

What is financial risk management?

It is important to know what financial risk management is all about. Basically, financial risk management is a process that deals with uncertainties that result from the financial markets. Financial risk management endeavours to increase and protect the economic value of an entity by exploiting financial instruments to manage the entity's exposure to risk, particularly credit risk and market risk.

It is essential that risk is addressed proactively since it provides an entity with a competitive advantage and ensures that the board of directors, management, key employees and influential stakeholders are all in agreement on key issues related to risk. Thus, financial risk management entails the assessment of the financial risks being confronted by an entity and most importantly, developing management strategies that are consistent with the priorities and policies established by executive management. In other words, it is necessary for an entity to identify the risk and have a specific strategy in place to address it.

The risk of failure is likely to affect not only the existence of the entity itself but the subsistence of many individuals with the consequence of causing financial ruin for them. Examples of such cases include the collapse of Barings Bank (1995), Enron (2001) and Madoff (2008).

In February 1995, Barings Bank, one of the oldest banks of the United Kingdom was declared bankrupt. The principal cause was one of the bank's traders in Singapore (Nick Leeson) who had lost $1.4 billion on derivatives trading against a capital of about $600 million as reported by the bank. Nick Leeson was a rising star in the bank where within a year of his appointment to Singapore in 1992, he generated 10 per cent of the bank's profitability. His spectacular performance resulted in senior management having enormous trust in his abilities, which resulted in giving him full authority over trading. Furthermore, because of the swift expansion of Barings Settlements, he instantly found himself in charge of both the front and back office. This was a terrible mistake on the part of the bank's management because internal control procedures broke down.

He would be trading on the futures market and simultaneously be responsible for booking and reporting the various trades. Typically, he would report for work in the Singapore Money Exchange (SIMEX) until trading closed at 2pm, and then would report to the office to conduct the back-office duties, where he would reconcile the day's trades with the actual sales. Normally, reconciliation would be performed by a different individual doing the back-office accounting, to detect any dubious deals. This abnormality provided Nick Leeson with the opportunity and power to make substantial losses without being revealed.

Nick Leeson's authorisation included arbitraging the Nikkei 225 futures agreements on the various exchanges, the Singapore International Monetary Exchange (SIMEX) and the Osaka Stock Exchange (OSE), buying the same futures at a low price in one exchange and selling simultaneously at a higher price on the other exchange. The huge futures position of Nick Leeson was basically part of his trading mandate and for the bank he was seemingly performing a trading strategy with little or no exposure to risk.

However, Nick Leeson was able to conceal his actual position in a secret account known as an 'Error' account because he was responsible for both front and back office. In a normal situation, a trader would not be able to use the 'Error' account because only the back office staff were authorised to use it for legitimate reasons.

The disastrous situation for the bank came to ahead when just three days after the earthquake in Kobe, Nick Leeson acquired a considerable number of contracts. He misjudged the market probably thinking that the money market had over reacted and that the fall of the Nikkei 225 from 20,000 to 18,950 was only temporary. However, the Nikkei continued to fall in value and by the end of February 1995, Nick Leeson had leveraged his position to $7 billion. Moreover, his status on the Simex was eight times bigger than the next largest position. Thus, his position became untenable with the margin calls being enormous and Barings Tokyo London had to immediately transfer a considerable amount of $835 million to Barings Singapore in January and February to cover the margin calls on Simex. These calls finally made Barings bankrupt as its reported capital was only $635 million. The above illustrates that the operational risk for Barings rose beyond expectations because management failed to maintain the internal control procedures that are considered normal practice in every industry.

A study of the Enron case reveals that the company took on a broad range of business risks by dubious management decisions and fraudulent accounting practices. Arthur Andersen, one of the five largest accounting firms in the United States, had a reputation for high standards and quality risk management. Through creative accounting practices under Arthur Andersen's supervision, Enron in the 1990s became one of the fastest-growing businesses in the world. The two major types of risk that Enron was able to conceal with Arthur Andersen's aid were accounting and internal control risks, and market risk.

Financial statements were systematically and constantly revised to show extra profitability. Enron established special-purpose entities (SPEs) to generate extra capital or assume debt; thus the company shifted problematic assets with its SPEs rather than show them on their accounts. Hence, offensive accounts were moved to these SPEs and were inadequately disclosed. By the end of the saga, Enron had thousands of SPEs. Arthur Andersen endorsed this practice with the application of reckless accounting standards. Hence, investors were not made aware of critical financial information.

This resulted in Enron's stock price increasing in value instead of declining. These practices resulted in the breakdown of the accounting and internal controls with the consequent exponential rise in the risks associated with them. Once fraud was revealed Enron's shares were trading at less than $1.

Additionally, the 1990s saw the emergence of numerous speculative entities; for instance the dot.com bubble was on a spectacular rise with innovative Internet stocks being valued at unbelievable amounts. Hence, this created an illusionary environment where typical investors and regulators acknowledged this situation as the new norm. Out of this chaos, Enron established Enron Online (EOL) in October 1999 as an electronic trading website that focused on commodities and where Enron was either the buyer or the seller. Investors were attracted to Enron due to its so called reputation, credit and expertise in the energy sector. EOL was conducting about $350 billion trading transactions by June 2000. The management of EOL showed extremely bad timing judgement when they invested hundreds of millions of dollars on the building of a high-speed broadband telecom networks at a time when the dot.com bubble burst, showing negligible returns on their investment. The recession that followed in 2000–2001 saw Enron having significant exposure to the most volatile parts of the market, resulting in huge losses for the many trusting investors and creditors.

In December 2008, as the financial and economic crisis continued on its de-structive course, the Madoff case broke out. This case illustrated that the risk management processes applicable at that time partially failed to prevent this scandal. The system developed by Madoff was known as a Ponzi scheme, which was based on a 'pyramidal' concept in the sense that the returns on investment of yesterday's investors were paid out of the deposits of today's investors rather than the true product of their investments. This went on for years, until (with the arrival of the financial crisis) a number of Madoff's clients wanted to pull out their capital, thus triggering the collapse of the entire scheme.

Madoff's scheme highlights the failure of operational risk management or more accurately, it highlights the failure of the quantitative measures applied to manage the risk associated with the so called investment by the asset management industry, particularly given the fact that the asset management firms are considered by the Basel Committee as low risk activities. According to Claussy et al. (2009), the Madoff fraud concerns the operational risk or more precisely, depending on the relation-ship between Madoff and the victim institution, it may be classified into different Basel II event type categories. For instance, research evidence suggests that this case involved type 1 risk (internal fraud), type 2 (external fraud) and type 4 (clients, products and business practices) through mis-selling or advisory failures by financial institutions.

Managing financial risk compels senior management to make decisions about risks to ascertain which risks are acceptable and which risks are not acceptable. Hence, there may be some risks that one may accept and carry on, however many risks are not acceptable and require immediate action. A passive strategy (or a wait-and-see attitude) that takes no action, in reality means that by default, the management is accepting all risks. Many entities control financial risk by using a variety of strategies and products, such as, hedging and outsourcing. However, it is important that management are aware and comprehend how these products and strategies work to reduce the risk an entity encounters, within the context of the entity's risk acceptance tolerance and objectives.

Very often the strategies for financial risk management focus on financial derivatives. Previously, we have seen that a derivative is a financial instrument or contract based on an underlying investment. The most common type of derivatives involves an option agreement, which entails the right to buy or sell the underlying instrument at an agreed price. For example, the underlying instrument (or asset) may include a crop of wheat with a fixed price agreement. It should be noted that derivatives are widely traded among financial institutions and on organised stock exchanges. The general rule is that the value of derivatives agreements, such as futures, forwards, options, and swaps, is achieved from the price of the underlying asset. What makes derivatives interesting is that they trade on a variety of financial aspects, such as, exchange rates; interest rates; commodities; equity and fixed income securities; and credit.

Theorists hypothesise that the extensive utilisation of derivatives intensifies the risk. However, a counter argument suggests that the existence of derivatives enables those who are risk averse, to pass the risk along to the risk seekers who recognise the conditions as an opportunity. For example, selling options at an agreed price would reduce the risk to the seller because of the agreed price, but would increase the risk to the buyer who will resell the resultant product on the open market at the price prevailing at that time of sale. This may result in a profit or loss to the buyer of the option depending on the market conditions. Hence, the risk is associated with the market conditions. Therefore, the ability to estimate the likelihood of a financial loss or gain is highly desirable. However, research shows that standard theories of probability often fall short when analysing financial markets. The major reason for this is that risks usually do not exist in isolation but have very complex interactions with many variables related to exposure. These complex interactions are at times difficult to predict, since many are dependent on human behaviour. Therefore, such variables need to be considered in understanding how financial risk arises so that an appropriate risk model is developed.

Financial risk management requires a continuous implementation process that involves the regular updating and refining of risk management strategies as the financial markets and associated activities are constantly changing. The regular updating and refining of risk management strategies reflect:

- Changing expectations about financial market rates brought about by unusual activities or more seriously, a financial crisis;
- Varying attitudes towards the business environment in particular a reaction to economic recession or growth;
- Shifting international political conditions. For example, the Arab Spring, where a revolutionary wave of demonstrations, riots, and civil wars in the Arab world spread throughout the countries of the Arab League and surroundings regions.

Generally, the financial risk management process may be summarised as consisting of four major activities:

- Risk identification;
- Risk quantification, including the determination of an acceptable level of risk tolerance and prioritisation;
- Formulating a risk response strategy;
- Implement risk response strategy (i.e. monitor, control and review as required).

The financial risk management process will be discussed in detail when examining in detail the financial risk management model.

Financial risk management model

Fundamentally, a financial risk management model has the objective of ensuring that an entity has in place, the appropriate strategies that enable it to manage the potential and existing risks associated with the financial markets. It should be noted that although a financial risk management model focuses on the risks associated with the financial markets, it still adheres to the basic principles of the standard risk management model. It must also be recognised that risk management is a dynamic process that needs to evolve as the entity and its business interests develop.

As such, financial risk management may implicate and influence various divisions of an entity. However, it particularly impacts the treasury function that has the specific task related to the management of an entity's funds regarding equity capital, working capital and the investment of surplus funds.

The Financial Risk Management Model (refer to Figure 7.1) illustrates that the model consists of three segments which are all inter-related. The three model segments are the inputs, processes and outputs.

The first model segment involves the analysis of the internal and external environment. The internal and external environments are the major inputs to the financial risk management model. The internal environment reflects the conditions within an entity that influence its activities and strategic choices. The factors influencing the internal environment include the entity's mission statement, leadership styles and its organisational culture. The internal factors may indicate

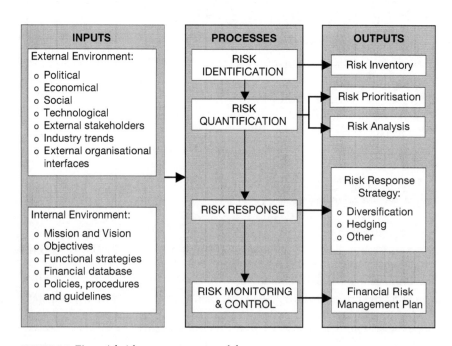

FIGURE 7.1 Financial risk management model

management's attitude to risk in terms of being a risk seeker or risk averse. The external environment reflects the situation or events that occur outside of the entity and are normally beyond its control. Examples of external driving forces might be, the financial industry itself; the economy particularly the fiscal and monetary policies that affect exchange and interest rates, capital inflows and outflows; demographics; competition; and regional political activities (Arab Spring). The examination of the external environment enables management to assess current and future economic trends.

The second model segment consists of four processes which are individually linked to prescribed outputs. The first process involves identifying the financial risks facing the entity and understanding their relevance by taking into consideration the analysis of the internal and external environments. The output from this process is an inventory of the financial risks that may occur.

The second process is to quantify the risks itemised in the financial risk inventory by conducting qualitative or quantitative risk analysis. This will enable management to measure and prioritise the various financial risks.

The third process is conducted once an understanding of the financial risks emerges so that appropriate financial risk strategies may be defined. For example, it might be possible to change where and how business is conducted, thus reducing the entity's exposure and risk. The entity may adopt some kind of hedging agreement to mitigate the risk of increasing interest rates or fluctuations in the exchange rates. The entity may consider adopting a diversification strategy to spread its risk exposure. Alternatively, existing risk exposures may be managed through derivatives or the entity may simply accept all the risks with the possibility of a loss or gain.

The fourth and final process is to define and implement a financial risk management plan in conjunction with the identified financial risk management policy. This process is closely linked to the risk response strategy task. The entity has basically four broad alternatives for managing financial risk:

- Do nothing and actively or passively accept all risks by default;
- Diversify the business activities;
- Hedge a portion of the risk exposures and identify the risk exposures that may and should be hedged;
- Hedge all risk exposures.

The measurement and reporting of financial risks provides managers with adequate information to enable them to make the appropriate decisions and monitor the outcomes. This establishes whether the implemented strategies are having the desired effect in mitigating the identified financial risks. Moreover, since the financial risk management is an ongoing process, the information reported and the feedback received may be utilised to review and refine the strategies. Let us now discuss in some detail each of the process within the financial risk management model.

Financial risk identification process

Financial risk identification basically addresses the question: What might go wrong? Hence, it specifically identifies the financial risks and their characteristics. This process provides the warning signs that indicate whether the identified risks are likely to occur and also gives management an opportunity to find better methods for achieving the entity's specific requirements and objectives. Information for the identification of financial risk may be obtained from various sources. For instance, banks, insurance firms and other financial institutions have the experience and the appropriate historical databases to identify the financial risk they are likely to encounter. However, a common approach is to conduct a workshop, where key stakeholders through brainstorming sessions, identify and review standard financial risk lists.

To compile a financial risk inventory, the entire operational processes of the entity are closely examined, meticulously looking for areas of uncertainty. For instance, a bank may want to examine the quality of its advances. An entity which mainly deals with imports or/and exports may need to examine its foreign currency exchange policies. Therefore, the objective of the brainstorming sessions would be to examine the operational processes to search for financial issues that may be a threat or opportunity to the entity.

There are various types of financial risks that are associated with a variety of different industries and individual entities. Therefore, it is important to identify the financial risks and decide on a process by process basis what to do about each type of financial risk. For instance, business risks are ongoing risks that are best resolved by the entity's financial division. For example, if the entity is seen as not meeting the cash-inflow financial targets, the financial division may need to examine the possibility of obtaining or extending the bank overdraft facilities. The response is likely to be a contingency plan developed by the financial division to acquire bank overdraft arrangements for a specified period.

The identification of financial risks may be viewed as being made up of two components: (a) the cause of the specific condition. For example, customers not meeting the payment schedule for services or goods received; and (b) the impact of the condition. For example, the cash inflow budget will not be met and short term bank financing may be needed. Therefore, a financial risk might be defined as: 'Customers not meeting the defined payment schedule will imply that the cash inflow predictions will not be met, thus resulting in cash flow short term shortage'. This method of financial risk identification will allow a standardised definition approach that will make it simple to define, remove duplicates and allow management to comprehend the risk. The financial risk identification process enables management to categorise financial risk under a number of major headings and compile a risk inventory. For example, the banking sector adhere to the Basel II Accord, which focuses on three types of risk, namely, credit risk; market risk; and operational risk. Hence, an inventory of financial risks may include:

- Credit risk: In any ongoing buyer-seller relationship, unless there is a cash exchange at the point of sale, one or other party will assume a certain degree of counterparty or credit risk. Bills of exchange play an important part in eliminating some of the uncertainty that is inherent in trade by providing increased security for the creditor (the seller) because (a) it is evidence that a demand for payment has been issued; (b) the debtor acknowledges that the debt exists due to the legal standing of bills of exchange; (c) it provides access to an established legal process in the event of default; and (d) a creditor can seek enhanced security by requiring the drawee's bank to guarantee the bill, thus the bank will ensure payment on maturity irrespective of the drawee's financial standing on that date. The risk losses from credit risk are due to borrowers submitting late payments or default to make payments.
- Market risk (or systematic risk) is the likelihood that an investor will experience losses due to factors that affect the overall performance of the financial markets. A concern with market risk is that it cannot be mitigated or eliminated through a diversification policy but one can hedge against it. For example, a consequence of a major natural disaster is a decline in the market as a whole. Other sources of market risk (risk of losses from shift in market prices) include recessions, political turmoil, changes in interest rates, terrorist attacks, changes in foreign currency exchange rates, changes in stock market investments value and commodity prices due to an imbalance in the supply-demand ratio.
- Operational risk is the risk of losses stemming from inadequate or failed internal processes, people and systems or from external events. Furthermore, operational risk includes legal risks but excludes reputational risk. Operational risk is entrenched in all banking products and activities and has always existed in all types of organisations. However, it has attracted greater significance due to the globalisation of trade and the globalisation of the financial system, increased complexity, and the recent materialisation of exceptional large losses. Risk of losses are to inadequate internal controls, such as unintentional human input errors and/or intentional fraud; external events, such as the Arab Spring; and legal grievances, such as a law suit or claim.
- Other risks: There are a host of other risks from which the risk of losses is due to liquidity concerns, such as inability to meet financial obligations or a bank unable to meet the demand of the depositors' withdrawals; business risk, such as a loss or decrease in the competitive position; and reputational risk, such as a loss or decrease in a bank's standing in public opinion.

In contrast to credit and market risk, the operational risk category is the most difficult to measure, manage and monitor. The reason for this is that operational risks are numerous, at times obscure and hence awkward to foresee, occasionally intricate to comprehend and often they are the most demanding to explicitly determine their impact on the entity. However, the methodology described above, regarding the organisation of workshops, focus group discussions or brainstorming sessions, where key stakeholders within the entity contemplate what may go wrong is an excellent way to identify this type of financial risk. Furthermore, many of the financial risks identified above are very common among many businesses, particularly financial institutions. The distinctive aspect is as a rule the operational risk category.

Financial risk quantification process

The financial risk quantification process may be viewed as consisting of two stages, namely, qualitative and quantitative risk analysis as depicted by Figure 7.2. Both methods help the Risk Analyst (RA) and particularly the Chief Risk Officer (CRO) to assess the financial risks being encountered by the entity.

Generally, Figure 7.2 illustrates that the first stage is the qualitative risk analysis, which aims at providing a prioritised list of all the major financial risks and their respective impact. The outcome from this stage is the financial risk probability and impact matrix. The second stage consists of conducting a quantitative financial risk analysis. However, a quantitative financial risk analysis is normally conducted if the financial activity being examined is complex or/and of substantial value. A quantitative financial risk analysis will likely require the use (and likely preparation) of a probability distribution and the selection of an appropriate risk analysis tool, depending on the financial activity being examined. This stage may also require specialised computer software for the analysis. The outcome from this stage is a computed probability distribution, including a measure of uncertainty (risk) and the expected value associated with the financial activity being examined. However, the outcome from the quantitative financial risk analysis is always dependent on the financial activity being examined (the concern), the analytical technique being applied and the computer software being used.

There are several techniques that may be applied to quantitative financial risk analysis. These include Monte Carlo simulation, expected monetary value analysis, decision tree analysis and sensitivity analysis. It should be noted that these analytical techniques are as a rule, applied to specific situations.

Qualitative risk analysis

Qualitative risk analysis is a method for assessing the significance of the identified financial risks and collates these risks in priority order for further analysis or direct mitigation. The RA or CRO would appraise each individual identified risk on two dimensions, namely, the probability of occurring and its impact.

The probability of occurring is basically deciding how uncertain the success of the financial activity is and the impact dimension measures the severity of the influence of the financial risk on the financial activity or/and entity. Hence, the process allows the identified financial risks to be sorted into the three categories of low, medium and high risk. The qualitative risk process consists of three phases:

1   Establish a financial risk probability ranking matrix as shown in Figure 7.3. The financial risk probability ranking matrix classifies risk into five scales.

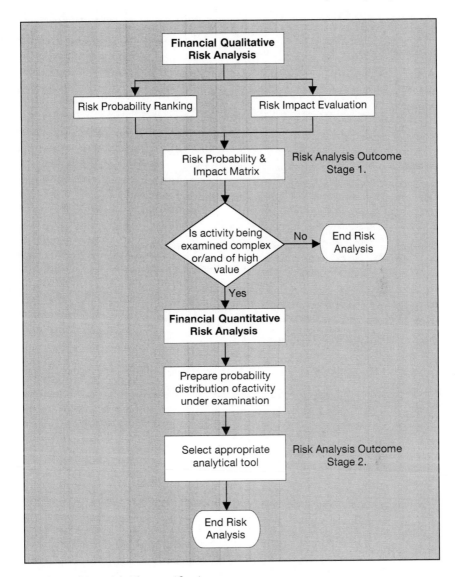

FIGURE 7.2 Financial risk quantification process

However, the probability of risk occurrence may be established to suit a particular financial activity or organisational environment. Moreover, an alternative ranking scale based on probabilities may also be applied.

2   Establish a financial risk impact matrix as shown in Figure 7.4. Let us assume that a Wholesaler provides merchandise to retailers on credit. Hence, in this type of industry and circumstance (i.e. credit rating of clients) this matrix would likely have two dimensions to match the financial activity objective of timely payment and avoiding payment default. The impact definition may be

Ranking Scale		Probability of Risk Occurrence	Alternative Scale
Very High	5	80-99%	.9 (.80 + .99 divide by 2 = .895)
High	4	60-79%	.7 (.60 + .79 divide by 2 = .695)
Medium	3	40-59%	.5 (.40 + .59 divide by 2 = .495)
Low	2	20-39%	.3 (.20 + .39 divide by 2 = .295)
Very Low	1	01-19%	.1 (.01 + .19 divide by 2 = .100)

FIGURE 7.3 Financial risk probability ranking matrix

Source: Adapted from Caltrans. (2003). *Project Risk Management Handbook* (1st edn). Sacramento, CA: Office of Project Management Process Improvement.

Financial Activity Goals	Risk Impact on Specific Financial Activity Goals				
	1 (Very Low)	2 (Low)	4 (Medium)	8 (High)	16 (Very High)
Timely Payment	Slight time increase	<15% increase in time	15-30% increase in time	31-50% increase in time	>50% increase in time
Payment Default	Highly unlikely	Unlikely	Vulnerable to changing conditions	Highly vulnerable to changing conditions	Expected default when payment is due

FIGURE 7.4 Financial risk impact evaluation matrix

Source: Adapted from Project Management Institute Standards Committee. (2004). *A Guide to the Project Management Body of Knowledge.* Upper Darby, PA: PMI.

established according to the particular requirements of the financial activity. In the example shown, the impact has five scales, with each scale being assigned the indicated value.

3   The financial risk probability ranking matrix (Figure 7.3) and the financial risk impact matrix (Figure 7.4) are combined in a two-dimensional matrix, that establishes whether each risk is low, medium or high as illustrated by Figure 7.5.

The contents of this matrix are calculated by multiplying the impact scale by the probability scale across all rows and columns. For instance, probability scale 5 (Row 1) times impact scale 1, 2, 4, 8 and 16 would give a value of 5, 10, 20, 40 and 80 respectively. Probability scale 4 (Row 2) times impact scale 1, 2, 4, 8 and 16 would give a value of 4, 8, 16, 32 and 64 respectively. This is conducted for each matrix row.

The following procedure is used to establish the three categories of low-risk, medium-risk and high-risk. The maximum value in the first column will establish

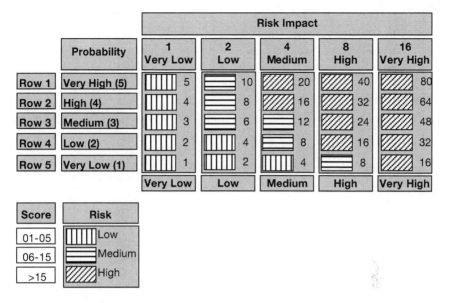

FIGURE 7.5 Financial risk probability and impact matrix

the maximum value for the low-risk category. Therefore, a score value of 5 and below is the low-risk category. The maximum value in the last column will establish the minimum value for the high-risk category. Therefore, a score value of 16 and above is the high-risk category. The remainder (what has not been allocated to the low and high risk category) are the medium-risk category.

This combined risk probability-impact matrix is applied by assessing a specific event. For example, a financial activity related to debtors is the event of 'late payment'. If the probability of this event occurring for a specific debtor, in the opinion of the RA, is very high but the impact is viewed as being low, then the risk is medium (score value of 10). Therefore, those events that have a score of 1 to 5 would be considered as low-risk, those with a score of 6 to 15 are viewed as medium-risk and a score greater than 16 would be classified as high-risk.

The above process provides a simple method for the Risk Analyst to classify a specific event according to the probability of occurrence and impact on the financial activity. The findings from this initial analysis may indicate if further investigation is warranted, such as, undertaking a quantitative risk analysis.

Quantitative risk analysis

Quantitative financial risk analysis is normally conducted when the financial activity being examined is complex or/and of substantial value or the qualitative risk analysis indicates that further detailed risk analysis is required. Quantitative financial risk analysis is a method for estimating the chance that a financial activity will achieve the established objectives. The risk identification process highlighted that financial risk management embraces a wide spectrum of financial activities and their associated risk. For instance, four major risk categories have been identified for most businesses (particularly those in the financial sector), including credit risk, market risk, operational risk and other risk types. Operational risks are the most misunderstood and challenging for the Risk Analyst to measure and assess, and are very suitable for simulation applications.

Furthermore, specialised simulation computer software is normally utilised to conduct this type of risk analysis. For instance, sophisticated artificial intelligence software may be applied for credit risk assessment, where a series of questions about the prospective debtor are to be answered and a diagnostic assessment of credit worthiness is made. However, spread sheet type software, such as EXCEL may also be used, as well as custom programmed systems that are designed for specific applications.

Quantitative risk analysis – Monte Carlo simulation

Quantitative risk analysis using Monte Carlo simulation applies statistical methods to simultaneously appraise the impact of numerous variables. The outcome of the analysis varies depending on the simulation objectives and model used. Simulation software provides a number of optional probability distributions that may be applied to the simulation model variables. These include the beta, triangular, uniform and normal distributions among others. Additionally, the input for these distributions may (but not necessarily) be based on a three parameter estimating method in which the estimate is represented by an optimistic, pessimistic and most likely value.

An issue that needs to be considered, before examining particular examples, is whether there is a distinction between risk and uncertainty. In practice, many business individuals tend to view risk and uncertainty as being the same. However, theorists make a distinction between the two terms. They view risk as being applied to circumstances where there is historical information to predict possible future outcomes. This implies that a particular situation has several possible outcomes, not just one outcome. On the other hand, they view uncertainty as being similar to risk with the exception that there is little historical data to predict the possible outcomes. Hence, the term '*uncertainty*' is applied to situations that are unique, where there is no previous experience. However, 'risk' is applied to situations where similar decisions have been previously made and that data is available so that the outcome from future analogous decisions may be predicted.

Unfortunately, many business decisions may be classified in the uncertainty category and therefore require a great deal of thought. Furthermore, it is important for decision makers to consider, which factors are not under their control and that may occur under different activity options. The uncontrollable factors are normally referred to as '*events*'. Hence, a probability is the possibility that an event will occur and is expressed as a value between 0 and 1 (or as a percentage between 0 per cent and 100 per cent). Therefore, the higher the value, there is a greater chance that the event will occur. In other words, a probability of 0.6 (or 60 per cent) means that the event is expected to occur six times out of ten. A probability distribution is basically a list of all the possible outcomes for a specific event and its associated probability of occurring.

Furthermore, there are probabilities that are computed objectively, through observation and measurement, such as, tossing a coin a hundred times and documenting the number of heads and tails. However, there are also subjective probabilities that are purely based on personal intuition. It is unlikely, with these types of probabilities, that two individuals will assign the same probability to a specific outcome. Hence, care should be used when applying subjective probabilities, since they are likely to result in a high degree of error. Objective probabilities are based on a scientific method of gathering data and provide a justification for the likely outcome.

Objective probabilities and their associated probability distribution can be of two types, namely, 'continuous' and 'discrete' probability distributions. If a variable can have any value between two specified values, it will generate a continuous distribution; otherwise, it will generate a discrete distribution. Unlike a discrete probability distribution, a continuous probability distribution cannot be expressed in tabular form. A continuous probability distribution is described by an equation or formula, which is often referred to as a probability density function. Examples of probability density functions are beta, triangular, uniform and normal distributions. Both 'continuous' and 'discrete' probability distributions are applicable in a Monte Carlo simulation method. However, 'discrete' probability distributions are more commonly applicable when dealing with expected monetary value analysis, which will be discussed later.

Example one: quantitative risk analysis – Monte Carlo simulation

The application of quantitative risk analysis using Monte Carlo simulation is best illustrated by an example. The following simulation example was developed by the author for a government energy entity, which had as one of its functions, the responsibility to trade crude oil (and its by-products) on the spot market. The simulation model was designed to be executed under two operational modes. The first operational approach was '*off-line*' simulation mode, using historical databases to estimate the individual probability distribution of the relevant simulation variables, and executing the simulation model based on these probability distributions. The second operational approach was '*real-time*' mode, using database information that was directly available at that moment in time. The 'real-time' operational mode provided the highest level of model accuracy, even though several variables still required an approximation of their respective probability distribution. The 'real-time' mode provided accurate results immediately and was used as the primary spot market crude oil procurement decision tool. The time factor for the 'real-time' mode was very important because the entity was competing against other entities exploiting spot market opportunities.

The simulation model for this example, as shown at Figure 7.6, has been simplified to facilitate explanation. The simulation model illustrates the integration of: (a) the parameters to execute the simulation model (simulation input parameters); (b) simulation databases, using 'real-time' data or historical probability distributions depending on the operational mode; and (c) simulation output results to enable the user to make an immediate decision or simulated decision depending on the operational mode.

A basic description of the various model variables is warranted at this stage to help the reader envisage the simulation model. The product demand data is a historical database of the local consumption of each crude oil by-product. This is a fairly static database which is easily converted into a cumulative probability distribution to predict local demand over a 12-month period. Like most cumulative probability distributions a random generator would sample the distribution for the demand for the listed by-products. The crude types and product yields database is

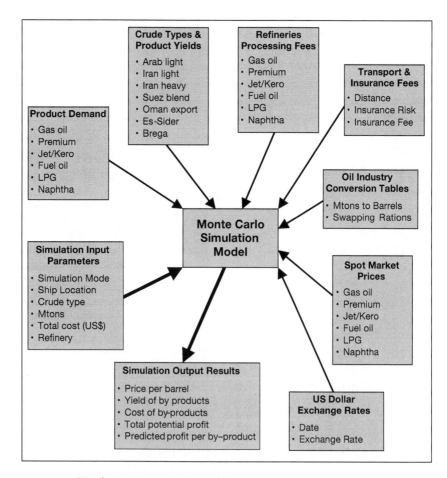

FIGURE 7.6 Simulation Monte Carlo model: spot market crude oil trade

very static. This database accurately indicates the production potential for each by-product, including production refinery losses. For example, the oil crude type regarding 'Arab Light' when refined usually produces: Gas oil, 22.1 per cent; Premium, 21.5 per cent; Jet/Kero, 9.4 per cent; Fuel oil, 33.9 per cent; LPG, 2.3 per cent; Naphtha, 3.4 per cent; and refinery losses, 7.4 per cent, totalling 100 per cent. Each crude type has its own individual by-product production percentages.

The refineries processing fees database contains the individual processing fee for each crude type per by-product. This is also a fairly static database. The transport and insurance fees database is relatively dynamic, with the level of fees being dependent on the geographical region (i.e. recognised trouble spots). Both of these databases are easily converted into a cumulative probability distribution to predict current costs and like similar applications, a random generator would sample the distribution for the likely refinery processing fee, and transport and insurance costs.

The oil industry conversion database is fairly static and provides the conversion ratios for converting Mtons to barrels (50 Mtons = 365 barrels) and the swap ratios (e.g. 1 Mton of naphtha may equal 0.25 Mtons of petroleum). This database is required because the local market may have a higher demand for a particular by-product, thus one may convert a low demand by-product for a higher demand by-product. However, this may affect profitability depending on the spot market prices for the by-products.

The spot market prices for the by-products are readily available and are very dynamic in nature. Hence, this database is always updated in 'real-time' mode. The behaviour of this database is dependent on the demand and supply of the by-products, and consists of a historical database with the prices for each crude oil by-product. This database is simply converted into a cumulative probability distribution to predict prices over a short-term period, say 12 weeks. The US dollar exchange rates database is also very dynamic, at times changing by the hour and thus requires constant and regular updating.

It should be noted that when the simulation model in executed in 'real-time' mode, the databases related to transport and insurance fees, crude oil by-products spot market prices and the US dollar exchange rates are directly accessed and contain up to the minute accurate data. The other databases are converted into cumulative probability distributions that are accessed by random number generators to predict the value of each variable in question. When the simulation model is executed in 'off-line' simulation mode, the databases with the exception of the crude type and product yields and the oil industry conversion tables are converted into cumulative probability distributions, which are accessed by random number generators to predict the value of each variable in question.

To execute the simulation model the user is required to input a number of simulation parameters, these include, the simulation mode; geographical location of the crude oil shipment that is up for sale on the spot market; crude oil type; the amount of crude oil available for sale in Mtons; total price of the shipment in US dollars; and the refinery that the crude oil is to be processed at. Once all the simulation input parameters are provided to the simulation model, the computer software using the data from various databases will compute the following: price per barrel; yield of crude oil by-products; the cost of the by-products; total predicted profit for shipment; predicted profit per crude oil by-product. This takes place instantly (a few seconds at the most) and provides the decision maker with the information to decide whether to bid for the crude oil shipment on the spot market.

Example two: quantitative risk analysis – Monte Carlo simulation

The following example illustrates how one may conduct a Monte Carlo simulation process using 'discrete' probability distributions. Later we will consider the same example but apply the 'expected monetary value analysis' approach, and therefore be in a position to compare the results under both methods.

Rothwell plc operates from a European Union country and is entering into a contract with a foreign firm estimated to be valued at €500,000. Management is considering whether the contract should be in euro (€); US dollar (USD); Swiss franc (CHF); Canadian dollar (CAD); or Australian dollar (AUD). The exchange rates against the euro at the time of signing the contact were 1.3281; 1.2311; 1.3684; 1.3777 respectively for the USD; CHF; CAD; or AUD. The contract delivery and payment is due in six months' time. Table 7.1 shows the available information regarding the average yearly exchange rates for the relevant currencies over the past 15 years published by the European Central Bank. This information is available to the management as an aid in making its decision.

Management have requested the Risk Analyst to recommend the foreign currency that should support the contract. After considering the information available, the Risk Analyst has decided that a Monte Carlo simulation method should be applied as a basis for the decision. Furthermore, the raw data does not follow a specific formula or equation and hence a 'discrete' probability distribution as distinct from a 'continuous' probability distribution is applicable.

The first step in a Monte Carlo simulation method is to design the simulation model. The simulation model is shown at Figure 7.7. As a general rule, the simulation model needs to be realistic so that it may provide accurate results.

Figure 7.7 illustrates a three stage process, namely, establishing the cumulative probability distribution for each relevant currency; providing simulation results for each individual currency by generating a random number between 0 and 1, and applying this random number to accessing the cumulative probability distribution, to give the indicated simulation results for that currency; and providing a combined simulation result with the objective of giving the risk ranking of each currency in comparison with each other. The simulation process may be conducted as many times as required by the Risk Analyst. In this case, the simulation model results are based on 100 simulation runs. Normally, the higher the number of simulation runs, the higher the accuracy.

The first stage process is to analyse the raw currency data provided and to convert this data into a cumulative probability distribution for each relevant currency. Basically, this process creates a table that consists of the following data items: the

TABLE 7.1 European Central Bank – average exchange rates against the euro

Year	US Dollar	Swiss Franc	Canadian Dollar	Australian Dollar
1999	1.0658	1.6003	1.5840	1.6523
2000	0.9236	1.5579	1.3706	1.5889
2001	0.8956	1.5105	1.3864	1.7319
2002	0.9456	1.4670	1.4838	1.7376
2003	1.1312	1.5212	1.5817	1.7379
2004	1.2439	1.5438	1.6167	1.6905
2005	1.2441	1.5483	1.5087	1.6320
2006	1.2556	1.5729	1.4237	1.6668
2007	1.3705	1.6427	1.4678	1.6348
2008	1.4708	1.5874	1.5594	1.7416
2009	1.3948	1.5100	1.5850	1.7727
2010	1.3257	1.3803	1.3651	1.4423
2011	1.3920	1.2326	1.3761	1.3484
2012	1.2848	1.2053	1.2842	1.2407
2013	1.3281	1.2311	1.3684	1.3777

probability range (start and end) and the likely gain/loss that is associated with this probability range.

To achieve the first stage process it is necessary to establish the probability distributions for the relevant variables. The variables being the USD; CHF; CAD; and AUD exchange rates against the euro. The data in Table 7.1 consists of several discrete exchange rate values. Therefore, the probability distribution that will be established is a 'discrete' probability distribution. However, if a detailed analysis of the data revealed that the exchange rates followed a mathematical pattern, such as, a 'normal distribution', then we would be able to have a 'continuous' distribution.

The issue is: How is a 'discrete' probability distribution established? This is accomplished by the following procedure:

1   Sort each individual variable (e.g. USD exchange rates) from smallest to largest. For example, if the USD data is sorted from smallest to largest, the following is obtained: 0.8956; 0.9236; 0.9456; 1.0658; 1.1312; 1.2439; 1.2441; 1.2556; 1.2848; 1.3257; 1.3281; 1.3705; 1.3920; 1.3948; 1.4708.
2   Calculate the range for the selected data by subtracting the smallest from the largest number of the sorted data. For example, using the sorted data for the USD exchange rates, the range is calculated by taking 1.4708 (that is the largest number) subtracting 0.8956 (that is the smallest number) from it, to give a result of 0.5752.

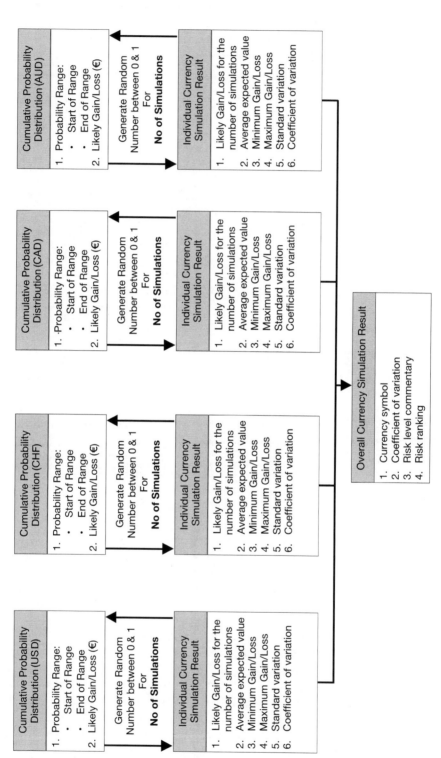

FIGURE 7.7 Monte Carlo simulation model: Rothwell plc foreign currency

3   Establish the number of required intervals. In this example the amount of data is limited to 15 per exchange rate data set, with a single data item representing one year. However, if the exchange rates available were monthly, over a 15-year period, the data items would amount to 180 (i.e. 12 months times 15 years) for each exchange rate data series. In situations where the data items within a data series are relatively large, the number of required intervals may be increased, and thus increasing the accuracy of the probability distribution. In this example having five intervals is considered sufficient (but this is a subjective judgement).

4   Calculate the specific data interval for the data set. This is calculated by taking the computed range and dividing it by the number of intervals. Taking the USD data set, the data range is 0.5752 (from step 2) and the number of required intervals is 5 (from step 3). Hence, the data interval is equal to 0.1150 (i.e. $0.5752 \div 5 = 0.1150$).

5   Calculate the valid range for each of the five intervals using the computed interval. This is achieved by starting with the smallest exchange rate within a data set and adding the calculated interval to it. This provides the end range number for that particular interval. The next interval range is obtained by using the end range number of the previous interval as the start range number and repeating the computation until the largest number within the data set is obtained. Hence, taking the USD data set, the valid range for the five intervals are as follows:

Interval-1 = 0.8956 + 0.1150 = 1.0107   Range is 0.8956 to 1.0107
Interval-2 = 1.0107 + 0.1150 = 1.1257   Range is 1.0107 to 1.1257
Interval-3 = 1.1257 + 0.1150 = 1.2407   Range is 1.1257 to 1.2407
Interval-4 = 1.2407 + 0.1150 = 1.3557   Range is 1.2407 to 1.3557
Interval-5 = 1.3557 + 0.1150 = 1.4708   Range is 1.3557 to 1.4708

Note that 1.4708 is the largest number for the USD exchange rate series.

6   Calculate the average value (or mid-point) within each of the calculated interval range. Taking the USD exchange rate intervals, the average value within each of the calculated interval range would be:

Interval-1: Range is 0.8956 to 1.0107   Average = (0.8956 + 1.0107) ÷ 2
Interval-2: Range is 1.0107 to 1.1257   Average = 1.0682
Interval-3: Range is 1.1257 to 1.2407   Average = 1.1832
Interval-4: Range is 1.2407 to 1.3557   Average = 1.2982
Interval-5: Range is 1.3557 to 1.4708   Average = 1.4132

7   Calculate the frequency of occurrence of a particular data set within each interval range. Taking the sorted USD exchange data set of 0.8956; 0.9236; 0.9456; 1.0658; 1.1312; 1.2439; 1.2441; 1.2556; 1.2848; 1.3257; 1.3281; 1.3705; 1.3920; 1.3948; 1.4708, examine the frequency of numbers that fit within each interval range. The resulting frequencies are as follows:

Interval-1: Range 0.8956 to 1.0107	0.8956	Frequency: 3
	0.9236	
	0.9456	
Interval-2: Range 1.0107 to 1.1257	1.0658	Frequency: 1
Interval-3: Range 1.1257 to 1.2407	1.1312	Frequency: 1
Interval-4: Range 1.2407 to 1.3557	1.2439	Frequency: 6
	1.2441	
	1.2556	
	1.2848	
	1.3257	
	1.3281	
Interval-5: Range 1.3557 to 1.4708	1.3705	Frequency: 4
	1.3920	
	1.3948	
	1.4708	

8 Calculate the probability of a particular data set within each interval range. This is computed by dividing each calculated frequency by the total number of data points in the data set. The total number of data points in each data set is 15. Hence, taking the USD exchange rates data set the probabilities are:

- $3 \div 15 = 0.20$;
- $1 \div 15 = 0.07$;
- $1 \div 15 = 0.07$;
- $6 \div 15 = 0.40$;
- $4 \div 15 = 0.26$.

The summation of the calculated probabilities must approximately add up to 1 (i.e. $0.20 + 0.07 + 0.07 + 0.40 + 0.26 = 1.0$).

9 Finally, calculate the expected outcome. In this case, this is achieved by applying the average currency rate for each interval to the initial contract value (to give the contract value at the contract payment time) and comparing this to the contract value at the time of signing the contract by applying the exchange rate when the contract was signed. The difference is the expected gain or loss. This gain or loss is converted to the original euro currency value. Hence, taking the USD data set the following calculations are carried out:

a   USD contract value at the time of signing the contract: 1.3281 (initial exchange rate) times €500,000 (contract value) = $664,050;

b   For each data set interval, apply the average exchange rate to the contract value:

- $0.9531 \times$ €500,000 = $476,571;
- $1.0682 \times$ €500,000 = $534,084;
- $1.1832 \times$ €500,000 = $591,596;
- $1.2982 \times$ €500,000 = $649,109;
- $1.4132 \times$ €500,000 = $706,621.

c   Compare each calculation at (b) with that of (a) to computed the expected gain/loss:

- $664,050 − $476,571 = -$187,479;
- $664,050 − $534,084 = -$129,966;
- $664,050 − $591,596 = -$72,454;
- $664,050 − $649,109 = -$14,941;
- $664,050 − $706,621 = $42,571.

d   Convert the calculated gain/loss back to euro so that we are able to compare the different national currencies:

- -$187,479 ÷ 0.9531 = -€196,696;
- -$129,966 ÷ 1.0682 = -€121,672;
- -$72,454 ÷ 1.1832 = -€61,236;
- -$14,941 ÷ 1.2982 = -€11,509;
- $42,571 ÷ 1.4132 = €30,123.

The procedure as described above, to obtain a probability distribution for the USD exchange rates against the euro, is shown at Figure 7.8.

Once the probability distribution (including the other various computations) is obtained, it is now necessary to establish the cumulative probability distribution so that the probability range (start and end) may be calculated. Taking the USD, at this point we know the probability (Pr.) of attaining a particular euro gain/loss:

- Pr. 0.200 for -€196,696;
- Pr. 0.067 for -€121,672;
- Pr. 0.067 for -€61,236;
- Pr. 0.400 for -€11,509;
- Pr. 0.267 for € 30,123.

Note that the summation of the probabilities is (approximately) 1.000. The cumulative probability distribution is obtained by commencing with the first probability and adding the next probability until the end of the list as follows:

- 0.200;
- 0.200 + 0.067 = 0.267;
- 0.267 + 0.067 = 0.333;
- 0.333 + 0.400 = 0.733;
- 0.733 + 0.267 = 1.00.

Hence, the cumulative distribution is: 0.200; 0.267; 0.333; 0.733; and 1.000. This provides the basis for probability range (start and end); hence the probability ranges associated with each euro gain/loss are as follows:

- Pr. 0 to 0.2000 = -€196,696;
- Pr. 0.2001 to 0.2667 = -€121,672;

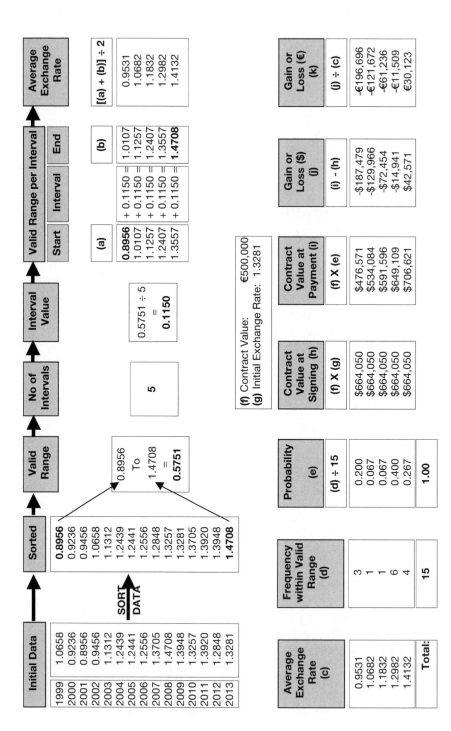

FIGURE 7.8 Probability distribution process using US dollar exchange rates

- Pr. 0.2668 to 0.3333 = –€61,236;
- Pr. 0.3334 to 0.7333 = –€11,509;
- Pr. 0.7334 to 1.0000 = € 30,123.

The resultant probability distribution (including the various computations) for the USD exchange rates against the euro is shown at Table 7.2. The above process is carried out for each of the currencies in question.

The second stage process is to provide the simulation results for each individual currency by generating a random number between 0 and 1, and applying this random number to accessing the probability ranges and associated euro gain/loss, thus giving the indicated simulation results for that currency. The simulation results for the 100 simulation runs for the USD currency data are shown at Table 7.3. The first and second stage processes would be repeated for each currency variable.

The final (third) stage process is to provide a combined simulation result with the objective of giving the risk ranking of each currency in comparison with each other. The combined simulation results and their relationship with the full simulation model are shown at Figure 7.9.

TABLE 7.2 Probability distribution – US dollar exchange rates against euro

Exchange Rates					Contract	Expected	Expected
Valid Range		Ave.			Value at	Gain/Loss	Gain/Loss
Start	End	Rate	Frequency	Probability	Payment	($)	(€)
0.8956	1.0107	0.9531	3	0.200	$476,571	-$187,479	-196,696
1.0107	1.1257	1.0682	1	0.067	$534,084	-$129,966	-121,672
1.1257	1.2407	1.1832	1	0.067	$591,596	-$72,454	-61,236
1.2407	1.3557	1.2982	6	0.400	$649,109	-$14,941	-11,509
1.3557	1.4708	1.4132	4	0.267	$706,621	$42,571	30,123
		Total:	15	1.00			

Gain/Loss	Probability	Cumulative	Probability Range	
(in Euro)		Probability	Start	End
-196,696	0.200	0.200	0	0.2000
-121,672	0.067	0.267	0.2001	0.2667
-61,236	0.067	0.333	0.2668	0.3333
-11,509	0.400	0.733	0.3334	0.7333
30,123	0.267	1.000	0.7334	1.0000
Total:	1.000			

TABLE 7.3 Simulation results for individual currencies – US dollar

Run No.	Random Number	Simulated Gain/Loss	Run No.	Random Number	Simulated Gain/Loss	Run No.	Random Number	Simulated Gain/Loss
1	0.5650	-11,509	34	0.7562	30,123	67	0.9877	30,123
2	0.1518	-196,696	35	0.1326	-196,696	68	0.2303	-121,672
3	0.9531	30,123	36	0.8211	30,123	69	0.4808	-11,509
4	0.6510	-11,509	37	0.7770	30,123	70	0.4998	-11,509
5	0.4094	-11,509	38	0.1272	-196,696	71	0.0609	-196,696
6	0.6495	-11,509	39	0.0027	-196,696	72	0.1680	-196,696
7	0.3346	-11,509	40	0.9041	30,123	73	0.9986	30,123
8	0.2701	-61,236	41	0.8660	30,123	74	0.8339	30,123
9	0.5824	-11,509	42	0.2944	-61,236	75	0.0123	-196,696
10	0.4927	-11,509	43	0.0711	-196,696	76	0.9061	30,123
11	0.4338	-11,509	44	0.2873	-61,236	77	0.5816	-11,509
12	0.6028	-11,509	45	0.3891	-11,509	78	0.3434	-11,509
13	0.2204	-121,672	46	0.7808	30,123	79	0.0077	-196,696
14	0.1048	-196,696	47	0.8673	30,123	80	0.7370	30,123
15	0.6163	-11,509	48	0.7169	-11,509	81	0.1937	-196,696
16	0.7081	-11,509	49	0.4261	-11,509	82	0.7054	-11,509
17	0.9532	30,123	50	0.2909	-61,236	83	0.1897	-196,696
18	0.3174	-61,236	51	0.5844	-11,509	84	0.5086	-11,509
19	0.2672	-61,236	52	0.8654	30,123	85	0.1290	-196,696
20	0.2516	-121,672	53	0.6550	-11,509	86	0.2520	-121,672
21	0.4435	-11,509	54	0.9022	30,123	87	0.8892	30,123
22	0.2937	-61,236	55	0.2677	-61,236	88	0.9736	30,123
23	0.5562	-11,509	56	0.9669	30,123	89	0.0764	-196,696
24	0.0761	-196,696	57	0.0198	-196,696	90	0.0949	-196,696
25	0.2989	-61,236	58	0.1365	-196,696	91	0.9557	30,123
26	0.8517	30,123	59	0.9957	30,123	92	0.5069	-11,509
27	0.2160	-121,672	60	0.7708	30,123	93	0.4786	-11,509
28	0.8370	30,123	61	0.2129	-121,672	94	0.7126	-11,509
29	0.9164	30,123	62	0.5914	-11,509	95	0.1828	-196,696
30	0.5006	-11,509	63	0.0322	-196,696	96	0.8183	30,123
31	0.1678	-196,696	64	0.4221	-11,509	97	0.7639	30,123
32	0.5545	-11,509	65	0.8197	30,123	98	0.2765	-61,236
33	0.1633	-196,696	66	0.1888	-196,696	99	0.8645	30,123
						100	0.5917	-11,509

Simulation Results Summary	
Ave. Expected Value:	**-€53,611**
Minimum value:	-€196,696
Maximum value:	€30,123
Standard Deviation:	±87,578
Coefficient of variation:	-1.63

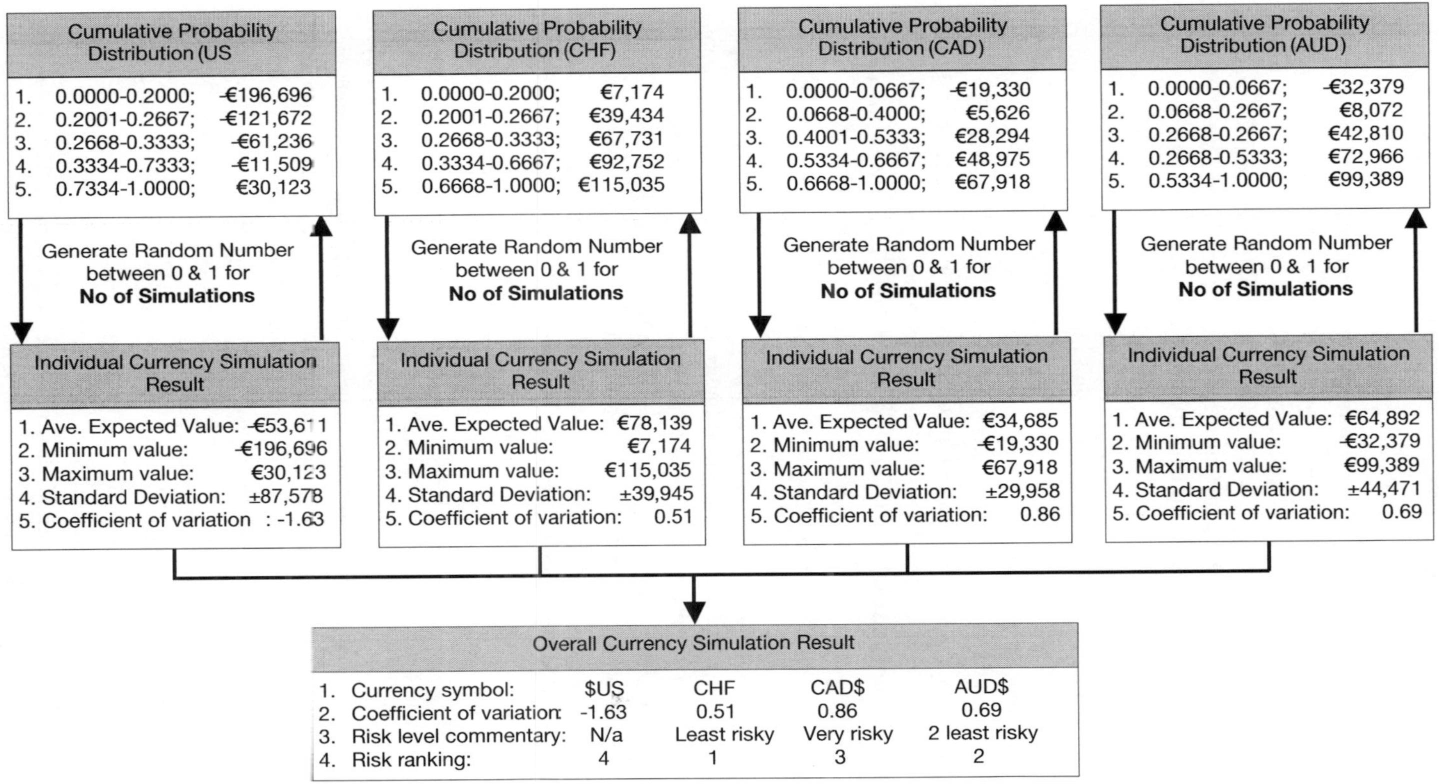

FIGURE 7.9 Simulation results for combined simulation – risk ranking

Cumulative Probability Distribution (US)

1.	0.0000-0.2000;	€196,696
2.	0.2001-0.2667;	€121,672
3.	0.2668-0.3333;	€61,236
4.	0.3334-0.7333;	€11,509
5.	0.7334-1.0000;	€30,123

Generate Random Number between 0 & 1 for No of Simulations

Individual Currency Simulation Result

1. Ave. Expected Value: -€53,611
2. Minimum value: -€196,696
3. Maximum value: €30,123
4. Standard Deviation: ±87,578
5. Coefficient of variation : -1.63

Cumulative Probability Distribution (CHF)

1.	0.0000-0.2000;	€7,174
2.	0.2001-0.2667;	€39,434
3.	0.2668-0.3333;	€67,731
4.	0.3334-0.6667;	€92,752
5.	0.6668-1.0000;	€115,035

Generate Random Number between 0 & 1 for No of Simulations

Individual Currency Simulation Result

1. Ave. Expected Value: €78,139
2. Minimum value: €7,174
3. Maximum value: €115,035
4. Standard Deviation: ±39,945
5. Coefficient of variation: 0.51

Cumulative Probability Distribution (CAD)

1.	0.0000-0.0667;	-€19,330
2.	0.0668-0.4000;	€5,626
3.	0.4001-0.5333;	€28,294
4.	0.5334-0.6667;	€48,975
5.	0.6668-1.0000;	€67,918

Generate Random Number between 0 & 1 for No of Simulations

Individual Currency Simulation Result

1. Ave. Expected Value: €34,685
2. Minimum value: -€19,330
3. Maximum value: €67,918
4. Standard Deviation: ±29,958
5. Coefficient of variation: 0.86

Cumulative Probability Distribution (AUD)

1.	0.0000-0.0667;	-€32,379
2.	0.0668-0.2667;	€8,072
3.	0.2668-0.2667;	€42,810
4.	0.2668-0.5333;	€72,966
5.	0.5334-1.0000;	€99,389

Generate Random Number between 0 & 1 for No of Simulations

Individual Currency Simulation Result

1. Ave. Expected Value: €64,892
2. Minimum value: -€32,379
3. Maximum value: €99,389
4. Standard Deviation: ±44,471
5. Coefficient of variation: 0.69

Overall Currency Simulation Result

	$US	CHF	CAD$	AUD$
1. Currency symbol:				
2. Coefficient of variation:	-1.63	0.51	0.86	0.69
3. Risk level commentary:	N/a	Least risky	Very risky	2 least risky
4. Risk ranking:	4	1	3	2

Concluding remarks: quantitative risk analysis – Monte Carlo simulation

There are two major concerns with quantitative financial risk analysis using Monte Carlo simulation, namely, the reliability and realism of the simulation model design and the robustness of the three parameter estimates and respective probability distributions selected for the various variables (if applicable). The simulation model must epitomise an accurate representation of the real world for the situation being examined. Furthermore, the mathematical probability distributions selected must approximate as much as possible the true and accurate behaviour of the variables that are included in the model.

The first concern related to the simulation model design reliability requires a careful analysis of the model outcomes and the respective processes to achieve them. Hence, the simulation model logic needs to be discussed with the relevant stakeholders who understand the process and are experts in their respective fields. The second concern is related to the realism of the probability distributions selected. Realism is achieved by collating and analysing relevant and accurate data. Data must be free from personal and institutional biases. Hence, this frequently requires focused group discussions with specialists in the field being examined.

The above discussion regarding quantitative financial risk analysis using the Monte Carlo simulation method revealed that there are three major processes, namely, the simulation model design; data gathering; and the simulation execution process. The simulation model design is highly dependent on the concern being investigated and requires experts who understand the specific phenomena being modelled. Data gathering is generally based on intensive and focused interviews. The interview process is conducted by a Risk Analyst or Risk Facilitator to a focus group of employees who possess expert knowledge of the particular area of concern. The Risk Facilitator must isolate motivational and cognitive bias so that the true risks are identified and assessed.

Motivational bias occurs when individuals or organisations have the aim of routing the inputs and resultant conclusions on a particular track. At times, participants tend to understate the risk so that a particular circumstance looks more feasible than it actually is. This practice is intentional and is very common in organisations. Hence the Risk Facilitator needs to be aware of any biased data. Cognitive bias is unintentional and usually results in underestimating the maximum ranges of the pessimistic and optimistic estimates or misdiagnosing the probability distribution type. Therefore, the Risk Facilitator must continuously question the data during the interview process to obtain more realistic estimate values. For instance, one needs to diagnose the data to see if it approximates a particular mathematical distribution. Statistical or mathematical software packages are usually used to assess the approximation of the data to a particular distribution or one needs to establish a '*discrete*' probability distribution.

Model simulation may be carried out using three basic methods. The first method utilises simulation tools that are add-ons to Excel spreadsheets for financial risk analysis, using a selection of probability distributions. The second method is the use of specific financial modelling simulation tools that permit the design of complex models to conduct financial risk analysis. The third method is to engage computer programmers to construct custom made software for a specific simulation model application. The second method is the most flexible and permits a wide variety of situations to be simulated.

Quantitative risk analysis – expected monetary value analysis

There are two common characteristics regarding business undertakings, namely, that financial decisions are continually being made; and when a decision is made, there is a risk associated with its financial outcome. Expected monetary value analysis is typically based on '*discrete*' probability distributions for the relevant variables and their associated payout (gain/loss). Unlike the Monte Carlo simulation approach, there is no random number generation to access the probability distribution to obtain the associated payout. The expected monetary value approach provides an approximate value of the outcome for an event. In other words, expected monetary value analysis may be viewed as being an average of the best and worst-case scenarios. It not only considers the monetary value assigned to each outcome but also for the likelihood of that outcome occurring. These concepts are best illustrated through an example.

Example one: quantitative risk analysis – expected monetary value analysis

Let us consider the Rothwell plc example that was analysed using the Monte Carlo simulation approach. As you may recall, Rothwell plc is entering into a contract with a foreign firm estimated to be valued at €500,000. Management is considering whether the contract should be in euro; USD; CHF; CAD; or AUD. The exchange rates against the euro at the time of signing the contact were 1.3281; 1.2311; 1.3684; 1.3777 respectively for the USD; CHF; CAD; or AUD. The contract delivery and payment is due in six months' time. Table 7.1 shows the available information regarding the average yearly exchange rates for the relevant currencies over the past 15 years published by the European Central Bank. This information is available to the management as an aid in making its decision.

The first step is similar to the Monte Carlo simulation method. We need to establish the probability distributions for the relevant variables. The variables being the USD; CHF; CAD; and AUD exchange rates against the euro. As we have already seen, the data at Table 7.1 consists of a number of discrete exchange rate values. Therefore, the probability distribution that will be established is a '*discrete*' probability distribution. The method to establish a '*discrete*' probability distribution has already been described previously.

The second step is to apply the calculated probability distributions for the relevant variables to compute the expected monetary value. However, with the expected monetary value method there is no need to determine the cumulative probability distribution and associated probability start/end range. What is required is the computation of the expected outcome (gain/loss) for each probability. The expected outcome is simply the multiplication of the gain/loss and its associated probability. Table 7.4 illustrates both steps applying the USD currency data from Table 7.1. The top portion of Table 7.4 demonstrates how the '*discrete*' probability distribution is established and the bottom portion of Table 7.4 shows the required computations to calculate the expected monetary value and the coefficient of variation.

The coefficient of variation is computed because it is not possible to compare the standard deviations of two probability distributions with different expected values. Hence, the scale effect can be removed by calculating the coefficient of variation, which normalises the standard deviation by dividing it by the expected

TABLE 7.4 Probability distribution and associated computations – USD data

Exchange Rates					Contract	Expected	Expected
Valid Range		Ave.			Value at	Gain/Loss	Gain/Loss
Start	End	Rate	Frequency	Probability	Payment	($)	(€)
0.8956	1.0107	0.9531	3	0.200	$476,571	-$187,479	-196,696
1.0107	1.1257	1.0682	1	0.067	$534,084	-$129,966	-121,672
1.1257	1.2407	1.1832	1	0.067	$591,596	-$72,454	-61,236
1.2407	1.3557	1.2982	6	0.400	$649,109	-$14,941	-11,509
1.3557	1.4708	1.4132	4	0.267	$706,621	$42,571	30,123
		Total:	15	1.00			

$$\sigma = \sqrt{\sum_{x=1}^{n} (A_x - \bar{A})^2 P_x}$$

Where:
σ = Standard Deviation
A_x = Gain/Loss observations
$\bar{A}$ = Expected or mean value
P_x = Probability of outcomes
n = Total number of possibilities

A_x	P_x	$A_x \times P_x$	$A_x - \bar{A}$	$(A_x - \bar{A})^2$	$[(A_x - \bar{A})^2]P_x$
Gain/Loss (€)	Probability	Expected Outcome	Deviation from Expected Value	Deviation Squared	Weighted Value
-196,696	0.200	-39,339	-148,592	22,079,565,572	4,415,913,114
-121,672	0.067	-8,111	-73,569	5,412,329,365	360,821,958
-61,236	0.067	-4,082	-13,132	172,451,305	11,496,754
-11,509	0.400	-4,604	36,595	1,339,176,594	535,670,638
30,123	0.267	8,033	78,227	6,119,458,256	1,631,855,535
Expected Value ($\bar{A}$):	-48,104			Total:	6,955,757,998

Std. Deviation (σ): ±83,401

Coefficient of Variation ($\sigma \div \bar{A}$): -1.73

value. This will also enable the risk ranking to be established. Therefore, the coefficient of variation is used to compare the degree of variation from one data series to another, even if the means are drastically different from each other. The coefficient of variation allows you to determine how much volatility (risk) that is being assumed in comparison to the amount of return that is expected. In other words, the lower the ratio of standard deviation to mean return, the better is risk-return. Furthermore, if the expected value in the denominator of the calculation is negative or zero, the ratio will not make sense. Hence, in the example, the degree of risk applicable to the USD cannot be determined and the CAD is very risky. The CHF followed by AUD, carry the least risk.

The third step, which is similar to the Monte Carlo simulation approach, provides a combined simulation result with the objective of giving the risk ranking of each currency in comparison with each other. The combined simulation results and their relationship with the full simulation model are shown at Figure 7.10.

Concluding remarks: quantitative risk analysis – expected monetary value

There are two major concerns with quantitative financial risk analysis using expected monetary value, namely, the subjective judgement in determining the number of probability intervals, thus limiting the accuracy; and its limited applicability regarding having a singular variable type.

The first concern may be addressed by increasing the number of probability intervals to increase the accuracy of the calculations. However, deciding the number of probability intervals would still be subjective, but a reasonable number of probability intervals enhance the accuracy of the model.

The second concern is more difficult to address. With Monte Carlo simulation models, numerous variables and various variable types are permitted. In fact, it is recognised that this approach allows unlimited number of variables and variable types. The major limitation when having unlimited number of variables and variable types is complexity. In other words, the simulation model may become unmanageable. Having said this however, the Risk Analyst may build very complex simulation models. The expected monetary value approach will allow variables of the same type. For instance, in the previous example, four foreign currencies were included in the model. The model could have included all the foreign currencies, but only a single variable type (currencies) is permitted. Therefore, the expected monetary value approach (by itself) can only handle very simple, one variable type applications. However, if used in conjunction with the '*decision trees*' method, very complex models may be designed and executed.

Quantitative risk analysis – decision trees

Decision tree analysis provides a way of presenting a balanced view of the risks and pay-outs associated with each possible alternative strategy. Decision tree analysis

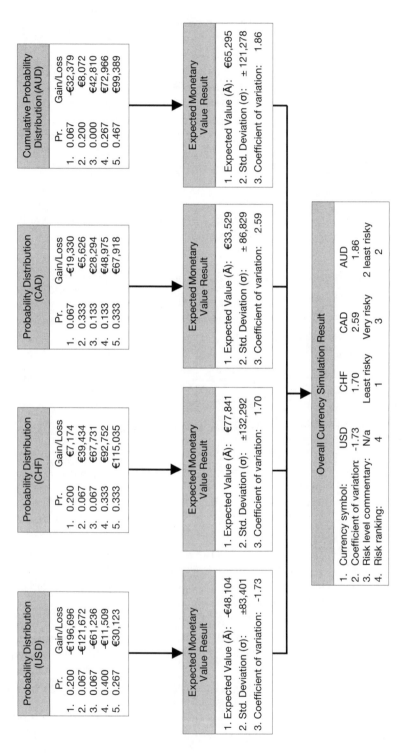

FIGURE 7.10 Expected monetary value combined results – risk ranking

may be based on the utilisation of the expected monetary value approach utilising *'discrete'* probability distribution function. However, sophisticated decision tree computer software is available that permits the application of a variety of *'continuous'* probability distribution functions, such as, normal, triangular and gamma distributions among many others.

There are a number of rules that must be adhered to, when applying the decision trees method. The following basic example has the objective of explaining these rules. Once, the basic principles are explained, a more complex example will be provided.

Assume that Sinclair Ltd has at its disposal $50,000 surplus cash that may be invested. However, any investment undertaken must not exceed 12 months because there are plans in the pipeline that require the use of the available capital within 12 months. Furthermore, there is a 0.15, 0.50, and 0.35 probability that the investment capital will be required in 3, 6 and 12 months respectively. After considering the matter, the Chief Financial Officer has itemised three options. These options include: (a) to keep the cash at bank at 1 per cent interest rate; (b) investing in fixed term deposits with a bank for 12 months with the probability of 0.3, 0.4 and 0.3 that the applicable interest rates will be 3 per cent, 3.5 per cent and 4 per cent respectively; and (c) purchasing 4.5 per cent government bonds on the stock market, maturing in 2030, and reselling them when the cash is needed. With the fixed term deposits option, the bank will permit the entity to borrow at 3.25 per cent interest should it need the investment capital before the 12-month maturity date.

With the government bond option, which originally cost $100 per bond, the bond's financial behaviour is as follows: a 0.05, 0.10, 0.25, 0.25, 0.15 and 0.20 probability of the bond price being $95, $96, $98, $104, $105 and $102, respectively. The interest on the bonds is paid annually to the bearer of the bonds. Further assume that the interest earned by the bonds was paid when Sinclair Ltd was not the bond bearer. The broker handling the government bond is paid a fixed fee of $250. The Chief Financial Officer has requested the RA to recommend the investment option that should be selected by Sinclair Ltd.

The first step in the decision tree process is to establish the various options available and the associated factual data. These are subsequently expressed in a pay-off probability matrix. In this case the facts are:

- Investment capital: $50,000;
- Investment period: 12 months or less;
- Investment period probabilities: 0.15, 3 months; 0.50, 6 months; 0.35, 12 months;
- Investment options: Keep in bank account; invest in fixed term deposits with bank or purchase government bonds;
- The investment capital would earn 1 per cent interest if it was kept in the bank account.

- The fixed term deposits would earn a higher interest rate. The likely interest rates applicable are: 0.30 per cent, 3 per cent; 0.40, 3.5 per cent; and 0.30, 4 per cent;
- If the investment capital is required before the maturity of the fixed term deposits, the bank will provide a cover loan for the period required at 3.25 per cent interest.
- Government bonds that may be traded, bear 4.5 per cent interest paid annually, maturing in 2030;
- Government bond cost: $100 each, hence $50,000 is equivalent to 500 bonds;
- Government bond market behaviour (probability/price): 0.05, $95; 0.10, $96; 0.25, $98; 0.25, $104; 0.15, $105; and 0.20, $102;
- Government bond broker's fee: $250.

The above factual information is converted to a pay-off probability matrix as shown at Table 7.5. Table 7.5 illustrates that the behaviour of the three options is unique to each individual option. Moreover, each option has one or more discrete probability distribution functions, which has resulted in the expected monetary value approach being incorporated within the pay-off matrix.

Note that because each of the three options functions differently, the 'Gain/Loss' computation also differs. For example, the first option (*keep cash in bank*) requires the calculation of the investment period based on the given probabilities. Once the investment period is computed, the interest rate is applied to calculate the gain/loss, which is $50,319 (or more precisely a gain of $319). The second option (*12 months fixed term deposit*) is more complex. First there is the need to determine the interest rate applicable based on the probability distribution function provided; after there is the need to determine when the investment capital would be required by the entity before the maturity of the fixed term deposits since the entity would need to take out a cover loan for the period in question.

Once these are determined, the gain/loss may be calculated, which is $51,161. Note that this option has two distinct probability distributions, one for the applicable interest rates and the other for the cover loan period. The third option (*government bonds*) is also complex. First there is the need to determine the interest earned by the 4.5 per cent interest bearing bonds. This depends on the period that the bonds are held for before they are sold. The period the bonds are held is computed from the investment period probability distribution function provided; after there is the need to determine the income received at the time the bonds are sold. This is calculated from the bond market response probability distribution function, which provides the bond price at the time of sale.

Hence, the income earned by the government bonds consists of two elements, namely the interest earned while the entity is holding the bonds, and the total capital received after selling the bonds at the determined selling price per bond. Once both income elements are determined, the gain/loss may be calculated, which is $51,684. Note that this option also has two distinct probability distributions, one

TABLE 7.5 Pay-off probability matrix: Sinclair Ltd investment decision

Keep Cash in Bank

Investment Amount	Interest Rate	Investment Period (months)							Gain/Loss
		Pr.	M	Pr.	M	Pr.	M	Period	
$50,000	1%	.15	3	.50	6	.35	12	7.65	$50,000 + ($50,000 x 1% ÷ 12 x 7.65) = $50,319

12 Months Fixed Term Deposit

Investment Amount	Interest Rate Applicable						% Rate	Income	Cover Loan Period (months)						Period	Gain/Loss
	Pr.	%	Pr.	%	Pr.	%			Pr.	M	Pr.	M	Pr.	M		
$50,000	.30	3	.40	3.5	.30	4	3.50	$51,750	.15	3	.50	6	.35	12	12 - 7.65 = 4.35	$51,750 – ($50,000 x 3.25% ÷ 12 x 4.35) = $51,161

30 Year Government Bonds

Investment Amount	Investment Period (months)						Period	Income
	Pr.	M	Pr.	M	Pr.	M		
$50,000	.15	3	.50	6	.35	12	7.65	$51,434

Bond Market Response												Sell Price (€)	Income	Gain/Loss
Pr.	€	Pr.	€	Pr.	€	Pr.	€	Pr.	€	Pr.	€			
.05	95	.10	96	.25	98	.25	104	.15	105	.20	102	101	(500 x $101) $50,500	$50,500 - $250 +1,434 = **$51,684**

for the applicable interest income earned and the other for the capital received on sale.

The second step in the decision tree process is to draw the resultant decision tree using the pay-off matrix (Table 7.5) as the information base. The object of the decision is to choose the appropriate investment strategy, that is: Should Sinclair Ltd keep the cash in the bank or invest in 12 months fixed term deposits with the bank or purchase long-term government bonds? Therefore, the basis of a decision tree is the decision that needs to be made. Figure 7.11 illustrates the decision tree that was drawn from the pay-off probability matrix.

The squares on the diagram typically represent decisions and the circles represent uncertain outcomes that are usually expressed in probabilities. The decision tree moves from left to right. In the example, Sinclairs' management team has three options with each option having its own individual alternative decisions. This illustrates that the decision tree method in combination with the expected monetary value approach can undertake complex decision making situations.

Similar to many other modelling techniques, obtaining an accurate representation of the model is an iterative process. Once the first version of the decision tree is achieved it must be reviewed by questioning each square and circle to determine whether there are any other solutions or outcomes that have not been considered. This process is repeated until a satisfactory decision tree is obtained.

Note that decision tree analysis is achieved through the application of an accurate decision tree diagram and the generation of the probability-payoff matrix for every option represented by the decision tree. This approach will indicate the option that has the greatest value for the company. The probabilities and values for the matrix are estimates based on historical data and financial market research. The branches stemming from each circle represent an uncertainty and will require a probability and the estimated outcome value to be assigned to them. Moreover, the probabilities of branches stemming from a specific circle must add up to 1 (100 per cent). Hence, the computation of the decision outcomes is calculated by using the decision tree and the probability-payoff matrix.

Starting from the right of the decision tree and moving towards the left, multiply the probability by the value of the outcomes on every node (decision square or uncertainty circle). For example, the option to invest in 12 months fixed term deposits shows that there is a .30 chance that the interest rate applicable is 3 per cent, a .40 chance of being 3.5 per cent and a .30 chance of being 4 per cent. Note that adding up the probabilities will give 1 (i.e. .30 + .40 + .30 = 1). Furthermore, multiplying the probabilities by their respective outcome will provide the probable interest rate applicable. For this example it will be: (.30 × 3 per cent) + (.40 × 3.5 per cent) + (.30 × 4 per cent) which equals to 3.5 per cent. Hence, applying 3.5 per cent to the investment capital of $50,000 will provide a total investment income of $51,750, of which $1,750 is interest. But the example for this option does not stop at this point. There is also a .15 probability that the investment period will be 3 months, a .50 probability it will be 6 months, and a .35 probability that the investment period will be 12 months. By multiplying

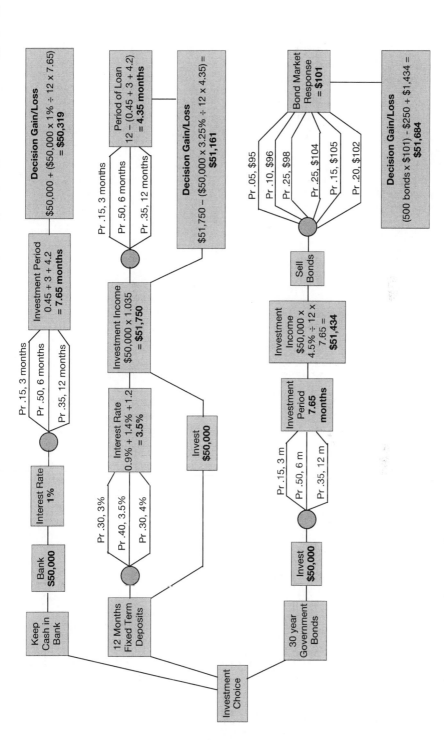

FIGURE 7.11 Decision tree analysis – Sinclair Ltd investment decision

the probabilities by their respective outcome will provide the probable investment period applicable. For this example it will be: (.15 × 3 months) + (.50 × 6 months) + (.35 × 12 months) which equals to 7.65 months. This means that the company will require its capital before the 12 months fixed term deposits maturity date. It also means that the company will need to take up the bank's offer for a loan at 3.25 per cent interest, to cover the 4.35-month period (12 months − 7.65 months) until the fixed deposits mature. Hence, the cover loan interest amounts to $589 (i.e. $50,000 × 3.25 per cent ÷ 12 × 4.35 months = $589) which is subtracted from $51,750 investment income to give an overall investment outcome of $51, 161. The other branches of the decision tree are computed in a similar fashion.

The decision tree analysis demonstrates that the third option (buying long-term government bonds) provides the better overall investment outcome at $51,684. Hence, the complete decision tree analysis process computes the best option. The Sinclair Ltd example illustrates that decision tree analysis beneficial because it:

- Visibly and unambiguously defines the decision to be resolved by showing all the options so that they may be systematically computed in terms of costs;
- Permits management to fully examine all likely consequences of a decision;
- Offers a feasible framework for calculating the outcome values and respective probabilities of achieving them;
- Helps management to evaluate estimates and available information to arrive at the best decisions by selecting the better alternative.

Like every other management tool, it takes experience and a rational approach in applying the method. This section has illustrated that decision tree analysis, which includes the expected monetary value approach is a powerful tool that management may apply for resolving concerns that involve risky situations. Let us now consider another example related to decision tree analysis.

Example one: quantitative risk analysis – decision tree analysis

Blumenthal plc is an electronics manufacturing company. Currently a division of the company specialises in making one particular unit (Unit-A) related to the defence industry. The division currently manufactures 20,000 items per annum of Unit-A. The cost structure is expected to remain unchanged in the foreseeable future if the division continues to manufacture the component.

Blumenthal's historical data indicates that the likely annual production cost to make 20,000 items of Unit-A is as follows: Pr .30, €310,000; .45, €320,000; and .25, €335,000. Blumenthal plc has currently completed the development work on a new product (Unit-B) which will shortly go into production with a similar production volume as Unit-A (20,000 items per annum). However, the company does not have the capacity to produce both Unit-A and Unit-B. The Industrial

Engineering Department at Blumenthal plc, estimates that the cost to produce 20,000 items of Unit-B is as follows: Pr .60, €280,000; .10, €250,000; and .30, €295,000.

Negotiations with the sub-contractor indicate that the likely cost for outsourcing Unit-A for 20,000 items is: Pr .35, €290,000; .40, €315,000; and .25, €320,000. While the cost for outsourcing Unit-B for 20,000 items is: Pr .45, €275,000; .20, €310,000; and .35, €320,000.

Blumenthal plc has a penalty clause for the late delivery of products to its clients. Historical data suggests that the likely penalty cost for the late delivery of Unit-A over a 12-month production period is as follows: Pr .50, €0; .50, €75,000. The company also estimates that since Unit-B is a new product, the penalty data is likely to be slightly different from that of Unit-A, and is estimated to be as follows: Pr .35, €0; .65, €75,000. Should the company manufacture Unit-B and outsource Unit-A, or should it manufacture Unit-A and outsource Unit-B?

Step-One: Establish the various options available and the associated factual data:

- Production cost to manufacture 20,000 items per annum of Unit-A is: Pr .30, €310,000; .45, €320,000; and .25, €335,000.
- A new product (Unit-B) which will shortly go into production with a similar production volume as Unit-A (20,000 items per annum).
- Production capacity does not permit both Unit-A and Unit-B.
- Production cost to manufacture 20,000 items per annum of Unit-B is: Pr .60, €280,000; .10, €250,000; and .30, €295,000.
- Cost for outsourcing Unit-A for 20,000 items is: Pr .35, €290,000; .40, €315,000; and .25, €320,000.
- Cost for outsourcing Unit-B for 20,000 items is: Pr .45, €275,000; .20, €310,000; and .35, €320,000.
- Penalty cost for the late delivery of Unit-A over a 12-month production period is as follows: Pr .50, €0; .50, €75,000.
- Penalty cost for the late delivery of Unit-B over a 12-month production period is as follows: Pr .35, €0; .65, €75,000.

Step-Two: Transform the various options available and the associated factual data into a pay-off probability matrix. The pay-off probability matrix is shown at Table 7.6. This matrix indicates the option that has the greatest value for Blumenthal plc. The probabilities and values for the matrix are estimates based on historical data and market research. When the pay-off probability matrix is transformed into a decision tree diagram, the probabilities for each depicted segment will result as branches stemming from a specific circle and must add up to 1 (100 per cent).

Step-Three: Express the pay-off probability matrix into a decision tree to depict the various options available and the pay-off (probability) matrix data. The resultant decision tree is shown at Figure 7.12. The computation of the decision outcomes is calculated by using the decision tree and the probability data from probability-payoff matrix. The decision tree analysis indicates that Blumenthal plc will generate

TABLE 7.6 Pay-off probability matrix: Blumenthal plc make–buy decision

	Blumenthal Plc Electronics Manufacturing Company: Make-Buy Outsourcing Decision																							
Production Option	Cost of Unit-A (probabilities/cost in 000's)							Cost of Unit-B (probabilities/cost in 000's)							Delivery Penalty for Unit-A (000's)					Delivery Penalty for Unit-B (000's)					Outcome Cost (000's)
	Pr.	€	Pr.	€	Pr.	€	Cost	Pr.	€	Pr.	€	Pr.	€	Cost	Pr.	€	Pr.	€	Cost	Pr.	€	Pr.	€	Cost	
Make Unit-A Outsource Unit-B	.30	310	.45	320	.25	335	**320.750**	.45	275	.20	310	.35	320	**297.750**	.50	0	.50	75	**37.5**	.35	0	.65	75	**48.75**	**704.75**
Outsource Unit-A Make Unit-B	.35	290	.40	315	.25	320	**307.500**	.60	280	.10	250	.30	295	**281.500**	.50	0	.50	75	**37.5**	.35	0	.65	75	**48.75**	**675.25**

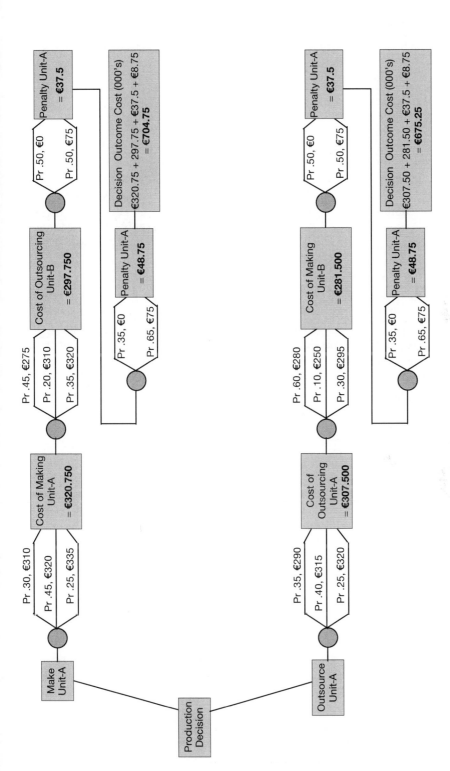

FIGURE 7.12 Decision tree analysis – Blumenthal plc make–buy decision

greater value to the approximate value of €29,500, if it outsources Unit-A and makes Unit-B in-house.

Concluding remarks: quantitative risk analysis – decision trees

The major concern with quantitative financial risk analysis using decision trees is similar to the other techniques that have already been examined, namely, the estimation of the probabilities associated with each decision outcome and accurate representation of the real world when depicting the decision tree model.

The first concern may be addressed by analysing historical data available to the organisation regarding the particular decision being made. If the historical data is not sufficient to estimate accurately the probability distribution, the entity will need to conduct an objective study. This type of study to be conducted depends on the circumstances. For instance, a probability distribution related to market response data will require extensive market research. Probability distributions regarding production costs may require a comprehensive study of the production process.

The second concern related to the accurate depiction of a decision tree model is more difficult and again will depend on the complexity of the problem to be resolved. The more variables are involved the more complex the behaviour of these variables and the respective depiction of their relationship with each other. Therefore, it is important that focus group discussions involving individuals, who have expert knowledge of the process, are undertaken to design the decision trees and to define the data extraction process and eventual transformation to a probability distribution.

Quantitative risk analysis – sensitivity analysis

Sensitivity analysis is a method that focuses on assessing the sensitivity of the expected monetary value or net present value (depending on the computation) to the changes in the underlying variable assumptions in the business model. Note that net present value (NPV) is basically the difference between the present value of cash inflows and the present value of cash outflows in the appraisal of the profitability of an investment or project as related to capital budgeting.

Sensitivity analysis applies as its starting point, a base-case scenario that is based on what are considered to be the most accurate values for the variables in the model. The values for these variables are the assumptions. For example, an assumption that may be made (based on historical data) is that the interest rate will be 4.5 per cent. Hence, to the knowledge of the Risk Analyst, who is defining the business model, the 4.5 per cent interest rate is considered to be the most accurate value for that particular variable. The difficulty arises, if the specific circumstance at the time the transaction is implemented change due to uncontrollable factors, such as, economic growth or recession, which may affect the borrowing interest rate.

Therefore, sensitivity analysis applies as its starting point, the base-case scenario, and from this point the various assumptions are changed to examine the effect of the changes on the resultant model, when compared to the base-case scenario. Depending on the confidence or tolerance in the assumptions, the Risk Analyst is in a position to determine the potential risk of an investment.

The focus of this section is sensitivity analysis but a technique that is closely related to it, is scenario analysis. Scenario analysis progresses the sensitivity analysis one step further by assigning probability distributions to the variables in the business model. The probability distributions may be '*discrete*' or '*continuous*' depending on the mathematical behaviour (or pattern) of the variables concerned, similar to the Monte Carlo simulation approach.

Hence, rather than just examining the sensitivity of the expected monetary value or net present value to the change in the variable assumptions, scenario analysis takes into consideration the probability distribution of the variables. Similar to sensitivity analysis, scenario analysis starts with a '*base case scenario*' business model and progresses the model to the '*worst-case scenario*'. The probabilities are assigned to the various scenarios and computed to arrive at an expected value.

Example one: quantitative risk analysis – sensitivity analysis

The Chief Finance Officer (CFO) of Rosewell Ltd is considering the implementation of two alternative investment development projects, namely Green Valley Retirement Village and White Rocks Lifestyle Village. The CFO has prepared the cash flow information using net present value, related to the two projects as shown at Table 7.7. The values at Table 7.7 are based on an Internal Rate of Return (IRR) of 7 per cent.

After conducting a sensitivity analysis, the CFO has determined that IRR would need to be 32.37 per cent for the two alternative projects to be at equilibrium. The sensitivity analysis was conducted by changing the IRR from 7 per cent (incrementing by 1 per cent or less) until the difference in the NPV for both projects approached or equalled zero. Table 7.8 and Figure 7.13 show the results of the sensitivity analysis.

Moreover, the CFO established that the best scenario would occur when the IRR was from 7 per cent to 15 per cent; the expected scenario would occur when the IRR was between 16 per cent and 24 per cent; and the worst scenario would occur when the IRR was between 25 per cent and 32.37 per cent. The sensitivity analysis indicates that the Green Valley Retirement Village project has a better NPV return under the best and expected scenarios, and the IRR would need to increase to 32.37 per cent for both projects to have the same NPV, which occurs at the worst scenario.

Example two: quantitative risk analysis – sensitivity analysis

Sentinel Cereals plc, a European Union (EU) based company, is negotiating a derivative contract with a USA based entity, namely, Excel Wheat Cooperative, for the supply of US wheat. After a number of lengthy negotiation sessions, the

TABLE 7.7 NPV cash flow information: Rosewell Ltd alternative projects

7% as initial IRR rate

Green Valley Development	NPV	0	1	2	3	4	5	6	7	8	9	10	Total
					Investment Project Cash Flow (€000's)								
Investment Cash-out Flow:	22,588	2,500	4,500	5,500	6,500	2,500	2,000	1,500	1,000	500	500	500	27,500
Primary Revenue Cash-in Flow:	115,104		10,695	13,505	15,520	16,593	17,035	17,720	18,433	19,173	19,945	20,745	169,363
Other Revenue Cash-in Flow:	9,680		439	1,040	1,355	1,503	1,534	1,585	1,658	1,714	1,793	1,876	14,497
Total:	102,196	-2,500	6,634	9,045	10,375	15,596	16,569	17,805	19,091	20,387	21,238	22,121	156,360

White Rocks Development	NPV	0	1	2	3	4	5	6	7	8	9	10	Total
					Investment Project Cash Flow (€000's)								
Investment Cash-out Flow:	40,888		5,500	6,500	7,500	8,000	9,000	6,500	5,500	4,500	1,000	1,000	55,000
Primary Revenue Cash-in Flow:	112,354	968	12,250	13,250	13,850	15,500	15,750	16,500	17,250	18,000	19,500	22,000	164,818
Other Revenue Cash-in Flow:	21,213	500	2,000	2,250	2,500	2,750	3,000	3,250	3,500	3,750	3,750	4,000	31,250
Total:	92,679	1,468	8,750	9,000	8,850	10,250	9,750	13,250	15,250	17,250	22,250	25,000	141,068

| Difference: | 9,517 | | | | | | | | | | | | 15,292 |

(Equilibrium Occurs at about IRR of 32.37%)

TABLE 7.8 NPV cash flow information: Rosewell Ltd sensitivity analysis

IRR	Green Valley NPV (€000's)	White Rocks NPV (€000's)	Difference NPV (€000's)
7.00%	102,196	92,679	9,516
8.00%	96,617	87,759	8,858
9.00%	91,441	83,208	8,233
10.00%	86,634	78,992	7,642
11.00%	82,164	75,082	7,081
12.00%	78,002	71,452	6,550
13.00%	74,124	68,079	6,046
14.00%	70,507	64,939	5,568
15.00%	67,128	62,014	5,114
16.00%	63,970	59,287	4,683
17.00%	61,014	56,740	4,274
18.00%	58,246	54,360	3,886
19.00%	55,650	52,133	3,517
20.00%	53,214	50,048	3,166
21.00%	50,925	48,093	2,832
22.00%	48,774	46,258	2,515
23.00%	46,748	44,535	2,214
24.00%	44,841	42,914	1,926
25.00%	43,042	41,389	1,653
26.00%	41,345	39,952	1,393
27.00%	39,743	38,598	1,145
28.00%	38,228	37,319	909
29.00%	36,795	36,111	683
30.00%	35,438	34,969	469
31.00%	34,153	33,889	264
32.00%	32,934	32,865	69
32.10%	32,816	32,766	50
32.20%	32,698	32,667	31
32.30%	32,581	32,569	12
32.35%	32,522	32,520	2
32.36%	32,511	32,510	1
32.37%	32,505	32,505	0

price that is being considered is $580 per bushel. An important issue for Sentinel Cereals plc is the exchange rate of the US dollar against the euro. Both companies have agreed to establish a fixed currency exchange rate of $1.3256 against the euro when signing the contract. The delivery of the product will take place in 12 months' time.

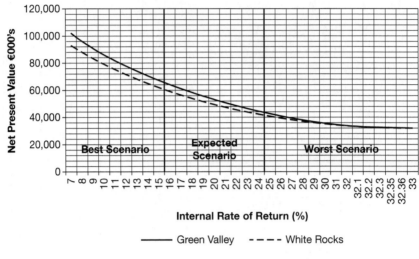

FIGURE 7.13 NPV cash flow graphs: Rosewell Ltd sensitivity analysis

The historical futures wheat prices as provided by the Chicago Board of Trade (CBOT) indicate that over the last 365 days, the average price of wheat was $625.94 per bushel and the maximum and minimum prices per bushel were $731.75 and $514.75 respectively.

The Chief Financial Officer (CFO) of Sentinel Cereals plc has requested the Risk Analyst (RA) to conduct a sensitivity analysis based on the official statistical range of the wheat prices per bushel and also on various scenarios that take into account the possible movements in the US$-euro exchange rate. The CFO considers that this analysis is essential for making the decision on whether to agree on the negotiation conditions prior to signing the contract.

In conducting a sensitivity analysis one needs to consider the variables that are likely to impact the final outcome. In this example, two major variables are identified, namely the price per bushel of wheat and the US$ exchange rate against the euro. Even though these two variables are at a fixed rate within the contract, they are likely to vary at the time the contract is implemented in 12 months' time. Hence, Sentinel Cereals plc needs to be careful in closing the deal so that it may maximise its eventual profit.

One should also note that the greater number of variables, the greater the complexity of the sensitivity analysis. However, the principles being demonstrated in this (and previous) example are the same.

Table 7.9 provides the initial business model for the sensitivity analysis. It shows the varying range of wheat prices per bushel (ranging from $500 to $740) against the fixed contract price. This provides a variety of percentage gain/loss for the various prices within the range. For instance, if the price per bushel at the delivery date is $560 per bushel, then Sentinel Cereals plc would make a loss of 3.57 per cent on the deal because the company could have purchased the wheat on the

TABLE 7.9 Sentinel Cereals plc: sensitivity analysis base scenario

Wheat Price per Bushel ($)			Exchange Rate of US$ Against €			
Price Range	Contract Price	% Gain/Loss	Actual Rate	Contract Rate	% Gain/Loss	Total % Gain/Loss
500.00	580	-16.00%	1.3256	1.3256	0.00%	-16.00%
520.00	580	-11.54%	1.3256	1.3256	0.00%	-11.54%
540.00	580	-7.41%	1.3256	1.3256	0.00%	-7.41%
560.00	580	-3.57%	1.3256	1.3256	0.00%	-3.57%
580.00	580	0.00%	1.3256	1.3256	0.00%	0.00%
600.00	580	3.33%	1.3256	1.3256	0.00%	3.33%
620.00	580	6.45%	1.3256	1.3256	0.00%	6.45%
640.00	580	9.38%	1.3256	1.3256	0.00%	9.38%
660.00	580	12.12%	1.3256	1.3256	0.00%	12.12%
680.00	580	14.71%	1.3256	1.3256	0.00%	14.71%
700.00	580	17.14%	1.3256	1.3256	0.00%	17.14%
720.00	580	19.44%	1.3256	1.3256	0.00%	19.44%
740.00	580	21.62%	1.3256	1.3256	0.00%	21.62%

open market at the prevailing price of $560 instead of $580. Table 7.9 also shows the impact of the exchange rate.

The scenario depicted by Table 7.9 shows no variation in the exchange rate because this is the base position of the sensitivity analysis. Hence, Table 7.9 basically demonstrates that a market price (at the time of product delivery) of greater than $580 (with no change to the exchange rate) will mean a gain for Sentinel Cereals plc. As was stated previously, Table 7.9 represents the base scenario.

Table 7.10 shows the same business model, including the range of wheat prices per bushel, however, the exchange rate of the US$ against the euro as specified in the contract is decreased by 10 per cent. The RA may view this as the worst case scenario, which shows that for Sentinel Cereals plc to register a gain, the wheat price per bushel at the time of delivery would need to be greater than $640 per bushel.

Furthermore, Table 7.11 shows the same business model, including the range of wheat prices per bushel, however, the exchange rate of the US$ against the euro as specified in the contract is increased by 10 per cent. Again, the RA may view this as the best case scenario, which shows that for Sentinel Cereals plc to register a gain, the wheat price per bushel at the time of delivery would need to be greater than $52 per bushel.

Note that the RA may execute any number of scenarios as desired. For instance, this example incremented the exchange rate by ±10 per cent from the base scenario. The increment could have been ±1 per cent from the base scenario (or any other

TABLE 7.10 Sentinel Cereals plc: sensitivity analysis worst case scenario

Wheat Price per Bushel ($)			Exchange Rate of US$ Against €			
Price Range	Contract Price	% Gain/Loss	Actual Rate	Contract Rate	% Gain/Loss	Total % Gain/Loss
500.00	580	-16.00%	1.1930	1.3256	-11.11%	-27.11%
520.00	580	-11.54%	1.1930	1.3256	-11.11%	-22.65%
540.00	580	-7.41%	1.1930	1.3256	-11.11%	-18.52%
560.00	580	-3.57%	1.1930	1.3256	-11.11%	-14.68%
580.00	580	0.00%	1.1930	1.3256	-11.11%	-11.11%
600.00	580	3.33%	1.1930	1.3256	-11.11%	-7.78%
620.00	580	6.45%	1.1930	1.3256	-11.11%	-4.66%
640.00	580	9.38%	1.1930	1.3256	-11.11%	-1.74%
660.00	580	12.12%	1.1930	1.3256	-11.11%	1.01%
680.00	580	14.71%	1.1930	1.3256	-11.11%	3.59%
700.00	580	17.14%	1.1930	1.3256	-11.11%	6.03%
720.00	580	19.44%	1.1930	1.3256	-11.11%	8.33%
740.00	580	21.62%	1.1930	1.3256	-11.11%	10.51%

TABLE 7.11 Sentinel Cereals plc: sensitivity analysis best case scenario

Wheat Price per Bushel ($)			Exchange Rate of US$ Against €			
Price Range	Contract Price	% Gain/Loss	Actual Rate	Contract Rate	% Gain/Loss	Total % Gain/Loss
500.00	580	-16.00%	1.4582	1.3256	9.09%	-6.91%
520.00	580	-11.54%	1.4582	1.3256	9.09%	-2.45%
540.00	580	-7.41%	1.4582	1.3256	9.09%	1.68%
560.00	580	-3.57%	1.4582	1.3256	9.09%	5.52%
580.00	580	0.00%	1.4582	1.3256	9.09%	9.09%
600.00	580	3.33%	1.4582	1.3256	9.09%	12.42%
620.00	580	6.45%	1.4582	1.3256	9.09%	15.54%
640.00	580	9.38%	1.4582	1.3256	9.09%	18.47%
660.00	580	12.12%	1.4582	1.3256	9.09%	21.21%
680.00	580	14.71%	1.4582	1.3256	9.09%	23.80%
700.00	580	17.14%	1.4582	1.3256	9.09%	26.23%
720.00	580	19.44%	1.4582	1.3256	9.09%	28.54%
740.00	580	21.62%	1.4582	1.3256	9.09%	30.71%

reasonable increment). The same may be said about the price range. In this example the price range was incremented by $20 but this could have been set at $5 or $10. The basic principle is to ensure that the business model depicts a fairly accurate realistic situation and most importantly that it is manageable. Hence, increasing the sensitivity increments by very small numbers may make the model unmanageable in terms of understanding what is in reality taking place.

Concluding remarks: quantitative risk analysis – sensitivity analysis

The different types of risks that confront an entity on a regular basis can have a significant impact on its bottom line, no matter what the size of that entity. Slight fluctuations in interest rates; foreign currency exchange rates; and/or commodity prices could affect an entity's financial statements. Without proper risk management analysis an entity may find itself in financial difficulty. With appropriate risk analysis, management can determine the risk and if appropriate, hedge against it.

Sensitivity analysis (or a what-if analysis) is a recent phenomenon that has become very common in the past few decades. The advantage of sensitivity analysis is that it is a relatively simple risk measurement tool to apply. However, it is important to gather the relevant factual data, to determine and depict an accurate business model and vary the model variables in a way that makes the output comprehensible and manageable. There is no point in generating a multitude of information if the information is not presented in a format that can be understood and interpreted. This will enable an entity to use sensitivity analysis to determine its hedging strategies if they are appropriate at that particular point in time.

Whatever the case, sensitivity analysis is evolving as an important tool to define an overall risk management strategy of an entity. One should note that no matter what type of entity is being considered, whether it is a public or private sector entity; whether it is a producer, importing raw materials; or a service-based company selling its wares internationally, it will encounter a multitude of risks. Some will be minor, others will be major. Interest rates, foreign currency exchange rates and/or commodity prices are constantly fluctuating. It is these fluctuations that create uncertainty and hence risk. These risks require entities to determine how these fluctuations will impact their business activity and eventually their bottom line.

Formulating a risk response strategy

Financial risk response has the objective of identifying the options available and defining the appropriate actions to enhance the opportunities and minimise the threats. The financial risk response phase takes into consideration all the identified risks and their quantification to determine the appropriate strategy for addressing the risks. It should be noted that the financial risk response phase will focus on the high risk items that were assessed and examined in the qualitative (and quantitative if conducted) risk analysis and has the added objective of assigning an owner to each risk requiring a response. Therefore, the financial risk response process identifies and assigns responsibility to an individual person or group of individuals as a team for each risk response. When dealing with risk there are basically four strategic options that are available to the Chief Risk Officer, these are:

1   Risk avoidance;
2   Risk transference;
3   Risk mitigation;
4   Risk acceptance.

Risk avoidance strategy

A risk avoidance strategy is based on the principle of doing something to remove the risk. This results in the removal of all vulnerable activities and exposures that can have a negative impact on the entity's assets. For instance, with a risk avoidance strategy, the Risk Analyst would eliminate the risk by not going ahead with the investment. Hence, a risk avoidance strategy seeks to avoid compromising trans-actions completely. Although the complete removal of risk is not usually achievable, a risk avoidance strategy aims to prevent as many threats as possible so that the consequences of costly and damaging events are evaded. In other words, if a number of investment options offer the same expected yield but have different risk characteristics, investors under a risk avoidance strategy, will choose the option with the lowest changeability (or fluctuation) in returns.

How does one decide whether or not a risky course of action is to be under-taken? This depends on the attitude to risk of the decision maker. Three possible attitudes have been identified, namely, aversion to risk; desire for risk; and indiffer-ence to risk. For example, consider the behaviour of two options under three different economic circumstances. The first option has three possible payout returns, namely €90, €100 and €110 under recession, normal and boom economic conditions respectively. The second option also has three possible payout returns, namely €0, €100 and €200 under recession, normal and boom economic conditions respectively. Let us assume that the three states of the economy are equally likely. Therefore, the expected value of each option is €100. That is: expected value option one = (€90 + €100 + €110) ÷ 3 = €100 and expected value option two = (€0 + €100 + €200) ÷ 3 = €100.

A risk-seeker would likely select the more risky option, which is option two. However, a risk-averter would likely select the less risky option, which is option one. A risk-neutral investor would be indifferent to both because they have the same return. Therefore, in examining a risk avoidance strategy, one needs to con-sider the attitude of the investors. Generally, research of the investment market indicates that: (a) the majority of investors are risk averse; and (b) most business managers are unlikely to be neutral to risk; they will either be risk averse or a risk seeker.

In deciding whether to adopt a risk avoidance strategy, it would be unwise for decisions to be made solely on expected values. The expected values computations are to be complemented with measures of dispersion, such as standard deviation and coefficient of variation. Moreover, investment decisions should take into consideration the comparison of the probability distributions for the various alternatives.

Risk transference strategy

Risk transference strategy shifts the responsibility of the risk from the entity to someone else. For example, an entity that specialises in cultivating wheat may enter into an agreement at a fixed price per bushel with an entity that trades in wheat. This is what is referred to as a derivative. A derivative is a special type of contract that derives its value from the performance of an underlying entity. In the example, the underlying entity is an asset, namely, the wheat crop. In this case, the derivative is used by the wheat cultivating entity to ensure that it will receive a predetermined fixed price irrespective of the market conditions at the time the transaction is implemented. This type of approach may also be used with foreign exchange rates for a specific currency in conducting international trade, where the terms of contract may stipulate a guaranteed exchange rate for the exporter or/and importer.

Another example of a risk transference strategy is taking out an insurance policy against financial failure or the re-insurance of a risky policy. In this case, the Risk Analyst would partially transfer the financial impact (consequences) of the risk to the insurance company. However, this risk strategy would lessen the risk only if the party taking on responsibility for the risk is better geared to take the necessary measures for risk reduction.

For example, a risky segment of the project may be outsourced. In this case, the project team would transfer the financial impact of the risk to a third party (i.e. the contractor). However, this strategy would lessen the risk of project management failure, only if the party taking on the responsibility for the risk is better geared to take the necessary measures for the reduction of the risk, otherwise the risk of failure would end up being higher.

Risk mitigation strategy

This strategy takes the appropriate steps to lessen the probability of the risk occurring or lowering the consequences of the risk if it occurs. For example, an investment company may diversify its investment portfolio across different industry types, particularly those that are negatively correlated to each other. For instance, one may invest in a beverage (soft drinks) entity, which peaks its revenue earning in summer but also invest in a chocolate producing entity that peaks its revenue earning in winter. This would insure that the investor has a regular earning stream throughout the financial year.

Another example of risk mitigation is hedging. This protects the financial objectives of an entity from the consequences of risk. Hedging is an investment position that is intended to offset possible losses/gains that may occur in the implementation of a variety of transactions. For example, fuel hedging is a common contractual tool that is used by large fuel consuming entities, such as energy generating companies that are dependent on fossil fuel for the generation of electricity. Fuel hedging permits these entities to reduce their exposure to unpredictable market conditions that could potentially lead to a substantial increase in fuel costs that would drastically impact their operating costs. These large fuel consuming companies would enter into hedging contracts to mitigate their exposure to future fuel prices that may be higher than current prices and/or to establish a known fuel cost for budgeting purposes. Furthermore, these companies may hedge part of their fuel requirements so that they can still take a partial advantage, should fuel prices fall during the hedging period.

Hedging contacts may operate in combination with fuel swaps and fuel call options. For example, if the energy generation entity buys a fuel swap and the price of fuel decreases, the entity would actually have to pay fuel prices that are above the market rate. However, if the energy generation entity acquires a fuel call option and the price of fuel increases, the entity would be given a return on the option that offsets their actual cost of fuel. Additionally, if the entity acquires a fuel call option but this option involves an upfront payment, similar to an insurance premium, and the price of fuel decreases, the energy generation entity would not receive a return on the option. However, it would benefit from buying the fuel at a lower cost at that moment.

Risk acceptance strategy

There are situations where the Risk Analyst may recommend the acceptance of certain risks, thus reacting to the specific risk if and when it occurs. This strategy is usually applicable when the risks involved (or their impact) are not significant enough to warrant the effort needed to address them proactively.

The aim of the Risk Analyst when dealing with a risk response is to select the best strategy to address each risk (that merits attention) and propose particular actions for implementing the selected strategy. Hence, the financial risk response stage identifies and defines the risk related tasks that need to be carried out; identifies the individual (or collective unit) responsible for executing the risk related tasks; and defines the schedule for the completion of the risk related tasks.

Financial risk monitoring and control

Financial risk management is a continuous process throughout the lifecycle of an entity. Hence, it is important that risks are monitored and controlled. Risk monitoring and control keeps a close scrutiny on all the identified risks, outstanding risks and new risks that may arise due to the changing external environment, such as a change in the economic conditions. This process ensures that the risk response plans are implemented effectively.

The continuous monitoring of risks will identify any change in the risk status, or if a particular risk has developed into an issue. The inventory of financial risks is not static and continually changes with time, thus new risks evolve and other risks disappear. Risk monitoring and control is best achieved by having frequent risk reviews to identify any outstanding actions; to update risk probability and impact; remove risks that are no long current; and to identify new risks.

Risk reviews allow the risk analyst to reassess and modify risk ratings and prioritisation. There may be a need to perform further risk response planning to control risk when an unforeseen risk becomes known or in the event that the risk impact is greater than anticipated. Those assigned responsibility for a particular risk must report regularly, highlighting the effectiveness of the response plan, any unforeseen affects and the course of action that must be taken to mitigate the risk. The outputs from the full financial risk management process establish the groundwork for the financial risk management plan. Therefore, the financial risk management plan is the culmination of the financial risk management process that is ultimately employed to achieve inclusive risk monitoring and control.

Financial risk management plan

Financial risk management need not be a complex task. However, it must be undertaken as part of a structured and systematic process. As has been illustrated in the previous sections, financial risk management planning consists of four components, namely, risk identification; risk quantification in terms of analysing and prioritising risk; risk response; and risk monitoring and control. Figure 7.14 provides a financial risk management plan template that may be adapted to a particular managerial environment.

| Investment Portfolio No: | | Investment Description | | | | Investment Manager: | | | Report Date: | / / |

Risk Identification						Qualitative Analysis			Quantitative Analysis			Risk Response Strategy		Risk Monitoring and Control		
Risk Rate	I.D	Category & Description	Date	Impact Area	Threat or Opp.	Causes of Risk	Risk Type	Pr.	Impact	Pr.	Impact	Result	Strategy	Measures	Task Manager	Status Period	Remarks
1	2	3	4	5	6	7	8	9	10	11	12	13	14	15	16	17	18

Col 01: Risk Rating (High=1; Medium=2; Low=3.)
Financial Risk Identification:
Col 02: Risk Identity Number (reference number)
Col 03: Risk category and description (refer to risk inventory)
Col 04: Date (date risk identified)
Col 05: Investment area affected
Col 06: Threat or Opportunity (impact on investment objectives)
Col 07: Cause of risk (the factors that may trigger the risk)
Financial Risk Qualitative Risk Analysis:
Col 08: Risk type (Specific activity goals - see Figure 7.4)
Col 09: Probability (Very high, High, Medium, Low, Very low.)
Col 10: Impact (Very high, High, Medium, Low, Very low.)

Financial Risk Quantitative Risk Analysis (only if necessary):
Col 11: Pr. (Probability range from +1 to -1)
Col 12: Impact (in terms of money)
Col 13: Result in terms of money (Col 11 x Col. 12)
Financial Risk Response Strategy:
Col 14: Strategy (avoidance, transference, mitigation, acceptance)
Col 15: Measures (response actions, benefits and shortcomings)
Financial Risk Monitoring and Control:
Col 16: Task Manager (person responsible i.e. risk owner)
Col 17: Status Period (interval period for checking activity at risk)
Col 18: Remarks (any relevant comments)

FIGURE 7.14 Financial risk management plan template

The financial risk management plan template consists of five segments. The first segment identifies the investment portfolio and the investment manager, implying that the report is prepared for a specific investment by the individual who has the overall responsibility for that investment. The four remaining report segments reflect the components that make up the financial risk management process.

The first column, entitled 'Risk Rating' can be one of three rates, namely, low, medium or high. The risk rating is obtained from the qualitative risk analysis (refer to Figure 7.5) and establishes the risk priority, hence the reason why this column for visual display purposes is shown as the first information item.

The segment headed 'Risk Identification' essentially describes each risk and its association with the investment. The column headed 'Threat or Opportunity' provides information regarding how the particular risk affects the defined investment objectives (or outcomes), while the column headed 'Causes of Risk' describes the factor(s) that would trigger the risk. For example, 'risk is occurring if the interest rates increase'.

The information for the segment headed 'Qualitative Analysis' is obtained from the qualitative risk analysis as illustrated by Figure 7.5. The risk type may be any number of factors depending on the risk element being considered (see example at Figure 7.4). The probability and impact columns both contain one of the following classifications, very low, low, medium, high or very high.

The '*Quantitative Analysis*' is usually conducted when the risk is high. Hence, this report segment may not always have information pertaining to a particular investment. If present, the information will describe the probability of the risk occurring expressed as a range from one to minus one; the impact in terms of gain or loss in monetary value; and the resultant outcome, which is calculated by the multiplication of the impact by the probability.

The 'Risk Response' segment itemises the selected risk strategy option and the response actions to be taken (including the benefits and shortcomings of the response action). It may be recalled, that the risk strategy options may include one of the following, risk avoidance; risk transference; risk mitigation; and at time risk acceptance.

The final report segment is 'Risk Monitoring and Control'. This provides the details of the individual (or unit) directly responsible for the risk, the status interval period for reviewing the risk and any relevant remarks regarding the response action.

Note that Figure 7.14 is meant to provide a sample template of a risk management plan. Therefore, the space allocated to each column will need to be adjusted to reflect a realistic and practical situation. It is worth remembering that without a risk management plan, the success of the investment and the credibility of the investment manager are at stake. The financial risk management process has the objective of increasing the chances of success for both the specific financial activity and the individuals who have the responsibility for its implementation.

Conclusion

Financial risk management strives to foresee and deal with uncertainties that threaten the objectives of a variety of financial undertakings. However, risk is not always bad. There are both opportunities and threats. Risk management is defined as a succession of processes, tools and methods that will aid management to increase the likelihood and impact of positive events and to decrease the probability and impact of negative events. This chapter has shown that financial risk management planning consists of four components, namely, risk identification; risk quantification; risk response strategy; and risk monitoring and control.

Risk identification

Risk identification basically addresses the question: What might go wrong? It identifies and names the financial risks and their characteristics that are relevant to the business activity being undertaken. The outcome of this phase is an itemised risk inventory. A risk inventory is generated by examining in detail the entire financial activity and systematically seeking areas of uncertainty and categorising risk under major sub-headings.

Risk quantification

Risk quantification assesses the magnitude of the identified risk and its impact. It consists of two distinct methods, namely, qualitative and quantitative risk analysis. The latter approach is usually applied for financial activities that are considered to have extremely high risks associated with them. Qualitative risk analysis provides the prioritisation of the risks and their respective impact so that all major risks are included. The outcome from this stage is the risk probability and impact matrix.

The quantitative approach normally uses mathematical probability distributions for defining a financial model and applies simulation techniques to determine the financial outcome of the undertaking. Other techniques that may be applied include expected monetary value analysis, decision tree analysis and sensitivity analysis.

Risk response

Risk response has the objective of identifying the options available and defining the appropriate actions to enhance the opportunities and minimise the threats. Thus, the process identifies and assigns responsibility to an individual or group for each risk response.

Generally, there are four strategic risk options that a project manager may choose, these are risk avoidance – doing something to remove the risk; risk transference – shifting the responsibility of the risk to someone else who is better at doing that a particular activity; risk mitigation – lessening the probability of the risk occurring or lowering the consequences of the risk if it occurs; and risk acceptance – to accept certain risks, thus reacting to the specific risk if and when it occurs. The objective is to select the best strategy for addressing each risk and propose particular actions for implementing the selected strategy.

Risk monitoring and control

Risk monitoring and control keeps a close watch on the identified risks, outstanding risks and any new arising risks. Risk monitoring and control ensures that the risk response plans are implemented effectively. The risk monitoring and control process regularly assesses the effectiveness of the risk response plans and is best achieved by having frequent risk reviews to identify any outstanding actions, update risk probability and impact, remove risks that are no long relevant and identify new risks.

One should note that the risk management plan is the product of the above four components. The financial risk management plan template provided at Figure 7.14 consists of five segments. The first part describes the investment activity and its respective manager, therefore the report is prepared for a specific investment or financial activity by the individual who has the overall responsibility for that activity. The four remaining report segments reflect the components that make up the financial risk management process. Without a realistic and reliable financial risk management plan, the success of financial undertakings and the credibility of the organisation and manager are at stake. The proper application of financial risk management will increase the chances of success for both the entity and the individuals who have the responsibility for the financial activity.

The next chapter will continue with the theme related to financial risk management and will focus when to use financial risk management, particularly the application aspects.

References

Banwait, Gurpreet. (2011). What's at risk? The use of sensitivity analysis to measure your portfolio's risk. *Insight, TMI*, 194, 37–41.

Begenau, J., Piazzesi, M. and Schneider, M. (2013). Banks' risk exposures. [Online] Available at: http://web.stanford.edu/~piazzesi/banks.pdf [accessed: 18 September 2014].

Berkowitz, Jeremy. (2001). Testing density forecasts, with applications to risk management. *Journal of Business & Economic Statistics*, 19(4), 465–474.

Best, Jacqueline. (2010). The limits of financial risk management: or what we didn't learn from the Asian crisis. *New Political Economy*, 15(1), 29–49.

Caltrans. (2003). *Project Risk Management Handbook* (1st edn). Sacramento, CA: Office of Project Management Process Improvement.

Claussy, P., Roncalliz, T. and Weisangx, G. (2009). Risk management lessons from Madoff fraud. *International Finance Review*, 10, 1–39.

Ernst & Young. (2013). *Remaking Financial Services: Risk Management Five Years after the Crisis – A Survey of Major Financial Institutions*. Ernst & Young, Global Ltd.

Marphatia, A.C. and Tiwari, N. (2003). *Risk Management in the Financial Services Industry: An Overview*. White Paper, TATA Consultancy Services.

Project Management Institute Standards Committee. (2004). *A Guide to the Project Management Body of Knowledge*. Upper Darby, PA: PMI.

8

FINANCIAL RISK
MANAGEMENT APPLICATIONS

> Risk is like fire: If controlled it will help you; if uncontrolled it will rise up
> and destroy you.
>
> Theodore Roosevelt, 26th President of the USA

This chapter will focus on financial risk management applications. Therefore, the major issue that will be addressed is when to use financial risk management. It has already been illustrated that all undertakings carry a certain magnitude of risk. However, frequent and thorough risk analysis and risk management techniques can help to resolve concerns before they arise or become serious.

Managers of all types of entities are confronted with many opportunities to create value for shareholders using financial risk management. The basic concept is to determine which risks are cheaper for the entity to manage than the shareholders. By and large market risks that result in unique risks for the entity are the best candidates for financial risk management. An important source of financial risk are those risks arising from an entity's exposure to changes in market prices, such as interest rates, exchange rates and commodity prices.

The major concern is to determine when to use financial risk management to mitigate the risk arising from the changes in interest rates, exchange rates and commodity prices. One should note that financial rates and prices are affected by a number of factors. Hence, it is essential to understand the factors that impact markets because these factors, in turn, impact the potential risk of an entity.

Diversification as a means to reduce risk

One way to reduce risk is through diversification. In other words, one should ensure not having all one's eggs in one basket. Traditionally, the risk level of an asset was assessed on the variability (or degree of fluctuation) of its financial returns. That is stability of returns versus the erratic behaviour of the returns. The degree of stability of the financial returns was associated with low risk whereas the erratic behaviour of the financial returns was viewed as high risk.

However, modern portfolio theory takes into account not only an asset's level of risk, but also its contribution to the overall level of risk of the portfolio to which it is added. What does this mean in practice? It means that entities are taking the opportunity to reduce risk as a result of risk diversification. But risk diversification does not only mean not having all one's eggs in one basket. It also results from having a diversified portfolio that contains assets whose returns are dissimilar. In other words, having a portfolio of assets, where the financial returns from these assets are negatively correlated with one another.

Consider the following example. Assume that an investor has purchased a soft drinks factory. Marketing data indicates that the factory has a regular cash inflow in summer but in winter sales for soft drinks has a downward trend. The investor is considering investing in another enterprise and is considering two options, either to invest in ice cream or chocolate production. A decision to invest in ice cream production would mean having a similar market demand trend as soft drinks. That is, regular cash inflow in summer with a downward trend in winter. In other words there is a positive correlation between soft drinks and ice cream sales. The sales trends behaviour is the same for both products. However, a decision to invest in chocolate production would mean having a regular cash inflow in winter with a downward trend in summer. In other words, there is a negative correlation between soft drinks and chocolate sales. Therefore, by investing in soft drinks and chocolate production, the investor would secure regular cash inflow throughout the year. Furthermore, if for instance, the investor decided to invest in soft drinks and ice cream production and there was a bad summer season with the demand for soft drinks and ice cream being lower than normal, the investor is likely to endure a financial loss, which if repeated over several seasons could mean the dilution of the entire investment.

Therefore, diversification does not only mean spreading the investment but to spread the investment on different products and industries. Diversification also means spreading sales over a diverse range of customers rather than focusing on a single large customer. The same principle applies to the diversification of suppliers as well as financing sources. The above illustrates that diversification is an important tool in managing financial risks. Hence, diversification among investment assets reduces the magnitude of loss if one issuer fails and diversification of customers, suppliers and financing sources reduces the possibility that an entity will have its business adversely affected by changes outside management's control. Although the risk of loss still exists, diversification may reduce the opportunity for large adverse outcomes.

Example of diversification as a means to reduce risk

A way of achieving risk diversification is through hedging using the correlation principle mentioned previously. Hedging is a business transaction that seeks assets or events that offset, or have a weak or negative correlation to an entity's financial exposures. Correlation is a statistical measure that determines the tendency of two assets to move, or not move, together. Correlation is the direction and level of association between two or more variables. This tendency is quantified by a coefficient between -1 and +1. Hence, a correlation of +1.0 signifies perfect positive correlation and means that two assets can be expected to move together in relation to each other. On the other hand, a correlation of -1.0 signifies perfect negative correlation, which means that two assets can be expected to move together in relation to each other but in opposite directions. Correlation does not reflect cause and effect. For example, a correlation between ice cream and soft drinks does not mean that the more ice cream an individual consumes, that more soft drinks are consumed. That is, one does not cause the other; the cause is the warm weather.

The concept of negative correlation is central to hedging and risk management. Risk management involves pairing a financial exposure with an instrument or strategy that is negatively correlated to the exposure. For example, to invest in a mixture of fixed term deposits which are government guaranteed and non-secure investment bonds. For instance a long futures contract which is used to hedge a short underlying exposure employs the concept of negative correlation. If the price of the underlying (short) exposure begins to increase, the value of the (long) futures contract will also increase, offsetting some or all of the losses that occur due to the increase in the price. Therefore, the extent of the protection offered by the hedge depends on the magnitude of the negative correlation between the two assets.

Let us take an example. A stock trader after assessing the financial market determines that the stock price of New Berry Ltd will likely increase over the next month, due to the company's new innovative method of production. Therefore, the stock trader would like to purchase shares in New Berry Ltd to gain from the expected share price increase in the near future (next month). However, the stock trader is also aware that New Berry Ltd forms part of a highly volatile industry where share prices are regularly fluctuating. It should be noted that the stock trader is specifically interested in New Berry Ltd and not the industry it represents. Hence, the stock trader would like to hedge against the industry risk by short selling an equal value of the shares (i.e. number of shares times the share price) of New Berry Ltd's direct competitor, namely, Ajax eCom Ltd.

In this example, there are two import terms or concepts that need to be understood, namely long selling and short selling of shares. Long selling of shares is the normal conventional trading. It basically means owning a security and profiting if the price of the security goes up (long-term investment). In other words, if one was to purchase a security, the owner of the security would hold on to the security and would only sell it when the price of the security is higher than when it was purchased. Hence, the objective is a long-term investment.

Contrary to long selling of shares, short selling of shares is purely speculative. The short seller anticipates to profit from a decrease in the share price in the short term. In this case, the short seller would buy and hold onto the shares until there is the anticipation that the price of the shares is likely to decrease in the near future.

Hence, the short seller would sell the shares now in anticipation that the price of the shares in the near future would decrease. If the share price does actually decrease, the short seller would repurchase them. Hence, the short seller will pay less to re-buy the shares than what was received on selling them.

In the example the stock trader is going to adopt a long sell strategy with New Berry Ltd and a short sell strategy with Ajax eCom Ltd. Note that New Berry Ltd and Ajax eCom Ltd are competitors. Therefore, the short seller will incur a loss if the price of the assets rises.

Let us assume that on the *first day* the stock trader's portfolio is: (a) 2,000 shares in New Berry Ltd at €2 per share, which is €4,000; and (b) 1,000 shares in Ajax eCom Ltd (short sell strategy) at €4 per share, which is €4,000. As stated in the narrative, the stock trader's intention is to pursue a long sell strategy for New Berry Ltd and a short sell strategy for Ajax eCom Ltd (i.e. New Berry shares are purchased and Ajax eCom shares are sold). By having this portfolio, the stock trader's objective is to mitigate the risk but not remove it entirely.

On the *second day*, a favourable story is published in the finance news media about the industry that both New Berry Ltd and Ajax eCom Ltd pertain to. This favourable financial publicity results in an increased value of all share prices related to that particular industry. However, since New Berry Ltd is a stronger company, its share prices increase by 10 per cent, while Ajax eCom Ltd's share price increases by just 5 per cent. The result is that the stock trader will make a speculative gain of €400 on the New Berry shares were the shares to be sold at this point. However, the stock trader would make a loss of €200 if the Ajax eCom shares were to be re-purchased at this stage because the re-purchase price would be higher than the price sold. The stock trader might regret the hedge on day two because a greater profit could have been made if the focus of the investment was specifically only New Berry shares.

On the *third day*, an unfavourable story is published in the general news media about the adverse health effects of the products being produced by the industry that both New Berry Ltd and Ajax eCom Ltd belong to. The reaction of the stock market to this story is that all stock in the industry crashed by 50 per cent. This situation means that the stock trader will make a speculative loss of €2,200 on the New Berry shares were the shares to be sold at this point. However, the stock trader would make a gain of €2,100 if the Ajax eCom shares were to be re-purchased at this stage because the re-purchase price would be much lower than the price they were sold for originally. Table 8.1 provides a summary of the stock trader's hedge position.

Without the hedging strategy, the stock trader would have made a loss of €1,800 by purchasing the shares in New Berry Ltd through adopting only the long sell strategy. However, using the short sell strategy, by trading in Ajax eCom Ltd's shares as a hedging mechanism, resulted in a gain of €1,900. Hence, the hedging strategy (long sell combined with short sell share trading strategy) resulted in an overall gain of €100 during the extraordinary market collapse. Thus, the risk of investment failure was mitigated by the stock trader's action.

TABLE 8.1 Summary of stock trader's hedge position

Stock Trading Day	New Berry Share Value	Ajax eCom Share Value
1	€4,000	€4,000
2	€4,400	€4,200
3	€2,200	€2,100
Gain/Loss if shares are sold at day 3:	€1,800 loss	€1,900 gain

Overall Gain/Loss Status:	€100 gain

Factors that impact interest rates

Interest rates are a key component that determine many market prices and are also viewed by economists and accountants as an important economic barometer. Interest rates basically reflect the cost of money. In other words, the price one pays to borrow money or the selling price for lending money.

The major issue to be examined in this section is related to the factors that impact the magnitude of interest rates. What causes interest rates to up or down? In other words, there is a need to know the elements that interest rates are composed of. For instance, the price that an entity pays for money (interest rates) will consist of the basic rate. Hence, it is logical to assume that interest rates reflect the supply and demand for funds. When the supply of money is limited, its price is likely to be higher. This is likely to determine the basic interest rate.

Another element that may influence the interest rate is the expected inflation, since inflation reduces the purchasing power of a lender's assets. Furthermore, uncertainty is higher depending on the duration to the loan or investment maturity. Hence, it is difficult to determine the inflation rate for a longer period of time, particularly exceeding three years or more. Apart from the base rate (money supply) and inflation (money dilution), an important element is credit risk. Credit risk relates to the level of reliability and credibility of the borrower to pay back the loan and the associated interest payments (credit worthiness). While the base rate and inflation elements are founded on general economic conditions, credit risk is more of an explicit factor that is dependent on the economic standing of the particular entity.

Interest rates are important to entities and governments alike because they are the key ingredient in the determination of the cost of capital. In the real practical world, the majority of entities private and public, including governments require debt financing for their expansion and to undertake the vast majority of capital projects. Hence, when interest rates increase or decrease, the impact can be significant on borrowers, since interest rates also affect prices in other financial markets. Therefore, the impact of an increase or decrease in interest rates is wide-ranging.

But there are other factors that influence the level of interest rates. For instance, a threat of political or sovereign risk can cause interest rates to rise drastically, as investors demand additional compensation for the increased risk of default. A threat of political or sovereign risk is based on a national level; for example the effects of 'Arab Spring' activities on the investment capital inflows to the countries involved. Other examples include the default in making full loan repayments to investors by the Argentine government in 2001; the financial crisis and subsequent bailouts for Greece and Cyprus in 2012; the collapse of all three of the country's major privately owned commercial banks in Iceland in 2008/2011; and the financial crisis in Ireland in 2008/2014.

It may be concluded that generally, the factors that influence the level of market interest rates include: general economic conditions; monetary policy and the stand of the central bank; expected levels of inflation; foreign exchange market activity; foreign investor demand for debt securities; levels of sovereign debt outstanding; and financial and political stability.

Developed countries through their respective treasury department, normally provide the interest yield curve. This yield curve provides a graphical or tabular depiction of interest yields for a range of terms to maturity. For example, a typical yield curve might illustrate interest yields for maturity duration of one day to 30 year terms. Moreover, the interest yield curve takes into consideration all the market forces, such as the various factors described previously.

The US Department of Treasury yield curve is normally the most reported yield curve. It compares the one-month, three-month, two-year, five-year and 30-year US Treasury debt. This yield curve is often utilised by many financial institutions as a benchmark for other debt in the market, such as mortgage rates or bank lending rates. The yield curve is also applied to forecast changes in economic output and growth.

Figure 8.1 illustrates that the yield curve shows the likely return on interest for the different maturity periods. Hence, since current interest rates reflect expectations, the yield curve provides useful information about the market's expectations of future interest rates. For example, using the rates for one- and two-year maturities, the expected one-year interest rate beginning in one year's time can be determined. Additionally, the yield curve is also often regarded to be a predictor of future economic activity and thus may signify expected change in economic conditions.

Figure 8.1 also illustrates that the yield curve normally slopes upward with a positive slope, as lenders and/or investors demand higher rates from borrowers for longer lending maturity terms. Furthermore, this upward slope reflects an increase in the likelihood that a borrower may default on payment as the term to maturity increases. As already explained, interest rates that encompass the yield curve are also affected by the likely inflation future inflation rate. Thus, if investors expect a higher future inflation rate, they will demand greater premiums for longer maturity terms to offset this uncertainty, resulting in an upward-sloping yield curve.

From time to time, the demand for short term funds may increase significantly, resulting in interest rates for short-term loans being greater than longer term interest

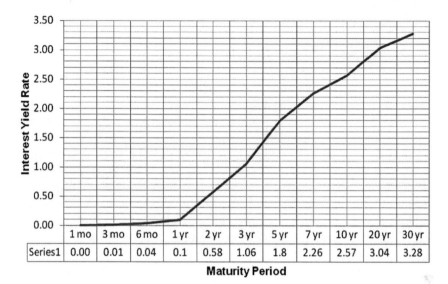

The following table corresponds to the chart:

Series1	1 mo	3 mo	6 mo	1 yr	2 yr	3 yr	5 yr	7 yr	10 yr	20 yr	30 yr
	0.00	0.01	0.04	0.1	0.58	1.06	1.8	2.26	2.57	3.04	3.28

Maturity Period

FIGURE 8.1 Example of interest yield curve

Source: US Treasury Department as at 22 September 2014.

rates. The effect of this phenomena is that the higher cost of funds for short-term loans may lower the expected gains that would result in the course of investment and expansion, and thus cause the economy to be at risk to a slowdown or recession. However, one should also note that rising interest rates are likely to weaken the demand for both short and long-term funds that may result in a reduction in all interest rates, which will cause the yield curve to return to its normal shape or curvature.

Interest rate determination theories

There are three major axioms that emerge when examining the interest yield curve: (a) interest rates for different maturities tend to move together over time; (b) yields on short-term bonds are more unpredictable (volatile) than yields on long-term bonds; and (c) long-term yield tends to be higher than short-term yields, hence the reason why the yield curve usually slopes upward. To explain these three axioms, four theories have been put forward that endeavour to account for the maturity term structure of interest rates and the resulting yield curve. These theories are: (a) the interest rate expectations theory; (b) the liquidity theory; (c) the preferred habitat theory; and (d) the market segmentation theory.

Expectations interest rate theory

The expectations interest rate theory suggests that forward interest rates are a mirror of what investors expect the future interest rates to be. Hence, as a result, the shape of the yield curve and the maturity term structure of rates reflect the market's aggregate expectations. The fundamental assumption for this theory is that the purchasers of bonds do not have preference for bonds of one maturity over another. Therefore, these purchasers will not hold on to any quantity of a bond if its expected return is less than that of another bond with a different maturity period. As a consequence, these bonds are viewed as perfect substitutes. The differentiation between short-term and long-term bonds is the inflation and interest rate risks, which the expectation theory in effect does not consider.

For example, assume that three months from today, a purchaser of bonds wants to buy a six-month treasury-bill. This purchaser would look at the forward rate on the six-month treasury-bill to determine its expected yield that would be projected in three months' time. Assume that the forward rate is 1.5 per cent for that specific treasury-bill. In this case, the expectations theory would suggest that the six-month interest rate, three months from today will be 1.5 per cent. In other words, investors tend to make decisions that are partly based on what they predict the level of interest rates to be in the future. Expectations theory suggests that investors that are attracted to long-term investments will make their decision to purchase a financial instrument based on whether the forward interest rates are less or more advantageous than the current short-term interest rates.

Liquidity interest rate theory

This theory suggests that investors will choose longer term investment maturities if they are provided with an additional yield that compensates them for lack of liquidity. As a result, liquidity theory supports the proposition that forward interest rates possess a liquidity premium and an interest rate expectation component.

This theory is more difficult to conceive. Financial instruments, such as bonds, that are default-free (i.e. fully secured) still carry a risk because of the uncertainty about the future rates of interest and also the uncertainty of inflation rates. This theory makes the point that investors (e.g. bond holders) are concerned about the purchasing power of the investment return. Hence, they are concerned with the real rate of return they receive from their investment, not just the nominal value of the interest payment. Therefore, the uncertainty about the inflation rate fuels doubt about the real return on the investment (i.e. bond), thus causing the investment to be risky. It is not a question of whether the interest payment will be received or not, but whether the value of the interest payment received in reality is at par with what was previously received, hence the effect of inflation on the real value of the investment return. Unfortunately, the further one looks into the future, the greater the level of uncertainly of inflation. This explicitly implies that an investment's inflation risk increases with its time to maturity.

Furthermore, the interest-rate risk is caused by the disparity between investor's investment horizon and the investment time to maturity. When a bondholder sells a bond before its maturity period, the variation in the interest rate will cause capital gains or losses. Hence, a longer maturity term will likely result in higher price changes for a given change in interest rates and the greater the probability for capital losses. Similar to inflation, the risk increases with the term to maturity of the investment, therefore, the investor expects higher compensation to safeguard against this risk. The purchaser of long-term bonds would require compensation for the risks they are taking in buying long-term bonds.

Contrary to the expectations theory where different investment maturities are viewed as substitutes, the liquidity theory views bonds of different maturities as substitutes. In other words, investors would prefer having short-term rather than long-term bonds because they are to a greater extent insulated from inflation and interest rate risks. Therefore, long-term investors will need to be paid a positive liquidity premium as compensation to hold long-term bonds. Consequently, the yield consists of two components, a component that is risk free similar to expectations theory and the other component being the premium for holding a longer-term bond.

Market segmentation theory

This theory assumes that markets for different-maturity term bonds are completely segmented. Therefore, the interest rate for each bond with a different maturity is determined by the market (the supply and demand for the bond), with no effects on the expected returns from other bonds with other maturities. In other words, long-term bonds that are influenced by inflation and interest rate risks are viewed as entirely different financial instruments from short-term bonds.

Thus, the market segmentation theory implies that various investors have different investment horizons that arise from the nature of their business or as a result of investment restrictions. These different investment horizons prevent these investors from changing maturity dates significantly to take advantage of the temporary opportunities in interest rates that may be relevant at the time. Therefore, the bonds of different maturities are not seen as substitutes, hence the expected income returns from a bond of one maturity is not viewed as having an impact on the demand for a bond of another maturity.

This attitude has the consequence that entities which have a long investment time horizon will likely be less interested in taking advantage of opportunities at the short end of the curve. Hence, this theory suggests that each borrower and lender have a particular timeframe in mind when purchasing or selling a debt instrument. For example, an entity undertaking a major construction project may want to issue long-term bonds that mature when the construction project is completed so that it has adequate liquidity to meet the demands of the creditors. Similarly, a financial institution may trade government bonds in the short-term to benefit from interest rate changes that may occur at the time.

Thus, bonds of shorter holding periods are likely to have lower inflation and interest rate risks. The segmented market theory predicts that the yield on longer term bonds will generally be higher, thus explaining why the yield curve is usually upward sloping. However, since markets for different-maturity bonds are completely segmented, there is no reason why the short and long yields should move together. Hence, the segmented market theory cannot explain why the short-term yields should be more volatile than the longer-term yields.

Preferred habitat theory

The preferred habitat theory is a combination of both the expectations and the market segmentation theories, so that the interest-rate and maturity-term relationship can be better explained. The preferred habitat theory suggests that investors who usually prefer one maturity horizon over another can be convinced to change maturity horizons if an appropriate premium is given. Thus, this theory implies that the yield curve shape depends on market participants' investment policies.

However, these investors will never prefer a long-term financial instrument over a short-term one with the same interest rate. Hence, as long as investors are compensated with a satisfactorily high interest rate, they will assign a greater value to an investment even though they may have a preferred maturity period over another. Additionally, the market is only partially segmented in that interest rates (in part) will add up over longer maturities.

Concluding remarks

From the above examination of the four theories, it may be concluded that interest rates, particularly the yield curve shape are affected by what the investors expect or perceive in the future; the opportunity cost through the loss of liquidity; the particular behavioural investment routine of investors, regarding their preference for long-term versus short-term maturity periods; and the specific industry to which the investors belong, which may influence them as to whether they indulge in long-term or short-term maturity periods.

Factors that affect foreign currency exchange rates

Similar to interest rates, foreign currency exchange rates are considered as an important element in the determination of market prices. Foreign exchange rates are determined by the supply and demand for currencies. However, the underlying variables that determine the supply and demand for currencies are economic factors, such as the inflation rate; foreign trade, particularly the level of imports and exports; and the activities of international investors in terms of capital inflows and outflows from one country to another. Typically, capital flows depending on their magnitude and mobility (i.e. ability to move about without currency exchange restrictions) are essential in determining the particular currency exchange rates.

As a general rule, factors that impact the level of interest rates also influence foreign currency exchange rates among floating or market-determined currencies. In fact, currencies are very sensitive to changes or anticipated changes in interest rates and to sovereign risk factors. For example, the Arab Spring uprising of 2010 and which spread throughout the countries of the Arab League and surrounding regions had a tremendous impact on both the interest rates and foreign currency exchange rates in these countries.

It should be noted that traditionally foreign trade was seen as the most significant influencing factor in determining foreign currency exchange rates. However, capital flows between countries (for investment objectives) have become an important element in the determination of foreign currency exchange rates. For example, a country that has higher interest rates than others will attract more capital inflows, because investors would desire a higher return on their capital, particularly if the country offering the higher interest rates is a stable one. In this case, investors would feel more secure in shifting their capital to a country having relatively high interest rates and which offers stability, such as in Australia when compared to Argentina which has a track record of defaulting on its foreign debt.

Research has shown that some of the key drivers that affect foreign currency exchange rates include the following: interest rate differentials net of expected inflation, namely the real interest rate; trading activity in other currencies with regard to imports and exports and the resultant balance of payments; international capital and trade flows, namely capital flows that fuel foreign investment; international institutional investor attitude in terms of banks opening in countries other than their parent country; financial and political stability in terms of whether the particular country has experienced or is in need of a financial bailout, such as in Portugal, Ireland and Greece; the monetary policy of the central bank in establishing the base interest rates or imposing foreign exchange restrictions; the domestic debt levels of a country in terms of the debt to GDP ratio in determining the creditworthiness of the country; and the economic conditions of the country in terms of whether it is experiencing a recession or growth. For eurozone countries some of these factors would need to be viewed from a regional perspective and others seen from a single country standpoint.

When trade in goods and services with other countries was the major determinant factor of foreign currency exchange rate fluctuations, market trade participants tended to monitor trade flow statistics closely for information about a particular currency future direction. However, given the growth of globalisation and the vast developments in information communications technology (ICT), capital flows have become very important and are also monitored closely. Hence, both trade in terms of the trade gap (the difference between imports and exports) and capital cash flows in terms of investment mobility are monitored closely to establish the future currency trends.

Furthermore, when other risk factors are considered equal, those currencies with higher short-term real interest rates will be seen as more attractive to international investors than those with lower interest rate currencies. Typically, currencies that are more attractive to foreign investors are countries that are viewed as the recipients of capital mobility. Hence, capital freedom, which allows an organisation to invest and divest internationally, is viewed as one that permits capital to seek a safe and opportunistic return. In other words, countries that have tight foreign exchange policies would not attract capital cash inflows. In fact, the more foreign currency exchange regulations are liberalised, the higher the requirement to monitor capital cash flows as an important determining factor in forecasting foreign currency exchange rates and movements.

There are some currencies, such as the Swiss franc, Canadian dollar and US dollar (and at one time the Japanese yen) that are particularly attractive during times of financial turbulence. These currencies are viewed as being stable and resilient. Additionally, the foreign currency exchange forward markets are also closely related to the interest rate markets. In freely traded currencies, such as the US dollar and euro, foreign currency traders tend to arbitrage between the forward currency markets and the interest rate markets to ensure interest rate uniformity. The practice of arbitrage is the simultaneous buying and selling of the same negotiable financial instruments, particularly currencies (it could also be commodities) in different markets in order to make an instant profit without risk. For example, a broker might buy Japanese yen when the yen to the US dollar ratio is increasing, then sells the yen and buys US dollars for a profit when the forward rate is higher, thus making an immediate profit on the transaction.

Currency exchange rate determination theories

Similar to interest rates, several theories have been put forward to provide an explanation of how exchange rates behave and are determined. There are basically five major theories (or approaches) that are presented that describe the behaviour and determination of exchange rates, namely the supply and demand approach; purchasing power parity approach; the balance of payments approach; the monetary approach; and the portfolio balance (or asset) approach.

Supply and demand approach

The supply and demand approach views the foreign currency exchange rate similar to a commodity, with its behaviour being determined by the level of supply and demand in the market. Hence, a foreign currency exchange rate is seen as being the price that one pays for a particular foreign currency in relation to another. In other words, an exchange rate is a swapping factor between foreign currencies. Therefore, its behaviour is comparable to commodities; hence, price is determined by the supply and demand forces. Admittedly, although international trade causes entities to swap one currency to another, it is currency speculation that mainly causes the change of the market forces. In other words, what the market expects the demand for a particular currency to be in the future.

As stated previously, the exchange rate, just like commodities, determines its price by responding to the supply and demand market forces. Hence, if for some reason there is an increase their demand for a particular currency, then the price will rise, provided the supply remains stable. On the contrary, if the supply is increased the price will decline, provided the demand remains stable. Therefore, the demand for a foreign currency occurs due to the level of imported goods and services imported; capital flows due to international investments in assets; and conventional international finance.

Purchasing power parity approach

The purchasing power parity approach is based in part on 'the law of one price'. It is also referred to as the inflation theory of exchange rates. According to 'the law of one price' the exchange rates are in equilibrium when the prices of goods and services (excluding capital flow mobility and other issues) in different countries are the same. In others words, to stabilise the foreign currency exchange rate there is a need to keep prices for goods and services at parity with the trading partners. Therefore, if local prices for goods and services increase more than the prices in the country we are trading with, for the same goods and services, the local currency would be expected to decline in value in relation to its foreign counterpart, assuming that no change in structural relationship between the countries has taken place.

The concern with this approach is the underlying assumption of the existence of an integrated, competitive product market with the implicit supposition of a risk-neutral world, in which the goods can be traded freely without transportation costs, tariffs, export quotas and other costs. Hence, it is not based on a realistic trading environment. In the real world of trade, each individual economy produces and consumes an unlimited number of goods and services, many of which have diverse prices from country to country due to normal activities, such as transport costs, customs tariffs and other trade barriers.

Balance of payments approach

The balance of payments is a process of recording all the international monetary transactions of a country during a specific period of time. These transactions are classified into three categories, namely the current account transactions, the capital account transactions, and the central bank transactions. Each transaction category can show a deficit or a surplus, but theoretically the overall payments of the three categories should be zero. However, this rarely happens.

The balance of payments approach implies that exchange rates result from trade and capital flow transactions that, in turn, affect the balance of payments. An equilibrium exchange rate is reached when both internal and external pressures are also in equilibrium. In other words, a country would need to keep its volume of exports and imports at parity with its trading partners. The change in the value of money, which in reality is the price depreciation or appreciation of a currency, directly affects the volume of a country's imports and exports. Hence, the probable rise and fall in the exchange rates may increase the balance of payments discrepancies.

Monetary approach

The monetary approach suggests that exchange rates are determined by a balance between the supply of, and demand for, money. When the money supply in one country increases compared with its trading partners, prices should rise and the currency should depreciate. The money supply is endogenously determined by domestic output, the foreign interest rate and foreign price level.

The monetary approach illustrates that the foreign currency exchange rate of a particular country depends on both current values as well as expected future values of related variables. These related variables being: (a) an increase in the domestic money supply and foreign interest rate raises both the domestic price level and nominal exchange rate level; and (b) that changes in real domestic income and the foreign price level have a negative effect on the domestic level and nominal interest rate.

Portfolio balance (asset) approach

The asset approach implies that currency holdings by foreign investors are chosen based on factors such as real interest rates, as compared with other countries. An important proposition of the asset approach is that exchange rates are likely to be much more variable than the prices for goods and services. This is consistent with reality, in that exchange rates react to changing circumstances in financial-asset markets and are not simply responding to changes in international trade for goods and services.

This approach assumes perfect capital mobility. In other words, capital flows freely between countries with no major transactions costs or capital controls to serve as barriers to investment. Hence, it assumes the full liberalisation of capital flow movement. In such a situation, covered interest arbitrage will ensure covered interest rate parity. Furthermore, this relationship will hold continuously, with spot and forward exchange rates as well as interest rates adjusting immediately to changing financial-market conditions.

Development of the futures market

The futures market originated some 150 years ago in a farming environment, where farmers would harvest their crops and then bring them to market in anticipation of selling them. However, without knowing the demand, very often either the supply often exceeded the requirements and the surplus crops were left to rot or the demand exceeded the supply and the products made from the crop became very expensive because of the shortage of availability.

This concern was to a certain extent addressed by the mid-nineteenth century where central grain markets were created. Thus farmers were able to deposit their commodities at a central marketplace and sell them either for immediate delivery (i.e. spot market trading) or for forward delivery, which is similar to today's futures contracts. Hence, this concept prevented many farmers from losing crops and profits. Furthermore, it also assisted in stabilising supply and prices in the off-season.

In the modern era, the futures concept has expanded and developed further into a global marketplace where all types of products apart from agricultural goods are traded. The futures marketplace deals with all types of metals and cereals, leather, currencies and financial instruments, such as treasury bonds and securities (securities futures). With the inception of ICT, a virtual futures market place has been created, which is viewed as a diverse meeting place of farmers, exporters, importers, manufacturers and speculators. ICT has made it possible for traders to access and view commodities prices around the world so that they can compete on the open market.

In 2006 the New York Stock Exchange entered into a strategic alliance with the Amsterdam-Brussels-Lisbon-Paris Exchanges 'euronext' electronic exchange, thus creating the first transcontinental futures and options exchange. This development has resulted in a rapid growth of internet futures trading platforms. The National Stock Exchange of India in Mumbai is the largest stock futures trading exchange in the world in terms of trading volume, followed by JSE Ltd in Sandton, Gauteng, South Africa.

A futures market can be visualised as a central financial exchange where persons may trade standardised futures contracts. In other words, they are a type of a contract to buy specific quantities of a commodity or financial instrument at a particular price with delivery set at a specified time in the future. These types of contracts are also referred to as derivatives and are valued according to the movement of the underlying asset, such as a physical commodity or stock, among others. The word 'derivatives' is used because the value of these instruments is derived from another class of asset. Viewed from a risk management perspective, futures markets provide limited income risk insurance to producers whose output is risky. However, futures are very effective insurance to commodity stockholders at unusually low cost. Speculators take up some of the risk but the practice of hedging seems to be driving most commodity markets.

Objective of the futures market

The objective of the futures market is based on competitive market economy principles. There is general consensus among economists that a market for a product would be perfectly competitive if three conditions exist, namely that many buyers and sellers met openly, with no single individual controlling the market; the commodity is homogeneous so that all market participants know the grade and quality of the product being traded; and buyers and sellers may freely enter the market and participants had full knowledge of available supply and demand for their product.

Futures markets, due to their highly competitive nature, come very close to satisfying the above three economic principles, namely:

- Futures trading is a very efficient means of determining the price level for a commodity because there are many potential buyers and sellers competing freely on the open market (i.e. concept of price discovery);
- Futures markets allow producers, processors and consumers of commodities, debt instruments and currency markets a means of transferring the price risks inherent in their businesses to traders who are willing to assume these risks (i.e. concept of hedging), thus ensuring a more efficient marketing system resulting in lower prices for consumers;
- Futures markets have developed into a national or worldwide phenomena, thus they facilitate the collection and dissemination of necessary market information and statistical data.

Hedging provides traders with an opportunity to lower their costs of doing business by allowing them to conduct an equal and opposite transaction, in order to reduce the risk of financial loss due to a change in price. Theoretically this makes it possible for hedgers to operate on narrower profit margins that may be caused by market competition. This reduces the risk of a loss and permit lower prices that may be passed on the consumer as savings and ultimately higher profits to the producer.

Hedging may also result in lower financing cost for traders. Some banks, particularly those lending to commercial borrowers, permit hedgers to borrow a higher percentage of the value of their commodity, typically at lower interest rates when compared with non-hedgers. The resultant lower cost financing in turn allows higher profit margins for the hedger and may provide lower prices for the consumer.

Having said the above, trading in futures is not meant to be applied as a means of transferring ownership of the actual commodity. Hence, few traders deliver on futures contracts because cash markets usually provide a more efficient method to exchange ownership of a commodity. Futures markets are more applicable as a means to establish a forward price to a commodity and to mitigate the risk of ownership.

Use of currency futures to hedge currency positions

Typically, foreign currency markets are viewed as being deep in that a large number of foreign currency dealings can be made without drastically affecting the price. They are also considered highly liquid and relatively inexpensive. In general, when managing currency risk exposures, one can follow a number of strategies namely hire the services of an overlay manager; trade over-the-counter (OTC) market currency forwards and options; or exchange-traded futures and options on futures. An overlay manager has the function of currency trading by taking an aggressive approach in managing a currency hedge mandate with the objective of maximising earnings, using currency futures, forwards and options contracts. However, the focus of this section is exchange-traded futures and options on futures, which provide a number of major benefits, including:

1   Removal of counterparty credit risk. Normally, when entering into exchange-traded currency contract, the counterparty acts as the exchange clearing house. For example, when processing currency transactions through a clearing house, the clearing house functions as the buyer to every seller and the seller to every buyer. This means that the market participants do not need to evaluate the credit worthiness of multiple counterparties. Hence, all clearing house participants support the trades at the exchange. Data from the GLOBEX at Chicago Mercantile Exchange indicates that there has never been a default experienced in the history of this exchange.

2   Price efficiency and transparency. Price efficiency refers to the price discovery process. This is achieved because futures and options exchanges function as a forum, bringing together in one central location, diverse types of buyers and sellers with the primary objective of establishing foreign exchange rates. Furthermore, the price discovery process entails having procedures that are open to scrutiny with the resultant rates being electronically disseminated across the globe; hence achieving a transparent process.

3   Ease of access for all types of market participants. The International Monetary Market was established in 1972 by the Chicago Mercantile Exchange. It initially traded in seven currency futures contracts, thus creating the world's first financial futures. The International Monetary Market provided universal access by permitting all types and size of participants, ranging from individuals to large commercial enterprises, to buy and sell currencies for future delivery or cash settlement.

Typically, foreign currency markets are viewed as being deep in that a large number of foreign currency dealings can be made without drastically affecting the price. They are also considered highly liquid and relatively inexpensive. However, foreign currency markets may carry a severe market risk, thus applying a suitable approach that mitigates this risk becomes essential.

Comparison of futures with forward contracts

The key distinguishing attribute between futures and forward contracts is that futures are publicly traded on an exchange while forwards are privately traded. Hence, forward contracts are traded privately over-the-counter, not on an exchange. This means that a forward contract is a bespoke contractual agreement, which is specially made between two private parties, where they agree to trade a particular asset with each other at an agreed explicit price and time in the future. The settlement date, notional amount of the contract and settlement form (cash or physical) is exclusively determined by the parties to the contract.

More specifically, a future contract involves two parties, namely the buyer and the seller. The buyer (who holds a long position) agrees to purchase the underlying asset (such as stocks, bonds, or commodities) on a specified date at a price that is agreed to when signing the contact. Hence, buyers benefit from price increases. On the other hand, the seller (who holds a short position) agrees to sell the underlying asset on a specified date at a price that is agreed to when signing the contact. Hence, sellers benefit from price decreases. One should note that since future contracts are transacted through a regulated exchange, prices are changing daily in the marketplace and are marked to market on this daily basis. At the agreed contract termination date, the buyer takes delivery of the underlying asset from the seller or the parties can agree to make cash settlement.

Therefore, a futures contract is similar to a forward contract in that it includes an agreed price and time in the future to buy or sell an underlying asset, however its format is standard (i.e. it is not tailor made) and is publicly traded on a futures exchange through brokerage firms. A futures contract includes standard terms and conditions related to trading and credit procedures; delivery location and dates; volume; and technical specifications.

Unlike forwards, futures do not have credit risk because a clearing house guarantees against default risk by matching both sides of the trade and 'marking to market' their positions every night. 'Mark to market' aims to provide a realistic appraisal of an entity's current financial situation. Hence, the 'mark to market' process converts daily gains and losses into actual cash gains and losses each night, such that as one party loses on the trade the other party gains, and the clearing house moves the payments for the counterparty through this process.

On the other hand, forwards may give rise to both market risk and credit risk because the risk exposure for over-the-counter derivatives arise from the default of the counterparty due to a failure in performing on a forward. As we have seen, this does not apply with futures because the exchange acts as the clearing house and guarantees the trade thus eradicating any risk involved in the process. However, the profit or loss on a forward contract is accomplished at the time of settlement, which means that the credit exposure can keep increasing.

Additionally, future contracts are regulated and typically fall under the responsibility of a single regulatory regime in one jurisdiction at the national or federal government level. This regulatory regime guarantees against manipulation, it ensures that the professionals in the market are qualified and behave honestly, and that the deals are reported in a timely manner. Since futures contracts are carried out through a regulated exchange, the counterparty on a futures contract is selected at random by the exchange.

On the other hand, trades involving forwards are conducted across jurisdictional precincts and are mainly managed by the contractual terms and conditions between the contracting parties. If physical delivery is specified in a forward contract, then it must stipulate the recipient of the physical object. One should note that forward contracts are normally carried out by regulated organisations. Moreover, a forward contract generates cash flows at the point of delivery, while futures contracts require margin requests, particularly periodic margin calls.

Mitigating risk through the use of currency futures

The application of foreign currency futures to currency hedging is an effective method for mitigating financial risk. The following provides an example of hedging euro foreign currency risk.

Let us assume that a US hedge fund finds that the Euro Area Treasury Bills (ECB) yields are attractive and decides to rollover an investment in ECB whose principal plus interest at maturity in six months will amount to 550 million euro.

However, the US hedge fund was aware that its all-in return depends on the US dollar versus euro exchange rate risk. Hence, the US hedge fund sought to hedge its risk exposure of converting the ECB investment back into US dollars. An appraisal of the available alternatives was conducted and the US hedge fund decided to hedge with exchange-traded euro futures contracts. The trading unit of the euro futures is 0.5 million euro.

Using this alternative, the US hedge fund on 1 January 2014, sells 1,100 June 2014 euro futures at $0.9208 per euro. This is equivalent to 550 million euro (i.e. 0.5 million euro trading unit times 1,100 contracts = 550 million euro).

During the six month period the US dollar exchange rate for the euro falls to $0.9145 per euro. Consequently, as the euro futures price decreases, the hedge fund's trading account at its clearing member firm is credited the gains on the position by the exchange clearing house. The price fluctuation from US$0.9208 to US$0.9145 per euro on the short euro futures position resulted in a positive gain of US$0.0063 per euro (i.e. 0.9208 minus 0.9145 = $0.0063).

This gain is equivalent to a profit of US$3,150 per contract times 1,100 contracts for a net position gain of US$3.465 million excluding brokerage or clearing fees that are normally related with exchange transactions (i.e. 0.5 million euro trading unit times positive gain of US$0.0063 per euro times 1,100 contracts = $3.465 million).

The outcome when US dollar profit is added to the US dollars amount due from the conversion at the lower dollar-euro exchange rate of US$0.9145 per euro in relation to the euro denominated ECB principal and interest, results in an effective rate equivalent to the euro futures price at the commencement of the hedge.

Mitigating financial risk due to currency exchange and interest fluctuations

The issue is to mitigate financial risk due to currency and interest fluctuations. Hedging of foreign currency and interest is a common approach for reducing risk. Foreign currency hedging is a risk reducing strategy to aid anyone involved with dealing in foreign currencies. The major concern with foreign currencies is that their exchange rates are very volatile and are constantly subject to change. Hence, this instability can transform into serious losses if there are adverse foreign currency exchange rates changes between the date of the transaction and date of actual receipt or payment.

One should bear in mind that the main concern for most businesses that focus on trading goods and services are the normal bread and better issues. In other words, how can the business secure more export/import contracts for the goods and services that are supplied? Does the enterprise have the logistical mechanisms in place to allow the effective and timely delivery of the goods and services being supplied? Foreign currency exchange rates are an added complication for these entrepreneurs. These entrepreneurs usually do not want to speculate on foreign currency exchange, they simply want to ensure that the contribution margin that was computed when signing an export/import contact in fact materialises. Hence, foreign currency hedging aims to minimise or eliminate this currency risk.

Like all hedging strategies, foreign currency hedging involves taking two offsetting, opposite positions, in two different parallel markets. The positions are such, that their end results offset each other. In other words, excess profit on one side of the equation is compensated by an extra loss in the other, leaving the entrepreneur with whatever was originally expected. Basically, the fundamental aim is that a business's income and expenditure does not get affected by any wayward foreign exchange rate or interest rate fluctuations.

The effect of currency devaluation on the home country is that it normally results in increasing the cost of imports and decreasing the cost of exports. Hence, an exporter who has a fixed rate contract to supply a foreign customer whose country has experienced currency devaluation would mean that the exports will cost more and hence a serious loss may occur.

Hedging of foreign exchange currency rates and interest rates

Basically, foreign currency hedging strategies may be achieved by taking either or a combination of two approaches, namely the internal approach or/and the external approach of hedging foreign trade risks. There are two most common internal approaches. The first is the leading and lagging of income and expenditures. Under this approach a trader can pay in advance (lead) or pay late (lag) on foreign currency payments, depending on the expectations of whether the foreign currency will appreciate or depreciate in the near future. The concept is based on the notion that foreign currency depreciation (home currency appreciation) will convert into lower returns and higher payments, respectively. Hence, if the trader expects that the foreign exchange rate will adversely change in the future, the likelihood would be that the trade will pay in advance.

The second approach is netting the receipts and payments. The notion with this approach is that it involves matching (or clubbing) the receipts and payments in a currency, so that any losses in receipts are compensated by the gains in payments and vice versa. In other words, the trader of goods and services would offset receipts and payments so that the amount of the transaction is reduced. This would result in reducing bank charges and at the same time mitigate the foreign currency exchange risk.

For example, let us assume that Ajax Ltd is a company in Australia and Sapphire Ltd is a company in the European Union. Both companies act as suppliers to each other (importing/exporting different goods). These companies enter into a contact at an agreed initial foreign exchange rate. Let us assume that at the end of an agreed financial period, Ajax Ltd owes Sapphire Ltd, €300,000 and Sapphire Ltd owes Ajax Ltd, €250,000. These amounts are calculated based on the initial agreed foreign exchange rate in the contract. Under the netting of receipts and payments concept, the companies would offset the amount of each respective transaction, so that what remains is the difference between €300,000 and €250,000 resulting in a transaction of €50,000. Hence, Ajax Ltd would make a bank transfer of €50,000 to Sapphire Ltd. The result is that only the €50,000 is subject to any resultant foreign currency exchange risk and additionally the bank transaction fee would be based on a reduced amount.

The concern with the internal approach is that there is a limit to the amount of foreign currency risk that can be hedged by the internal strategies. Hence, the external foreign currency hedging strategies are more popular since they offer a broader scope.

There are many external foreign currency exchange hedging strategies. This section focuses on two, namely, foreign currency exchange swaps and interest rate swaps. Generally, foreign currency swaps are exchange transactions that take place in real time. In other words, the currency exchange is immediate without any lapse or delay in the time period. The concept is based on having both the principal and payments of a fixed interest contract in one currency that are swapped for the principal and payments of an equal loan in another currency. This effectively means swapping one currency with fixed payment obligations with another currency with also fixed payment obligations, so that both parties to the transaction will be dealing in the currency in which they have more faith. This would reduce the foreign currency exchange risk that may occur between them.

On the other hand, interest rate swaps are basically contracts that allow two parties to swap their particular interest rate exposure with another. Note that this is not a risk neutralising strategy, but the rationalisation of the interest rate risk exposure. Interest rate swaps often exchange a fixed payment for a floating payment that is directly linked to an interest rate standard such as the London Interbank Offer Rate (LIBOR) or the Euribar. LIBOR is the interest rate offered by London banks on deposits made by other banks in the euro-dollar markets. The Euro Interbank Offered Rate (Euribor) is a daily reference rate, published by the European Banking Federation, based on the averaged interest rates at which euro-zone banks offer to lend unsecured funds to other banks in the euro wholesale money market (or interbank market). The market for interest rate swaps frequently (but not always) utilise LIBOR or Euribar as the base for the floating rate. An entity will generally use interest rate swaps to limit or manage exposure to fluctuations in interest rates, or to obtain a marginally lower interest rate than it would have been able to get without the swap.

Hedging of foreign exchange currency swaps

The best way to explain foreign exchange currency swaps is through a practical example. A foreign currency exchange swap may easily take place, particularly when the entities involved have subsidiary companies in each of their respective countries.

Let us assume that Golden Bay UK Ltd is a company established in the United Kingdom (UK) and Parkland Canada Ltd is a company that is established in Canada. Both of these companies have subsidiary companies in their respective country, that is Golden Bay UK Ltd has a subsidiary company in Canada known as Golden Bay Canada Ltd and Parkland Canada Ltd has a subsidiary company in the UK known as Parkland UK Ltd. Both companies would like to invest in the subsidiary companies as part of their expansion programme. This example will illustrate what is known as 'Parallel Loan'.

Assume that the typical borrowing costs are 10 per cent in the UK and 11 per cent in Canada. The Board of Directors of the UK parent company (Golden Bay UK Ltd) would like to secure funds to finance their expansion of its Canadian subsidiary company (Golden Bay Canada Ltd). Golden Bay Canada Ltd is not well known in Canada so it would likely be penalised a 2 per cent risk premium over the normal rate (i.e. normal rate is 11 per cent plus 2 per cent risk premium = 13 per cent effective rate). The Board of Directors of the UK parent company view a 13 per cent interest rate as being too high.

On the other hand, the Board of Directors of the Canadian parent company (Parkland Canada Ltd) is in a similar circumstance, in that they would like to secure funds to finance their expansion of their UK subsidiary company (Parkland UK Ltd). Similarly, Parkland UK Ltd is not well known in the UK so it would likely be penalised a 3 per cent risk premium over the normal rate (i.e. normal rate is 10 per cent plus 3 per cent risk premium = 13 per cent effective rate). The Board of Directors of the Canadian parent company view a 13 per cent interest rate as being unacceptable. Figure 8.2 depicts the situation of the companies involved.

Both parent companies are unwilling to agree to the anticipated interest rates for the business expansion to take place at their respective subsidiary companies. Hence the parallel loan solution to this dilemma would be for the UK parent company (Golden Bay UK Ltd) to borrow the amount required by Canadian subsidiary (Parkland UK Ltd) in UK at 10 per cent in pounds sterling, and thus re-lend the money to the Canadian subsidiary (Parkland UK Ltd) in UK. Moreover, the Canadian parent company (Parkland Canada Ltd) would borrow the amount required by the UK subsidiary (Golden Bay Canada Ltd) in Canadian dollars at 11 per cent and re-lends this money to the UK subsidiary in Canada (Golden Bay Canada Ltd). Since no foreign currency leaves the UK there is no foreign currency transfer tax. Additionally, during the loan period, the UK subsidiary in Canada (Golden Bay Canada Ltd) would earn Canadian dollars to pay the interest and principal. Similarly, the Canadian subsidiary in UK (Parkland UK Ltd) would earn pounds sterling to pay back the interest on the loan and eventually the principal.

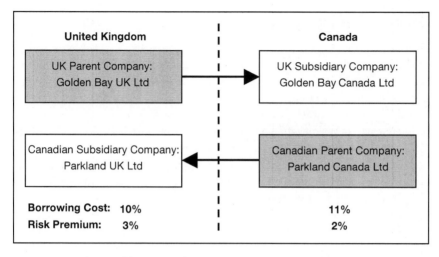

FIGURE 8.2 Hedging of foreign exchange currency swaps – parallel loan

The end result is that the UK subsidiary in Canada (Golden Bay Canada Ltd) would end up paying 11 per cent interest instead of 13 per cent, thus saving 2 per cent and the Canadian subsidiary in UK (Parkland UK Ltd) would pay 10 per cent interest instead of 13 per cent, thus saving 3 per cent. Figure 8.3 depicts the above solution regarding the parallel loan of the companies involved.

What is the concern with this arrangement? For this arrangement to be equitable to both parties concerned, they would both need to have comparable credit rating. In other words, the risk of the default of either party would need to be similar.

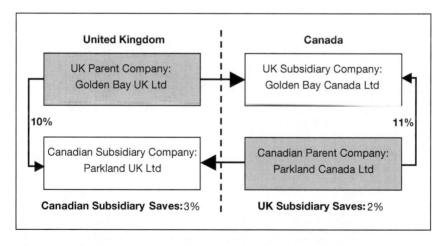

FIGURE 8.3 Hedging of foreign exchange currency swaps – parallel loan

Hedging of interest rate swaps

We have already seen that hedging involves mitigating financial risk by passing it on to someone else. Hence, hedging removes the uncertainty of cash flows, which assists management with budgeting, decreases the probability of financial failure, gives more confidence to management to undertake investment, and alleviates the concerns of employees who have a risk-averse characteristic.

Interest rate swaps operate is a similar way as foreign exchange currency swaps. The object of hedging is always to counter adverse movements, such as higher costs and reduced income. Interest rate swaps in particular tries to mitigate the concern of risk that takes place from future movements in interest rates. Like other hedging activities it is a two-way risk because interest rates can change up or down. In other words interest rates may change to have an adverse impact on the entity but they can also have a favourably affect, particularly if there is an increase in rates above what was agreed upon.

Let us now examine a practical example of an interest rate swap to see how it impacts entities. On 31 December 2012, Rubenstein Textiles Ltd and Novetal Ltd signed a five year interest swap agreement. It was agreed that Rubenstein Textiles Ltd would pay Novetal Ltd an amount equal to 6 per cent per annum (fixed rate) on a national principal of €20 million. However, it was further agreed that Novetal Ltd would pay Rubenstein Textiles Ltd an amount equal to one-year LIBOR plus 1 per cent per annum (floating rate) on a national principal of €20 million. Hence, we have what is referred to as a 'plain vanilla' interest rate swap, that is, fixed rate to floating rate interest rate swap. For simplicity, let us assume that the two entities involved in the agreement, exchange payments annually on 31 December, beginning in 2013, with the last payment being in 2017.

As a general observation, it is likely that Rubenstein Textiles Ltd has in place a loan at a floating rate of interest with a financial institution and is therefore trying to hedge its interest rate by swapping the interest conditions with Novetal Ltd at a fixed rate. It is also likely that Novetal Ltd is in a similar position, but its interest is fixed, so it is hedging by having a floating rate with Rubenstein Textiles Ltd. Figure 8.4 illustrates that above agreement.

As stated previously, 'plain vanilla' interest swap means the exchange of fixed rate interest rate to a floating interest rate. It also means that there are no other conditions in the agreement. In other words, it is just a simple straight forward transaction without any strings attached.

Table 8.2 shows the interest computations and payments that would be made by the entities involved. For instance, if the entities did not hedge the interest rates, Rubenstein Textiles Ltd would be liable to pay $6 million in interest payments over the five-year period and Novetal Ltd would be liable to pay $6.33 million. However, by hedging using the interest swap method (fixed to floating rate and floating to fixed rate) they both end up paying the same amount. Obviously, we are examining the situation in hindsight. For example, the LIBOR rate could have changed every year (up or down) more drastically. The point is

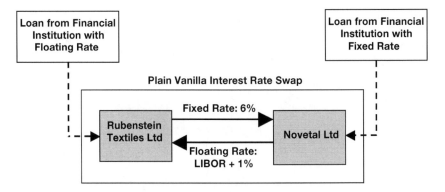

FIGURE 8.4 Hedging of interest rate swaps – plain vanilla swap

that both companies do not want to take the risk; they would rather know their position (i.e. stability). In fact, this is what risk financial management is all about; the minimisation of fluctuations (uncertainty).

In a plain vanilla interest rate swap, the floating rate method (i.e. whether to use LIBOR or some other approach) is usually determined at the beginning of the settlement period. Normally, swap contracts allow for payments to be netted against each other to avoid unnecessary payments. Hence, in the first year, Novetal Ltd pays \$66,000, and Rubenstein Textiles Ltd pays nothing. However, in the second year because the LIBOR rate decreased, Rubenstein Textiles Ltd pays \$50,000, and Novetal Ltd pays nothing. At no point does the principal change hands, which is why it is referred to as a 'notional' amount.

Other hedging approaches

There are many other hedging approaches that business enterprises may consider to mitigate their risk exposure. One should note that trading companies are interested in trade, that is, the business activity related to selling and buying goods and services. Fluctuations in foreign currency exchange rates and interest rates are a complication for them. In other words, most consumer goods and services trading entities want to limit their business domain to the business segments that they are expert at; they do not want to gamble with foreign currency exchange rates and interest rates. This is the primary reason why the vast majority of EU business enterprises support the European Monetary Union (EMU) because the EMU removes the foreign currency exchange risk element for those entities whose primary trading partners are within the EU.

Hedging using forward contracts

Forward contracts are the most popular means of foreign currency hedging in the world of finance. These are contracts that lock in a fixed foreign currency exchange

TABLE 8.2 Hedging of interest rate swaps – plain vanilla swap

No Hedging

Rubenstein

Year	Fixed Interest Payments
1	$1,200,000
2	$1,200,000
3	$1,200,000
4	$1,200,000
5	$1,200,000
Total:	$6,000,000

Novetal

Year	LIBOR Rate	Premium	Interest Rate	Interest Payments
1	5.33%	1.00%	6.33%	$1,266,000
2	4.75%	1.00%	5.75%	$1,150,000
3	4.90%	1.00%	5.90%	$1,180,000
4	5.00%	1.00%	6.00%	$1,200,000
5	5.50%	1.00%	6.50%	$1,300,000
			Total:	$6,096,000

With Hedging*

Rubenstein

Year	LIBOR Rate	Premium	Interest Rate	Interest Payments
1	5.33%	1.00%	6.33%	$1,266,000
2	4.75%	1.00%	5.75%	$1,150,000
3	4.90%	1.00%	5.90%	$1,180,000
4	5.00%	1.00%	6.00%	$1,200,000
5	5.50%	1.00%	6.50%	$1,300,000
			Total:	$6,096,000

Novetal

Fixed Interest Payments
$1,200,000
$1,200,000
$1,200,000
$1,200,000
$1,200,000
$6,000,000

*Rubenstein Textiles Ltd & Novetal Ltd swap interest rate from fixed to floating and vice-versa

Summary of Hedging Position

	Interest Paid	
	Fixed	Floating
Rubenstein Textiles:	$6,000,000	$6,096,000
Novetal Ltd:	$6,000,000	$6,096,000
Total Difference:	$0	$0

rate, for the receipts and payments. The foreign currency exchange rate is usually the market determined forward exchange rate that has the aim of ensuring the stability of receipts and payments, since the trading parties involved know precisely how much is required to be paid or received. Therefore, the everyday exchange rate on the date of the transaction becomes irrelevant. However, this not only mitigates the losses but also confines the extra profits that could have been made, had the exchange rate on the transaction settlement date been more favourable than the predetermined forward rate.

As was stated previously, trading companies are interested in trade, that is, the business activity related to selling and buying goods and services. They do not want to be troubled about fluctuations in foreign currency exchange rates and interest rates, which are an unwarranted complication for them. Apart from using forward contracts for hedging foreign currency and financial instruments, they are also used to trade commodities like cereals, crude oil, natural gas, electricity, precious metals, leather, meat, wool, cotton and fruit crops. As explained above, forward contracts have a payoff that is symmetric. This basically means that when one purchases any of these instruments and the underlying exchange rate increases, the purchaser gains proportionally; however, when the rate decreases, the purchaser would also make a proportionate loss. In other words, the payoff of these instruments is symmetric.

Forward contracts are best explained using an example. Gilroy Ltd is a commercial grower of maize. This entity is planning to grow 10,000 bushels (approximately 254,000 kg) of maize next season. This entity has two basic choices, either to sell its maize for the going price when it is harvested or it could enter into a forward contract with Kellogg's (or Quaker Oats) to sell its crop after the harvest at a fixed price, which is determined now. Hence, by securing the price now, Gilroy Ltd has removed the risk of falling maize prices. Conversely, should maize prices rise afterwards, Gilroy Ltd will receive the forward contract value. On the other hand, the cereal manufacturer (Kellogg's or Quaker Oats) may desire to purchase a forward contract to control its costs. The cereal manufacturer may pay more or less for the maize crop depending on the market price when it takes delivery of the maize. However, through this process both parties achieve price stabilisation.

Let us take the example further. Assume that Gilroy Ltd is located in Australia and the cereal manufacturer (Kellogg's or Quaker Oats) is located in the United Kingdom. A new variable is now introduced in the transaction. Apart from having a fixed price for maize, Gilroy Ltd and the cereal manufacturer may also agree on a fixed currency exchange rate for the Australian dollar and pound sterling. Let us assume that the forward contract stipulates a price of AUD 2.50 per bushel with a currency exchange rate of one Australian dollar to GBP 0.54. Further assume that at the time of delivery the market price of maize was AUD 2.00 per bushel and that 10,000 bushels of maize are ready for delivery and the currency exchange rate of one Australian dollar to GBP 0.50.

This situation is complicated by the fact that the hedging process is based on two variables, namely the price of maize and the currency exchange rate. Table 8.3

illustrates that Gilroy Ltd gains AUD 5,000 (or GBP 10,000) and the cereal manufacturer (Kellogg's or Quaker Oats) makes an equal loss due to the price hedging concept (symmetric result). In other words, Gilroy Ltd receives $5,000 more and Kellogg's (or Quaker Oats) pay $5,000 more. However, the currency exchange rate hedging works in favour of the cereal manufacturer in that the loss is reduced by £741 sterling and the gain for Gilroy Ltd is similarly reduced by the same amount.

Hedging using foreign currency options

Foreign currency options (referred to as FX option or currency option) are financial instruments that allow the holder of these options to achieve asymmetric returns. This means that the gain or loss experienced by the holder is not proportional. These options are financial instruments that are much more flexible for hedging and speculating. A foreign currency option is a contract giving the option purchaser (the buyer) the right, but not the obligation, to buy or sell a fixed amount of foreign exchange at a fixed price per unit for a specified time period. In other words, foreign currency options provide their holder the right but not the obligation to purchase (call option) or sell (put option) a specific foreign currency.

These options safeguard the holder's interest, since the holder would only exercise the option if it is favourable to do so. Furthermore, no matter what, the holder will definitely be receiving (or paying) an amount that is better than what would have been received (or paid) without this foreign currency hedging strategy.

TABLE 8.3 Hedging using forward contracts

Particulars (Data)	Value
Bushels to be delivered:	10,000
Price agreed per bushel (AUD$):	$2.50
Market price per bushel at delivery (AUD$):	$2.00
Agreed currency exchange rate £stg per AUD$:	£0.54
Currency exchange rate at delivery £stg per AUD$:	£0.50

Calculations	Gilroy Ltd (Receive)	Kellogg's (Pay)
No Hedging (10,000 X AUD$2.00):	$20,000	$20,000
No Hedging (convert to £ sterling)	£40,000	£40,000
Hedging (10,000 X AUD$2.50):	$25,000	$25,000
Gain/Loss by hedging on price: ($25,000 - $20,000)	**$5,000 more**	**$5,000 more**
Gain/Loss by hedging on price (convert to £ sterling)	**£10,000 more**	**£10,000 more**
Gain/Loss by hedging on currency: (convert $5,000 to £ sterling)	£9,259	£9,259
Actual Gain/Loss by hedging on currency:	**£741 less**	**£741 less**

However, to enter into such an agreement, the holder would pay a modest fee to take out the option.

Let us consider an example. Assume that Sinclair Ltd has entered into an agreement where it has the right to sell £1.50 million and buy $3.50 million on 31 December 2014. Further assume that the agreed currency exchange rate is USD 2.25 per GBP (or GBP/USD 2.00 as it is often referred to) and the notional amounts are £1.50 million and $3.50 million.

The agreed currency exchange rate is often referred to as the strike price. The strike price is the price (or rate) at which the Sinclair Ltd can exercise an option. In this case the strike price is USD 2.25 per GBP. Moreover, the notional amounts are the amount of each currency that the option allows Sinclair Ltd to sell or buy. In this case the amounts are £1.50 million and $3.50 million.

A foreign currency options contract is both a 'call' on US dollars and a 'put' on pound sterling, hence it is often referred to as 'GBPUSD put', since it is a 'put' on the exchange rate. However, it may likewise be termed a 'USDGBP call'. Note that a 'call' option is where the buyer has a right to purchase an asset at a set date and price. In other words the date and price are fixed. On the other hand a 'put' option is where the financier (in this case Sinclair Ltd) has the right to sell an asset at a fixed date and price.

Let us assume two scenarios, namely that on 31 December 2014: (a) the USD is 2.00 per GBP; and (b) the USD is $2.35 per GBP. Under the first scenario the US dollar is stronger and the pound sterling is weaker, hence Sinclair Ltd would exercise its option. Thus Sinclair Ltd would sell the pounds sterling at 2.25 and instantaneously repurchase the pounds sterling in the spot market at 2.00. The spot market price is the price of the asset at the time of the trade. This would allow Sinclair Ltd to earn a profit of USD375,000 (i.e. 2.25 GBPUSD – 2.00 GBPUSD) X £1,500,000) in the course of action. Therefore, if Sinclair Ltd converted the earned profit to pound sterling without delay, this would be equal to GBP187,500 (i.e. USD375,000 ÷ 2.00). Under the second scenario, Sinclair Ltd would not exercise its option since it would make a loss of USD150,000 (i.e. 2.25 GBPUSD – 2.35 GBPUSD) × £1,500,000) or GBP75,000 (i.e. USD150,000 ÷ 2.00).

Foreign currency options are commonly used by companies to hedge against uncertain future cash flows in a foreign currency. The normal practice is to hedge certain foreign currency cash flows with a 'forwards' contract, and uncertain foreign currency cash flows with an 'options' contract. As you may recall, 'forwards' contracts lock in a fixed exchange rate, for the receipts and payments, with the rate usually being the market determined forward exchange rate. On the other hand, an 'options' contract gives their holder the right but not the obligation to purchase (*call option*) or sell (*put option*) a specific foreign currency.

Let us consider another hedging example. Belview Ltd is a machinery manufacturing company located in the United Kingdom. This company has completed an order and is preparing a shipment of machines to one of its clients. The machines are due to be delivered in 60 days, at which point Belview Ltd will be paid USD350,000. The management is aware that if the pound sterling strengthens against the US dollar over the next 60 days, Belview Ltd will lose money on the exchange of US dollars to pounds sterling. On the other hand, management is also aware that the opposite applies and Belview Ltd will make a gain if the pound sterling weakens against the US dollar.

Therefore, Belview Ltd is exposed to foreign currency exchange risk. However, Belview's management would like to focus on their machinery export business and do not want to be apprehensive about foreign currency issues. As a result, to mitigate this risk and since the cash flow is certain, Belview's management have decided to enter into a forward contract for the delivery of USD350,000 in 60 days' time, in exchange for pound sterling at the current forward rate (the exchange rate of the currency for delivery at a future time). If the cash flow takes place when expected (in 60 days), this would perfectly match Belview's risk exposure, hence flawlessly hedging their foreign currency exchange risk.

However, in circumstances where it is doubtful that the cash flow will take place when agreed (60 days), a forward foreign currency exchange contract would expose Belview Ltd to risk in the opposite direction. Therefore, if the receipt of the cash flow is in doubt, Belview Ltd would be better off by taking an 'options' contract. A foreign exchange option gives the holder the right to sell cash in one currency and purchase cash in another currency at a fixed time and relative price. This would mean that Belview Ltd can purchase 'pound sterling call/US dollar put' option, thus giving it the entitlement to sell part or all of their expected revenue for pounds sterling at a predetermined rate. Hence, this mechanism would shield the pound sterling value which Belview Ltd expects in 60 days' time, assuming that the cash is received. The only added cost for Belview Ltd under an 'options' contract would be the option premium.

On the other hand, a forward foreign currency exchange contract would result in unlimited losses should the expected cash flow not materialise, whereas an options contract would yield a profit if the expected cash flow is not received but foreign currency exchange rates move in Belview's favour.

A general principle that may be applied is that if the cash flow is certain, a *forward* foreign currency exchange contract is the best hedging alternative; however if the cash flow is uncertain a foreign currency exchange *option* is the best hedging alternative.

Hedging using interest rate options

Interest rate options operate in a similar fashion to foreign currency exchange options. They give the option holder the right but not the obligation to purchase or sell a specific interest rate contract. Hence, the parties involved in the transaction, particularly when cash flows are uncertain, are fully aware of their payment and receipts responsibility. An interest rate option has a fixed cost in terms of an 'option premium', but it provides an excellent cover against interest rate movements, especially if a company is holding an uncovered position (referred to as a naked position).

Interest rate options are normally utilised by interest rate speculators, such as large banks and therefore, is not generally used as a retail vehicle for hedging against interest rate fluctuations. The reason why interest rate options are restricted between reputable banks and other financial institutions may be due to the concern related with the issue of creditworthiness.

Hedging using spot contracts

The most effective method to hedge against foreign currency risk is to not take the risk. Spot contracts can be used as a mechanism to protect entities or sole traders from adverse fluctuations in currency exchange rates or interest rates. Spot contracts are based on what is known as the spot price. The spot price is the price of the asset at the time of the trade. Hence, with spot contracts, the contract payments and receipts are settled preferably on the day they are made. Therefore, by having the payments and receipts settled on the same day means that the foreign currency exchange rate at the time of trade is the same as that at the time of the settlement of the payment or receipt. In other words, there is no time duration for the foreign currency exchange rate to fluctuate, with the consequence that no risk is taken.

A variation of spot contracts is to settle the contract payments and receipts on T+n settlement terms, where 'T' is the time of the trade and '+n' is the number of days after the time of the trade. Hence, when 'n' is zero no risk is taken because there is no possibility for foreign currency exchange rate fluctuation. However, the higher the value of 'n' the greater the risk of foreign currency exchange rate fluctuation (i.e. uncertainty or risk). Therefore, a small duration does not allow for massive foreign currency exchange rate or interest movements and thus safeguards against foreign currency exchange risks.

The basic principle with this method is to settle the transaction at the time it takes place. This ensures that foreign currency exchange rates do not have the time or opportunity to change.

Examples of hedging approaches

When dealing with foreign investment there are two major elements to be anxious about, namely the price fluctuation of the asset itself (e.g. fluctuation in the stock price) and fluctuations in the foreign currency exchange rate. The focus in this section is the mitigation of the adverse impact of foreign currency exchange or/and interest rate fluctuations.

Foreign currency exchange rate hedging mitigates the following exposures:

• To counter foreign currency exchange rate risk exposure. When companies undertake trading in foreign countries, these entities will be exposed to foreign currency exchange rate movements. This can be mitigated by foreign currency exchange rate hedging.

- To counter interest rate risk exposure. When money is borrowed or loaned to somebody in a foreign country, the interest payments or receipts are likely to be affected by interest rate variation in that country. Considerable fluctuations in interest rates during a predetermined contractual period may cause abnormal losses to the parties concerned in the transaction.
- To counter foreign investment valuation exposure. Trading in foreign stocks or stock markets exposes the investor to both speculative risk and to foreign currency exchange rate risk. Speculative risk occurs when the stock prices vary unfavourably, while foreign currency exchange rate risk transpires when stock is sold or matures and funds are repatriated to the source country.
- To counter open speculative positions. The main purpose of speculation is to profit from gambling on the direction in which an asset will be moving. However, hedging involves taking an offsetting position in a derivative in order to balance any gains and losses to the underlying asset. Hence, any open position (i.e. a position that will remain open until an opposing trade has taken place), in any market can be neutralised through the foreign currency exchange rate hedging instrument.

The above suggests that anyone exposed to the risks of operating in various different countries or stock markets requires the support of foreign currency hedging vehicles. Open positions are extremely risky and precarious. Examples of open positions include having a forward contract that has not been liquidated or settled by an offsetting contract or by the delivery of the underlying asset or a trading condition where the assets and liabilities are not at equilibrium or symmetric. Therefore, foreign currency exchange rate hedging mechanisms make all transactions much safer. Anyone holding these positions is highly likely to require foreign currency exchange rate hedging strategies to reduce the effect of the extra risks being picking up.

Example 1: plain vanilla foreign currency swap

Plain vanilla foreign currency swap involves exchanging the principal and fixed interest payments on a sum borrowed in one currency for the principal and fixed interest payments on a similar loan in another currency. Unlike an interest rate swap, the parties to a currency swap will exchange the principal amounts at the beginning and end of the swap period. The two particular principal amounts are established at approximately equal value to one another, given the currency exchange rate at the time the swap was initiated.

Let us take an example. Belair Ltd is a company located in the USA and Conrad Ltd is a European firm. These two companies enter into a five-year currency swap agreement for $65 million. Assume the exchange rate at the time of the agreement was established at $1.25 per euro (i.e. dollar is worth €0.80).

Step 1: The companies will exchange the principal values. Therefore, Belair Ltd pay $60 million and Conrad Ltd pay €52 million. This complies with each

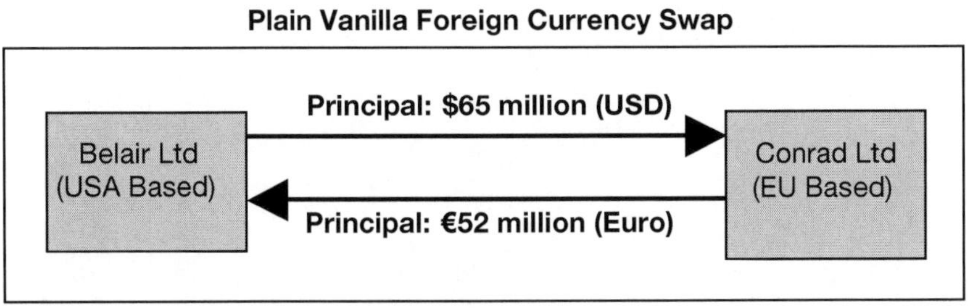

Plain Vanilla Foreign Currency Swap

FIGURE 8.5 Example 1: Step 1 – plain vanilla foreign currency swap

company's requirement for cash denominated in another currency, thus satisfying the objective of the currency swap. This position is illustrated by Figure 8.5.

Step 2: To simplify matters, let us assume that in the swap agreement the two companies agree to exchange the interest payments yearly, commencing one year from the exchange of the principal. Therefore, every year (as specified in the swap agreement) Belair Ltd and Conrad Ltd exchange interest payments on their respective principal amounts. Since Belair Ltd has borrowed in the euro currency, it must pay interest in euro based on a euro interest rate. Similarly, Conrad Ltd which has borrowed in US dollars, will pay interest in US dollars, based on a dollar interest rate. Let us assume that the agreed US dollar denominated interest rate is 8 per cent, and the euro denominated interest rate is 3.75 per cent. Therefore, each year Belair Ltd pays Conrad Ltd €1,950,000 (i.e. €52,000,000 @ 3.75 per cent). On the other hand, Conrad Ltd pays Belair Ltd $5,200,000 (i.e. $65,000,000 @ 8 per cent). Similar to interest rate swaps, the two companies will net the payments by offsetting against each other at the then-prevailing exchange rate. Therefore, if at year one, the prevailing currency exchange rate was $1.40 per euro, then Belair's Ltd interest payment would be $2,730,000 (i.e. €1,950,000 × $1.40) and Conrad's Ltd payment would be $5,200,000. Hence, due to the off-setting mechanism, Conrad Ltd would pay the net difference of $2,470,000 to Belair Ltd ($5,200,000 − $2,730,000). The position for the five years is illustrated by Table 8.4 assuming that the exchange rates for year 2 to year 5 are $1.30, $1.40, $1.45 and $1.35 respectively.

Step 3: At the end of the swap agreement (often also the date of the final interest payment), Belair Ltd and Conrad Ltd would re-exchange the original principal amounts. These principal payments are unaffected by currency exchange rate at the time because the currency exchange rate was agreed upon at the commencement of the swap agreement (refer to Figure 8.6). In this example the companies involved in the foreign currency swap agreement are hedging their position on the exchange rate.

Example 2: interest rate swap

An interest rate swap is classified as a derivative in that one party (Firm 'A') enters into an agreement with another party (Firm 'B'). Firm 'A' would pay interest to

TABLE 8.4 Example 1: Step 2 – plain vanilla foreign currency swap

Parameters		
Agreement Period:	5 years	
Principal Amount:	Belair Ltd $65,000,000	Conrad Ltd €52,000,000
Exchange Rate:	$1.25	€0.80
Interest Rate:	8.00%	3.75%

Year	(a) 8% X $65 Mil. Belair Ltd Interest Payment ($)	(b) 3.75% X €52 Mil. Conrad Ltd Interest Payment (€)	(c) Currency Exchange Rate	(d) (b) x (c) Conrad Ltd Interest Payment ($)	(a) – (d) Net Payment to Belair Ltd	Net Payment to Conrad Ltd
1	$5,200,000	€1,950,000	$1.40	$2,730,000	$2,470,000	Nil
2	$5,200,000	€1,950,000	$1.30	$2,535,000	$2,665,000	Nil
3	$5,200,000	€1,950,000	$1.40	$2,730,000	$2,470,000	Nil
4	$5,200,000	€1,950,000	$1.45	$2,827,500	$2,372,500	Nil
5	$5,200,000	€1,950,000	$1.35	$2,632,500	$2,567,500	Nil
Total:	$26,000,000	€9,750,000		$13,455,000	$12,545,000	Nil

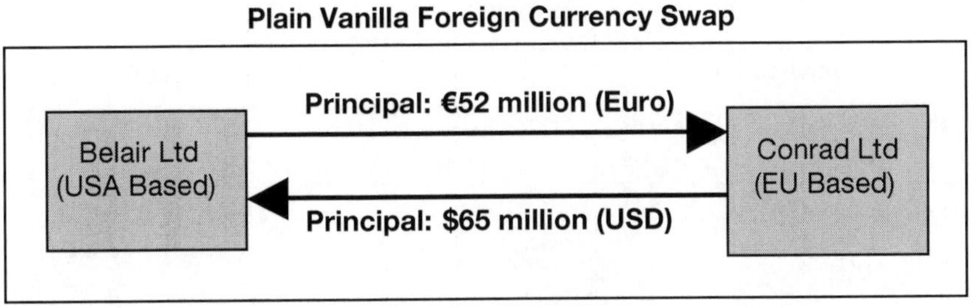

Plain Vanilla Foreign Currency Swap

FIGURE 8.6 Example 1: Step 3 – plain vanilla foreign currency swap

Firm 'B' at a fixed rate in exchange for receiving a floating interest rate. On the other hand, Firm 'B' would pay interest to Firm 'A' at a floating interest rate in exchange for receiving at a fixed interest rate. This mechanism is referred to as a fixed-to-floating interest rate swap of the same currency. Note that the underlying principal value does not change between the parties concerned. In other words, the principal value is a notional amount used only as a basis to determine the interest payment. Being a notional value ensures that there is no risk on the principal value.

Let us assume that there are two banks, namely FMS Bank Ltd and Mid-Med Bank Ltd. FMS Bank Ltd receives interest on a US$1.5 million bond at 7 per cent fixed and pays interest on a US$1.5 million loan at Euribor + 25 basis points (bp). Mid-Med Bank Ltd receives interest on a US$1.5 million at Euribor + 50 bp (0.50 per cent) and pays interest on a US$1.5 million term deposit at 4.75 per cent fixed. The Euribor (Euro Interbank Offered Rate) is the rate at which the Euro Interbank Term Deposits are being offered by one prime bank to another within the EMU zone. Table 8.5 shows the position of both banks when they are not hedging their position assuming that the current Euribor is 5.75 per cent.

Therefore, FMS Bank's position is: (a) an asset for USD1.5 million bond at 7 per cent fixed interest earning $105,000; and (b) a liability for USD1.5 million loan at Euribor 5.75 per cent + 0.25 per cent (25 basis points) paying interest of $90,000. Hence, the gain margin is of 1 per cent (7 per cent − 6 per cent) on $1,500,000 = $15,000.

On the other hand, Mid-Med Bank's position is: (a) an asset (cash in bank) for USD1.5 million at Euribor 5.75 per cent + 0.50 per cent (50 basis points) earning $93,750 ($1,500,000 × 6.25 per cent); and (b) a liability for US$1.5 million term deposit at a fixed rate of 4.75 per cent paying interest of $71,250 ($1,500,000 × 4.75 per cent). Hence, the gain margin is of 1.50 per cent (6.25 per cent − 4.75 per cent) on $1,500,000 = $22,500.

Let us now examine the effect of interest rate fluctuations on the unhedged position. Assume that interest rate increased by 15bp, hence new rate is 5.90 per cent (Euribor 5.75 per cent + 0.15 per cent). Table 8.6 shows the position of both banks when they are not hedging their position assuming that the current Euribor has now increased to 5.90 per cent.

TABLE 8.5 Example 2: interest rate swap (FMS Bank and Mid-Med Bank)

Unhedged Position			Assume Euribor = 5.75%	
Financial Instrument	**Amount US$**	**Interest Rate**	**Interest %**	**Margin US$**
FMS Bank Ltd Position:				
Asset: US$ Bond	1,500,000	Fixed coupon 7.00%	7.00%	105,000
Liability: US$ Loan	1,500,000	Euribor + 25pb = 5.75% + 0.25%	6.00%	(90,000)
Margin ———————————▶ **Margin**			1.00%	15,000

Financial Instrument	**Amount US$**	**Interest Rate**	**Interest %**	**Margin US$**
Mid-Med Bank Ltd Position:				
Asset: US$ Bank A/c	1,500,000	Euribor + 50pb = 5.75% + 0.50%	6.25%	93,750
Liability: US$ Term Dep.	1,500,000	Fixed coupon 4.75%	4.75%	(71,250)
Margin ———————————▶ **Margin**			1.50%	22,500

TABLE 8.6 Example 2: interest rate swap (interest rate increase)

Unhedged Position	Assume rates rise by 15bp = (5.75 + 0.15) = 5.90%			
Financial Instrument	**Amount US$**	**Interest Rate**	**Interest %**	**Margin US$**
FMS Bank Ltd Position:				
Asset: US$ Bond	1,500,000	Fixed coupon 7.00%	7.00%	105,000
Liability: US$ Loan	1,500,000	Euribor + 25pb = 5.90% + 0.25%	6.15%	(92,250)
Margin ———————————▶ **Margin**			0.85%	12,750

Financial Instrument	**Amount US$**	**Interest Rate**	**Interest %**	**Margin US$**
Mid-Med Bank Ltd Position:				
Asset: US$ Bank A/c	1,500,000	Euribor + 50pb = 5.90% + 0.50%	6.40%	96,000
Liability: US$ Term Dep.	1,500,000	Fixed coupon 4.75%	4.75%	(71,250)
Margin ———————————▶ **Margin**			1.65%	24,750

FMS Bank's position is: (a) an asset for US$1.5 million bond at 7 per cent fixed interest earning $105,000; and (b) a liability for USD1.5 million loan at Euribor 5.90 per cent + 0.25 per cent (25 basis points) paying interest of $92,250. Hence, the gain margin is of 0.85 per cent (7 per cent − 6.15 per cent) on $1,500,000 = $12,750. A decrease of $2,250 from previous position.

The position of Mid-Med Bank is: (a) an asset (cash in bank) for USD1.5 million at Euribor 5.90 per cent + 0.50 per cent (50 basis points) earning $96,000 ($1,500,000 × 6.40 per cent); and (b) a liability for USD1.5 million term deposit at a fixed rate of 4.75 per cent paying interest of $71,250 ($1,500,000 × 4.75 per cent). Hence, the gain margin is of 1.65 per cent (6.40 per cent − 4.75 per cent) on $1,500,000 = $24,750; an increase of $2,250 from previous position. Therefore, FMS Bank had unfavourable outcome and Mid-Med Bank had a favourable outcome.

Let us assume that the interest rate decreases by 10bp, hence new rate is 5.65 per cent (Euribor base rate of 5.75 per cent − 0.10 per cent = 5.65 per cent). Table 8.7 shows the position of both banks when they are not hedging their position assuming that the current Euribor has now decreased to 5.65 per cent.

FMS Bank's position is: (a) an asset for USD1.5 million bond at 7 per cent fixed interest earning $105,000; and (b) a liability for USD1.5 million loan at Euribor 5.65 per cent + 0.25 per cent (25 bp) paying interest of $88,500. Hence, the gain

TABLE 8.7 Example 2: interest rate swap (interest rate decrease)

Unhedged Position	Assume rates decrease by 10bp = (5.75 - 0.10) = 5.65%			
Financial Instrument	**Amount US$**	**Interest Rate**	**Interest %**	**Margin US$**
FMS Bank Ltd Position:				
Asset: US$ Bond	1,500,000	Fixed coupon 7.00%	7.00%	105,000
Liability: US$ Loan	1,500,000	Euribor + 25pb = **5.65% + 0.25%**	5.90%	(88,500)
Margin ⟶ **Margin**			1.10%	16,500

Financial Instrument	**Amount US$**	**Interest Rate**	**Interest %**	**Margin US$**
Mid-Med Bank Ltd Position:				
Asset: US$ Bank A/c	1,500,000	Euribor + 50pb = **5.65% + 0.50%**	6.15%	92,250
Liability: US$ Term Dep.	1,500,000	Fixed coupon 4.75%	4.75%	(71,250)
Margin ⟶ **Margin**			1.40%	21,000

margin is of 1.10 per cent (7 per cent − 5.90 per cent) on $1,500,000 = $16,500; a decrease of $3,750 from previous position.

The position of Mid-Med Bank is: (a) an asset (cash in bank) for USD1.5 million at Euribor 5.65 per cent + 0.50 per cent (50 bp) earning $92,250 ($1,500,000 × 6.15 per cent); and (b) a liability for US$1.5 million term deposit at a fixed rate of 4.75 per cent paying interest of $71,250 ($1,500,000 × 4.75 per cent). Hence, the gain margin is of 1.40 per cent (6.15 per cent − 4.75 per cent) on $1,500,000 = $21,000; an increase of $3,750 from previous position. Therefore, FMS Bank had favourable outcome and Mid-Med Bank had a unfavourable outcome.

The overall unhedged position as a consequence of the interest rate fluctuation resulted in FMS Bank making a loss of $1,500 and Mid-Med Bank made a gain of $1,500.

Let us now see the situation when FMS Bank and Mid-Med Bank agree to hedge interest rate positions using interest rate swaps. FMS Bank would like to switch from a fixed to floating interest rate arrangement. FMS Bank achieves this arrangement by swapping the fixed receivables into floating receivables. Mid-Med Bank on the other hand, changes from floating to fixed interest rate and attains this by swapping floating receivables into fixed receivables. They agree the following terms: (a) FMS Bank receives Euribor + 125bp (1.25 per cent) but pays a fixed rate of 7.00 per cent; and (b) Mid-Med Bank receives a fixed interest rate of 7 per cent but pays Euribor + 125bp (1.25 per cent). Figure 8.7 illustrates the interest rate swap agreement.

Let us now examine the effect of this arrangement on the position of both banks. Table 8.8 and Table 8.9 illustrate that by hedging using an interest rate swap

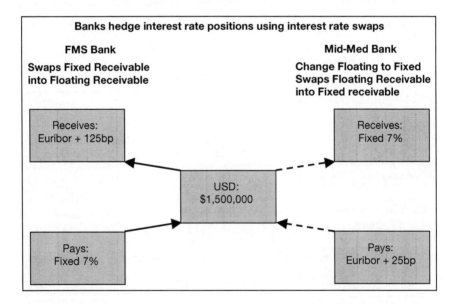

FIGURE 8.7 Example 2: Interest rate swap agreement

TABLE 8.8 Example 2: FMS Bank hedged position

FMS Bank Ltd Position:	Unhedged Asset/Liability	Hedged Interest Rate Swaps	Net Gain/Loss
Current position – Euribor 5.75%			
Receive:	7.00%	7.00%	
Pay:	-6.00%	-7.00%	
Margin:	1.00%	0.00%	1.00%
Current position – Euribor 5.75% + 10bp			
Receive:	7.00%	7.10%	
Pay:	-6.10%	-7.00%	
Margin:	0.90%	0.10%	1.00%
Current position – Euribor 5.75% - 10bp			
Receive:	7.00%	6.90%	
Pay:	-5.90%	-7.00%	
Margin:	1.10%	-0.10%	1.00%

TABLE 8.9 Example 2: Mid-Med Bank hedged position

Mid-Med Bank Ltd Position:	Unhedged Asset/Liability	Hedged Interest Rate Swaps	Net Gain/Loss
Current position – Euribor 5.75%			
Receive:	6.25%	7.00%	
Pay:	-4.75%	-7.00%	
Margin:	1.50%	0.00%	1.50%
Current position – Euribor 5.75% + 10bp			
Receive:	6.35%	7.00%	
Pay:	-4.75%	-7.10%	
Margin:	1.60%	-0.10%	1.50%
Current position – Euribor 5.75% - 10bp			
Receive:	6.15%	7.00%	
Pay:	-4.75%	-6.90%	
Margin:	1.40%	0.10%	1.50%

arrangement, FMS Bank's position and that of Mid-Med Bank is stable, showing a consistent net gain of 1 per cent and 1.5 per cent respectively, every time the interest rate changes. When one examines the unhedged column, there is a consistent fluctuation ranging from 0.90 per cent to 1.10 per cent for FMS Bank and 1.40 per cent to 1.60 per cent for Mid-Med Bank. Moreover, when the hedged position column is examined, there is a net impact of zero per cent gain/loss, with a very small fluctuation range of -0.10 per cent to +0.10 per cent for both banks. This demonstrates that a hedging arrangement attempts to stabilise real and potential fluctuations. In this case the net resultant change is zero.

Example 3: foreign exchange currency swap

A currency swap is an agreement by two or more parties to exchange aspects of a loan in one foreign currency for an equal loan in another foreign currency. In a currency swap the loan characteristics include both the principal and/or the interest in one currency in exchange for another currency. Companies agree on a currency swap because they typically provide a comparative advantage. A currency swap is regarded as a foreign exchange transaction but is not required by law to be recorded on a company's balance sheet. Historically currency swaps were conducted as a way of avoiding exchange controls. However, currently currency swaps are utilised because they are considered to be a very simple and adaptable method for conducting certain foreign exchange transactions that are negotiable for at least 10 years.

Their simplicity is best explained by an example. Suppose a company located in Japan needs euros and a French based company requires Japanese yen. By having a currency swap, these two companies may enter into an agreement to swap currencies by establishing a mutually approved principal and interest rate, and a common maturity date for the exchange. A currency swap is different from an interest rate swap because in a currency swap, both the principal and interest of the loan are swapped over from one company to another company for mutual benefits.

Currency swaps may be utilised by companies to mitigate exposure by hedging against foreign currency exchange rate fluctuations; and to guard against financial instability by permitting a particular country that may be experiencing liquidity concerns to have access to money from other sources with its own currency. Currency swaps may also be a method of acquiring a cheaper source of funds by borrowing at the most advantageous rate of interest irrespective of the currency and then exchanging the borrowed funds for the required currency.

Let us consider an example in which only the principal is taken into account. Albatross Ltd has entered into an agreement to sell Helios Ltd $2.5 million US dollars in exchange for €1million euro. Albatross Ltd also made a separate agreement to purchase £1.5 million pounds sterling from Xeronet Ltd in exchange for €1 million euro. The foreign currency exchange rates at the time the agreements were made were as €1.00 at USD2.50 and €1 at £1.50 (pound sterling).

Furthermore, on maturity the foreign currency exchange rates were €1 at USD2.55 and €1 at £1.40 (pound sterling). It should be noted that without this hedging arrangement Albatross Ltd has an open position. The issue is to examine the impact of the above transactions for Albatross Ltd.

The agreements between the three companies are illustrated at Figure 8.8. Note that without hedging, Albatross Ltd would have an open position.

Let us first consider the position of Albatross Ltd with no hedging. In other words the company has an open or naked position. Albatross Ltd unhedged position is illustrated at Table 8.10. Table 8.10 shows that when Albatross Ltd eventually settles its position at maturity, the company will make an exchange loss of €91,036.

Table 8.11 illustrates the hedged position of Albatross Ltd. Albatross Ltd will sell a US$ forward to Helios Ltd and on maturity, Albatross Ltd will receive $2.5 million, which at the currency exchange rate applicable at the time is equivalent to €980,392 therefore making an exchange loss of €19,608. However, Albatross Ltd has a contract to sell Helios Ltd $2.5 million at a price of €1.00 million. Hence, instead of exchanging the $2.5 million it received, Albatross Ltd will pass the $2.5 million to Helios Ltd, who in turn will pay Albatross Ltd the agreed price of €1.00 million.

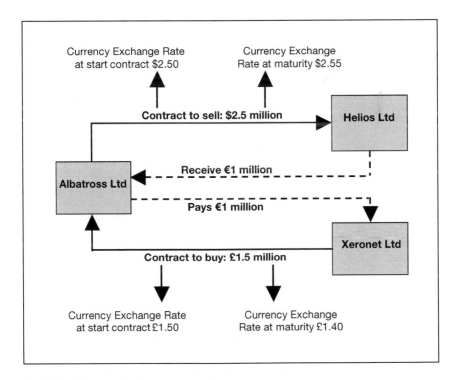

FIGURE 8.8 Example 3: Currency swap between three companies

TABLE 8.10 Example 3: Albatross Ltd with no hedging (open position)

Transaction Type	Amount in Foreign Currency	Today's Exchange Rate	Today's € Equivalent	Exchange Rate at Maturity	€ Equivalent	Exchange Gain/Loss	Transaction Destination
Asset USD	$2,500,000	$2.50	€1,000,000	$2.55	€980,392	(€19,608)	Transaction with Helios Ltd
Liability GBP	(£1,500,000)	£1.50	(€1,000,000)	£1.40	(€1,071,429)	(€71,429)	Transaction with Xeronet Ltd
If Albatross Ltd had to settle today:			€0				
When Albatross Ltd eventually settles (asset is received and liability is paid):						(€91,036)	Short on pound sterling (£)

TABLE 8.11 Example 3: Albatross Ltd with hedging

Albatross Ltd: To sell a US$ forward to Helios Ltd

Transaction Type	Amount in Foreign Currency	Today's Exchange Rate	Today's € Equivalent	Exchange Rate at Maturity	€ Equivalent	Exchange Gain/Loss	Transaction Destination
Asset USD	$2,500,000	$2.50	€1,000,000	$2.55	€980,392	(€19,608)	Transaction with Helios Ltd
Forward Sale of:	($2,500,000)		(€1,000,000)		(€980,392)	€19,608	Transaction with Helios Ltd
If Albatross Ltd had to settle today:			€0				
When Albatross Ltd eventually settles (asset is received and liability is paid):						€0	

Albatross Ltd: To buy a GBP forward from Xeronet Ltd

Transaction Type	Amount in Foreign Currency	Today's Exchange Rate	Today's € Equivalent	Exchange Rate at Maturity	€ Equivalent	Exchange Gain/Loss	Transaction Destination
Liability GBP	(£1,500,000)	£1.50	(€1,000,000)	£1.40	(€1,071,429)	(€71,429)	Transaction with Xeronet Ltd
Forward Buy of:	£1,500,000		€1,000,000		€1,071,429	€71,429	Transaction with Xeronet Ltd
If Albatross Ltd had to settle today:			€0				
When Albatross Ltd eventually settles (asset is received and liability is paid):						€0	

The consequence of this is that Albatross Ltd has made a loss on one transaction and a gain on the other of the same amount, which cancel out each other. There is the risk that the exchange rate moves in the other direction, which would have resulted in Albatross Ltd making an exchange gain had it not entered into a currency swap arrangement. However, the objective of the agreement is to mitigate exchange losses and achieve some sort of exchange stability. Therefore, whether the currency exchange rate moves in the opposite direction or not, Albatross Ltd will remain in the same position, which represents its maximum risk exposure.

Furthermore, Table 8.11 also shows that Albatross Ltd will buy a pound sterling forward from Xeronet Ltd and on maturity will pay £1.5 million pounds sterling. At maturity and applying the exchange rate at the time, this would be equal to €1,071,429, thus making an exchange loss of €71,429. Given that Albatross Ltd has also entered into an agreement to buy £1.5 million pounds sterling at a price of £1.0 million, then on maturity it will pay Xeronet Ltd €1.0 million in return for £1.5 million pounds sterling and then settle the liability in pounds sterling. Here again, the two transactions off set each other and hence Albatross Ltd will remain in the same position, which represents its maximum risk exposure.

Example 4: currency swap

Assume that Blue Star Ltd a United Kingdom (UK) based company plans to issue five-year bonds valued £150 million pounds sterling at 8 per cent interest to finance the setting up of a subsidiary company in Canada. Therefore, Blue Star Ltd requires the equivalent of $225 million Canadian dollars given that the current currency exchange rate is $1.50 per pound sterling. Furthermore, assume that Penguin Services Ltd, a Canadian company also plans to issue $225 million in bonds at 10 per cent, with a maturity of five years. However, it requires this finance to

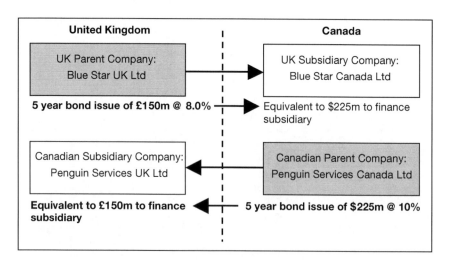

FIGURE 8.9 Example 4: Currency swap between Blue Star and Penguin Services

establish a subsidiary company in the UK. Hence, its real financing need is about GBP150 million. These two companies consult with FSP Bank Ltd as clients to find an appropriate solution to their financing situation. FSP Bank Ltd specialise in currency swap transactions. Figure 8.9 illustrates the current financing requirements of Blue Star Ltd and Penguin Service Ltd.

FSP Bank Ltd observes that the transactional requirements of Blue Star Ltd and Penguin Services Ltd complement each other. Therefore, FSP Bank Ltd decided to bring the two parties together and draft three separate agreements related to initiating the financing; paying the interest payments; and repayment of principal at maturity.

It was agreed that Blue Star UK Ltd would take out a five-year bond issue for GBP150 million at 8 per cent interest rate. The actual amount collected from the

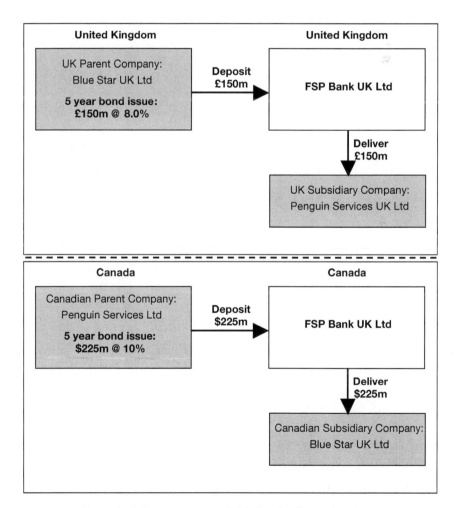

FIGURE 8.10 Example 4: Currency swap – initiating the finance requirements

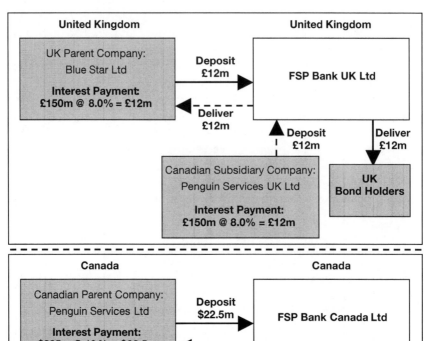

FIGURE 8.11 Example 4: Currency swap – paying interest payments

bond issue by Blue Star UK Ltd amounted to $150 million, which was deposited at FSP Bank (UK) Ltd, who in turn would loan the deposited amount to Penguin Services (UK) Ltd. The same method was adopted for Penguin Services Ltd. Penguin Services (Canada) Ltd would take out a five-year bond issue for $225 million at 10 per cent interest rate. The amount collected from the bond issue by Penguin Services (Canada) Ltd amounted to $225 million, which was deposited at FSP Bank (Canada) Ltd, who in turn would loan the deposited amount to Blue Star (Canada) Ltd. Figure 8.10 illustrates the bond issue transactions for both companies.

It was also agreed that the Canadian subsidiary company (Penguin Services UK Ltd) would pay the 8 per cent interest on £150 million amounting to £12 million

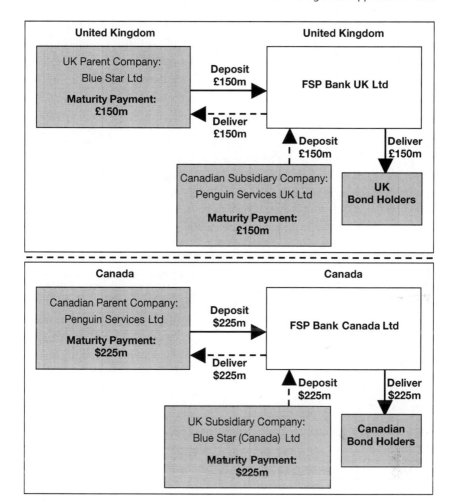

FIGURE 8.12 Example 4: Currency swap – repayment of principal

to FSP Bank UK Ltd who will pass it on the UK parent company (Blue Star Ltd) so that the UK bond holders can be paid. On the other hand, the UK subsidiary company (Blue Star Canada Ltd) would pay the 10 per cent interest on $225 million amounting to $22.5 million to FSP Bank Canada Ltd who will pass it on to the Canadian parent company (Penguin Services Ltd) so that the Canadian bond holders are paid their interest payments. Figure 8.11 illustrates the above agreement.

The final agreement is related to the repayment of the principal by both companies. At maturity the Canadian subsidiary company (Penguin Services UK Ltd) would repay the principal of £150 million to FSP Bank UK Ltd who will pass it on the UK parent company (Blue Star Ltd) so that the UK bond holders can be paid. On the other hand, the UK subsidiary company (Blue Star Canada

Ltd) would pay the $225 million to FSP Bank Canada Ltd who will pass it on to the Canadian parent company (Penguin Services Ltd) so that the Canadian bond holders are repaid their principal. Figure 8.12 illustrates the above arrangement.

Conclusion

This chapter has focused on financial risk management applications and has addressed the major issue of when and how to use financial risk management. It was amply illustrated that all transactions carry a certain magnitude of risk. However, frequent and thorough risk analysis and risk management techniques can help to resolve concerns before they arise or become serious.

A number of risk mitigating techniques have been shown through examples illustrating the use of diversification, particularly the application of hedging. Other examples were utilised to demonstrate the application of interest rate and foreign currency rate options, forward contracts and spot contracts. Moreover, the use of interest rate swaps and currency swaps were also shown, to further illustrate that businesses can achieve high degree of stability in conducting their financial transactions if risk mitigating measures are correctly applied.

References

Hakkio, Craig S. (1986). Interest rates and exchange rates – what is the relationship? *Economic Review, Federal Reserve Bank of Kansas City*.

Hnatkovska, Viktoria, Amartya, Lahiri and Vegh, Carlos A. (2008). *Interest Rates and the Exchange Rate: A Non-Monotonic Tale*. National Bureau of Economic Research, Working Paper No. 13925, Cambridge, MA.

Mishkin, Frederic S. and Eakins, Stanley G. (2011). *Financial Markets and Institutions*. Prentice Hall.

Stockman, Alan C. (1980). A theory of exchange rate determination. *The Journal of Political Economy*, 88(4), 673–698.

Sutton, Gregory D. (2000). *A Defence of The Expectations Theory as a Model of US Long-Term Interest Rates*. Bank for International Settlements, Monetary and Economic Department, Basel, Switzerland.

9

BUSINESS AND FINANCIAL ANALYSIS

Numbers have an important story to tell. They rely on you to give them a clear and convincing voice.

Stephen Few
Author

The focus of this chapter is the analysis of the business concern. In the context of this chapter, the 'analysis of the business concern' means the examination and assessment of both the external and internal environment. The basic premise is that an organisation's business and financial performance are influenced by their internal and external environment. Hence, how the organisation responds to these environments (whether reactive or proactive) will determine its business and financial performance.

The analysis of an entity's external environment will look at all outside factors that may affect an organisation. These factors envelop an organisation and have a direct impact on its operational activities, strategic choices, and influence its opportunities and risks. On the other hand, the assessment of an entity's internal environment will principally concentrate on the analysis of the entity's financial statements based on ratio analysis. In other words, the analysis of the internal environment will apply ratio analysis to the financial statements to examine various elements, including liquidity, profitability, asset utilisation, investment, working capital management and capital structure. Figure 9.1 provides the analytical framework for this chapter illustrating that an organisation's performance is greatly influenced by the external and internal environments in which it exists.

The external environment

The external environment of an entity reflects those factors that are outside the entity but have an impact on the entity's ability to operate. Some of these external

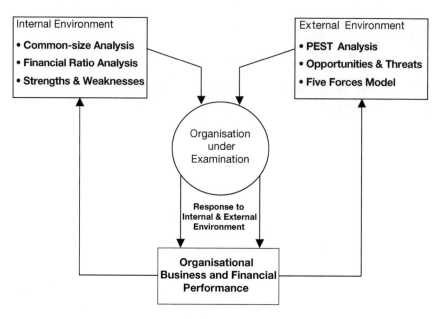

FIGURE 9.1 General analytical framework

factors can be controlled through a marketing campaign but many other factors require the organisation to make adjustments to its mode of operations. One must recognise that a business does not exist in isolation but exists within an external environment consisting of the actions of many other players who exist outside the business.

The external environment consists of competitors; the socio-economic system; and the political and legal systems. Competitors will continuously search for ways to gain a competitive advantage over each other, by diversification, differentiating their products and services, and by finding ways to improve value for money. Hence, the behaviour of competitors will directly affect the capacity of an entity to generate profits.

Socio-economic development emphasises progress in terms of economic and social factors that influence an organisation or a geographical unit. Therefore, economic development is the process by which the level of prosperity increases through the growth of production, distribution and consumption of goods and services. Business enterprises know that the economy goes through a cycle, varying from growth-recession-growth. Hence, an entity needs to be aware of the status of this economic cycle and to be careful in how it allocates its scarce resources. A business will flourish when the economy is booming and the conditions in which people live, especially in terms of their level of material comfort and rising disposable income. On the other hand, social development is concerned with the complexity of the various social inter-relationships that focus on social concerns of people and people-centric participative approaches to development. Above all, businesses are vulnerable to consumer attitudes and behaviours that vary according to the demographics of the population, such as, the age structure and the nature of work and leisure.

The monetary system complements the socio-economic system by facilitating business exchange through monetary activity that is derived from consumer earnings, spending, saving and borrowing. Such activity necessitates the involvement of businesses with the supply chain that includes financial institutions, creditors, debtors, customers and suppliers. The cost of money (interest rate) is a primary monetary impact factor for a business, since higher interest rates increase finance servicing costs that slow down consumer spending which result in weakening the economy.

Moreover, the political and legal system defines the framework and resultant rules within which a business operates. Government policy through its rule setting mechanism (public service and parliament) provides the magnitude of thrust for various business activities. Hence, certain business sectors may be promoted and actively supported, such as financial services, while others are restrained, particularly those that generate undesirable outcomes such as noise, odours and other pollutants. This aspect is also closely related to the environmental system. Businesses are more conscious (through civil and government intervention) of the relationship that exists between economic activity and sustainable development. Economic development needs to coexist with the restraints demanded by the environmental system.

The analysis of the external environment examines the above factors and applies a number of models to determine the trend and general impact that these identified factors will have on the entity's operating ability. The models that will be examined include the PEST (political, economic, social and technological) analysis; SWOT analysis, and five forces model.

PEST (political, economic, social and technological) analysis

According to Mind Tools (2011), the PEST analysis enables management to understand the 'big picture' of the environment in which an organisation operates, and forces them to think about the opportunities and threats that lie within it. Hence, they argue that by understanding the environment, the organisation can take advantage of the opportunities and minimise the threats. Mind Tools (2011) identify several advantages of the PEST analysis, such as facilitating the positive alignment of the entity's activities with the forces of change to increase the likelihood of success; helps to avoid activities that are destined to failure for reasons beyond management's control; and aids to break free of unconscious assumptions by quickly adapting to the new realities.

However, Thakur (2010) identifies a number of limitations. First, he views the external factors as being very dynamic; hence the PEST findings, in his opinion, have a very short life span and need to be regularly reviewed. The suggested resolution for this weakness is to mitigate uncertainty through the application of risk management practices. The presentation of the PEST analysis is seen as being too simplistic; hence it is suggested that the attributing factors are to be critically examined for their degree of impact. Thakur (2010) posits that to conduct a comprehensive PEST analysis is considered to be costly due the enormous amounts of information that are required. However, this may be remedied by ensuring the use of accurate and timely updates. A serious weakness highlighted by Thakur (2010) is that factors mentioned in the PEST analysis are often based more on assumptions and less on actual facts; hence there is a need to have a cross-verification mechanism in place. Finally, Thakur (2010) posits that the PEST analysis is insufficient for strategic planning, because it scans only the external environment; therefore it is important that the PEST analysis is used in conjunction with other tools, such as SWOT.

The above illustrates that the PEST analysis is a tool to evaluate external factors. Hence, it is often helpful to complete a PEST analysis prior to a SWOT analysis. One should note that a SWOT analysis measures a business unit; while a PEST analysis measures trends and changes in the market. Table 9.1 provides an example of the PEST analysis for a commercial bank operating in a small European Union (EU) member state. The situation being analysed is to assess how well this bank is coping in operating in a post EU membership environment in terms of its strategic position in the member state's banking industry.

The findings of the PEST Analysis are found at Table 9.2. The analysis provides a general view of a particular industry of interest on the four aspects (political, economic, social and technological). Hence, it helps management to understand the 'big picture' of the environment in which the bank in question is operating. For instance, the PEST analysis highlights that there are likely changes to be made related to the banking regulatory provisions, such as higher capital quality, higher quality liquid assets and an increase in the net stable funding ratio to over 100 per cent. All of these anticipated these measures are likely to present a challenge (threat) to the banking industry.

On a national level, the PEST analysis highlights that the bank's client base (anticipated and existing) has a relatively high level of technology awareness and utilisation, but the older section of the community is a concern. This may indicate that the bank has an opportunity to introduce more electronic (including mobile phone) banking services to increase its client penetration base and lower its operating costs. In other words, the PEST analysis forces management to think about the opportunities and threats that lie within the industry. This enables management to understand the environment the entity is operating in, with the consequence that the entity can take full advantage of the opportunities and minimise the threats.

SWOT analysis

According to von Franz and Schall (2004), SWOT is used to identify and analyse an entity's strengths and weaknesses, as well as the opportunities and threats that reflect its external environment. Its main aim is to determine the strategies that will

TABLE 9.1a Example of PEST analysis: bank operating in the EU

Political	Economical
Global	*Global*
Changes to Basel III CRD IV is under consultation (McKinsey, 2012):	Reduced Chinese economic activity, with consequential reductions in demand for commodities to fuel that output, could have a knock-on effect on many world-wide economies (Deloitte, 2012a).
• Capital quality rules now disallow a number of forms of capital e.g. capital held by insurance subsidiaries, defined-benefit pension-fund assets, investments in unconsolidated financial institutions and deferred-tax assets.	Bankers likely will continue to be challenged to find profit in an environment of low interest rates, and thus low net interest margins (Deloitte, 2012a).
• 2013 New capital ratios with a total requirement of 8%.	*European*
• A liquidity coverage requirement to be introduced in 2015 due to uncertainty about unintended consequences and will require high-quality liquid assets to meet short-term needs.	European economy continues to weaken (Deloitte, 2012a). Europe's retail banks are recovering (ATKearney 2012).
• By 2018 the net stable funding ratio (NSFR) to be greater than 100% to promote more medium and long-term funding of assets.	With the exception of banks in three countries (Portugal, Spain, Italy) risk provisions have rebounded, but profits remain nearly 15% below pre-crisis levels (ATKearney 2012).
European	Banks have focused on cost containment, but not adopting substantial measures to reduce costs, (ATKearney 2012).
EU directive on credit agreements relating to residential property to harmonise mortgage lending across EU and to foster competition (McKinsey, 2012).	Nordic banks have focused more attention on digital transformation and cost containment, recording better financial results (ATKearney 2012).
Markets in Financial Instruments Directive (MiFID) to strengthen investor protection with respect to advisory services (McKinsey, 2012).	Stopgap measures have been adopted, but a long-term resolution of the economic instability in Portugal, Ireland, Italy, Greece, and Spain is not evident (Deloitte, 2012a).
Single Euro Payments Area (SEPA) to harmonise rules for processing cross-border payments (McKinsey, 2012).	

generate an entity's particular business model, with the objective of aligning the entity's competencies and resources to the needs of the environment in which the entity operates in (NetMBA, 2011).

Von Franz and Schall (2004) contend that a SWOT analysis helps in strategic planning by:

- Acting as an information source for strategic planning.
- Developing an organisation's strengths and overturning its weaknesses.
- Exploiting an organisation's response to opportunities and surmounting its threats.
- Helping to ascertain an entity's core competencies and setting its strategic planning goals.

TABLE 9.1b Example of PEST analysis: bank operating in the EU (continued)

Social	Technological
European (Local)	*International*
Low unemployment relative to other European countries (CIA World Factbook, 2013).	The financial services industry is becoming a technology business. As such, the effective and creative utilisation of the massive amounts of data that banks have could become a characteristic of future winners and losers in the industry (Deloitte, 2012a).
Life expectancy at birth: females, 82 years and males 78 years (UN Data).	
Education: Government expenditure is 6.4% of GDP (UN Data).	*European (Local)*
Pensioners prevail among owners of stocks and shares.	75% of households connected to internet with 66% of population use internet.
15% invest their money in shares.	90% of age group <35years use internet once or more per week.
7% do not have a bank account – most of them working class respondents.	97% with formal education use internet once a week and 49% with no or low formal education use internet once a week.
36% have a pension fund.	
21% covered by non-state health insurance.	40% of younger respondents have shopped over the internet with 8% of older respondents have shopped over the internet.
	52% with tertiary education have done some internet shopping.
	19% with secondary level schooling have done some internet shopping.

Figure 9.2 illustrates that the SWOT framework reviews the past and antici-pates the future, classifying the strengths and opportunities as positive elements, while the weaknesses and threats are viewed as the negative factors.

Silva (2012) claims that the results of the PEST analysis should be included in the SWOT opportunities and threats section (see Figure 9.3). Additionally, von Franz and Schall (2004) argue that SWOT has its limitations; it may cause organisa-tions to over simplify the situation, hence neglecting some key strategic links.

Furthermore, SWOT tends to be subjective and does not indicate how an organ-isation can identify the four aspects. Moreover, there are limitations that are not under management's control, such as price fluctuations; economic environment; and government legislation. Internal limitations include inadequate industrial relations; deficient research and development facilities; unsatisfactory products due to weak quality control; and insufficient skilled and efficient labour. However, the internal limitations which are normally under management's control may be overcome by involving employees through focus group discussions, together with meticulous workmanship.

The findings of the SWOT Analysis related to the example regarding a commercial bank operating in a small EU member state, is found at Table 9.3.

TABLE 9.2 Example of PEST analysis findings: bank operating in the EU

PEST ANALYSIS FINDINGS:

The PEST Analysis illustrates that banking regulations will continue to be strengthened, with changes to Basel-III, by requiring higher capital quality; higher quality liquid assets; and increasing the net stable funding ratio to over 100% (McKinsey, 2012).

EU regulatory changes include mortgage lending harmonisation; strengthening investor protection; and harmonising rules for processing cross-border payments (McKinsey, 2012).

Globally, bankers will continue facing a hostile economic environment, with low interest rates and low net interest margins (Deloitte, 2012a). The European economy continues to weaken, with a long-term resolution to economic instability in Portugal, Ireland, Italy, Greece, and Spain not being evident (Deloitte, 2012a). However, with the exception of these countries, retail banks are recovering, and risk provisions have rebounded, but profits remain 15% below pre-crisis levels (ATKearney, 2012).

Banks have focused on cost containment not cost reduction; however, Nordic banks have achieved better financial results by focusing on digital transformation (ATKearney, 2012).

On a national level, the growing financial services sector has avoided contagion from the financial crisis, because its debt is mostly domestic and banks have low exposure to sovereign debt of peripheral European countries (CIA World Factbook, 2013).

Nationally, there is an aging population with 64% being over 60 years (UN Data). A survey has shown that 93% of the population have a bank account, with 30% having several accounts with different banks; 36% have a pension fund; pensioners are the predominant owners of stocks and shares. 75% of the local households have internet connection. However, 90% of internet users are less than 36 years old, in contrast to 11% of those older than 64 years. 97% of those with a formal education are internet users, in contrast to 49% with no or low formal education.

SWOT analysis is the most recognised mechanism for evaluating the overall strategic position of a business entity and its environment. This is the reason why the SWOT analysis complements the PEST analysis and should be conducted concurrently or very closely with it.

The primary objective of the SWOT analysis is the identification of the strategies which will generate a robust business model for optimising the alignment of

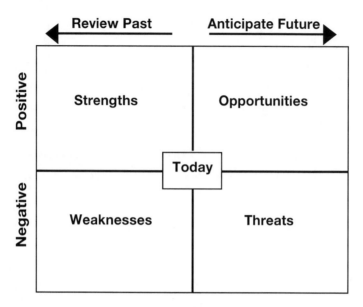

FIGURE 9.2 SWOT analysis framework

Source: von Franz, Johannas and Schall, Nikolaus 2004, *Practitioner's Guild: Strengths, Weaknesses, Opportunities, Threats (SWOT)*, Deutsche Gesellschaft für Technische Zusammenarbeit (GTZ) GmbH.

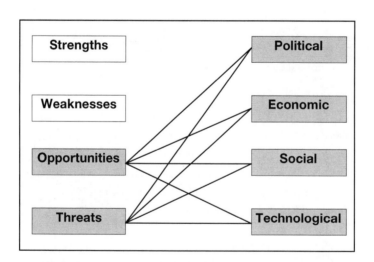

FIGURE 9.3 Relationship between SWOT and PEST analyses

Source: Silva, N. (2012). SWOT Analysis Vs PEST Analysis and When to Use Them, viewed 13.03.2013, http://creately.com/blog/diagrams/swot-analysis-vs-pest-analysis/.

TABLE 9.3 Example of SWOT analysis: bank operating in the EU

Strengths:	Weaknesses:
Risk exposure is spread among individual clients and not a few banks.	Large cash inflows from investing activities; should focus more on enlarging core operating activities.
Growing customer base despite high competition.	Growing credit impairment losses perhaps due to creditworthiness policy.
Better profitability and cash inflow trends.	Dividend payments exhibit downward trend due to profitability decline.
More efficient by reducing personnel and administration expenses.	Vulnerable to paying cost of long-term borrowing from profit.
Effective use of human resources and fixed assets.	Declining investment earnings.
Adequate liquidity to meet working capital requirements.	Advances portfolio needs more diversification to lower risk.
High financial strength and lower vulnerability to business cycle downturns.	**Threats:**
Better investment earnings performance and earnings retention for future expansion.	Changes to Basel-III may increase compliance costs (Political).
Capital adequacy is twice international benchmark.	Government policies fostering financial services may promote new entrants (Political).
Opportunities:	Continuing economic downturn may hinder profitability (Economic).
New EU harmonisation rules may provide level-field to compete with larger banks (Political).	EU inaction to resolve economic instability in Portugal, Ireland, Italy, Greece, and Spain may delay economic recovery (Economic).
Pending recovery with normal risk provisions may lead to pre-crisis profitability levels (Economic).	Digital divide may hinder remote/virtual banking (Technology).
Digital transformation and cost reduction may achieve better financial results (Economic).	Low capital requirements for establishing banks may attract new entrants.
Aging population a source of increased capital (Social).	Poaching of human capital by bigger banks may lead to talent drain/higher training costs.
Retirement fund management business has scope for growth (Social).	Switching costs may prevent customers from seeking smaller banks.
Remote/virtual banking has growth potential since most households and individuals have internet connection (Technology).	Insurance, mutual funds or fixed income securities being offered by non-banking financial services companies.
Technology is major weapon in competitive rivalry strategies.	High competition may lead to undertaking high-risk projects exposing bank to heavy losses.

the resources and competencies of an entity with the requirements of the environment in which the entity operates. Table 9.3 illustrates that the bank being analysed is in a very strong financial position by diversifying its exposure risk; increasing its customer and profitability base; reducing operating expenditure; and having sufficient liquidity to cover its working capital. These strengths are reflected in the bank's capital adequacy level, which is twice the established Basel benchmark. Furthermore, the bank under examination needs to diversify its advances portfolio further and control the growth in credit impairment losses by reviewing its creditworthiness policy.

The SWOT analysis highlights that the bank will likely see an increase in compliance costs due to the amendments to the Basel-III accord and an increase in competition, specifically due to new entrants and the increase in financial services being offered by non-banking financial institutions. However, these threats may be countered by the new EU harmonisation rules that are aimed at providing a level playing field in the banking industry. Finally, the SWOT analysis suggests that technology is a major weapon in competitive rivalry strategies.

Five forces model (analysing competitive forces)

Porter (2008a) argues that in the long-term, it is the industry structure that drives competition and profitability, and not whether an industry produces a product or service, is emerging or mature, high tech or low tech, and regulated or unregulated. He contends that understanding the competitive forces and their underlying causes

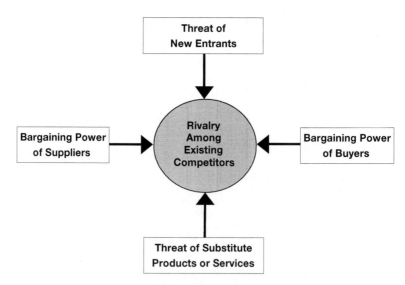

FIGURE 9.4 The five forces that shape industry competition

Source: Porter, M.E. (2008a). Leadership and strategy: the five competitive forces that shape strategy, *Harvard Business Review*, January, 78–93.

as shown in Figure 9.4, reveals the roots of an industry's current profitability while providing a framework for anticipating and influencing competition (and profitability) over time and is essential to effective strategic positioning.

Porter (2008b) suggests that entities must reshape the forces in their favour. He argues that organisations are to use tactics designed specifically to reduce the share of profits leaking to other players by:

- Neutralising supplier power through standardising specifications for provisions so that they can switch more easily among suppliers.
- Countering customer power via expanding services so it is harder for customers to change to a rival.
- Mitigating price wars initiated by rivals through investing more in product differentiation.
- Thwarting new entrants through an increase in the fixed costs of competing by escalating R&D expenditures.
- Diminishing the threat of substitutes by offering better value through wider product accessibility.

However, some researchers contend that the five forces model has a number of weaknesses. Brandenburger and Nalebuff (1997) argue that the 'impact of complementors' is lacking from Porter's model. They view complementors as entities that are outside the industry that sell goods or services, which complement industry competitors. Hence, they argue that the five forces model does not account for the impact of strategic alliances. Morstan (2012) notes that Porter's model does not consider the unique resources and capabilities that a firm brings to the industry. It is argued that the five forces model should be supplemented by the application of the Grant (1991) resources and capabilities model.

Despite these criticisms, the five forces model is generally viewed as an aid to management, for it not only helps managers to comprehend the competitive forces that are at play but also provides an insight of their underlying causes. The results of the five forces analysis related to the example regarding a commercial bank operating in a small EU member state, is found at Table 9.4. The results from the five forces model at Table 9.4 are applied by management to ascertain the bank's position related to the services it provides to its customers compared with the local and international banking trends.

For instance, the five forces analysis in the example indicates that a threat of new entrants is high, because establishing a bank in this particular EU member state requires relatively low capital, with conditions for registering a bank not being very complex. The analysis also suggests that the power of banks is low because customers have a wide choice. However, the threat to suppliers is related to human capital; if talented individuals are working for a smaller bank, there is the likelihood of these persons being enticed to the bigger banks that would offer better conditions and career opportunities. Moreover, it is suggested that the power of suppliers will increase by merging to form larger banks.

TABLE 9.4 Example of five forces model: bank operating in the EU

---

1. Threat of New Entrants.

Threat of new entrants is high since minimum capital requirement to establish a bank is relatively low and the conditions set for registering a bank are not very complex.

Banks are fearful of being squeezed out of the payments business.

Insurance companies pose a threat by offering mortgage and loan services.

The possibility of a mega bank entering into the market with smaller banks being taken.

---

2. Power of Suppliers.

The threat of suppliers luring away human capital. Talented individuals working for smaller regional banks are likely to be enticed away by bigger banks and investment firms.

The threat of suppliers merging to become larger banks. The impact of regulation, combined with strategic repositioning, may force a variety of mergers and divestitures across the banking sector.

---

3. Power of Buyers.

Having a wide range of suppliers, customers can move within the many operators and can also decide to switch to other financial institutions for various services.

Power of buyers is impacted by high switching costs. If a person has a mortgage, car loan and mutual funds with one particular bank, it can be tough for that person to switch to another bank.

Large corporate clients have high power.

---

4. Availability of Substitutes.

There are many substitutes in the banking industry. Insurance, mutual funds or fixed income securities are being offered by non-banking financial services companies.

---

5. Competitive Rivalry.

Banks entice clients away from competitor banks by offering lower financing, preferred rates and investment services.

In the long run, there is likely to be more consolidation in the banking industry with larger banks preferring to take over or merge with another bank.

Competitive rivalry will be based on how customers interact with banks and how this impacts revenue streams in retail banking.

Technology will make an impact on: services to be offered; size of branches that are likely to be smaller with innovative approaches to staffing focused on building relationships, growing sales and helping customers resolve more difficult problems; branch technology such as having a touch-friendly interface and a 'virtual teller'; taping into the virtual gaming ecosystem or charge a fee for facilitating end-to-end payments of virtual currencies; and increase focus on senior citizens since they have considerable savings and want simple products, and are likely to be more loyal.

Additionally, the analysis illustrates that the power of buyers is high because customers can switch suppliers for various services. The switching costs are a limiting factor to the power of buyers (normal consumer), particularly if a customer has a mortgage or other type of loan. However, large corporate clients have high power and banks would offer them better terms and conditions. Substitutes are indicated as being high in the banking sector; for instance, insurance, mutual funds or fixed income securities are being offered by non-banking financial services companies, with large car dealerships also offering preferred financing to customers.

Finally, the five forces analysis in the example suggests that the banking industry has very high competitive rivalry. This competitive forces analysis indicates that apart from enticing banks to undertake high-risk projects, competitive rivalry will likely lead to more consolidation, with larger banks preferring take-overs or mergers with another bank to enlarge their customer base. Moreover, the analysis indicates that banking competitive rivalry may be based on offering the best and fastest services; the interaction of customers with banks; and how this interaction impacts revenue streams in retail banking. As such, technology has a major role in competitive rivalry strategies.

External environment concluding remarks

The previous sections have applied a number of analytical models to examine the external environment of the organisation. This process is viewed as important because the external environment of an entity reflects those factors that are outside the entity but have an impact on the entity's ability to operate.

The models that were examined included the PEST (political, economic, social, and technological) analysis; SWOT analysis and five forces model. These models were applied to an actual example for a commercial bank operating in a small EU member state to demonstrate their utility.

The internal environment

The internal environment of an organisation is reflected in how management makes the most of the resources under its control so that it may implement the agreed organisational strategy. Typical resources include physical, financial, human and technological. Moreover, the utilisation of the organisation's resources must be aligned with the organisation's strategy otherwise the applied resources are not being used to their optimal level. In addition, when competing with other entities, the strategy needs to be in place, which fundamentally reflects the internal environment. In other words, management must estimate and apply the appropriate magnitude of internal resources to ensure that the entity's strategy is successfully implemented.

The organisation's mission and leadership style are also considered to be factors that influence the internal environment. However, the focus of this section will be on the analysis of the organisation's financial statements since they reflect the effective application of the organisation's resources by management. This section shall address the following:

- Understanding the meaning of ratio analysis;
- The users of the financial ratios;
- The application of financial ratios;
- Applying financial ratios to interpret an organisation's financial statements.

Furthermore, the analysis of the internal environment will be illustrated by an example using a factitious organisation as a case study as the basis for common-size analysis and financial ratio analysis.

Understanding the meaning of ratio analysis

Financial ratio analysis refers to the computation and comparison of relative amounts or values (ratios) that are acquired from information in a company's financial statements. Therefore, the fundamental basis for financial ratio analysis is the financial statements, namely the statement of financial position (balance sheet), statement of financial performance (profit and loss statement) and the statement of cash flows. The term 'comparison of ratios' may take on two distinct meanings. It could refer to the comparison of ratios for the same company with previous years' data or it could also refer to the comparison of ratios with other companies for the current year or the year under examination.

If properly utilised, financial ratios may be used to examine historical trends so that certain conclusions or deductions can be made about a company's financial status and circumstances, its operational effectiveness and its potential as an investment opportunity. However, one must also recognise that like every other computation method, the financial ratio analysis is regulated by the GIGO (garbage-in garbage-out) rule. Hence, the data needs to be accurate, timely and applicable to the situation that is being measured. For example, there is little point in comparing a company that operates in the car manufacturing industry with one that operates a chain of supermarkets. There is simply no comparison between these two industries and the companies involved in them.

Financial ratios are calculated from one or more items of information from a company's financial statements. For example, the 'gross margin' is the gross profit from operations divided by the total sales or revenues of a company, expressed in percentage terms. However, a financial ratio on its own is meaningless and there-fore must not be viewed in isolation. A financial ratio becomes useful when it is compared to other data, particularly benchmarks. For instance, stating that a company's profitability increased by 20 per cent is not very meaningful. However, if we know that other companies within the same industry had their profitability increase by only 5 per cent, then we know that the company with an increase of 20 per cent is more profitable than its industry peers and therefore has a very favourable financial performance.

Moreover, knowing that a company's profitability is constantly increasing over a number of financial accounting periods is indicative of good financial management, particularly in implementing effective business strategies. Therefore, it is not just a matter of calculating financial ratios, but there is a need to understand their underlying meaning in relation to the company's own performance by examining historical trends, the particular industry the company is participating in, and its competitors.

Financial ratios are a way of presenting voluminous data in a concise format that provides a clear and meaningful representation of a particular company's financial situation. However, one needs to be on the lookout when examining figures, particularly absolute amounts. For example, assume that there are two companies, one reports a profit of €20,000 and the other reports a profit of €30,000. The issue is who is the most profitable. The company that registers a profit of €30,000 appears to be the most profitable. However, let us assume that the first company had capital of €100,000 and the other company had capital of €1.5 million. Hence, the return on capital employed of the first company is 20 per cent (20,000 ÷ 100,000 = 20 per cent) and for the second company it would be 2 per cent (30,000 ÷ 1,500,000 = 2 per cent). Therefore, numerical data must not be considered on its own, it needs to be related to other figures, so that it may be examined from the appropriate viewpoint. The data indicates that the first company is much better in terms of the return on capital employed and hence appears to have better investment prospects.

When using financial ratio analysis for decision making purposes, one also needs to take into consideration the circumstances. For instance, a company that has recently undergone a restructuring programme may initially go through a decline before making a come-back. Similarly, a company that has completely replaced its business processes using a high technology solution will need to time for the new technology to provide its full benefits. Therefore, for comparison purposes make sure that companies being compared are in similar industries and are operating in similar circumstances.

When carrying out financial ratio analysis make sure that the appropriate ratios are selected for the purpose they are being used. For instance, a creditor would place more importance on liquidity and gearing ratios to ascertain the company's financial risk exposure. Furthermore, ensure that comparison between companies is based on similar industries and similar circumstances. Additionally, compare the internal divisions of the company under examination, particularly for those firms that are structured according to product (or service) lines.

It is also important that a conclusion or deduction is made based on what the financial ratios reveal. Hence, make a strong attempt to interpret the financial ratio analysis. Moreover, to carry out a full investigation of the company there is a need to ask relevant questions. For instance, why is debt high? Why is it taking so long for the company to pay its creditors? Why is it taking so long for the company to collect its accounts receivables?

Finally, management must take appropriate action as necessary based on the financial ratio analysis. However, this depends on the function of the analyst making the financial ratio disclosure. For instance, if the analyst is part of the company being examined, the action may be related to measures that would improve the weakness being disclosed, for example improving liquidity. However, if the analyst is representing a bank or a trade creditor to decide whether to approve a loan or credit, the action may be to examine liquidity and not approve the loan or credit if liquidity is a concern.

Users of financial ratios

The users of financial ratios are varied and depend on their particular function. Hence, the financial ratios that are selected for a specific analysis will depend on the objective of the financial analysis. As stated previously, a creditor or bank would be more interested in financial ratios that disclose the liquidity and gearing level of the company.

There are basically two types of users of financial ratios, those that are employed by the company or are shareholders (internal) and those that exist outside the company but all the same have a vested interest in the company (external). For example, the management would make use of financial ratios to analyse previous results for determining trends in expenditure, revenue and sales, among others; to prepare business plans, including operational budgets; and to monitor and control business activities and performance. In addition, the company shareholders would want to examine whether their investment in the company is giving an adequate return and to investigate whether the dividend trend is likely to remain stable, decline or grow. This would permit them to determine whether they should hold on or sell their shareholdings.

The external users are many and have diverse functions, such as financial analysts employed by the financial press, trade unions and trade associations; and government, including tax regulatory authorities and national statistical institutions. Other external users include competitors who desire to compare their position with others in similar industries and circumstances; banks and creditors who would focus on liquidity and gearing levels to determine the creditworthiness of the company; and potential investors or equity analysts who would like to determine the current and future dividend policies of the company as a comparative basis with alternative investments.

Financial ratios must be meaningful to be of use and therefore they must demonstrate that there exists a direct relationship between the variables that constitute the particular ratio. For instance, stating that two companies have a profitability of €20,000 and €30,000 respectively and that their capital is €100,000 and €1.5 million respectively does not tell us very much. However, it is when we examine the relationship between profitability and the capital employed that provides a better basis for determining which company is the most profitable. Hence, when profit is divided by capital employed, this gives us the return on capital employed (i.e. €20,000 ÷ €100,000 = 20 per cent and €30,000 ÷ €1,500,000 = 2 per cent) and is used as the basis for concluding that one company is better than the other based on profitability.

One must also recognise that a major objective of the published financial statements of a company is to provide a true and fair view of the economic performance of the company under examination and to determine its financial status. On the other hand, the objective of financial ratio analysis is to assist all types of users to interpret the information provided in the financial statements by establishing trends; aiding in the identification of the underlying causes that have contributed to the strengths and weaknesses of the company; and actually disclosing the strengths and weaknesses of the organisation being examined. In other words, financial ratios are used to help management to establish benchmarks and to use these benchmarks as a comparative basis; assess the performance of particular divisions or sub-divisions within the company being examined; and to compare the company with other entities, particularly its major competitors.

Application of financial ratios

Figure 9.5 provides a summary of the financial ratios that are the focus of this chapter. Moreover, Figure 9.5 also illustrates that financial ratio analysis groups the various ratios into categories that attempt to explain the diverse aspects of a company's operational circumstances and financial condition. Figure 9.5 demonstrates that financial ratio analysis may be applied to five distinct and related areas, namely:

- Asset utilisation ratios that provide an indication of the company's operational efficiency and how well it utilises its assets;
- Profitability ratios that show aspects related to the return on sales and capital employed; and depicts a company's ability to generate cash flow and honour its financial obligations;
- Liquidity ratios that describe a company's short term financial status in terms of solvency (the degree to which the current assets exceed the current liabilities);
- Capital structure ratios that describe how the company is financing its operational activities (through equity and/or borrowing);
- Investment ratios that describe the rate of return earned on the company's shares.

One should note that financial ratios have their limitations. Financial ratios may indicate that a concern exists but they do not provide the cause or the solution to the concern; hence further analysis would be required. Additionally, the veracity of the financial ratios depends upon the quality of the information provided in the financial statements. Therefore, financial statements that are qualified by the auditor may not provide an accurate basis for the calculation of all or some of the financial ratios. Furthermore, the required information may not always be disclosed in the financial statements and at times financial statement headings may be misleading.

When financial ratios are used to compare two or more companies, make sure that these companies belong to the same industry sector and approximately exist under the same circumstances (i.e. undergoing restructuring or merger). Financial ratios are purely a computation they do not take into consideration that certain enterprises are seasonal and hence may experience a wide spectrum in terms of stock levels and debtors. For example, some companies may encounter low or high

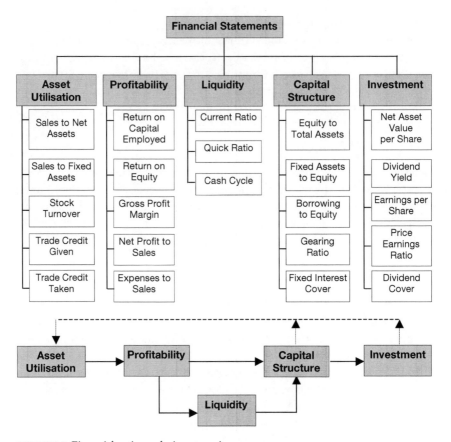

FIGURE 9.5 Financial ratio analysis categories summary

stock and debt levels at the end of the financial year due to seasonal fluctuations (e.g. ice cream manufacturers). Not adjusting the values in the financial statements for inflation may provide misleading financial ratios. For instance, a company may indicate an increase in sales turnover of 5 per cent, however, if the inflation rate throughout the financial year was hovering at around 4 per cent, then in reality the increase in sales turnover is only 1 per cent.

Applying financial ratios to interpret an organisation's financial statements

Table 9.5 itemises the key financial ratios, including their formulae that are applicable to each identified category, namely, asset utilisation, profitability, liquidity, capital structure and investment. These financial ratios are described in more detail blow.

TABLE 9.5a Financial ratios by application category

Financial Ratio	Formulae	Remarks
Liquidity:		
Current Ratio	Current Assets ÷ Current Liabilities	A current ratio of between 1.5:1 and 2:1 is generally considered practical although this depends on the nature of the business. Current assets should always be greater than current liabilities.
Liquid Ratio (Quick Ratio or Acid Test)	(Current Assets − Stock) ÷ Current Liabilities	A liquid ratio of 1:1 is normally considered satisfactory but may be allowed to fall to 0.9:1 if the debtors pay promptly and there is a regular inflow of cash from them.
Profitability:		
Return on Capital Employed (ROCE)	$\dfrac{\text{Profit Before Interest and Tax}}{\text{Capital Employed}} \times 100$	This ratio indicates management efficiency because it contrasts the earnings with the funds utilised to generate that profit. As a minimum management will aim to maintain the ROCE level. Capital Employed = Total Assets − Current Liabilities.
Return on Equity (ROE)	Profit Before Tax (after preference dividends) ÷ (Ordinary Share Capital + Reserves)	The ratio measures profitability by revealing how much profit a company generates with the money shareholders have invested. Net income is for the full fiscal year (before dividends paid to common stock holders but after dividends to preferred stock.) Shareholder's equity does not include preferred shares.
Gross Profit Margin	Gross Profit ÷ Sales	The ratio shows the margin that is being earned on sales. It measures a company's manufacturing and distribution efficiency during the production process. Note that gross margin tends to remain stable over time.
Net Profit to Sales	Profit Before Interest and Tax ÷ Sales	The ratio indicates the overall performance of the company.
Expenses to Sales: *Operating Expenses* *Selling/Distribution Cost* *Administrative Expenses* *Finance Charges*	Total Operating Expenses ÷ Sales Selling & Distribution Expenses ÷ Sales Administrative Expenses ÷ Sales Finance Charges ÷ Sales	Only four ratios are shown and focus on the performance of the company in terms of the proportion of each particular expense is to sales. Other ratios may include any other expense item. These ratios provide a view of the company's cost structure.

TABLE 9.5b Financial ratios by application category (continued)

Financial Ratio	Formulae	Remarks
Asset Utilisation:		
Sales to Net Assets	Sales ÷ Net Assets Where: Net assets = Total Assets − Total Liabilities.	Unless the firm is over trading, a high ratio is a healthy indication. A low ratio may indicate unused capacity especially if accompanied with a high ratio of fixed overheads to sales.
Sales to Fixed Assets	Sales ÷ Net Fixed Assets Where: Net Fixed Assets = Purchase price − Depreciation + Leasehold Improvements − Total Liabilities.	Measures the utilisation of fixed assets. A low ratio may suggest ineffective use of fixed assets. However, this may also be due to recent fixed capital investment. One may consider using the book value of the fixed assets for net fixed assets.
Stock Turnover (days)	(Average Stock ÷ Cost of Sales) x 365 days Average Stock = (Opening Stock + Closing Stock) ÷ 2	Shows the number of days stock held before it is sold.
Trade Credit Given (days)	(Average Debtors ÷ Sales) x 365 days Average Debtors = (Opening Debtors + Closing Debtors) ÷ 2	Measures the collection period in days of debtors.
Trade Credit Taken (days)	(Average Creditors ÷ Purchase) x 365 days Average Creditors = (Opening Creditors + Closing Creditors) ÷ 2	Measures the payment period in days of creditors.
Cash Cycle Duration (days)	Stock Turnover + Credit Period Given − Credit Period Taken	Measures the period of time between the purchase of stocks and receipt of cash from debtors for goods sold.
Capital Structure:		
Equity to Total assets	(Capital + Reserves) ÷ Total Assets	Shows the percentage of total assets financed by the shareholders.
Fixed Assets to Equity	Net Fixed Assets ÷ (Capital + Reserves)	Shows the percentage of fixed assets financed by the shareholders.
Borrowing to Equity	(Long Term Liabilities + Current Liabilities) ÷ (Capital + Reserves)	Shows the proportion of external financing versus internal financing.
Gearing Ratio	Long Term Liabilities ÷ (Capital + Reserves)	Measures financial leverage, demonstrating the degree to which a firm's activities are funded by owner's funds versus creditor's funds.
Fixed Interest Cover	Net Profit Before Interest ÷ Fixed Interest Expense	Indicates how easily a firm can pay interest on outstanding debt.

TABLE 9.5c Financial ratios by application category (continued)

Financial Ratio	Formulae	Remarks
Investment:		
Net Asset Value per Share	Net Assets ÷ No. of Ordinary Shares Where: Net assets = Total Assets − Total Liabilities.	Represents the value of a share and may be viewed as the price at which shares are bought and sold.
Dividend Yield	Dividend per Share ÷ Market Price per Share.	Measures the real rate of return on an investment since it is based on the market price and not the nominal value.
Earnings per Share	Net Profit After Tax ÷ No. of Ordinary Shares	Indicates level of profitability, but it is limited when compared to dividend yield since number of shares remain constant.
Price Earnings Ratio	Market Price per Share ÷ Earnings per Share	The lower the price earnings ratio, the quicker the capital outlay is recovered.
Dividend Cover	Net Profit After Tax ÷ Net Dividend	It shows the amount available for distribution and demonstrates the plough back and dividend distribution policies of the company.

Company's asset utilisation position

The asset utilisation ratios indicate management's effectiveness in the utilisation of the assets under their responsibility, including working capital management and fixed assets. The financial ratios of particular interest are asset turnover (sales to net assets); sales to fixed assets; stock turnover; trade credit given; and trade credit taken. The last three financial ratios, namely stock turnover, trade credit given and trade credit taken provide an insight into working capital management, particularly the calculation of the cash cycle duration. These are discussed under Liquidity Ratios.

The asset turnover ratio shows the rate of revenue (sales) to net assets, where net assets are total assets minus total liabilities. A low asset turnover ratio may suggest that the company has idle capacity; particularly if a low ratio is complemented with a high fixed overhead costs to sales ratio. The higher the ratio the more effectively the capital is being employed, unless the company involved is over trading. Overtrading is a condition where a company tries to enlarge turnover at a hurried pace to a point where working capital becomes insufficient. Note that a company selling products with a low profit margin must turn its stock over more quickly than an enterprise that earns a high profit margin if it is to achieve the same net profit percentage.

The sales to fixed assets ratio provides a measure of the utilisation of fixed assets (e.g. fixed assets include machinery, equipment and property). A low sales to fixed assets ratio, suggests an unproductive use of the fixed assets. However, it may also be indicative of recent fixed capital investment in the company. For example, a company may have recently invested a significant amount in new technology, which has not had adequate time to generate sufficient improvement is sales.

Stock turnover is an important ratio since it highlights the number of days that stock is held by the company before it is sold. Therefore, this ratio indicates the level of efficiency in the use of stock, particularly if the company keeps a breakdown of the stock into raw materials, works in progress and finished goods. To be useful, the stock turnover ratio should be compared with the gross profit margin ratio. If the gross profit margin ratio is low, then a high stock turnover ratio is desirable (e.g. supermarket). Therefore, entities such as supermarkets have low operating leverage, which means that they must have high sales turnover at a low profit margin. However, car dealers selling luxury cars, have high operating leverage, where they would have low sales turnover but very high profit margins.

The trade credit given computation measures the collection period of debtors. This measure is essential for management to plan its cash flow and also provides an indication of the possibility of bad debts. One should note that the longer it takes to collect the debt, the higher the probability of bad debts. However, one needs to consider the nature of the business of the entity under examination in relation to seasonal fluctuations. There is also the risk that the real working capital value is less than what appears on the balance sheet.

The trade credit taken computation measures the payment period of creditors. This measure is also important for planning cash flow. The trade credit taken period is the cheapest form of finance if used in moderation. However, if payments are not made in time, a trader may lose the trade discount. Furthermore, a high trade credit taken period may send a signal to creditors that the company is experiencing a period of tight liquidity, which could adversely affect the operations of the entity (i.e. loss of good will by creditors).

As stated previously, stock turnover, trade credit given, trade credit taken are the three components for calculating the cash cycle (cash flow) and working capital management, which are discussed under the liquidity ratios. The cash cycle duration is calculated by: Stock Turnover plus Credit Period Given to Debtors minus Credit Period Taken from Creditors.

Company's profitability position

The profitability ratios examine a company's profit margins and returns for the past financial periods, approved budgets, and other divisions within the company. There are a number of key ratios under this heading; these include return on capital employed (ROCE); return on equity (ROE); gross profit margin; net profit to sales; and various expenses to sales.

ROCE is an important financial ratio that indicates management's efficiency by contrasting the return on capital employed with the funds utilised to generate the profit. It illustrates how much profit has been earned on long-term capital. Generally, earnings (or profit) are calculated before interest and tax (EBIT) to ensure better comparability. At minimum, management would want to maintain a stable ROCE level. One should note that a low ROCE indicates that an entity's profitable situation could easily be transformed into a loss making enterprise. Moreover, if the interest rate is higher than the percentage return on capital, than further borrowing will have an unfavourable effect upon profitability.

ROCE can also act as a benchmark to measure the accounting rate of return when assessing existing business activities or alternative projects. Hence, if the return on capital cannot be improved, then any business undertaking with a percentage return below the average for the business as a whole, may be considered for disposal or termination. When using ROCE as a comparative measure, ensure that the companies being assessed have the same line of business and analogous operations. For example, a company that produces personal computers and manufacturers the entire component parts itself will be more capital intensive than a company that simply assembles sub-contracted parts.

ROE is a slight variation from the ROCE since the ROE excludes all long-term liabilities from the denominator. ROE demonstrates the return made by business for the proprietor but it is not considered as an overall measure of profitability. However, gross profit margin ratio provides an overall guide of efficiency of production (goods and services). Its limitation is the fact that selling and distribution expenses are excluded from the calculation. The gross profit margin will also vary with the type of business. A business that requires high volume turnover to survive (e.g. supermarket) will operate on a lower gross profit margin to encourage sales. However, a car dealer will have a lower volume of sales but will aim for a higher gross profit margin. A lower than expected gross profit margin may be due to a number of reasons, such as not passing an resulting increase in the cost of goods sold to clients; lowering the selling price to dispose of obsolete or slow moving stock items (e.g. sales); giving special prices or bulk discounts to the larger customers; pilfering of stock that has not been included as part of cost of sales; and achieving a sales mix that is different from what was predicted in the sales budget (e.g. selling more products that have low margin in comparison to selling high margin ones).

Another financial ratio under this category is the net profit to sales ratio. This ratio provides an overall performance of the firm and is widely used. Once again, when using net profit to sales ratio for comparing different companies, it is important to ensure that they are in the same line of business. For example, a vegetable retailer needs to dispose of stock quickly due to the perishable nature of the goods and will therefore operate on a small profit margin. However, a company that sells classic jewellery will sell fewer items but at a much higher profit margin. Finally, the various expenses to sales ratios allow more detailed analysis to be carried out if and when required. These financial ratios assist management to identify and focus on vulnerable expense areas. Furthermore, these various ratios may be utilised as a basis for a SWOT analysis.

Company's liquidity status

The two key liquidity ratios are the current ratio and the acid test. These ratios determine the ability of a company to meet its current liabilities from its working capital. The term liquidity refers to those assets which belong to a particular company and are easily transformed into hard cash so that the company can honour the payments as they fall due. Hence, the current ratio measures a company's ability to pay its short-term obligations. The higher the current ratio, the more capable the company is of paying its debt.

The notion of honouring payments as they fall due is closely linked to the concept of working capital management, which aims to ensure that the company generates a regular supply of cash inflows to meet the demand for a regular flow of cash outflows. In other words, working capital management ensures that a company has sufficient cash flow to meet its short-term debt commitments and operating expenses. The issue that needs to be addressed is whether the company is generating sufficient cash to finance its business activities or if it is depending on short-term borrowing (i.e. trade creditors, bank overdrafts etc). Hence, the current ratio is used to indicate whether a company's operating cycle is efficient. A company's operating cycle being the company's ability to turn its product into cash quickly. Companies that have difficulty getting paid on their receivables or have long inventory turnover may have liquidity concerns since they are unable to reduce their debt and mitigate their debt risk exposure.

The Current Ratio (or Working Capital ratio) also indicates whether a firm is using its own generated funds to finance its current assets or if it is using current liabilities, through its creditors, to finance its current assets. Hence, a company's level of debtors and creditors show the extent to which the company is financing itself or being financed by external company sources.

A question that is often asked is related to what should an ideal current ratio level be. There is no ideal current ratio level, but it is desirable that current assets are greater than the current liabilities in order to provide sufficient cover in case there are cash flow problems. One should note that liquidity concerns may seriously hold back the operation of a business. Having said this, the current ratio level normally depends on the industry sector, but a ratio of between 1.5:1 and 2:1 may generally be considered practical. A current ratio under one suggests that a company would be unable to pay its obligations if they all came due at that particular point in time. While this shows the firm is not in good financial health, it does not necessarily mean that it will go insolvent, since there are many ways for a company to obtain financing.

The other liquidity ratio is the acid test (or liquid ratio or quick ratio). The acid test ratio measures the ability of a company to meet all of its current liabilities from liquid resources. This is the reason why stocks are subtracted from the current assets but the computation includes all debtors even those that are considered to be sluggish in honouring their payments. This ratio provides a practical indicator regarding the solvency position of a company. Hence, a liquid ratio of 1:1 is generally considered satisfactory and may be allowed to fall to 0.9:1 if debtors pay promptly and there is a regular inflow of cash. However, to improve liquidity a company may consider selling trading investments (even at a loss) to increase its cash holdings. A business which sells almost wholly for cash (supermarket) but enjoys normal credit terms for its purchases may have a liquid ratio of 0.5:1 or less. Therefore, the level of the liquidity ration depends on the industry sector.

The issue of liquidity is also closely related to the concept of overtrading and the cash cycle duration (working capital management). Overtrading is a condition where a company tries to enlarge turnover at a hurried pace to a point where working capital becomes insufficient. Note that stock piling (over trading) may improve the current ratio but worsen the quick ratio because the numerator in the current ratio calculation includes all current assets. Indications that a company is overtrading include situations where creditors increase in relation to debtors; there is increased borrowing; the company is constantly struggling to have sufficient cash; there is an increase in stock but this is not followed by an increase in turnover; there is a decline in gross and/or net profit; and experiencing very high expenditure on fixed assets.

The cash cycle duration measures the period of time between the purchase of stocks and the generation of cash from debtors for goods and services sold. The cash cycle duration is calculated by: Stock Turnover plus Credit Period Given to Debtors minus Credit Period Taken from Creditors.

Company's capital structure

The capital structure ratios indicate how the company is being financed in terms of internal and external financing, and whether the financing method utilised is of a short- or long-term nature. There are five primary ratios under this category, namely, equity to total assets; fixed assets to equity; borrowing to equity; gearing leverage; and fixed interest cover.

The equity to total assets ratio provides the percentage of the total assets being financed by the shareholders; in other words, financing from an internal source. This ratio indicates the internal financial strength of the company. Hence, a deterioration of this ratio may require a reduction in dividend payments to shareholders and an increase in the amount of profits that are ploughed back into the company. However, one needs to be careful in interpreting this ratio because an investment in fixed assets financed by long-term loans would result in a weakening of this ratio. An important ratio is the fixed assets to equity ratio. This shows the percentage of fixed assets financed from internal sources (the shareholders). Preferably, fixed assets should be financed by equity (shareholders) or other long-term borrowing (bonds/debentures) in order that the working capital is not stressed.

The borrowing to equity ratio is a significant indicator because it shows the proportion of funds that are provided for the business from external sources in relation to internal sources. Hence, a low ratio is desirable. A primary ratio under this category is the gearing ratio. The gearing ratio is a measure of financial leverage, demonstrating the degree to which a company's business activities are funded by internal sources (owner's funds) versus external sources (creditor's funds). One should note that a highly geared company is considered to be very risky. However, an acceptable level of gearing is established by comparing a company's gearing ratio with that of other companies in the same industry. For instance, the construction industry has a tendency to have high gearing. However, one should note that a high geared company is more exposed to downturns in the business cycle since the company must continue to service its debt regardless of how bad its sales are. This is the basic reason why construction companies are more susceptible in national economic downturns. A higher equity level provides a cash buffer and is thus viewed as a measure of financial strength.

During a period of increasing profits, the rate of increase in profits available to shareholders in a highly geared firm is greater than that of a low geared firm. Therefore, a drop in profits in a high geared firm affects the ordinary shareholders more severely than in a low geared company. Hence, investment in the ordinary shares of a highly geared company may present a greater risk than an investment in a low geared company, with the consequence that a financial institution, such as a bank, may be reluctant to provide a loan to a highly geared company on the grounds that the ordinary shareholders should be prepared to finance the company. In other words, a bank should not be expected to take a risk, which the shareholders themselves are unwilling to take.

A ratio that is closely related to gearing is the fixed interest cover ratio because it indicates how easily a company is able to meet its interest payment obligations on outstanding debt. The extent a company is burdened by debt servicing costs will be reflected in a low fixed interest cover ratio. Hence, the lower the fixed interest cover ratio, the higher the company's problem to service its debt. As an indicative measure, an interest coverage ratio of 1.5 or less means that a company's capacity to pay it interest obligation may be questionable. Moreover, an interest coverage ratio below 1.0 suggests that the company is not generating adequate earnings to comply with the interest expenses.

Company's investment status

The investment ratios represent the final category of the ratios under discussion. These ratios are of great consequence because they address three critical issues, namely, the security level of the investment; the return yield the investor is receiving for the investment; and the payback period of the investment (i.e. how soon the capital outlay is recovered). There are five ratios under this category, namely, net asset value per share; dividend yield; earnings per share; price earnings ratio; and dividend cover.

The net asset value per share (where net assets are the difference between total assets and total liabilities) is the share value, that is, the price at which shares are bought and sold. Hence, it indicates the security level of the investment. In other words, a high share price is indicative of high security.

A primary investment ratio is the dividend yield. The dividend yield measures the real rate of return on an investment because it is based on the market price and not the nominal value. This investment ratio is also viewed as indicating the security level of the investment, since typically, a high yield return is synonymous to a higher risk. Moreover, a potential investor may match different yield returns from various investment types to ascertain investment opportunities depending on whether the particular investor desires high security with a lower return or low security but with a high return.

The earnings per share ratio basically indicates the return yield that the investor is receiving. Thus, the earnings per share ratio is viewed as a measure of company success. However, when compared to dividend yield the use of this ratio is limited because the number of shares in the denominator of the computation remains constant. Whereas, the dividend yield ratio computation uses the market price per share, which is more realistic. The earnings per share computation is normally included in the published financial statements of a company and indicate the profitability level of the company.

The price earnings ratio provides an indication of the payback period of the investment. In other words, the lower the price earnings ratio, the quicker the capital outlay is recovered. For instance, if the market price per share was $2.50 and the earnings per share is $0.50, then the payback period would be five years (i.e. $2.50 ÷ $0.50 = 5 years) subject that the earnings per share remain at the level of $0.50. This ratio is a measure of investor confidence in the future of the company.

Another key investment ratio is the dividend cover. This ratio is important for both existing and potential investors because it shows the amount available for distribution, thus revealing the dividend distribution policy of company and the amount of earnings that are being ploughed back in the company. In other words, the higher the dividend cover would suggest that the profit being generated by the company is being held in reserves, which may be utilised for future expansion. Therefore, a high dividend cover may indicate a cautious dividend policy, which suggests that the company should be able to maintain the present level of dividend to ordinary shareholders even if profits decline temporarily. Conversely, a low dividend cover indicates that a relatively small reduction in profits may put the ordinary dividend at risk. Consequently, this ratio may be used to estimate the security of dividend payments. A low dividend cover ratio may be viewed as putting at risk future dividend distributions (no reserves), while a high ratio would affect the dividend yield unfavourably.

However, the interpretation of this ratio depends on the objective of the investor. For instance, investors that desire capital gains would welcome a high dividend cover ratio because it indicates that the company has the capacity for future expansion (i.e. high reserves due to low dividend outflow). On the other hand, investors that want immediate income would prefer a lower dividend cover ratio because it indicates that the company has a higher level of dividend payment. Therefore, the use of the dividend cover ratio depends on what the investor desires.

It should be noted that the ordinary shareholders are interested in the return on their investment and the value of their shares. However, ordinary shareholders take third place after debenture holders and preference shareholders. For instance, debenture (or bond) holders are entitled to the interest payment on their investment, whether the company makes a profit or not, while preference shareholder take precedence over ordinary shares. Therefore, the dividend payment of the ordinary shareholders is at risk if their company's long-term capital is to a large extent provided by holders of debentures and/or preference shares.

Common-size analysis

Common-size analysis basically adjusts the financial statements for various companies as a percentage of a selected or common figure. For example, to common-size the statement of financial position, one would use the total assets figure as a basis for the percentage calculation. This allows companies of different sizes to be compared over time. Thus, by using common-size financial statements, investors may recognise trends that a normal financial statement may not reveal.

Common-size: statement of financial position

Common-size analysis of the statement of financial position (balance sheet) may take two distinct forms, namely vertical or horizontal common-sizing. A vertical common-size balance sheet is generated by dividing each balance sheet item by the same financial period's total assets and expressing the result as percentage. This approach draws attention to the structure of the balance sheet in terms of the assets mix being utilised; the comparative basis of the balance sheet structure with other companies in the same industry; and the reasons for the differences that may be revealed between the balance sheet structures under examination. On the other hand, a horizontal common-size balance sheet is obtained by calculating the change (increase or decrease) in percentage terms of each balance sheet item from the previous year. Hence, it indicates those balance sheet items that have suddenly changed or have remained unchanged even though they were predicted to change.

Consider the example at Table 9.6 which shows a segment of a vertical common-size balance sheet for two accounting periods. The data presented shows that the accounts receivables have increased from 40 per cent to 63 per cent of the total assets.

The issue that needs to be addressed is the reasons that have caused this change. The possible reasons for the upward change of the accounts receivable may be due to a review of the client credit procedures by not aggressively chasing outstanding debts; a significant increase in the credit sales as distinct from cash sales; a review of the revenue recognition policies; and a sudden decrease in the level of inventory due to a sales clearance of slow moving or obsolete items. One may also compare the growth trend in the accounts receivable with that of sales to establish a likely reason for the change. Table 9.6 illustrates that the company has experienced a decline in its cash position due to the increase in accounts receivables and a decrease in inventory. It is likely that the company in question is clearing inventory of old stock in preparation for the new upcoming sales season.

The common-size analysis of the balance sheet can also reveal the company's capital structure strategy in comparison with its competitors. Hence, prospective investors may be able to examine the capital structure for a particular industry and compare this to the company of interest.

TABLE 9.6 Vertical common-size statement of financial position

Particulars	Period-1 % of Total Assets	Period-2 % of Total Assets
Cash at Bank	20	10
Accounts Receivables	40	63
Inventory	30	15
Fixed Assets (book value)	10	12
Total Assets:	**100**	**100**

Common-size: statement of financial performance

The common figure used in common-sizing the statement of financial performance (income statement) is normally total revenue but total assets may also be used in particular instances, such as, for companies that are classified as financial institutions. Table 9.7 illustrates a common-size income statement for a company with two different time periods. When there are diverse revenue sources, the breakdown of the revenue by source may better reveal the reasons why certain changes have occurred.

The common-size income statement at Table 9.7 shows that the earnings from the different services are not proportional. For instance, there is a wide difference between period one and two for the earnings from maintenance of equipment 'B' (i.e. from 27 per cent to 42 per cent). Once again, there is a need to examine the possible reasons for this change in growth in sales and the impact of this growth on the reported sales mix. The possibility of management implementing a strategic decision to sell more maintenance services for equipment 'B', because it is more profitable does not seem plausible due to the decline from 55 per cent to 47 per cent in the earnings before interest, taxation, depreciation and administrative costs.

TABLE 9.7 Vertical common-size statement of financial performance

Particulars	Period-1 % of Total Revenue	Period-2 % of Total Revenue
Revenue from sales of services:		
1. Equipment 'A' maintenance revenue	20	17
2. Equipment 'B' maintenance revenue	27	42
3. Equipment 'C' maintenance revenue	28	29
4. Equipment 'D' maintenance revenue	15	7
5. Equipment 'E' maintenance revenue	10	5
Total Revenue from Sale of Services:	**100**	**100**
Less Operating Costs (Excl. depreciation:		
1. Personnel emoluments	12	22
2. Administrative costs	18	16
3. Building rent cost	15	15
EBITDA:	**55**	**47**
Less Depreciation and Amortisation	5	5
EBIT:	**50**	**42**
Less Interest Paid	9	9
EBT:	**41**	**33**
Less Income Tax Provision	15	12
Net Income:	**26**	**21**

EBIT (Earnings before interest and tax)

Personnel emoluments, which have increased from 12 per cent to 22 per cent of total revenue, appear to be the main reason for the decline in profitability. A likely explanation is that the growth in personnel cost as a resource may have been diverted towards the selling of more maintenance services for equipment 'B'. One would need to investigate further to see whether equipment 'B' requires unskilled or specialist skilled workers, with the requisite training needs depending on the skill requirements level.

Cross-sectional analysis

Financial ratios and common-size financial statements are more meaningful when used as a comparative measure either when contrasting specific companies as competitors or as a benchmark for a particular industry.

Cross-sectional analysis compares a particular variable (e.g. line item in a balance sheet) of a specific company with that of another company or group of companies in the same industry. Therefore, this approach permits comparative studies to be undertaken across a spectrum of companies despite the fact that these companies are considerably different in magnitude and/or operate in different currencies.

Table 9.8 shows a segment of a vertical common-size balance sheet for two companies as at a particular period ending date. The first company exhibits better liquidity since the asset item 'cash at bank' is much higher than that of the other company in percentage terms (30 per cent of total assets versus 10 per cent).

This may indicate that Company 'A' is not using its cash asset very efficiently, since hard cash is very low yielding. On the other hand, Company 'A' may be anticipating a decline in the current operating circumstances and is therefore preparing for harder times. Of concern is the high percentage of accounts receivables for Company 'B'. This may suggest a more relaxed customer credit policy than that of Company 'A' which may turn out to be a serious concern should the industry endure economic difficulties in the near future. Hence, the cross-sectional analysis suggests that Company 'A' is more risk averse than Company 'B' and is more likely to withstand an economic down turn should this occur in the future.

TABLE 9.8 Vertical common-size statement of financial position of two firms

Particulars	Company 'A' % of Total Assets	Company 'B' % of Total Assets
Assets:		
1. Cash at Bank	30	10
2. Accounts Receivables	36	51
3. Inventory	30	26
4. Fixed Assets (book value)	2	3
5. Investments	2	10
Total Assets:	**100**	**100**

Trend analysis

The trend analysis of financial statement analysis is typically related to the comparative examination of financial data over a number of accounting periods (i.e. 5 to 10 years) and does not involve statistical methods, such as time-series analysis. Trend analysis focuses on historical performance. Hence, for trend analysis to be of utility, requires an adequate lengthy history of accurate seasonal data, which may be applied for planning and forecasting purposes.

Horizontal common-size balance sheets are useful because they emphasise structural changes that have taken place in an enterprise. It is an axiom that historical trends are not necessarily an accurate predictor of the future, particularly in a turbulent economic environment. One should note that the economic or competitive environment is constantly changing. However, historical trend analysis can still be of assistance to companies that are seeking business opportunities, particularly if the analysis indicates that the established trends are likely to continue or change direction.

Comparative studies that compare a particular company to the industry it operates in provide an indication of the level of success being enjoyed by that particular company. Hence, a company that experiences a growth rate higher than the industry average it operates in provides a clear measure of success. This type of success measure is important because companies that demonstrate faster growth are able to attract equity capital. On the other hand, investors need to be cautious, because companies that enjoy rapid growth may encounter difficulties, since their administrative systems, including the management information systems, are unable to cope with the rapid rate of development.

Comparative studies may also be conducted between horizontal common-size financial statements. For example, one may compare the growth rate of assets for the company with its growth in revenue during the period under examination. Hence, a company whose revenue is increasing at a higher rate than its assets may suggest that the company is improving its operating efficiency.

For example, assume that a company has the following year-over-year percentage changes: revenue, +15 per cent; net income, +20 per cent; operating cash flow -7.5 per cent; and total assets, +25 per cent. The information illustrates that net income is increasing at a more rapid rate than revenue, which suggests that the company is increasing its profitability. In spite of this indicative increase in profitability, management would be wise to investigate further and establish whether the faster growth rate in the net income is a consequence of continuing operations or from other sources, such as disposal of assets, which generate revenue on a once off basis. Likewise, the decrease in operating cash flow of 7.5 per cent, when revenue and net income are on the rise are a concern, because this may suggest that cash is not being collected at the desired rate from the company's debtors. Furthermore, the asset structure needs to be examined because the company's efficiency could be diminishing, since the percentage increase in revenue is not at par (but below) the growth rate in the company's assets.

Concluding remarks: common-size analysis

A key benefit of a common-size analysis is its flexibility. Vertical analysis can be conducted over a single time period, such as monthly, quarterly or annually for each line item in the respective financial statement. Additionally, the horizontal analysis can be conducted over a much longer time period, such as five years or longer. But it greatest benefit is that it allows benchmarks to be established (in percentage terms) for the whole industry and permits companies of diverse sizes to be compared with each other and the industry in general.

Common-size analysis allows an investor to identify changes in a company's financial status. It allows investors to readily reveal swift increases or decreases in profits and other numerous line items from all the financial statements during one quarter or year.

A common-size analysis can also provide clues about the different strategies that companies may be implementing. For example, a company may be prepared to forgo profit margins for an increase in market share by having a higher turnover but at lower gross, operating or net profit margins. But for this type of strategy to be successful, it would need to be complemented with faster growth.

As with many other financial tools made available to management, common-size analysis on its own is not likely to provide a comprehensive and clear conclusive picture of a particular company. The analysis of a particular company or group of companies needs to be conducted in a systematic manner, taking into consideration an overall financial statement analysis, including the financial ratio analysis. Analysts must be aware of short-term versus long-term disparity. For instance, a short-term drop in profitability may only indicate a short-term failure, rather than a long-term and continuing decline in profit margins.

Case study example: internal environment

Financial ratio analysis is a primary tool for analysing a company's financial performance. The financial ratios help to formulate a company's plans by establishing and assessing its financial performance trends. Moreover, financial ratio analysis facilitates the comparison of a particular company with another company or group of companies within the same industry to ascertain its performance in comparison to the others.

Financial ratio analysis assists management to understand the financial position of a company so that appropriate decisions may be taken by a variety of users, including management, investors, trade creditors and financial institutions. Financial ratios are also important to appraise the efficiency level of a company in terms of its operations and management, particularly, how well it is able to utilise its assets and earn profits. Additionally, financial ratios are an effective method of highlighting the weakness of the company's operations, irrespective of the fact that overall performance may be adequate. Once weaknesses are highlighted it is the responsibility of management to take corrective action to resolve them.

Case study information

The case study that is presented below is aimed at illustrating how financial ratio analysis may be used to determine a company's financial position and performance. Assume that you have been provided with the financial data pertaining to Jacobson Accessories Ltd that is shown at Table 9.9, Table 9.10 and Table 9.11, which provide the Statement of Financial Position as at 31 December, 2013 and 2014; Statement of Comprehensive Income for 2013 and 2014; and the Statement of Changes in Equity for 2013 to 2014 respectively.

   You are to prepare a report to the directors of Jacobson Accessories Ltd comparing 2013 and 2014 by using financial ratio analysis. In your report, you are to comment about the following segments of financial activity, namely, profitability, asset utilisation, liquidity, capital structure and investment.

Case study solution

The financial ratios, including their formulae and general interpretation guidelines, which are to be calculated for this case study, are found at Table 9.5. Moreover, Table 9.12 shows all the applicable variables (i.e. the numerators and denominators of the formulae used in Table 9.5) together with their respective value and the applicable financial ratio(s).

TABLE 9.9 Jacobson Accessories Ltd statement of financial position as at 31 December 2013

	2013		2014	
Non-Current Assets	€	€	€	€
Property, Plant and Equipment (net book value)		20,000		80,000
Current Assets				
Stock	12,200		17,550	
Trade Debtors	9,550		15,430	
Cash at Bank	3,520	25,270	nil	32,980
		45,270		112,980

	2013		2014	
Equity				
Ordinary Shares of €0.50 each	22,000		27,000	
Retained Earnings	4,659	26,659	11,306	38,306
Non-Current Liabilities				
10% Debenture Stocks		nil		40,000
Current Liabilities				
Trade Creditors	12,673		24,205	
Bank Overdraft	4,000		5,000	
Taxation	1,938	18,611	5,469	34,674
		45,270		112,980

TABLE 9.10 Jacobson Accessories Ltd statement of financial performance – year 2013

	2013		2014	
	€	€	€	€
Sales (Note 1)		105,000		139,650
Less: Cost of Goods Sold				
Opening Stock	11,750		12,200	
Purchases (all on credit)	78,050		104,950	
	89,800		117,150	
Less: Closing Stock	(12,200)	77,600	(17,550)	99,600
Gross Profit		**27,400**		**40,050**
Less: Selling and Distribution Expenses	(8,925)		(11,032)	
Less: Administrative Expenses (Note 2)	(12,578)	(21,503)	(8,942)	(19,974)
Operating Profit		**5,897**		**20,076**
Less: Interest Payable		(360)		(4,450)
Profit Before Tax		**5,537**		**15,626**
Less: Taxation		(1,938)		(5,469)
Profit After Tax		**3,599**		**10,157**
Ordinary Dividend Declared and Paid:		**1,540**		**3,510**

Note 1: Assume that 75% of sales are made on credit and the remaining 25% on a cash basis.

Note 2: Other Information Available	2013	2014
The administrative expenses include:		
Rent	€5,000	nil
Depreciation	€1,000	€4,000
Market Price of Shares:	€2.00	€4.75

Additionally, the financial ratios, including their computations for 2013 and 2014 together with the remarks and interpretation of the respective ratios are found at Table 9.13 to Table 9.16 inclusive.

The objective of the case study was to prepare a report to the directors of Jacobson Accessories Ltd comparing 2013 and 2014 by using financial ratio analysis. This report was also expected to contain comments about the financial activity of the entity regarding profitability, asset utilisation, liquidity, capital structure and investment. Tables 9.12 to 9.16 provided the necessary information for the report to the directors of Jacobson Accessories Ltd, comparing 2013 and 2014, to be prepared. A proper report should contain the following structure:

1 Head page that identifies clearly the title of the report, author and/or organisation preparing the report and report preparation date.

TABLE 9.11 Jacobson Accessories Ltd statement of changes in equity – year 2013

	Ordinary Share Capital	Retained Earnings	Total
	€	€	€
As at 1ˢᵗ January 2013	22,000	2,600	24,600
Profit for the year		3,599	3,599
Ordinary Dividend Paid		(1,540)	(1,540)
As at 31ˢᵗ December 2013	**22,000**	**4,659**	**26,659**
As at 1ˢᵗ January 2014	22,000	4,659	26,659
Issue of Ordinary Shares	5,000		5,000
Profit for the year		10,157	10,157
Ordinary Dividend Paid		(3,510)	(3,510)
As at 31ˢᵗ December 2014	**27,000**	**11,306**	**38,306**

2   Executive summary.
3   Report contents.
4   Report narrative which is segmented according to appropriate headings.
5   Report conclusion.
6   Appendices (if any).

A brief report to the directors of Jacobson Accessories Ltd is found at Table 9.17. Due to space restriction, only the body of the report is shown at Table 9.17. However, it contains sufficient information to demonstrate how the findings from the financial ratios may be used to make certain conclusions.

Conclusion

This chapter has focused on the analysis of the business concern in terms of the examination and assessment of the external and internal environment. It is posited that the extent an organisation responds to these environments (whether reactive or proactive) will determine its business and financial performance.

The analysis of an entity's external environment examined all external factors that may affect an organisation and that have a direct impact on its operational activities, strategic choices, and influence its opportunities and risks. On the other hand, the assessment of an entity's internal environment focused on the analysis of the entity's financial statements based on financial ratio analysis and examined various elements, including liquidity, profitability, asset utilisation, investment, working capital management and capital structure.

The examination of the external and internal environments was based on numerous examples some of which pertained to existing enterprises. Space limitation

TABLE 9.12 Applicable variables for use in the financial ratio analysis

Ratio Numerator Or Denominator	2013 Value (€)	2014 Value (€)	Ratio Applicable
Sales	105,000	139,650	Sales to net assets; Sales to fixed assets; Trade credit given; Gross profit margin; Net profit to sales; Expenses to sales
Current assets	25,270	32,980	Current ratio; Quick ratio
Current liabilities	18,611	34,674	Current ratio; Quick ratio; ROCE
Net assets	26,659	38,306	Sales to net assets; Net asset value per share
Total assets	45,270	112,980	Sales to net assets; Equity to total assets; ROCE
Total liabilities	18,611	74,674	Sales to net assets;
Net fixed assets	20,000	80,000	Sales to fixed assets; Fixed assets to equity
Stock	12,200	17,550	Quick ratio
Average stock	11,975	14,875	Stock turnover
Cost of sales	89,800	117,150	Stock turnover
Opening stock	11,750	12,200	Stock turnover
Closing stock	12,200	17,550	Stock turnover
Purchases	78,050	104,950	Trade credit taken
Average debtors	9,550	12,490	Trade credit given
Opening debtors	9,550	9,550	Trade credit given
Closing debtors	9,550	15,430	Trade credit given
Average creditors	12,673	18,439	Trade credit taken
Opening creditors	12,673	12,673	Trade credit taken
Closing creditors	12,673	24,205	Trade credit taken
Credit period given	33.20	32.65	Cash cycle period
Credit period taken	59.27	63.25	Cash cycle period
Stock turnover	48.67	46.35	Cash cycle period
Equity	26,659	38,306	Equity to total assets; Fixed assets to equity; Borrowing to equity; Gearing; Return on equity
Borrowing	0	40,000	Borrowing to equity
Long-term liabilities	0	40,000	Gearing ratio
Net profit before interest & tax	5,897	20,076	Fixed interest cover; ROCE; Return on equity; Net profit to sales; Earnings per share; Dividend cover
Fixed interest expense	360	4,450	Fixed interest cover
Gross profit	27,400	40,050	Gross profit margin
Various expenses	Various	Various	Expenses to sales
Dividend per share	0.035	0.065	Dividend yield
Market price per share	2.00	4.75	Dividend yield; Price earnings ratio
Net dividend	1,540	3,510	Dividend cover
No of ordinary shares	44,000	54,000	Net asset value per share; Earnings per share

TABLE 9.13 Profitability ratios for Jacobson Accessories Ltd

Financial Ratio	2013	2014	Remarks
Profitability Ratios			
a) Return on Capital Employed (ROCE)	22.12%	25.64%	The analysis shows an improvement in profitability from 2013 to 2014 mainly due to increase in sales. The improvement in profitability from 2013 to 2014 is 3.52%.
b) Return on Equity	20.77%	40.79%	This ratio measures a corporation's profitability by revealing how much profit a company generates with the money shareholders have invested. The return on equity shows a very large improvement between 2013 and 2014. Note that long term loan capital is not included in the denominator, hence, the significant increase between 2013 and 2014.
c) Return on Total Capital Employed (i.e. total fixed & current assets)	13.03%	17.77%	This recognises short term creditors as suppliers of finance to the business. The analysis indicates an improvement from 2013 to 2014 of 4.74%.
d) Net Profit Percentage	5.62%	14.38%	The net profit percentage taking into consideration operating expenses shows a big improvement between 2013 and 2014 of 8.76%.
e) Gross Profit Percentage	26.10%	28.68%	This ration shows the margin which is being earned on sales. The gross profit margin is a measurement of a company's manufacturing and distribution efficiency during the production process. Note that gross margin tends to remain stable over time.
f) Operating Expenses to Sales	20.48%	14.30%	Operating expenses as a percentage of sales have decreased, indicating an increasing in operating efficiency.
g) Selling & Distribution Expenses to Sales	8.50%	7.90%	This shows that the company has increased efficiency in its selling and distribution processes. Selling and distribution expenses normally vary with sales but not necessarily proportionately.
h) Administrative Expenses to Sales	**11.98%**	**6.40%**	A significant decrease in administrative expenses shows a definite increase in efficiency.
Rent:	4.76%	0.00%	There has been a real decrease in rent even when taking into consideration interest payable.
Depreciation:	0.95%	2.86%	The significant decrease in the administrative expenses are rent decrease of 4.76%; depreciation increase of 1.91%; and other administrative expenses decrease of 2.73%.
Other:	6.26%	3.54%	
i) Finance Charges to Sales	0.34%	3.19%	There is an increase in finance charges due to increased borrowing. However, borrowed money is expected to generate revenue. The increase is due to the 10% debentures in 2014 to finance the increase in fixed assets, namely, property, plant and equipment. Note that Profit before tax to sales (thus taking into account finance charges) still shows an increase from 5.27% in 2013 to 11.19% in 2014.

TABLE 9.14 Utilisation of assets ratios for Jacobson Accessories Ltd

Financial Ratio	2013	2014	Remarks
Utilisation of Resources			
a) Utilisation of Capital Employed	3.94 times	1.78 times	The analysis shows a decline in this ratio suggesting a reduction in the effectiveness of the capital employed. This decrease is mainly due to the issue of €40,000 debentures that were needed to finance the growth in fixed assets. The interest payable (€4,450) in the income statement indicates that the debentures were issued at the start of the financial period. However, the attained assets may not have earned revenue until later in the year (although a reduction of the rent expense is evident). Hence, a full year's incremental revenue later in the year (although a reduction of the rent expense is evident). Hence, a full year's incremental revenue as a return on the additional capital employed would not materialise.
b) Utilisation of Total Assets	2.32 times	1.24 times	A decrease in total assets usage confirms the decline in the utilisation of capital employed.
c) Utilisation of Total Fixed Assets	5.25	1.75	Note that the main cause of asset under utilisation is due to the fixed assets, since the recurrent asset utilisation ration has a slight improvement. This tends to confirm that the fixed assets in 2009
d) Utilisation of Total Current Assets	4.16 times	4.23 times	may have not achieved a full year's incremental revenue return on the additional acquired assets. However, it may also indicate ineffective use of the fixed assets.
e) Utilisation of Net Working Capital (NWC)	1577%	−8244%	The deterioration of this ratio in 2014 is a major concern since this ratio measures the operating liquidity available for a company to use in developing and growing its business. Working capital allows companies to grow smoothly and make necessary improvements to their corporate operations. On the other hand, operating with negative working capital may not have the financial support or flexibility to grow and/or improve, even when such developments would be indicated. Hence, working capital can be an indicator of the overall strength of a company. In this case the company appears to be fairly weak with trade creditors being a major concern.
f) Stock Turnover	48.67 days	46.35 days	There is a decrease in the stock turnover that may improve profitability. However, since the nature of company's business is not known it is difficult to assess whether the turnover rate is acceptable.
h) Trade Credit Given	33.20 days	32.65 days	Given the deterioration of the NWC it is important that the trade credit given is reduced significantly to ensure better cash flow management and avoid the possibility of bad debts.
i) Trade Credit Taken	59.27 days	63.25 days	Note all purchases are on credit with the creditors' ratio being too high. While this may be a cheap method of obtaining finance, this could mean the forfeiture of trade discounts. It may also indicate tight liquidity which may result in creditors insisting on trading on a cash basis only.

TABLE 9.15 Liquidity and capital structure ratios for Jacobson Accessories Ltd

Financial Ratio	2013	2014	Remarks
Liquidity Ratios			
a) Working Capital Management (cash cycle)	33.66 days	15.94 days	The time period between the purchase of stocks and receipt of cash from debtors has been reduced by almost 18 days. This reduction is mainly due to an increase in the trade credit period taken and not by a significant improvement in the stock turnover period or reduction in trade credit given.
b) Current Ratio	1.36 : 1	0.95 : 1	A current ratio of between 1.5:1 and 2:1 is generally considered practical although this depends on the nature of the business. The current ratio for 2013 and 2014 is not satisfactory. Current assets must be greater than current liabilities. The raise in creditors in relation to debtors, increased borrowing, low cash and high expenditure on fixed assets suggest that the entity is overtrading; it is attempting to expand turnover at a fast rate, to a point where working capital is becoming sparse.
c) Liquid Ratio (Acid Test)	0.70 : 1	0.45 : 1	A liquid ratio of 1:1 is satisfactory but may be allowed to fall to 0.9:1 if debtors pay promptly and there is a regular inflow of cash from them. Given that 75% of the sales are on credit it is unwise to allow the liquid ratio to fall below the acceptable level. Hence, the company's solvency is threatened.
Capital Structure Ratios			
a) Proprietary Ratio	58.89%	33.91%	The proprietary ratio has declined sharply in 2014 suggesting a weakening of internal financial strength. This decline is likely due to the investment in fixed assets financed by the debentures.
b) Fixed Assets to Equity	75.02%	208.8%	The large increase in the fixed assets to equity ratio in 2014 is a result of financing the fixed assets by long term borrowing, namely, debentures. The aim being not to weaken working capital further.
c) Gearing Ratio	0.00%	51.08%	The gearing and debt to equity ratios indicate that in 2014 the company is highly geared. When profits are increasing, the rate of increase in the profits available for the shareholders in a highly geared entity is greater than that of a low geared one. However, investment in the ordinary shares of a highly geared company may present a greater risk than investment in a low geared company.
d) Debt to Equity Ratio	0%	104.4%	
e) Borrowing to Equity Ratio	69.81%	194.9%	This ratio shows a high increase due to the 2014 debenture issue. This confirms the high gearing status of the entity. A bank may be reluctant to provide a loan to such a company on the basis that the ordinary shareholders ought to be prepared to put more of their own money into the company.
f) Interest Cover	16.38 times	4.51 times	The interest cover ratio suggests that the company's ability to pay the cost of its long term borrowing out of profit has been drastically weakened. While the 4.51 times for 2014 is above the normal limit of at least 3 times, it should be noted that inflation from the previous year is not considered. Hence, the 4.51 times may be very close or below the normal acceptable limit. A low interest cover is a warning to ordinary shareholders that their dividend may be endangered if profits are not maintained.

TABLE 9.16 Investment ratios for Jacobson Accessories Ltd

Financial Ratio	2013	2014	Remarks
Investment Ratios			
a) Net Asset Value per Share (NAVPS)	€ 1.03	€ 2.09	The NAVPS referred to as book value per share has risen to €2.09 from €1.03 due to the large increase in fixed assets relative to a lower increase in ordinary shares. The book value per share is usually below the market price per share due to the historical cost accounting principle, which tends to understate certain asset values, and the stock supply and demand forces valuations of the marketplace generally push prices above book value per share.
			In general, the net asset value per share is the price an investor would receive when selling a fund's shares back to the fund.
b) Earnings per Share (EPS)	€ 0.08	€ 0.19	The earnings price per share has improved in 2014 from €0.08 to €0.19. Indicating that the company was substantially more successful in 2014.
c) Price Earnings Ratio (PER)	25.00	25.00	The price earnings ratio has not changed indicating that the level of confidence of investors in the future of the company has not increased even with the substantial increase in fixed assets.
d) Dividend Cover	2.34	2.89	The dividend cover has slightly increased in 2014. The ratio shows that the dividend paid to shareholders could have more than doubled indicating that the current level of dividend could still be maintained should profits temporarily decline.
			Furthermore, shareholders looking for future growth in the capital value of their investment would be assured that the firm is retaining back profits to re-invest in the business.
e) Dividend Yield	1.75%	1.37%	The dividend yield is low for 2013 and 2014, and has declined in 2014. This indicates (in the absence of capital gains) that the return on investment for a share is poor. Shareholders seeking cash flow from their shares would be unhappy about this result.
f) Earnings Yield	4.09%	3.96%	The earnings yield has decreased in 2014 from 4.09% to 3.96% indicating that the earnings of the company per share have decreased.
			It is normal practice to compare the prevailing interest rates (e.g. current 10-year Treasury yield) with the earnings yield. If the earnings yield is less than the rate of the 10-year Treasury yield, stocks as a whole may be considered overvalued, however if they are higher, stocks may considered undervalued.

TABLE 9.17a Report to the directors of Jacobson Accessories Ltd

---

1. Introduction

This report evaluates Jacobson Accessories Ltd by comparing the financial data for year 2013 and 2014 using ratio analyses pertaining to profitability, resource utilisation, liquidity, capital structure and investment. The financial data provided is found at Table 9.9 to Table 9.11, while Table 9.12 to Table 9.16 shows the detailed ratio analyses for the relevant assessment factors.

2. Company Profitability

Return on capital employed shows that the efficiency and profitability of the firm's capital investments have improved in 2014 by 3.52%. However, the soundness and strength of the firm's growth becomes a concern if this increase is inadequate to cover inflation. The return on equity shows an increase of 20% in 2014 implying that profit generated by shareholders' funds is high. Due to the lack of industry data it is not possible to assess its relationship to the industry average. Growth in profitability is also indicated when short term creditors are taken into consideration, showing an increase in the return on total capital employed of 4.74% in 2014. Likewise, gross profit percentage which determines the operating performance of the firm, particularly its productivity and distribution efficiency is high for both 2013 and 2014 (26.10%, 28.68%). Given that gross margin tends to remain stable over time, the improvement of 2.58% for 2014 is acceptable in the absence of industry data. Growth in profitability, taking into account operating expenses, is confirmed by the increase of 8.76% in the net profit rate for 2014. A study of cost factors reveal a slight decline in selling and distribution cost (0.6%) with a significant saving in administrative costs of 5.58%, indicating more efficiency. This saving is due to a reduction of rent and other costs. Finance charges to sales have increased in 2014 by 2.85% due to borrowing for financing the growth in fixed assets, which are expected to generate future revenue and/or decrease operating cost. In spite of this, profit before tax to sales (taking into account finance charges) still shows a significant increase of 5.92% for 2014 confirming the company's increase in profitability.

3. Resource Utilisation

The analysis shows a decline in the utilisation on capital employed from 3.94 to 1.78 in 2014. This decrease is mainly due to the debenture issue to finance the growth in fixed assets. Interest payable in the income statement implies that the debentures were issued at the start of the year but the attained assets may not have generated revenue until later. The utilisation of total asset ratio declined in 2014 from 2.32 to 1.24. A closer study of this ratio suggests that the utilisation of fixed assets had a major decline from 5.25 to 1.75; while the utilisation of current assets showed a slight increase. This suggests that fixed assets acquired in 2014 may have not achieved a full year's incremental revenue return, however it may also indicate ineffective use of the fixed assets. A major concern is the deterioration of the Net Working Capital ratio (NWC) from 1576.81% to a negative 8243.80% in 2014. NWC measures the operating liquidity available to a firm for use in developing and growing its business, thus indicative of overall company strength. The volume of trade creditors are a major concern in this regard. Operating with negative working capital suggests that the company may not have the financial support or flexibility to grow and/or improve, even if it has the potential to do so. The small advance in stock turnover may improve profitability. However, the debtor's ratio has increased to 53.77 days in 2014. Given the decline of the NWC it is critical that the trade credit given is reduced to ensure better cash flow management and avoid the risk of bad debts. Likewise, the trade creditors' ratio has worsened during 2014 increasing to 84.18 days. While trade credit taken may be a cheap way of acquiring finance this may result in the forfeiture of trade discounts. Moreover, it may be sending the message that the firm has tight liquidity, with the consequence that creditors may insist on trading on a cash basis.

4. Liquidity

The cash cycle (working capital management) that measures the period of time between the purchase of stocks and receipt of cash from debtors for goods sold has decreased by 18 days. However, this was achieved mainly by increasing the trade credit period taken and not through an improvement in the stock turnover period or reduction in trade credit given. This is confirmed by the current ratio, which is not satisfactory for 2013 and 2014, with 2014 being worst at 0.95:1. A current ratio of between 1.5:1 and 2:1 is deemed realistic but depends on the nature of the business. Moreover, current assets should always be greater than current liabilities. The rise in creditors in relation to debtors; increased borrowing; minimal cash; and heavy expenditure in fixed assets are indicative of overtrading.

TABLE 9.17b Report to the directors of Jacobson Accessories Ltd *(continued)*

---

4. Liquidity (continued)

In other words, the firm is trying to expand turnover at a fast rate to a point where working capital is becoming inadequate. Likewise, the liquid ratio has deteriorated to 0.45:1 in 2014. The liquid ratio may be allowed to fall to 0.9:1 if the debtors pay swiftly and there is a regular inflow of cash from them. However, since 75% of the sales are on credit and the debtor's ratio for 2014 is 54 days, it is unwise to allow this ratio to fall below the acceptable level of 1:1 because this would threaten the company's solvency.

5. Capital Structure

The proprietary ratio has declined sharply in 2014, due to the added fixed assets financed by debentures, suggesting a weakening of internal financial strength. Financing fixed assets by a debenture issue has increased the fixed assets to equity ratio to 209% in 2014, thus avoiding a further weakening of working capital. On the other hand, both the gearing and debt to equity ratios indicate that in 2014 the company is highly geared. This means that when profits are increasing, the rate of increase in profits available to shareholders is greater than for a low geared firm. However, investment in ordinary shares may present a greater risk for highly geared firms, with the consequence that financial institutions may be reluctant to provide loans on the basis that the shareholders should be prepared to put more of their own money into the firm. The decline in the interest cover ratio from 16.38 to 4.51 times in 2014 suggests that the company's ability to pay for the cost of its long-term borrowing out of profit has been severely weakened. Normally a suitable limit is at least 3 times. Hence, if inflation is taken into account, the interest cover ratio for 2014 may be very close or below this limit. Moreover, the low interest cover is a warning to ordinary shareholders that their dividend may be endangered if profits are not maintained.

6. Investment

Net asset value per share (NAVPS) has risen to €2.09 in 2014 due to the growth in fixed assets relative to a lower rise in ordinary shares, hence reflecting an increase in the book value per share. Earnings price per share has improved in 2014 from €0.08 to €0.19, illustrating that the firm was much more successful in 2014. However, the price earnings ratio has not changed indicating that the level of confidence of investors in the firm's future has not increased despite the high growth in fixed assets. The dividend cover has slightly risen in 2014 to 2.89, indicating that the dividend paid in 2014 could have more than doubled, implying that the present dividend would continue if profits temporarily decline. Shareholders looking for future growth in the capital value of their investment would be assured that the firm is retaining profits to reinvest in the business. However, the dividend yield is low for 2013 and 2014, and has declined in 2014 to 1.37%, indicating that the return on investment per share is poor. Shareholders seeking cash flow from their shares would be adversely affected. Likewise, the earnings yield has decreased in 2014 to 3.96%. If the earnings yield is less than the 10-year Treasury yield, stocks as a whole may be considered overvalued.

7. Conclusion

The firm's efficiency and profitability improved in 2014, but the soundness and strength of a company's growth becomes a concern if this increase is inadequate to cover inflation. The firm must utilise its fixed assets more fully to increase profitability further. Liquidity is a serious concern that must to be addressed with urgency. There are indications of overtrading, in other words, the firm is trying to expand turnover rapidly to a point where working capital is becoming insufficient. The current capital structure is depending on outside financing with the ability to pay the resulting interest being weakened and putting further pressure on the firm's liquidity. Financial institutions may be reluctant to provide further financing on the basis that the shareholders should be prepared to put more of their own money into the firm. Although, the company was more successful in 2014, this is not reflected in an increase in shareholder confidence despite the high growth in fixed assets and the implication that the firm could have potentially almost tripled its dividend. The return on investment per share is low; however this would need to be compared with the prevailing interest rates to determine if the stocks are overvalued. To overcome the concerns, the company may need to increase shareholders equity by increasing retained earnings (which may mean paying no dividend) and/or by increasing the outstanding number of shares.

and providing information on existing enterprises is a major concern when writing a chapter of this nature. However, despite these restrictions, this chapter provides the reader with extensive information, particularly an analytical framework to be able to apply the material contained in this chapter to actual and practical situations.

References

AT Kearney, Johannsen, Matthias and Pratz, Andreas 2012. *Retail Banking Radar: Change Looms in Europe*, A.T. Kearney Inc. viewed 30.03.2013, www.atkearney.com/documents/10192/419855/2012_Retail_Banking_Radar.pdf/b647969f-fa13–48f8–999e-4d278d6e0866.

Brandenburger, A.N. and Nalebuff, B.J. 1997. *Co-Opetition: A Revolution Mindset That Combines Competition and Cooperation: The Game Theory Strategy That's Changing the Game of Business*, Crown Publishing Group.

Deloitte. 2012a, 2013. *Banking Industry Outlook Moving Forward in the Age of Re-Regulation*, Deloitte Centre for Financial Services, New York, USA.

Deloitte. 2012b, 2013. *International Tax: Malta Highlights 2012*, Deloitte Global Services, UK.

Grant, R.M. 1991. Resource-based theory of competitive advantage: implications of strategy formations. *California Management Review*, Spring 1991, 114–135.

Kumbirai, Mabwe and Webb, Robert. 2010. A financial ratio analysis of commercial bank performance in South Africa. *African Review of Economics and Finance*, 2(1).

McKinsey. 2012. *Banking and Securities (Europe): Day of Reckoning for European Banking*, Frankfurt.

Mills, R.W. 1994. *Finance, Strategy and Strategic Value Analysis*, Mars Business Associates, Lechlade, Glasgow.

Mind Tools Ltd. 2011. *Understanding 'Big Picture' Forces of Change: PEST Analysis*, viewed 12.03.2013, www.mindtools.com/pages/article/newTMC_09.htm.

Morstan, M. 2013. *Strengths and Limitations of Porter's Five Forces Model*, viewed 13.03.2013, http://voices.yahoo.com/strengths-limitations-porters-five-forces-model-11498296.html?cat=3.

NetMBA. 2011. *SWOT Analysis*, viewed 10.03.2013, www.netmba.com/strategy/swot/.

Porter, M.E. 2008a. Leadership and strategy: the five competitive forces that shape strategy. *Harvard Business Review*, January, 78–93.

Porter, M.E. 2008b. The five competitive forces that shape strategy. *Harvard Business Review*, January, 24–41.

Randell, H. 1996. *Advanced Level Accounting*. London: Letts Educational.

Robinson, T.R., van Greuning, H., Henry, E. and Broihahn, M.A. 2009. *International Financial Statement Analysis*. Hoboken, NJ: John Wiley and Sons.

Silva, N. 2012. *SWOT Analysis vs PEST Analysis and When to Use Them*, viewed 13.03.2013, http://creately.com/blog/diagrams/swot-analysis-vs-pest-analysis/.

Thakur, S. 2010. *Limitations of a PEST Analysis*, viewed 12.03.2013, www.brighthubpm.com/project-planning/100700-limitations-of-a-pest-analysis/.

von Franz, Johannas and Schall, Nikolaus. 2004. *Practitioner's Guild: Strengths, Weaknesses, Opportunities, Threats (SWOT)*. Deutsche Gesellschaft für Technische Zusammenarbeit (GTZ) GmbH.

Wahlen, J.M., Stickney, C.P., Brown, P.R., Baginski, S.P. and Bradshaw, M.T. 2011. *Financial Reporting, Financial Statement Analysis, and Valuation: A Strategic Perspective*. Mason, OH: South-Western Cengage Learning.

Wood, Frank and Sangster, Alan. 2007. *Business Accounting*. London: Prentice Hall.

10

VALUATION OF A BUSINESS

I never guess. It is a capital mistake to theorise before one has data. Insensibly one begins to twist facts to suit theories, instead of theories to suit facts.

Sir Arthur Conan Doyle
Author of Sherlock Holmes stories

There are many instances when an objective and accurate assessment of a company's value is required. Business valuation is a process and a set of procedures employed to approximate the economic value of an owner's interest in a business. In the valuation of a business, the most important question that requires a response is how much is the business worth? This may seem easy, but the correct process to conduct a valuation of a business takes a great deal of effort, planning and reflection. Additionally, the difficulty in answering this question is that there are no precise methods to value a private business, because the term 'business value' means different things to different people. The tendency is for one party of a transaction to increase the value, and for the other to drive the price down.

The determination of the value of a business also depends on the valuation assumptions. For instance, a business owner may assume that a strong linkage between the business and its client base (i.e. goodwill) is worth a great deal. On the other hand, an investor may have the perception that the business value is entirely defined by its historic income stream. Therefore, it all depends on why the valuation is taking place and the circumstances the business is encountering. For example, one should make a distinction between a business that is being sold as a going concern and is part of a well-planned marketing effort to attract many interested buyers, and a quick sale of business assets at an auction.

While there are somewhat straightforward approaches to value particular segments of the business, such as stock and fixed assets (e.g. land, machinery, equipment, etc.), there may be significant intangible components that are difficult to value. These intangible components include 'goodwill', such as trademarks, a business client base and the reputation of the entity. It is these components that are extremely difficult to value, and in many cases, the value of a business will be based upon the eagerness of a potential buyer to acquire the business in question.

This chapter will be focusing on a number of valuation methods that will be classified under two main categories, namely non-going concern (an entity that will not remain in business) and a going concern (an entity will remain in business for the foreseeable future). There is only one method under the non-going concern category, namely the asset break-up approach. However, the going concern category contains a number of different valuation methods that are commonly used. These include:

- The asset approach, consisting of three techniques, namely book value, replacement cost, and book value plus goodwill;
- The yield basis, consisting of three techniques, namely earning yield, price-earnings ratio, and dividend yield);
- The economic value, namely the discounted cash flow technique.

This chapter will examine the above valuation methods and explore how other factors may influence the value of a business at any given time.

Significance in valuing a business

The valuation of a business implies that the financial market participants determine the price they are willing to pay or receive to fulfil their obligations as a consequence of the sale of a business. Furthermore, the financial interest of ownership in a business is equated to the recorded value of net assets in the statement of financial position (i.e. balance sheet). One should note that the recorded value of the net assets is equal to the value of the total assets minus the value of the total liabilities.

For example, assume that a company reported $12 million in assets and $4.5 million in total liabilities, then the company's net assets would be $7.5 million (i.e. $12m − $4.5m = $7.5m). According to the accounting standards, the majority of a company's assets and liabilities on the balance sheet are recorded at their book value and not at their fair market value. Hence, the net asset value may not in reality signify the cash that the company would have in its possession if it sold all of its assets and paid all the outstanding liabilities. In other words, the value of the net assets is practically equivalent to shareholders' equity, because both reflect the difference between what the company owns and what it owes. Therefore, a high net assets value of the company reflects a higher worth of that company. However, the true price of a business is the one established when the buyer and seller agree to transact. In other words, the true value of a business is dictated by the market.

Often, the valuation of a business is required to resolve disputes. However, more specifically, business valuations may be required in case of business amalgamations, including both friendly and hostile takeovers; the private issuance of new shares in an established company; the flotation of shares on the stock exchange; the private sale of existing shares; regulatory obligations, such as inheritance and taxation regarding estate or gift tax; as collateral for financing the company through short- or long-term loans; selecting between alternative investment options; and the private sale of a company, subsequently followed by the floatation of shares on the stock exchange.

Factors that impact the valuation of a business

A major consideration in assigning a value to a business is to formally articulate the reason for the business valuation and circumstances the business is encountering at the time. This is what is referred to as the business value standard and premise of value. The standard of value is the hypothetical conditions under which the business will be valued. For instance, is the business being valued due to taxation regulatory obligations or due to a merger or is it due to some financing arrange-ments with a financial institution or is the business being forcibly sold due to liquidation procedures? Hence, the standard of value establishes the theoretical state of affairs under which the business is being valued.

On the other hand, the premise of value is associated with the assumptions that are being made in valuing the business. For instance, will the business continue in its current form when it is sold (i.e. going concern) or is the value of the business based upon the earnings from the disposal of its total asset base less any outstanding debt? As one may conceive, the resultant business valuation amount will differ considerably depending upon the choice of both the standard of value and the premise of value.

When an actual sale of a business takes place, the buyer and seller will have their own individual motives for conducting the transaction. It is these individual motives that would lead to an optimal outcome and result in a convergence of their own individual value expectations with the fair market value of the business.

Additionally, the value of a business may be influenced by the synergy of merging a business with another. For instance, a firm that produces goods may have an incentive of purchasing another firm that controls the distribution channel for the goods being sold by it. Hence, the firm may be willing to pay a price for the business above the fair market value to obtain the distribution channels. Moreover, fair market value does not incorporate discounts for lack of control or marketability, but it is possible to achieve a fair market value for a business asset, which is being liquidated in its secondary market, by using the break-up value approach.

The above emphasise the divergence between standard value and premise of value, in that the assumptions made probably do not reflect the actual market conditions when the business is being sold. Having said this, the theoretical conditions are assumed because they yield a uniform standard of value, after applying generally accepted valuation techniques, which allow meaningful comparison to be made between businesses that are similarly positioned. There are basically five considerations that need to be taken into account when conducting the valuation of a business. These include:

- Type of business. Here one needs to determine whether the business structure is a sole trader (i.e. free to dispose of the business); or a partnership (one that may require agreement between several partners; or a limited liability company, where there may be restrictions in the memorandum and articles of association about what the company can and cannot do.
- Size of the stake in the company being bought or sold. This factor is applicable to limited liability companies and assesses whether the seller or buyer will have a minority holding and having no influence or a minority holding having a significant influence through an associate status; or acquiring control (having greater than 50 per cent) or having full control.
- Potential growth of the company being sold or bought. This factor would assess the status of the order book; the firm's contacts; and the economic and industry prospects in terms of whether the industry is experiencing an economic downturn, in which case, caution would be exercised.
- Reason for the sale. This factor would examine whether the sale is forced (i.e. liquidation), hence any valuation methods are bound to be discounted to encourage a quick sale.
- Reality of the estimated business value. The golden rule is that a business is only worth what someone is willing to pay for it. Hence, one will need to be realistic about the true value of the company.

The business valuation framework

The objective of having a business valuation framework is to be able to formulate the Business Valuation Report. This section has the objective of providing a brief description of the contents of the Business Valuation Report. The Business Valuation Report will be covered in more detail in the next chapter. Figure 10.1 provides the business valuation framework, which shows four major components, namely, the description of the economic conditions (external environment); financial analysis (internal environment); normalisation of the financial statements; and the valuation approach. Note that the upper half of Figure 10.1 is similar to Figure 9.1 (General Analytical Framework). The business valuation approach varies, depending on whether the business under examination is a going concern or otherwise. Under the on-going concern category, there are seven distinct methods for valuating a business.

Description of the economic conditions

A business valuation report typically begins with a description of the economic conditions existing as of the valuation date, which also describes the conditions of the particular industry the entity operates in. A common and useful source of

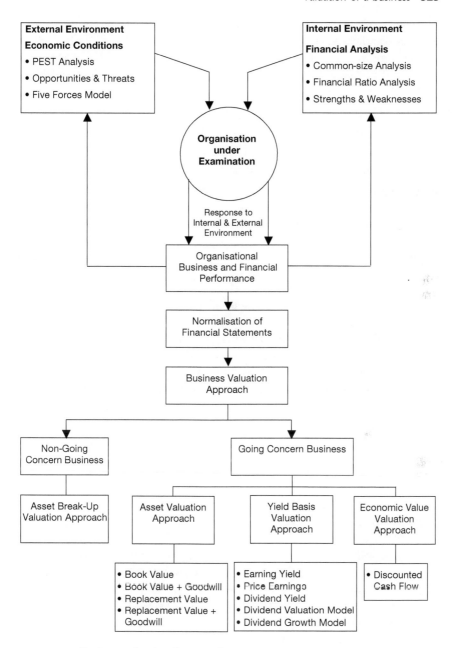

FIGURE 10.1 Business valuation framework

economic information is obtained from the Central Bank Report and the National Statistics Office. The description of the economic conditions is basically an analysis of the external environment, which has been illustrated at Chapter 9. The typical analysis at this stage included the PEST analysis, five forces model and the SWOT analysis.

Financial analysis

The financial analysis is the analysis of the internal environment, which has also been described in Chapter 9. The financial analysis involves common-size analysis, ratio analysis and the strengths and weaknesses from the SWOT analysis. Furthermore, if warranted, trend analysis and industry comparative analysis are also conducted. This permits the comparison of subject entity with entities in the same or similar industry, to reveal the trends affecting the entity and/or the industry over time. Basically, trend analysis is conducted by comparing an entity's financial statements for different periods, which reveals the growth or decline in revenues or expenses and the changes that transpire in the capital structure, or other financial trends.

Common-size analysis transforms the line items appearing in the financial statements as a percentage of a key figure (referred to as the base value). The base value is usually the total assets for the statement of financial position and total sales (or revenue) for the statement of financial performance. Comparing the entity under examination with the industry will help to conduct a risk assessment; determine the discount rate (the internal rate of return); and the selection of market multiples (i.e. the firms used for comparison).

Normalisation of financial statements

Normalisation of the financial statements is the process of adjusting the financial statements for non-economic or non-recurring items; non-operating assets or liabilities; and other incongruities or unusual items to facilitate uniform comparison. The most common normalisation adjustments (among others) fall into four categories:

- Comparability Adjustments. This results from adjusting the financial statements of the company being valued to make comparison with businesses in the same industry easier. For instance, the companies being compared may have different depreciation policies or revenue recognition policies. Hence, there is a need to compare like with like.
- Non-operating Adjustments. Non-operating assets, such as excess cash and investments are usually removed from the statement of financial position.
- Non-recurring Adjustments. The financial statements of the company being valued may be influenced by dealings that are not expected to recur, such as the procurement or disposal of assets, receipts or payouts due to court cases, or an extraordinarily large revenue or expenditure item. Hence, there is a need to remove one-off items that may distort the normal position of the

company. Therefore, non-recurring items are adjusted to ensure that the financial statements will better reflect the management's expectations of future performance.

- Discretionary Adjustments. There are a number of expense and revenue items, among others that need to be adjusted according to industry standards to enable the determination of the fair market value of the business. These include owner's compensation and benefits; bonuses to senior management staff; and directors' fees. Rent and lease payments made by the company being valued, particularly if the property being rented or leased belongs to the company's owners, will need to be examine closely.

Valuation approach

The valuation approach and respective methods will be examined in detail in the sections below. However, the focus of the valuation methods will be the following:

1   The non-going concern valuation approach will consist of the Break-Up Valuation method.
2   The going concern valuation approach will consist of:

- The asset approach, which has three methods, namely the book value method; the replacement value method; and the book value plus good will.
- The yield basis approach, which has three methods, namely the earnings yield method; the price earnings ratio; and the dividend yield method.
- The economic value approach, which consists of the discounted cash flow method.

Ultimately, a fair valuation of a business will depend on whether the market is practical and efficient. The difficulties arise when trying to value an enterprise that has major assets that are of a unique nature, such as antiques, specialist equipment and skills or there is no active market, such as companies that are not quoted in the stock exchange. In fact, the value of companies quoted on the stock exchange is typically determined by the stock market. In other words, the going share price at that the time.

A total of eight business valuation methods have been itemised above. However, no single method is infallible and therefore, each of the methods that will be described and illustrated below will very often provide dissimilar outcomes. Hence, it is often the practice to determine the mean (average) value and the corresponding standard deviation to obtain the full spectrum of the business valuations for a particular business enterprise. Having said this, ultimately, the transacted business value will depend on the negotiations between the parties concerned, which may involve factors that are not of a monetary value. Hence, the valuation methods are viewed as providing an indicative range of values for a particular business, to be used as a negotiating starting point.

Non-going concern business valuation: asset break-up valuation method

The asset break-up valuation method views the business enterprise as an assorted collection of assets that may be disposed of, on an individual basis, in a collective or progressive manner. Therefore, the owners of the business will eventually receive the residue value after discharging their obligations towards the third parties.

The asset break-up valuation method normally arises due to liquidation. Hence, liquidation values are based on the assumption of forced sale proceeds of individual assets. Typically, a company going through liquidation procedures is not likely to obtain fair market value for its assets. The asset break-up value is, therefore, the forced sale value of the assets less the liabilities and less the liquidation costs. Consequently, the break-up value per share is the asset break-up value, which represents the value of ownership, divided by the number of shares (i.e. Break-Up Value per Share = Value of Ownership ÷ Number of Shares).

From the above, it may be observed that the residual value is the asset break-up value, because it is the value of the assets after deducting the liabilities and liquidation costs. Therefore, the outcome, if it is positive, is the residual value that belongs to the owners of the enterprise.

Furthermore, the residual value is the value that the asset would be, after it has been depreciated (or amortised). Hence, the point of interest is the book value of the asset. For the sake of accuracy, the residual values used for computing depreciation are to be considered separately for each asset and often for the various components of the asset. For example, a building containing escalators that have a shorter expected economic life shorter than the building itself, should be depreciated separately from the rest of the building. Moreover, various tangible fixed assets may not be fit for sale and/or their disposal value is taken up by the costs to remove them. Intangible assets, such as, expired patents or other rights would have no residual value. Therefore, determining the asset break-up value (or residual value) is relatively easy but it takes quite a great deal of effort to calculate. An added complication is the residual value of assets that are leased. The residual value of assets that are leased is the cost of the asset, less any repayments of the capital, less the interest component made over the life of the lease. Additionally, it is common practice to permit the holder of the lease to procure the leased assets at the residual value.

Limitations of the break-up valuation method

The break-up valuation method does not take into account the going-concern principle and implies the minimum valuation for the assets in question. It also overlooks the possibility that the value of the assets collectively (as a group) may surpass the aggregate total value of each individual asset. There is also the risk of inaccurate valuations because costs associated with the sale of the individual assets, including liquidation expenses are estimates, which will only be accurately known when all the assets are sold. Generally, the break-up valuation method ignores the opportunity of the business to generate future earnings. Hence, the reason it is often used in situations when liquidating a business.

Going concern business valuation: asset approach

As stated previously, the going-concern asset approach consists of three individual methods, namely, the asset book value, asset replacement cost and the asset book value plus goodwill.

Asset book-value method

The main advantage of the asset book-value method is its factual basis. The factual values and amounts are based on historical cost that is easily obtained from the company's financial statements and that are also verifiable due to the existence of audited accounts. However, similar to other methods, it has a number of limitations.

The asset book-value method may disregard various key intangibles. For example, an accounting firm may have very few assets, but it often has considerable market value because the people it employs are key 'assets', whose expertise and relations with the respective clients result in earning power. Although historical cost is not viewed as being relevant to current valuation, it provides a factual basis upon which certain assessments and computations may be made.

Care should be taken when valuating stocks. As such, stock values are often unreliable, particularly when dealing with apparel (i.e. clothing), which may represent a correct and accurate value in the balance sheet, but does not represent reality, since apparel loses value rapidly. However, stock that consists of antiques may significantly appreciate in value.

Another factor to be aware of is debtors, more precisely, the transformation of debtors to hard cash, since not all debtors are easily converted to cash, particularly outstanding debtors extending many weeks and months. As a general rule, the older the debtor becomes, the greater the risk that the debt will not be collected. Therefore, an analysis of the ageing of debtors becomes particularly important in this valuation scenario.

However, the most serious limitation is that Net Asset Value (NAV) is derived from the valuation of the separate assets. NAV dispenses with the concept that the assets may be worth more than their book value, and therefore there is the tendency for this valuation method to devalue the earning power of the assets, particularly for lucrative businesses.

Asset replacement value method

The asset replacement cost method is another asset based valuation approach, where the assets are valued at their replacement cost. To obtain the valuation of a business applying this approach, the purchaser has the option of fitting together a matching assortment of assets for valuation purposes. Hence, in replacement cost accounting, assets and liabilities are valued at how much it would cost to replace them.

Moreover, when replacement costs are applied for determining the value of assets, then the replacement method of depreciation to adjust the value of an asset as it is utilised over time, is also applied. Thus, the depreciation amount is determined as the accumulation of the historical cost depreciation, in addition to a percentage of the difference between the historical cost and the replacement cost. In other words, the depreciation amount is determined by a combination of its historical cost and its replacement cost. Consequently, the replacement cost method often provides a more accurate value of the company's assets, than the present book value of the assets. Hence, it is the usual practice for a company seeking to acquire another, to obtain an estimated value of the company being acquired, using the replacement cost method, before making a purchase offer.

One should note that the objective of the asset based valuation methods is to measure the resources that are owned by the business. However, the purpose of owning a business is to produce income, and as such, the purchaser does not just acquire a collection of assets but also the earning potential of the company's resources. Therefore, the value of an asset is intended to reflect its earnings potential. This is a serious limitation with asset based valuation methods. Valuation methods that are based on historical costs and depreciation, do not take into account such factors as inflation, among others. However, despite this weakness, the replacement cost method is more likely to accurately reflect the economic conditions that can affect the value of a company's assets. The serious limitations of the asset replacement cost method are associated with its disregard for intangible assets, such as research and development, and goodwill.

Asset book value plus goodwill method

The asset book value plus goodwill method is the final technique to be discussed under the asset based approach. Basically, this method is an asset based valuation but makes an adjustment for the value of goodwill; hence, it attempts to take into consideration the earnings potential of the entity. Furthermore, the purchaser of the entity is not only paying for tangible assets, but is also paying for the earnings potential as represented by the value recognised to goodwill. The difficulty with this method is the valuation of goodwill. First, it is necessary to consider what the accounting standards declare about goodwill. The accounting standards characterise goodwill as follows:

- IFRS 3: This defines goodwill as the excess of the cost of the business combination over the acquirer's interest in the net fair value of the identifiable net assets.
- IAS 36: This standard views goodwill as arising on acquisition representing a payment made by an acquirer in anticipation of future economic benefits.

- IAS 38: This standard considers goodwill as representing future economic benefits from synergy between identifiable assets or from intangible assets that do not meet the criteria for recognition as an intangible asset.

The general implication of the above three definitions is that goodwill consists of the excess of cost over fair value; the cost of future economic benefits; and the cost of synergy. However, the above also illustrate that goodwill is something that is not easily described. Typically, it generally means having a good reputation and wide business connections that help a business to earn more profits than the profit that could be earned by a newly started business. Hence, one may conclude that goodwill is a desirable influence, which brings in customers to an old place of business (i.e. repeat or returning customers). Furthermore, goodwill is viewed as an intangible but valuable asset, and can include brand name and logo recognition, trademarks and patents, employees and their skill competencies, a customer database and ensuing relationships.

In a lucrative commercial enterprise, goodwill is not some fabricated asset, but represents a monetary value associated with the advantage of earning more profits. In other words, goodwill facilitates a company to increase its potential earnings. There are a number of methods for determining the value of goodwill. However, this chapter will focus on two key methods, namely the super-profits approach and the weighted average profits approach. These methods will be discussed in detail below.

However, similar to the other methods, the asset book value plus goodwill method has a number of limitations. For instance, the parameters for calculating goodwill, particularly super-profits, require the use of subjective judgement, which may not accurately reflect reality. In addition, the method still makes use of historical balance sheet values that may distort the computation of goodwill.

Calculating goodwill: super profits approach

The value of the business based on the super-profits approach is the value of the net assets plus the goodwill. The value of goodwill is the capitalisation of super-profits, which is equivalent to 'n' years' purchase of super-profits. The value of super-profits is the average earnings of the business less the fair return or expected return on the book value of the assets. The calculation of goodwill using the super profits approach is best illustrated by an example.

Assume that the Maxwell Ltd on 1 January 2014 had €425,000 as the value of its capital employed and the profits for the last five years (2010 to 2014) respectively were €45,000, €55,000, €65,000, €60,000 and €75,000. Calculate the value of goodwill, based on three years' purchase of the super profit of the business given that the normal rate of return is 10 per cent. The capital employed is basically the investment in the company. In other words, the issued share capital plus reserves plus long-term loan capital. The determination of goodwill is shown at Table 10.1. The goodwill is calculated at being €52,500.

TABLE 10.1 Calculation of goodwill using super profit method

Years	Profits
1. 2010	€45,000
2. 2011	€55,000
3. 2012	€65,000
4. 2013	€60,000
5. 2014	€75,000
Total:	€300,000

Average Profit =	€300,000 ÷ 5 = **€60,000**
Normal Profit =	Capital Employed x Rate of Return
	€425,000 x 0.10 = **€42,500**
Super Profit =	Average Profit – Normal Profit
	€60,000 - €42,500 = **€17,500**
Goodwill =	'n' years' purchase of Super Profits
	3 years x €17,500 = **€52,500**

It should be noted that this method of determining goodwill is very subjective due to a number of judgemental parameters, namely, the 'n' years' purchase of super profits and the normal rate of return.

Calculating goodwill: weighted average profits approach

The value of the business based on the weighted average profits approach is net assets plus goodwill. However, unlike the super-profits approach, the value of goodwill is the capitalised value of all earnings less the net assets employed. The calculation of goodwill using the weighted average profits approach is best illustrated by an example.

Assume that the Maxwell Ltd had the following profits for the last four years, €40,000; €32,000; €29,000; and €43,000. Calculate the value of goodwill, based at twice the weighted average profits of the last four years. The determination of goodwill using this approach is shown at Table 10.2. The goodwill is calculated at being €72,600.

This method of determining goodwill is also very subjective due to the judgemental parameters, namely, the number of years used to calculate the weighted average profits and the number of times that is used to determine the goodwill once the weighted average profits have been computed

TABLE 10.2 Calculation of goodwill using weighted average profit method

Profits	Year	Weighted Value
€40,000	1	€40,000 x 1 = €40,000
€32,000	2	€32,000 x 2 = €64000
€29,000	3	€29,000 x 3 = €87,000
€43,000	4	€43,000 x 4 = €172,000
Total:	**10**	**€363,000**

Weighted Average Profit =	€363,000 ÷ 10 = **€36,300**
Goodwill =	€36,300 x 2 (twice) = **€72,600**

The year column is used as the weight being applied to calculated weighted profit.

Going concern business valuation: yield basis approach

The yield based approach consists of three methods, which are all based on the earnings potential of the business as a going concern. The three methods include, earnings yield, price earnings ratio and dividend yield.

Earnings yield method

This method is based on the valuation of a business using the earnings yield of the company's shares as the computational basis. The valuation is based on the dividend amount available for distribution to ordinary shareholders. Therefore, this method does not take into consideration the company's assets (i.e. their book value) and does away with their resulting built-in limitations. The earnings yield method emphasises the concept that the purchaser is acquiring the 'right to profits'. Hence, the earnings yield method links the profit to the amount being invested. This method is particularly applicable when acquiring a majority shareholding in a company.

The earnings yield method is very subjective because it is based upon the forecast of future maintainable earnings, which will vary with risk. The value of the business using this method is the predicted future earnings divided by the earnings yield, where the earnings yield is computed by the dividend yield (i.e. dividend per share divided by the market price per share) times the dividend cover (i.e. profits available to pay ordinary dividend divided by the ordinary dividend paid).

An alternative method to calculate the business value using the earnings yield method is illustrated by the following example. Assume that Bellview Ltd on 1 January 2015 had €350,000 as the value of its capital employed and the profits for the last five years (2011 to 2015) respectively were €40,000, €52,000, €60,000,

€62,000 and €70,000. The value of goodwill calculation is based on three years' purchase of the super profit of the business given that the normal rate of return is 10 per cent. The capital employed is basically the issued share capital plus reserves plus long-term loan capital. Furthermore, assume that the number of ordinary shares is 200,000. The calculations necessary to compute the value of the business using the earnings yield method are found at Table 10.3. The value of the business is calculated at €218,000, thus the value per share using the earnings value method is €1.09.

Similar to most of the valuation methods, this approach has its limitations. First, as stated previously, it requires the forecast of future earnings, which is linked to the risk level applicable and is very subjective. Furthermore, the method may use past profits as a basis for forecasting earnings, but yield valuations are based on the ability to earn future earnings, hence, historical profits may not be a good basis for forecasting earnings. Moreover, the determination of the capitalisation rate requires judgement, hence, it becomes subjective.

TABLE 10.3 Calculation of earnings value method

Years		Profits
1.	2011	€40,000
2.	2012	€52,000
3.	2013	€60,000
4.	2014	€62,000
5.	2015	€70,000
Total:		**€284,000**

Average Profit =	€284,000 ÷ 5 = **€56,800**
Normal Profit =	Capital Employed x Rate of Return €350,000 x 0.10 = **€35,000**
Super Profit =	Average Profit – Normal Profit €56,800 - €35,000 = **€21,800**

Earnings Yield

Estimated Average Future Profits (Super Profit) =	€21,800
Average Earning Yield (Required Rate of Return) =	10%
Valuation (Estimated Ave. Future Profits ÷ Ave. Earning Yield) =	€21,800 ÷ 0.10 = **€218,000**
Number of shares =	200,000
Value per share (Valuation ÷ No of shares) =	**€1.09**

Price-earnings ratio method

The price-earnings ratio method is also based on an earnings-based valuation approach. It basically relates the share price to the payback period and as such is often used for the valuation of listed companies. Similar to the previous method, this approach disregards the book value of the assets and thus does away with the inherent limitations posed by the book value approach. When valuing an unquoted company, it is best to use the average price-earnings ratio of a similar listed company or better still to use the average price-earnings ratio of a similar group of listed companies.

Similar to the other yield based methods, the price-earnings ratio method requires the prediction of future maintainable earnings. Hence, the value of business is calculated by the estimation of future earnings times the price earnings ratio, where the price earnings ratio is computed by the market price per share divided by the earning per share.

An alternative method to calculate the business value using the earnings yield method is illustrated by the following example. Consider the previous example regarding Bellview Ltd. Let us assume that quoted companies that operate in the same industry have an average price-earnings ratio of 8.50. The calculations necessary to compute the value of the business using the price-earnings ratio method are found at Table 10.4. The value of the business is calculated at €185,300, thus the value per share using the earnings value method is €0.93. One should observe that this method provides a lower valuation of the business than the earnings valuation method discussed previously.

An issue that needs to be addressed is why the price-earnings ratio method provides an indication of the payback period of the investment. Consider the following example. Assume that a company has an earnings price per share of €0.45 and the share price is €5.25, thus giving a price-earnings ratio of 11.66 (i.e. €5.25 ÷ €0.45 = 11.66). This implies that the market is prepared to hang on for almost 12 years to recover the share price. A high price-earnings ratio suggests that the share market anticipates the earnings tendency to grow, consequently decreasing the payback period.

This approach has two major limitations. First, the method involves a great deal of subjectivity in predicting future earnings; and Second the magnitude and strength of listed companies make their shares more desirable to the share market, and therefore, more highly priced than the unlisted shares.

Dividend yield method

The dividend yield method is the final methodology under the yield based approach, which is based on an estimation of the anticipated company's earnings in the future. Basically, this valuation method is based on the dividend amount that is to be distributed to the ordinary shareholders. Similar to the other yield based methods this methodology does not take into account the book value of the assets.

TABLE 10.4 Calculation of price-earnings ratio method

Years		Profits
1.	2011	€40,000
2.	2012	€52,000
3.	2013	€60,000
4.	2014	€62,000
5.	2015	€70,000
Total:		**€284,000**

Average Profit =	€284,000 ÷ 5 = **€56,800**
Normal Profit =	Capital Employed x Rate of Return €350,000 x 0.10 = **€35,000**
Super Profit =	Average Profit − Normal Profit €56,800 - €35,000 = **€21,800**

Price-Earnings Ratio Method

Estimated Average Future Profits (Super Profit) =	€21,800
Average Market Price-Earnings (P/E) ratio =	8.50
Valuation (Estimated Ave. Future Profits x Ave. Market P/E ratio) =	€21,800 x 8.50 = **€185,300**
Number of shares =	**200,000**
Value per share (Valuation ÷ No of shares) =	**€0.93**

The basic premise is that a shareholder is entitled to receive future dividends. This method is frequently applied to situations related to the acquirement of a minority holding in a company. Hence, the dividend yield relates the dividend declared to the amount invested. When valuing an unquoted company it is suggested that the average dividend yield of a similar listed companies is utilised. The dividend yield is calculated by division of the dividend for the year by the market price, expressed as a percentage. Thus, the value of the business is the total annual dividend payout divided by the dividend yield.

Let us consider an example. Assume that a company has 200,000 ordinary shareholders and declares a dividend of €0.45 per share. Further assume that the market price per share at the time the dividend was declared is €4.75. Hence, the dividend yield would be equal to 9.5 per cent (i.e. [€0.45 ÷ €4.75] × 100 = 9.47 per cent). Using this dividend yield calculation, the value of the business would be approximately equal to €950,370 (i.e. [200,000 × €0.45] ÷ 0.0947 = €950,370).

There are a number of significant limitations regarding this method. The relationship between the value of a business and the dividend declared is dissimilar for listed and unlisted companies (i.e. little basis for comparison). For instance, listed companies may use the dividend payout rate to preserve the share price, whereas unlisted companies are likely to distribute a smaller proportion of earnings and increase their reserves for future expansion. However, a company's growth financed by retained earnings would lead to a higher level of future dividend payouts. Furthermore, past declared dividends may not be representative of future expectations, with many other factors having an impact on the amount of dividends to be declared, such as the state of the national and global economy. Since the dividend yield is vital to the calculation, a decisive issue with this method is the value of a business that does not declare a dividend payment (i.e. does it have a value).

Dividend business valuation model

The dividend valuation model is very similar to the dividend yield method and inherits its limitations. The dividend valuation model has a slightly different equation to the dividend yield model. The value of a business is computed by the division of the declared annual dividend payout by the required rate of return (i.e. Annual Dividend ÷ Rate of Return). This method is based on the concept of valuing a perpetuity. A perpetuity being defined as a constant stream of identical cash flows with no end.

For example, assume that a company is expected to pay a dividend of €0.28 through time, and an investor required a rate of return of 12 per cent, then the share price would approximately be €2.33 (i.e. €0.28 ÷ 0.12 = €2.33 per share). The serious limitation with this approach is that it is not practical to assume constant dividend payments in perpetuity.

Dividend growth business valuation model

The dividend growth business valuation model is also one of the methods falling under the yield based business valuation approach. This model is an enhancement to the dividend business valuation model because it allows for a dividend growth into the future. In other words it is not static but provides for some dividend growth flexibility.

For example, assume a company declares and pays a dividend today of €0.45. Further assume that after the financial year the company will retain 40 per cent of its earnings, which are invested at a return of 10 per cent. However, the management are seeking a required rate of return of 12 per cent. The dividend growth valuation model is expressed as P = [D (1 + g)] ÷ (k − g); where: P is the share price today; D is the dividend paid today; g is the growth rate; k is the required rate of return. Moreover, g = (b × R); where b is retention ratio and R is Return on invested earnings. Therefore:

a   g = (40 per cent × 10 per cent) = 0.40 × 0.10 = 0.04
b   P = [D (1 + g)] ÷ (k – g)
c   P = [0.45 (1 + 0.04)] ÷ (0.12 – 0.04) = 0.468 ÷ 0.08 = €5.85 per share

There are some issues that need to be addressed regarding this model. First, there is the difficulty in valuing the business if the company does not pay a dividend; second, it is difficult to ascertain whether there will always be an adequate amount of worthwhile projects in the future that the company may invest at the fixed return on invested earnings rate (R); and finally a difficulty arises if the growth rate 'g' exceeds required rate of return 'k', hence the denominator in the equation becomes negative.

Going concern business valuation: economic value approach

The economic value approach is the final method that will be considered under the going-concern business valuation category. This approach is based on the discounted cash flow technique, which is a cash flow based valuation method that recognises the time value of money. This method disregards the asset book values and accounting profit but focuses instead on the income stream potential (future cash flows) of the company.

This technique is a widely used and acknowledgeable investment appraisal method for valuing a project, company, or asset using the concepts of the time value of money. In other words, €1 today is preferred to €1 in the future, unless the delay in receiving the €1 is compensated by an interest factor. Hence, all future cash flows are estimated and discounted to give their present values. Therefore, it is the future amount of money that has been discounted to reflect its current value, as if it existed today. Thus, the method computes the net present value by taking the cash flows under examination and applying a discount rate.

The discount rate used is generally the appropriate weighted average cost of capital that takes into account the cost of financing the investment and reflects the risk of the cash flows; or the opportunity cost approach which takes into account alternative returns. The former discount rate method is cost oriented, while the latter is income oriented. The discount rate reflects two things, namely the time value of money (risk-free rate); and a risk premium reflecting the risk that the cash flow might not materialise.

A conservative discount rate is the long-term government bond rate since it takes into account the interest rate, risk premium and often inflation. However, no matter which method is used, the discount rate applied may give rise to subjectivity. The issue of subjectivity may be mitigated by testing the financial model under different stress or sensitivity conditions, thus one would end up with a spectrum of business values depending on the low and high discount factors applied. Notwithstanding the application of a range of discount factors, the discounted cash flow method's main weakness is still subjectivity, because the model requires the forecast of future cash flows assuming acquisition takes place and the forecast of future cash flows assuming acquisition does not take place.

Under this method the value of the business is equal to the present value of the purchased cash flow plus the present value of the changes in acquirer's cash flow (due to rationalisation). Rationalisation is the increased efficiency due to the cost savings initiated by the new owner or/and greater synergies. Thus, the value of the business would be equal to the present value of the net cash flow arising to buyer from acquisition.

An issue that needs to be addressed is the determination of the company's cash flow from the acquisition. For instance, with a majority holding, the cash flow would consist of the cash generated by the operations of the company, which equates to the earnings, adjusted for depreciation, acquisitions and disposals of fixed assets and capital redemptions. On the other hand, with a minority holding, the cash flow is mainly from the dividend flow being received.

The cash flow discounting formula provides the future value of an investment after 'n' years at 'r' rate of compound interest. This is expressed as: $A = P(1 + r)^n$ where A is the future value; P is the present value; 'r' is the percentage rate of interest per year; and 'n' is the period of the investments in years. The future value of €1 at 7 per cent interest per year at end of four years would be €1.31 (i.e. €1.00 $(1 + 0.07)^4$ = €1.31). The subject of the equation in this case is 'A', which is the future value.

However, if the present value is to be determined (i.e. the subject of the equation), which means the value today of a sum of money to be received in 'n' years' time then the equation would be: $P = A \div (1 + r)^n$. Therefore, the present value of €1.00 received in four years' time and discounted at 7 per cent is €0.76 (i.e. €1.00 $\div (1 + .07)^4$ = €0.76). This and the other methods discussed under this chapter will be illustrated in practical examples later in the chapter. Table 10.5 provides a summary of all the business valuation approaches and their respective methods.

Other factors that impact business valuation

The purpose of the various business valuation approaches and their respective methods are to provide a spectrum of values that one may negotiate around. It was stated earlier in the chapter that the various valuation methods provide a diverse selection of business values. Therefore, no single method is reliable and all have their limitations. In other words the various valuation techniques give different results and hence, agreement on the eventual price that a business is sold for arises from negotiations and various compromises by the parties involved in the transaction.

Therefore, the business valuation methods establish a reasonable spectrum within which negotiations may progress. Additionally, negotiations are also dependent on the availability of information and its interpretation regarding the business being sold. Typically, having less information available, results in a longer

TABLE 10.5 Summary: business valuation approaches and respective methods

Business Valuation Approaches Categories and Respective Methods
Non-Going Concern Valuation Approach: Break-Up Valuation Approach
Value of Ownership = Forced Sale Value of assets − Liabilities − Liquidation Costs
(a) Break-Up Value per Share = Value of Ownership ÷ No. of Shares
Going Concern Valuation Approach: Asset Approach
Book Value: Value of business based on valuation of assets (historical cost).
Replacement Cost: Value of business based on the replacement cost of assets.
(a) Book Value plus Goodwill and (b) Replacement Cost plus Goodwill
Value of the Business = Net Assets + Goodwill.
Goodwill: (i) Super-Profits Approach or (ii) Weighted Average Profits Approach
Going Concern Valuation Approach: Yield Basis Approach
(a) Earning Yield: Value of Business = Future Earnings ÷ Earnings Yield
(b) Price-Earnings Ratio: Value of Business = Future Earnings x Price Earnings Ratio.
Dividend Yield: (Dividend for year in cents ÷ Share Market Price) x 100
(c) Value of Business = Annual Dividend ÷ Dividend Yield
(d) Dividend Valuation Model:
Value of Business = Annual Dividend ÷ Required Rate of Return
(e) Dividend Growth Model: Value of Business Share Price (P) = $[D (1 + g)] \div (k - g)$
P = Price Today; D = Dividend Today; g = Growth rate; k = Required rate of return.
g = (b x R) Where: b = retention ratio; R = Return on invested earnings.
Going Concern Valuation Approach: Economic Value Approach
(a) Discounted Cash Flow: Value of Business = PV of purchased cash flow + PV of changes in acquirer's cash flow (due to rationalisation) = PV of net cash flow arising to the buyer from acquisition.
Future value of investment (P) at end of Year n: $A = P (1 + r)^n$
Present value of investment (P) at end of Year n: $P = A \div (1 + r)^n$
A = Future Value; P = Present Value; r = interest % p.a.; n = investments in years.

negotiating process. This is the reason why a data room is normally established for the company being sold, particularly if it is being sold as a going-concern. The concern with having a data room is related to security of information. A genuine purchaser requires information to make a decision, however a buyer who purports to be a genuine purchaser, particularly one who is a competitor may be just probing for information about employees and customers of the company being sold without the intention of concluding a transaction.

Information is required to examine whether the area of operations of the business domain being sold is increasing or decreasing in substance. For example, video rental businesses are decreasing in importance due to interactive TV and the internet.

Other factors that need to be examined are related to the market and industry the business being sold is participating in, that is whether the market is experiencing growth or contraction; the product or service demand; current or anticipated regulatory restrictions; and the prospect of forward industry integration by the seller (i.e. the potential of the seller becoming a future competitor). All the above factors need to be taken into consideration.

Practical example: business valuation and sale of Trident Ltd

Determining the value of a business is not a simple matter, mainly due to the fact that there are no precise ways to value a private business. Furthermore, the stock market will establish a value of the shares for a public company. However, the eventual price paid by the party interested to acquire the business may be more than the market share price. It all depends on the motive of the acquiring party.

Often the valuation of a business does not involve the sale of the business in question. It could be related to obtaining a bank loan or complying with regulatory measures, such as inheritance tax. Hence, it all depends why the valuation is taking place. In any case, the various valuation methods provide a spectrum of business values that one may negotiate around. As we have seen there are many ways to value a business, the application of which will be illustrated by the example below.

Example narrative: business valuation and sale of Trident Ltd

Wellington Ltd has shown an interest in acquiring a controlling share in Trident Ltd. Hence, they approached the directors of Trident Ltd and offered them the price of €3.50 per share. The Chief Financial Officer (CFO) of Trident Ltd has been requested to determine the business value of the company, particularly the value of each share using various methods and to prepare a brief report to the directors comparing the results of the valuation with the offer received from Wellington Ltd. The CFO has also been requested to comment on the valuation findings and advise the directors whether they should accept the offer made by Wellington Ltd. The information regarding Trident Ltd is found at Table 10.6.

The various methods that will be applied to determine the business valuation of Trident Ltd include the following:

1   Non-going concern:

    a   break-up valuation approach

2   Going concern:

    a   book value
    b   book value plus goodwill method (i)
    c   book value plus goodwill method (ii)
    d   book value plus goodwill method (iii)

TABLE 10.6 Trident Ltd: available business valuation information

Statement of Financial Position as at 31 December 2014	
Assets:	€000
Freehold land and property (at net book value)	106
Plant and equipment (at net book value)	186
Investment in 5% stocks 2022 (at cost)	159
Investment in Mohawk Ltd (40,000 shares at cost)	95
Net current assets	90
Total Assets:	**636**
Financed by:	
Share capital (200,000 ordinary shares of €0.50 each)	106
Share premium	53
Retained earnings	371
Long term loan	106
Capital employed:	**636**

Other Information:

Investments:

1. The 5% stocks 2022 were issued at par on 1 January 2010. Trident Ltd acquired a holding of 159,000 (at 100 each) and has since carried this asset at cost. The latest quoted price for this stock is: 110 each.

2. Mohawk Ltd's annual financial statements for the third year running have shown a decline in the company's status. The latest stock market data shows that Mohawk's shares are being traded at €2 each.

Trident Ltd Data:

3. Trident Ltd has reported a growth in profitability since it has been benefitting from a government subsidy of €18,000 per annum for the five years 2009–2014.

4. Profit for the year ended 31 December 2014 was €100,000. This level of profitability is expected to remain for the foreseeable future.

5. Profit for years 2010 to 2013 were €80,000; €95,000; €98,000; €100,000.

6. Average profit reported for the industry in general is €60,000 per annum.

7. Goodwill is to be calculated as four years' purchase of estimated future super profits and once of the weighted average profits.

8. Companies operating in the same industry have an average P/E ratio of 8.5.

9. The average return for the industry is 10% per annum (i.e. required rate of return)

10. The market value of fixed assets owned by Trident Ltd are as follows:

Freehold land and property value: Balance Sheet, €100,000; Current Market, €140,000

Plant and equipment value: Balance Sheet, €175,000; Current Market, €160,000

11. Company paid a dividend of €0.30 and share market price is currently €2.50.

12. Estimated retention ratio of 15% and return on invested earnings 7%.

e   replacement value

f   replacement plus goodwill method (i)

g   replacement plus goodwill method (ii)

h   replacement plus goodwill method (iii)

i   earning yield

j   price-earnings ratio

k   dividend yield

l   dividend valuation model

m   dividend growth model

n   economic value (without subsidy)

o   economic value (with subsidy)

Non-going concern: break-up valuation approach

The break-up valuation approach is the only method under the non-going concern situation. The break-up valuation approach perceives a business as a collection of assets that may be disposed of gradually individually or as a group. Hence, the owners of Trident Ltd will receive the residue value after discharging their commitments to third parties. Normally, the break-up valuation approach is applicable to companies being liquidated and therefore there is the presumption that the assets are being sold under forced-sale conditions.

Under a liquidation situation, the break-up value is the value of the assets under forced sale conditions less the liabilities, less the liquidation costs. This provides the value of the ownership. Hence, the break-up value per share is the value of ownership divided by the number of ordinary shares. In this case, Trident Ltd is not in a liquidation position therefore, the break-up value (value of ownership) is the book value of the assets less equity, less the long-term loan (i.e. €636,000 − €265,000 = €371,000). The estimated share price under this method is €1.86 (i.e. €371,000 ÷ 200,000 ordinary shares = €1.86). The calculations are shown at Table 10.7.

TABLE 10.7 Trident Ltd: non-going concern break-up valuation approach

Book value of total assets:		€636,000
Less:		
	Share Capital: €106,000	
	Share Premium: €53,000	
	Long Term Loan: €106,000	€265,000
Value of Ownership:		**€371,000**
	Number of Shares = 200,000	
Estimated Value per Share (Valuation ÷ No of Shares) =		**€1.86**

Going concern valuation: book value

The book-value method is one of the asset based valuation approaches. Its advantage is related to the use of factual figures that are easily obtainable from the company's financial statements, which are verifiable (i.e. audited).

The book value for Trident Ltd is obtained from Table 10.6 (total assets) which is €636,000. Therefore, the estimated share value under this method is €3.18 (i.e. €636,000 ÷ 200,000 ordinary shares).

Determination of goodwill

The other methods under the asset based approach include book value plus goodwill and replacement value plus goodwill. Hence, there is a need to determine the value of goodwill of Trident Ltd. Furthermore, there are a number of ways to compute goodwill. In this example we shall demonstrate three techniques. The use of these techniques depends on the information available. Basically, according to the accounting standards, goodwill consists of an excess of cost over fair value, the cost of future economic benefits and the cost of synergy. Table 10.8 shows the methods for determining goodwill in the case of Trident Ltd.

The first method utilises the current profitability of Trident Ltd as compared with the industry average profitability. Hence, the excess of Trident Ltd's current profitability over the industry average profitability is viewed as super profit. Goodwill is the super profit at four years' purchase as stated in the information provided (see Table 10.6), which in this case is computed to €88,000.

The second method utilises historical profitability (five years) figures for Trident Ltd less the subsidy for each year of €18,000 as provided in the information to provide Trident Ltd's average profit over the five years. This is compared to Trident Ltd's normal profit, which is based on the rate of return applied to the capital employed. Hence, the excess of Trident Ltd's average profit over normal profit is considered to be super profit. Goodwill is the super profit at four years' purchase, which in this case is computed to €52,000. Note that the parameters for the computation of goodwill are found in the information provided (see Table 10.6).

The third method is based on the weighted average method, which also uses historical profitability (four years) figures for Trident Ltd less the subsidy for each year of €18,000 as provided in the information. Note that in this case the historical profitability figures are based on four years. The number of years depends on the data available. In this case, five years could have been used. The method is illustrated at Table 10.8, showing the estimated goodwill as being valued at €78,400.

The estimated goodwill figures will be applied to the various business value calculations as shown below.

TABLE 10.8 Trident Ltd: methods for determining goodwill

(i) Super Profit Method €'000:	€000
Trident's Profit for 2014:	100
Less: Government Subsidy:	18
Profit less Subsidy:	82
Less: Industry Average Profitability:	60
Super Profit:	22
Goodwill = Super Profit at 4 years' purchase (22 x 4 years):	88

(ii) Super Profit Method €'000:

Year	Profit	Profit less Subsidy
1	80	62
2	95	77
3	98	80
4	100	82
5	100	82
		383

Average Profit =	76.6	
Capital Employed=	636	
Rate of Return=	10%	
Normal Profit =	63.6	Capital Employed x Rate of Return
Super Profit =	13	Average Profit – Normal Profit
Goodwill = Super Profit at 4 yrs' purchase:	52	(13 x 4 years)

(iii) Weighted Average Method €'000:

	(a) Year	(b) Profit	(c) Profit less Subsidy	(d) Weighted Value
Weighted Value = (a) x (c)	1	80	62	62
	2	95	77	154
	3	98	80	240
	4	100	82	328
	10			784

Weighted average value: 78.4

Goodwill at once weighted average profits of last 4 years: 78.4   (78.4 x 1)

Going concern valuation: book value plus goodwill method (i), (ii) and (iii)

The findings for the book value plus the goodwill method for three ways of calculating goodwill (i, ii and iii) are found at Table 10.9. In this example, goodwill represents the intangible assets of the entity.

TABLE 10.9 Trident Ltd: book value plus goodwill (method i, ii, and iii)

Book Value:	€636,000	€636,000
	Share value:	**€3.18**
Book Value + Goodwill method (i)	€636,000 + €88,000	€724,000
	Share value:	**€3.62**
Book Value + Goodwill method (ii)	€636,000 + €52,000	€688,000
	Share value:	**€3.44**
Book Value + Goodwill method (iii)	€636,000 + €78,400	€714,000
	Share value:	**€3.57**

Going concern valuation: replacement value

The replacement cost business valuation method is also an asset based valuation approach. However, the entity's business assets (resources) are valued at their replacement cost. Therefore, with this approach the purchaser may want to bring together an identical collection of the entity's assets for valuation purposes. Since only the replacement value of the business assets is being applied, the intangible assets, such as goodwill, are disregarded at this stage.

Table 10.10 shows the replacement cost of the business assets (net tangible assets valuation) taking into consideration the current market replacement value of certain assets as given at Table 10.6 (Trident Ltd: Available Business Valuation Information). Note that the net assets valuation as provided in the statement of financial position is €530,000 which is calculated by subtracting the long-term loan from total assets (i.e. €636,000 – €106,000 = €530,000). The investment in 5 per cent stock at market price is calculated by multiplying the number of stocks by the current market value per stock (i.e. 1590 × €110 = €174,900 rounding to €175,000).

Going concern valuation: replacement plus goodwill method (i), (ii) and (iii)

The findings for the replacement value of the business assets plus the goodwill method for three ways of calculating goodwill (i, ii and iii) are found at Table 10.11. Including goodwill as part of the business valuation approach attempts to account for intangible assets and introduces the concept of the earning potential of the assets. Hence, the ultimate purpose of owning a business is to produce income, which means that the buyer of the business not only owns a group of assets but also their earning potential.

TABLE 10.10 Trident Ltd: asset replacement value

	€'000	€'000
Net Assets per Balance Sheet:		€530
Adjustment for investments:		
Investment in 5% stock at cost:	€159	
Investment in 5% stock at market price:	€175	€16
Investment in Mohawk Ltd (40,000 shares) at cost:	€90	
Investment in Mohawk Ltd (40,000 shares) at market price:	€80	(€10)
		€536
Add Revaluation of assets:		
Assets at book value:	€275	
Assets at current market value:	€300	€25
Valuation = Net assets adjustment:		**€561**
Number of shares =	200,000	
Estimated Value per Share (Valuation ÷ No of Shares)=	**€2.81**	

TABLE 10.11 Trident Ltd: replacement value plus goodwill (method i, ii, and iii)

Replacement Cost:	€561,000	€561,000
	Share value:	€2.81
Replacement Cost + Goodwill method (i)	€561,000 + €88,000	€649,000
	Share value:	€3.25
Replacement Cost + Goodwill method (ii)	€561,000 + €52,000	€613,000
	Share value:	€3.07
Replacement Cost + Goodwill method (iii)	€561,000 + €78,400	€639,000
	Share value:	€3.20

Going concern valuation: earnings yield

The earnings yield method is based on the amount that Trident Ltd has made available to ordinary shareholders. Hence, this method is recognising the right of the purchaser of the business to share in the company's profit. In other words the earnings yield method links the profit of the company to the amount invested. Table 10.12 shows the value of the business, including the value per share using the earnings yield method. Since, this example applies three methods of computing

TABLE 10.12 Trident Ltd: yield basis approach – earnings yield method

Super profit (a):	€88,000
Super profit (b):	€52,000
Super profit (c):	€78,400
Average Super Profit (as estimate of future earnings):	**€72,800**
Estimated average future profits (super profit) =	€72,000
Dividend paid per share:	€0.30
Share Market Price:	€ 2.50
Ave. Earning Yield (Dividend Yield = Dividend paid per share ÷ Share market price) =	12%
Valuation (Estimated Ave. Future Profits ÷ Ave. Earning Yield) =	€607,000
Number of shares =	200,000
Earning Yield Value per Share (Valuation ÷ No of Shares) =	**€3.03**

super profit, it is best to calculate the average super profit and use this average super profit value in the determination of the earnings yield value per share (i.e. [€88,000 + €52,000 + €78,400] ÷ 3 = €72,800). Furthermore, if the dividend or/and share market price are not known, and therefore the average earning yield (i.e. Dividend Yield = €0.30 ÷ €2.50 = 12 per cent) cannot be calculated, use the required rate of return as an estimate of the dividend yield.

Going concern valuation: price-earnings ratio

The benefit of using the price-earnings ratio method is that it relates share value to the payback period for the investment made. Hence, it is a useful method particularly for the valuation of listed companies. The method may be adapted to unlisted or unquoted companies by using the average price-earnings ratio of a similar individual company or group of listed companies. Table 10.13 shows the value of the business, including the value per share using the price earnings ratio method.

In the case of Trident Ltd, the price-earnings ratio (P/E ratio) is given as part of the provided information (P/E ratio = 8.5). The P/E ratio method requires the prediction of future maintainable earnings, which in this case is based upon the average super profit (as estimate of future earnings) that is valued at €72,800. Therefore, in Trident Ltd's case, the value of the business is equal to €619,000 (i.e. €72,800 × 8.5 P/E ratio), giving a share price value of €3.09. Note that the P/E ratio is based on the average for the industry. This means that normally, the payback period for a share is 8.5 years. If the dividend paid per share and the market value of the share is used, the P/E ratio is 8.33 (i.e. payback period of 8.33

TABLE 10.13 Trident Ltd: yield basis approach – price-earnings ratio

Future Earnings:	€72,800
Price Earnings Ratio (average for the industry):	8.5
Value of Business (Future Earnings x Price Earnings Ratio):	€619,000
Number of Shares =	200,000
Price-Earnings Value per Share (Valuation ÷ No of Shares) =	**€3.09**
Payback Period (using industry average price earnings ratio) =	8.5 years
Payback Period (share market value ÷ share dividend = €2.50 ÷ €0.30) =	8.3 years
Payback Period (calculated share value ÷ share dividend = €3.09 ÷ €0.30) =	10.3 years

years), which is similar to the industry average. However, if the dividend paid per share and the calculated share price value is used, the P/E ratio is 10.3 (i.e. payback period of 10.3 years). Hence, the payback period for the investment is estimated to be between 8.33 years and 10.3 years.

Going concern valuation: dividend yield

The dividend yield valuation method is based on the total dividend amount distributed to ordinary shareholders. This approach recognises the owners' right to receive future dividends. However, this method can only be used when a dividend is declared. Hence, a concern arises when the company does not declare and pay any dividends, since its business value cannot be computed. When valuing an unlisted company, the average dividend yield of similar listed companies is applied. Table 10.14 provides the computations necessary for this method. The business value of Trident Ltd under this method is calculated at €500,000 with a share value of €2.50.

TABLE 10.14 Trident Ltd: yield basis approach – dividend yield method

Dividend Paid per Share:	€0.30
Share Market Price:	€ 2.50
Dividend Yield = (Dividend Paid per Share ÷ Share Market Price) x 100:	12%
Total Annual Dividend= Dividend Paid per Share x Number of Shares:	€60,000
Value of Business = Total Annual Dividend ÷ Dividend Yield	€500,000
Number of Shares =	200,000
Price-Earnings Value per Share (Valuation ÷ No of Shares) =	**€2.50**

Going concern valuation: dividend valuation model

The dividend valuation model is similar to the dividend yield model except that the required rate of return is used instead of the dividend yield. Hence, the dividend yield is calculated by dividing the dividend paid per share by the share market price, whereas the required rate of return is given in the information from Trident Ltd. If the required rate of return is not available, the average return for the industry may be used. The value of business is calculated by dividing the total annual dividend by the required rate of return. However, it is unrealistic to assume constant dividends in perpetuity. Table 10.15 shows the computations necessary for this method. The business value of Trident Ltd under this method is calculated at €600,000 with a share value of €3.00.

Going concern valuation: dividend growth model

The dividend growth model does not maintain a static dividend payout but makes an allowance for a growth in the dividend payment to shareholders. This approach has a similar difficulty to the methods that use the dividend payment as the basis for the business valuation calculations. In other words, this method can only be used when a dividend is declared. Therefore, a concern arises when the company does not declare and pay any dividends, since its business value cannot be computed. Table 10.16 shows the value of the business, including the value per share using the dividend growth model method.

The data for the computation to calculate the share price of Trident Ltd is given in Table 10.6. The share price of Trident Ltd is calculated at €3.39 per share. The valuation of the business is estimated by multiplying the calculated share price by the number of shares, which amounts to €678,000 (i.e. €3.39 × 200,000 = €678,000).

Going concern valuation: economic value (with and with no subsidy)

The economic business valuation approach is based on cash flows and recognises the time value of money. However, this method requires the prediction of cash flows that are to be generated by the investment, discounted at an appropriate rate to account for the time value of money. In this example, the discount rate for Trident

TABLE 10.15 Trident Ltd: yield basis approach – dividend valuation model

Total Annual Dividend = Dividend Paid per Share x Number of Shares:	€60,000
Required Rate of Return (given in Trident Ltd's information sheet):	10%
Value of Business = Total Annual Dividend ÷ Required Rate of Return:	€600,000
Number of Shares:	200,000
Dividend Valuation Value per Share =	**€3.00**

TABLE 10.16 Trident Ltd: yield basis approach – dividend growth model

Share Price (P) = [D (1 + g)] ÷ (k – g)
Where: P = price today; D = dividend today; g = growth rate; k = required rate of return.
g = (b x R)   Where: b = retention ratio; R = return on invested earnings.
D = dividend today: €0.30
k = required rate of return: 10%
b = retention ratio: 15%
R = return on invested earnings: 7%
(g) = retention ratio x return on invested earnings = (15% x 7%) ÷ 100 =   1.05%
Share Price (P) = [D (1 + g)] ÷ (k – g) =   **€3.39**
Value of Business = Share Price x Number of Ordinary Shares =   **€678,000**

Ltd is provided at Table 10.6, which is the average return for the industry, given as 10 per cent per annum (or the required rate of return).

The two common approaches to determine the discount rate are the opportunity cost approach, which takes into account alternative returns and tends to be income oriented; and the cost of capital approach, which takes into account the cost of financing investment and is cost oriented. The average rate of return for the industry or the required rate of return may be used as an estimate of the present value discount rate if the appropriate information is not available to calculate it by the opportunity cost and cost of capital approaches.

The economic value approach has been calculated using two methods. The first method (shown at Table 10.17) removes the effect of the €18,000 annual subsidy from the expected net income. This shows the business value of Trident Ltd at €287,000 with a share value of €1.44 each. The second method (shown at Table 10.18) includes the €18,000 annual subsidy as part of the expected net income. This shows the business value of Trident Ltd at €355,000 with a share value of €1.78 each.

Summary of business valuation findings

The results of the practical example using various approaches and methods regarding the business valuation and sale of Trident Ltd are summarised at Table 10.19 and Figures 10.2 and 10.3. The findings show that the average business value for all methods is €578,000 with an average share value of €2.89. The findings also indicate that the share value ranges from a minimum of €1.44 to a maximum of €3.62 per share.

Table 10.19 also provides the average and standard deviation of all the business valuation methods. This allowed the computation of the spectrum related to the dispersion (standard deviation) from the average, which was calculated as

TABLE 10.17 Trident Ltd: economic value approach – without subsidy

Present value of investment (P) at end of Year 'n': $P = A \div (1 + r)^n$

Where: P = present value; A = expected net income; r = rate of return; n = year

Economic Value Approach without government subsidy of €18,000:

n Year	A Expected Net Income	Profit Less Subsidy	$(1+r)^n$ Discount Factor	P Present Value
1	80,000	62,000	1.1	56,000
2	95,000	77,000	1.21	64,000
3	98,000	80,000	1.331	60,000
4	100,000	82,000	1.4641	56,000
5	100,000	82,000	1.61051	51,000
				Total: 287,000

Value of business = €287,000

Number of shares = 200,000

Value per share = €1.44

TABLE 10.18 Trident Ltd: economic value approach – with subsidy

Present value of investment (P) at end of Year 'n': $P = A \div (1 + r)^n$

Where: P = present value; A = expected net income; r = rate of return; n = year

Economic Value Approach with government subsidy of €18,000:

n Year	A Expected Net Income	$(1+r)^n$ Discount Factor	P Present Value
1	80,000	1.1	73,000
2	95,000	1.21	79,000
3	98,000	1.331	74,000
4	100,000	1.4641	68,000
5	100,000	1.61051	62,000
			Total: 355,000

Value of business = €355,000

Number of shares = 200,000

Value per share = €1.78

the arithmetic average (mean) plus or minus three standard deviations from the mean (i.e. share value spectrum = €2.89 ±3 × €0.66 = €0.91 to €4.87). This provided the classification of the share value into the following scales, namely extremely low (€0.91 to €1.56); very low (€1.57 to €2.22); low (€2.23 to €2.88); average (€2.89); high (€2.90 to €3.54); very high (€3.55 to €4.20); and extremely

TABLE 10.19 Trident Ltd: summary of business value for all methods

Approach and Method	Business Value (€'000)	Share Value
Non-Going Concern: Break-Up Valuation Approach	371	€1.86
Average for Asset Break-up Approach:	**371**	**€1.86**
Going Concern Valuation: Book Value	636	€3.18
Average for Asset Book Value Approach:	**636**	**€3.18**
Going Concern Valuation: Book Value + Goodwill method (a)	724	€3.62
Going Concern Valuation: Book Value + Goodwill method (b)	688	€3.44
Going Concern Valuation: Book Value + Goodwill method (c)	714	€3.57
Average for Asset Book Value + Goodwill Approach:	**709**	**€3.54**
Going Concern Valuation: Replacement Value	561	€2.81
Average for Asset Replacement Value Approach:	**561**	**€2.81**
Going Concern Valuation: Replacement + Goodwill method (a)	649	€3.25
Going Concern Valuation: Replacement + Goodwill method (b)	613	€3.07
Going Concern Valuation: Replacement + Goodwill method (c)	639	€3.20
Average for Asset Replacement Value + Goodwill Approach:	**634**	**€3.17**
Going Concern Valuation: Earning Yield	607	€3.03
Going Concern Valuation: Price-Earnings Ratio	619	€3.09
Going Concern Valuation: Dividend Yield	500	€2.50
Going Concern Valuation: Dividend Valuation Model	600	€3.00
Going Concern Valuation: Dividend Growth Model	677	€3.39
Average for Asset Yield Basis Value Approach:	**601**	**€3.00**
Going Concern Valuation: Economic Value (without subsidy)	287	€1.44
Going Concern Valuation: Economic Value (with subsidy)	355	€1.78
Average for Asset Economic Value Approach:	**321**	**€1.61**
Average Business Value (all methods):	**578**	**€2.89**
Standard Deviation from Average Business Value:	**132**	**€0.66**
Minimum:	**287**	**€1.44**
Maximum:	**724**	**€3.62**

high (€4.21 to €4.87). Moreover, the average of each approach was plotted using the calculated spectrum (or scale) as shown in Figure 10.4.

Figure 10.4 illustrates that four approaches, namely yield basis, replacement value plus goodwill; book value; and book value plus goodwill are classified as providing a high share value. The other approaches, namely replacement value; asset break-up; and economic value are classified as low to very low share value. The asset replacement business valuation method and the yield basis approach are ranked as being the closest to the average share value.

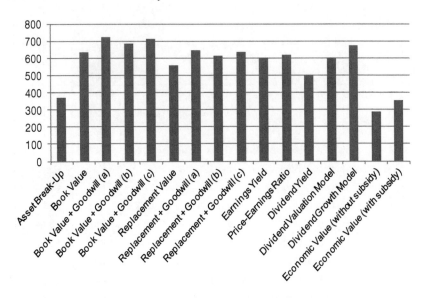

FIGURE 10.2 Trident Ltd: summary of business valuation for all methods

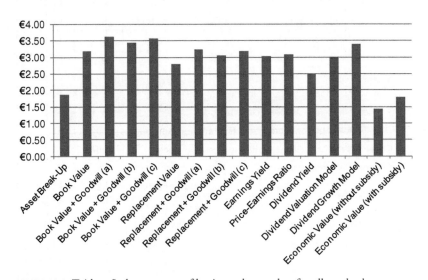

FIGURE 10.3 Trident Ltd: summary of business share value for all methods

Comments regarding business valuation findings for Trident Ltd

The findings indicate that the lowest share prices are related to the economic value, asset break-up value, and asset replacement value methods. One should note that the economic value method in this example applied a very low required rate of return of 10 per cent. In the case of the asset break-up and asset replacement, no consideration for future earnings is taken into account for these methods.

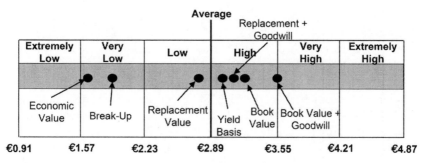

FIGURE 10.4 Trident Ltd: classification of resultant business share valuation

The business valuation methods that apply a goodwill value take into account of the fact that Trident Ltd has reported a profit that is higher than the industry average. Note that the goodwill calculation adjusted the profit figure by removing the impact of the subsidy received by the company.

It would also be appropriate to adjust the asset valuation if the shares in Mohawk Ltd are to be written off due to the persistent losses. These losses would result in a decrease of the value per share to €2.41 for replacement cost and €2.77 for replacement cost plus goodwill. In other words, if Mohawk Ltd shares are written off (€80) the value of assets is decreased to €481 and €554 respectively (i.e. replacement cost, [€561 − €80] ÷ 200 = €2.41; replacement cost plus goodwill using average figures, [€634 − €80] ÷ 200 = €2.77). The same adjustment would also apply the book value and book value plus goodwill methods.

Generally, the business valuation using the yield basis approach has provided a high valuation measure for Trident Ltd, particularly the dividend growth model. These methods reflect their recognition that the purchaser of the business has a right to share in the company's profit. In other words these methods link the profit of the company to the amount invested. Furthermore, dividend growth model also makes an allowance for a growth in the dividend payment to shareholders.

Other factors that may impact the share value are whether a company is listed or unlisted and whether the purchaser is acquiring control of the company. Hence, listed companies tend to be less risky than unlisted shares, so the price would be expected to be higher for listed companies. Moreover, acquiring control of a company will likely escalate the asking price.

Trident Ltd has a return on equity (ROE) of 15.47 per cent. ROE is calculated by dividing net profit by the shareholder fund after adjusting the profit for the subsidy. Therefore, the profit of €100,000 less the subsidy of €18,000 is adjusted to €82,000. The shareholder fund consists of the shareholder capital plus the share premium plus the retained earnings (i.e. €106,000 + €53,000 + €371,000 = €530,000). Thus, ROE is the net profit divided by the shareholder fund (i.e. €82,000 ÷ €530,000 = 15.47 per cent). Taking into account that Trident has a higher return on equity (ROE) of 15.47 per cent and the industry average is 10 per cent, then a relatively high value per share is justified. Additionally, the return on capital employed (ROCE) is calculated at 12.89 per cent. ROCE is calculated by dividing net profit by the capital employed (see Table 10.6) after adjusting the profit for the subsidy (i.e. €82,000 ÷ €636,000 = 12.89 per cent).

Taking into consideration the high ROE and ROCE, Trident Ltd should seek the highest price possible. Table 10.19 indicates that the highest business valuation share price is calculated at €3.62. Hence, even though the offer of €3.50 per share offered by Wellington Ltd is close to the maximum calculated value of €3.62 and given the fact that Wellington Ltd are interested in acquiring a controlling share in Trident Ltd, the Directors of Trident should try to negotiate a share value of at least €3.62, preferably even higher, particularly if Trident Ltd's management are confident that the current level of profitability and growth can be maintained.

Conclusion

This chapter has focused on a number of concepts regarding the valuation of enterprises, particularly businesses. Businesses are being continually traded or more accurately transacted, like every other commodity. Therefore, there are numerous situations when an objective and accurate assessment of a business's value is required. Business valuation provides an approximate economic value of an owner's interest in a particular business. Hence, a set of procedures are required to ascertain the valuation of a business. This chapter had the objective of explaining and illustrating these procedures, with the aim of establishing a simple but realistic process by which the value of a business may be determined.

However, one should note that there are no precise ways of valuing a private business, since the term 'business value' means different things to different people, which meaning is dependent on the basic assumptions that are made by them in the valuation. These assumptions may be related to the objective of the trans-action, the purpose of the valuation (i.e. why is the valuation taking place), past business performance, goodwill, and the circumstances the business is encountering. Intangible assets are a common cause of concern in the valuation process because of their inherent subjectivity.

This chapter has focused on many valuation approaches and methods, with a number of methods having some alternative methodology, due to a variety of tech-niques that are applied for the determination of the value of the intangible assets, such as goodwill. Table 10.19 illustrates that a total of 16 methods, classified under four major business valuation approaches have been explained and demonstrated through an example. Apart from the explanation of various business valuation methods, this chapter also explored how other factors may influence the value of a business at any given time, particularly the negotiating ability of the individuals involved in the transaction.

References

Bird, Davis. 2007. *Business Valuation Methods*, Business Focus Reference Sheet, Bendigo Bank, Bendigo, Victoria, Australia.

Koller, Tim, Goedhart, Marc and Wessels, David. 2010. *Valuation: Measuring and Managing the Value of Companies*, 5th edn. McKinsey.

Pignataro, Paul. 2013. *Financial Modeling and Valuation: A Practical Guide to Investment Banking and Private Equity*. Hoboken, NJ: Wiley.

Pratt, Shannon and Niculita, Alina V. 2008. *Valuing a Business*, 5th edn. New York: McGraw-Hill.

11

BUSINESS VALUATION REPORT AND RELATED ISSUES

A point of view can be a dangerous luxury when substituted for insight and understanding.

Marshall McLuhan
Canadian philosopher of communication theory and a public intellectual

The application of the analytical information that was the object of a number of previous chapters is the Business Valuation Report. It is therefore appropriate to focus on this aspect to provide the reader with a more comprehensive explanation of the format and contents of the Business Valuation Report using best practice criteria.

Business Valuation Report: format and content

As has been explained in the previous chapter, businesses are being continually transacted, like every other commodity. Therefore, there are numerous situations when an objective and accurate assessment of a business's value is required. Moreover, the previous chapter focused on the procedures to establishing a simple but realistic process by which the value of a business may be determined. This chapter will take the topic of business valuation a step further. It will explain the format and content (i.e. presentation) of the Business Valuation Report based on best practice criteria. The documentation related to the Business Valuation Report consists of a number of segments as shown at Figure 11.1.

Business Valuation Report: preliminary segment

The preliminary segment of the Business Valuation Report consists of three elements that will be described below.

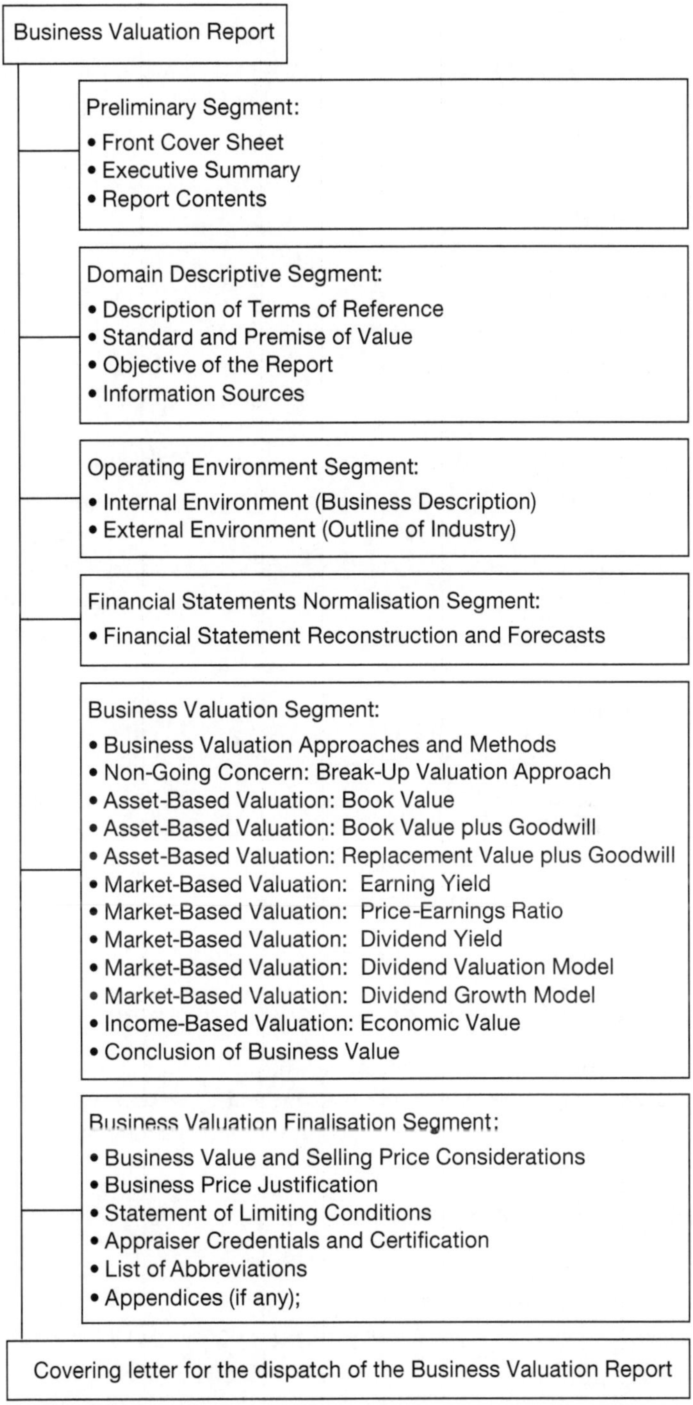

```
┌──────────────────────────────┐
│ Business Valuation Report    │
└──────────────────────────────┘
        │
        │   ┌────────────────────────────────────────────────┐
        ├───│ Preliminary Segment:                           │
        │   │ • Front Cover Sheet                            │
        │   │ • Executive Summary                            │
        │   │ • Report Contents                              │
        │   └────────────────────────────────────────────────┘
        │
        │   ┌────────────────────────────────────────────────┐
        │   │ Domain Descriptive Segment:                    │
        │   │ • Description of Terms of Reference            │
        ├───│ • Standard and Premise of Value                │
        │   │ • Objective of the Report                      │
        │   │ • Information Sources                          │
        │   └────────────────────────────────────────────────┘
        │
        │   ┌────────────────────────────────────────────────┐
        │   │ Operating Environment Segment:                 │
        ├───│ • Internal Environment (Business Description)  │
        │   │ • External Environment (Outline of Industry)   │
        │   └────────────────────────────────────────────────┘
        │
        │   ┌────────────────────────────────────────────────┐
        ├───│ Financial Statements Normalisation Segment:    │
        │   │ • Financial Statement Reconstruction and Forecasts │
        │   └────────────────────────────────────────────────┘
```

Business Valuation Segment:

- Business Valuation Approaches and Methods
- Non-Going Concern: Break-Up Valuation Approach
- Asset-Based Valuation: Book Value
- Asset-Based Valuation: Book Value plus Goodwill
- Asset-Based Valuation: Replacement Value plus Goodwill
- Market-Based Valuation: Earning Yield
- Market-Based Valuation: Price-Earnings Ratio
- Market-Based Valuation: Dividend Yield
- Market-Based Valuation: Dividend Valuation Model
- Market-Based Valuation: Dividend Growth Model
- Income-Based Valuation: Economic Value
- Conclusion of Business Value

Business Valuation Finalisation Segment:

- Business Value and Selling Price Considerations
- Business Price Justification
- Statement of Limiting Conditions
- Appraiser Credentials and Certification
- List of Abbreviations
- Appendices (if any);

Covering letter for the dispatch of the Business Valuation Report

FIGURE 11.1 Business Valuation Report Framework

Front cover sheet

The front cover sheet addresses five information requirements, namely, the name of the entity responsible for the preparation of the report; the report title; client details; report preparation date; and author details.

Executive summary

The executive summary should include the major details of the report. The analysis, diagrams, tables, numbers and reviews are not to be included in the executive summary. The executive summary is used to convey a brief explanation of the report findings and its recommendations. Hence, the executive summary should only contain those things that are considered important and things that are not essential are to be discarded.

The executive summary is a critical opportunity to entice the reader to read the entire document. In fact, in many instances, the executive summary is the only section of the report that is read. Thus having a strong and convincing executive summary is a key critical success factor. The executive summary should contain a brief financial summary. The financials are to include the valuation of the deal, thus allowing the reader to immediately assess the risks and the returns.

Report contents

A contents page is required only if the report is longer than about ten pages. The contents page is an itemised list of the headings, tables, figures and appendices of the report. Whether the list of tables, figures and appendices is shown separately depends on the complexity and length of the report. The author should ensure that the contents of the report have the correct page numbers that match the content description.

Business Valuation Report: domain descriptive segment

This segment basically provides a description of the report boundary, in terms of the assignment terms of reference; the standard and premise of value; the report objective and the information sources utilised in the preparation of the report.

Description of terms of reference

The terms of reference specifies the terms and conditions of the assignment and the resultant report. For example, the terms of reference may specify that the report is to estimate the fair market value of a particular company on a marketable, controlling ownership basis as at a particular date assuming a going concern.

Furthermore, the terms of reference will signify the purpose of the particular appraisal. For example, it may stipulate that the objective of the appraisal is to provide an independent valuation opinion with the aim of assisting the client in placing the business for sale, thus providing the client with a valuation basis for the negotiation phase. Hence, the valuation report is for the internal use of the client.

Finally, the terms of reference would specify the valuation standard being applied. For example, the Consulting Services Executive Committee of the American Institute of Certified Public Accountants (AICPA) has issued a detailed statement on standards for valuation services. Another valuation standard setter is the International Valuation Standards Council (IVSC). The IVSC is responsible for developing the International Valuation Standards and associated technical guidance. The IVSC is an independent, not-for-profit, private sector standards organisation incorporated in the USA but with its operational headquarters in London, UK. This organisation develops international technical and ethical standards for valuations to help investors and other organisations determine the veracity of the business valuation process. The IVSC standards are utilised by over 78 institutions spread over 53 countries. It is significant to note that Deloitte and Touche, Ernst and Young, Grant Thornton and KPMG are sponsors of the IVSC valuation standards.

Standard and premise of value

The valuation report must indicate the standard and premise of value. In other words, this section must articulate the reason for the business valuation and circumstances the business is encountering at the time. As we have seen in the previous chapter, the standard of value is the hypothetical conditions under which the business will be valued.

For instance, the appraisal report may indicate that its basis is the use of fair market value as the standard of value. In addition, the valuation report is to define the meaning of fair market value. For example, fair market value may be defined as the expected price that the business being sold would change hands between a consenting buyer and a consenting seller, neither being forced or under pressure to conclude the transaction and both having full knowledge of all the relevant facts. This definition is basically the same as that found in International Valuation Standards in defining market value. However, when an actual sale of a business takes place, the buyer and seller will have their own individual motives for conducting the transaction. Therefore, the standard of value establishes the theoretical state of affairs under which the business is being valued.

The premise of value is associated with the assumptions that are being made in valuing the business. For example, the appraisal may be performed under the premise of value in continued use as a going concern business enterprise. Therefore, this premise of value represents the highest and best use of the subject business assets.

Report objectives

This section basically describes the scope of the report. For instance, the valuation report may be conducted on a limited scope basis, as it is defined in the AICPA or IVSC standards. If the valuation report is prepared on a limited scope basis, this section would specifically state the limitations and departures. For example, the departures taken during the preparation of the valuation report may be related to not conducting a site review of the business premises being sold and not undertaking a specific audit of the reviewed business financial statements; thus relying on the financial statements provided by management and its financial advisors. Hence the limitation may be related to assuming that the financial statements provided are true and accurate.

Information sources

This section describes the sources of information that were used in preparing the valuation report. The sources of information may be classified into two major categories, namely external and internal information sources.

The external information sources include:

1   Economic data from the government statistics office or other similar agencies related to national, regional and local economic sectors.
2   Research information related to comparative business sale transaction data, including private company and publicly traded company sale databases.
3   Information sources related to cost of capital data for estimating suitable discount and capitalisation rates.

The internal information sources include:

1   Interviews with the subject business client (business proprietor and management team).
2   The most recent four years of audited business financial statements and tax records of the subject business. These are utilised to estimate the business's current performance and outlook for continued income generation.
3   Historical financial statements of the subject business, particularly the income statements and balance sheets. These are reconstructed (i.e. normalised) to determine the business earning power and provide inputs for the selected business valuation methods.

Business Valuation Report: operating environment segment

This segment provides a description of the internal (business description) and external (outline of industry sector) environments.

Internal environment (business description)

This section would describe the subject business being valued, particularly the business domain and primary business activities. For example, the subject business being valued may be a retail chain of supermarkets catering for the general consumer market, located in primary shopping malls in various suburbs of a specific city (e.g. Melbourne, Australia).

It would also describe its geographical location and legal jurisdiction the subject business is operating under. For example, the subject business's headquarters may be the city of Melbourne, with supermarket outlets in various suburbs, such as Cheltenham, Altona North, Chadstone, Maribyrnong and Victoria Gardens. The legal jurisdiction of the subject business in this example would be the laws of the State of Victoria, Australia.

This section would also include the number of issued shares and an itemised list of the major shareholders and the size of their shareholding. One would also include the organisation structure showing the top management posts, such as the Chairperson of the Board, Chief Executive Officer, Chief Finance Officer and other senior positions. The organisation structure should also indicate in a tabular format the total number of the employees engaged in the subject business classified by salary scale.

A general description of the clientele would also be included. For example, business may be primarily generated through customer loyalty (repeat business) with a customer retention rate of 80 per cent of the customers continuing to do business with the company for two years or more after the initial contact with the company.

Finally, some key financial trends data for the last five years would be provided in this section, such as the percentage annual revenue growth; the customer base volume; total annual sales turnover; average monthly value of creditors; and average monthly gearing status. Other data trends may be included depending on the nature of the business and the industry. For further details regarding the internal environment analysis refer to Chapter 9 (Applying financial ratios to interpret an organisation's financial statements).

External environment (outline of industry sector)

The industry overview is basically a description of the external environment. The methodology for the full appraisal of the external environment is found at Chapter 10 (The business valuation framework: description of the economic conditions).

As an overview, this section would contain key demographic data about the industry that the subject business belongs to. For example, similar to the previous section, the subject business being valued may be a retail chain of supermarkets catering for the general consumer market, located in primary shopping malls in various suburbs of a specific city (e.g. Melbourne, Australia). Hence, the industry overview would provide the estimated number of supermarket establishments in the State of Victoria, Australia and the total number of persons being employed within these establishments. Moreover, an estimated value of the total annual sales that the industry generates would be provided, together with the average sales value that is generated by a typical supermarket at a specific staff level.

Depending on the industry, one would also categorise the statistics by employment level. For example, supermarkets employing 30 people or fewer comprise 75 per cent of the total number of supermarket businesses. These businesses produce about 40 per cent of the total industry revenues. Similar statistical data would be provided for supermarkets within the Melbourne district as a distinct business geographical region. In addition, an opinion would be provided about the industry's life cycle status. For example, the supermarket industry continues to provide solid opportunity for growth. The supermarket business relies upon a high level of marketing and logistics professional practitioners to provide a high level of service to their customers at competitive prices. Industry consolidation is high with the top 30 supermarket companies responsible for over 80 per cent of the industry total revenues. The previous five years have seen the industry registering a continual growth of 15 per cent per year on average.

This section would also contain a discussion of the market factors and forces affecting the subject business in the specific industry of interest and providing a summary of the industry consolidation trends and growth prospects.

Business Valuation Report: financial statement normalisation segment

Financial statement reconstruction and forecasts

This section involves making various adjustments to the subject business financial statements for analytical and forecasting purposes. Chapter 10 provides a detailed treatment of common-size analysis and a methodology for the normalisation of the financial statements.

As accurate estimate of the business value of the subject business is highly dependent on its financial performance. This section of the Business Valuation Report looks to the future. Hence, while examining past financial statements is essential, business value is based upon the ability of the subject business to continue generating the required economic benefits for its owners.

It is therefore important that the historical financial statements represent a realistic financial position of the subject business. This is fundamental for determining an accurate business value. Hence, a company's historic financial statements, such as its income statements and balance sheets will need to be closely examined to ascertain whether they require certain adjustments. For example, a significant one-off sale of an asset belonging to the subject business may distort the income statement. Hence, the effects of this one-off sale will need to be removed from the financial statements. Consequently, the objective of these adjustments is to reconstruct the historic financial statements in order to reveal the true economic potential and earning power of the subject business.

For example, cash on hand may be adjusted down to the amount required to support normal business operations and amounts deemed uncollectible would be removed from the value of the debtors (or accounts receivable). Likewise, the value of the fixed assets may be questioned if the depreciated value is based on replacement cost basis and shareholder loans would need to be removed from the long-term liabilities.

Business Valuation Report: business valuation segment

A comprehensive treatment of the business valuation methods is found in Chapter 10. Chapter 10 also provided a detailed practical example related to the business valuation and sale of Trident Ltd. There are many ways of measuring the value of a business or professional practice, which, however, are classified under three categories, namely, the asset approach, market (yield) approach and income (economic method) approach.

As explained in Chapter 10, under each category, a number of methods are available that may be used to determine the value of a business enterprise. Each business valuation method uses a specific process to determine an estimate of the business value.

However, one should note that no one business valuation approach or method is perfect. Therefore, it is common practice to apply a number of business valuation methods under each approach. This will provide a general estimate that one may use when negotiating with the interested party or buyer.

Conclusion of business value

The estimated business value is determined by merging the results acquired from the methods applied. As explained in Chapter 10 (see Figure 10.4) the computed average and standard deviation of the business value within each business valuation category allow a graphical representation of the different valuations to be made. Hence, providing a useful range of measurements related to the value of the subject business to be used in the negotiating process.

TABLE 11.1 Example: weighted approach to determine business value

Business Valuation Method	Approach	Business Value	Weight	Weighted Value
Book Value + Goodwill Approach	Asset	709,000	20%	141,800
Replacement + Goodwill Approach	Asset	649,000	20%	129,800
Price-Earnings Ratio	Market	619,000	20%	123,800
Dividend Growth Model	Market	677,000	20%	135,400
Discounted Cash Flow	Income	355,000	20%	71,000
			Estimated Business Value:	**601,800**

One can apply a weighted approach, instead of using the average and standard deviation to determine a particular estimated business valuation figure as shown in Table 11.1. This process of concluding the business value of the subject business is often described as the business value synthesis.

Business Valuation Report: business valuation finalisation segment

This segment provides the concluding sections of the Business Valuation Report and consists of four major subdivisions, namely:

- Business value and selling price considerations;
- Business price justification;
- Statement of limiting conditions;
- Addendums.

Business value and selling price considerations

The selling price of a business is affected by a number of considerations, such as how the purchaser will finance the acquisition of the business; the terms and conditions of the sale of the business; and the motivation of the seller and purchaser.

Financing the acquisition of a business could be a mixture of debt and equity capital. Debt financing often involves a commercial bank loan. Hence, the procedure to obtain a loan will depend on the amount being sought and will definitely require the comprehensive preparation of a business strategy and business plan for the proposed venture. Equity capital also depends on the magnitude of the business being acquired. For example, a small business may be fully financed by the purchaser. However, the merger and acquisition of publicly traded companies requires a different financing strategy. For instance, publicly traded companies have direct access to public capital markets which facilitates the attainment of the required capital. Therefore, access to adequate debt and equity capital required to successfully secure the transaction is a key qualification to a successful sale of a business.

The business sale terms and conditions have an impact on the selling price. A buyer and seller of a business expect a return on their investment. However, the type of return expected impacts the business acquisition price. For instance, do the seller and/or purchaser of a business expect a capital or income return? Debt financing terms will impact the cash flow of the business and consequent profitability resulting in a lower income generation for the investor. Hence, the seller of a business may offer payment terms that minimise the impact on the cash flow position of the business being acquired making the business acquisition more feasible. Furthermore, these favourable sale terms and conditions may result in a higher selling price.

The motivations of the seller and the buyer impact the price a business sells for. There are a multitude of reasons a business why a business is offered for sale. These include:

- Insufficient financial performance with lower than expected return;
- Inadequate investment capital being driven into the business;
- Disputes between the owners of the business;
- Retirement, death or poor health of owner;
- Seeking new business growth and opportunities.

The ideal situation for maximising the sale price of the business is when the business is in its growth life cycle. The worst case scenario is selling the business when the business and the industry it belongs to are in decline. However, the individual circumstances of the owners involved may force them to sell the business when the market conditions are not favourable and thus not optimal to attain the most advantageous selling price. On the other hand the buyer may be motivated in particular by the investment opportunities and goals.

Business price justification

This section addresses the issue of whether the computed business selling price is reasonable in relation to the depicted theoretical business sale. Hence, the aim is to assess the cash flow that the business should generate to reasonably support its acquisition.

A key assumption is made when reviewing the business price justification, namely, that the purchase is based on an arms-length transaction which does not consider the benefits that may be derived from synergy by the business buyer. Moreover, the buyer acquires the underlying business assets without the supposition of its liabilities. Apart from the acquisition price and working capital to revitalise normal business operations, the business purchaser will also encounter transaction costs in relation to licenses and permits, professional and brokerage fees, financing charges and other related costs. These cash outflows will need to be covered by cash inflows from a reasonable return from the business.

Statement of limiting conditions

This section itemises the Business Valuation Report constraints. These constraints provide an insight into further assumptions that limit the domain of the Business Valuation Report. In other words, this section identifies the dependent and restraining conditions. For example, the author of the Business Valuation Report would not question legal title ownership for the assets being included in the report. The same applies to the accuracy of the information that is made available as the basis of the report. The author cannot offer any assurances as to the accuracy of the information provided by the client and other related parties; the information

TABLE 11.2 Limiting conditions affecting the Business Valuation Report

1.	Declaration of non responsibility for legal concerns, such as assets title issues.
2.	Assumption that business assets are in good and marketable condition.
3.	Assumption that business assets are free and clear of any impediment and ownership claims, unless stated otherwise.
4.	Assumption that all information provided by the client and other parties is accurate.
5.	Assumption that no assurance is provided about the completeness and accuracy provided in the report.
6.	Assumption of compliance with laws and regulations (unless otherwise stated).
7.	Assumption that no hazardous conditions or materials exist which could affect the subject business or its assets.
8.	Declaration of lacking competencies related to hazardous conditions or materials.
9.	Declaration of the standard being applied in the compilation of the Business Valuation Report that delimits the scope of the assignment.
10.	Declaration of the standard being applied in the compilation of the Business Valuation Report that delimits the disclosure of information sources, methodologies and discussions utilised to arrive at the conclusion of the business asset value.
11.	Declaration of limited use of the Business Valuation Report for the purpose it was intended.
12.	Disclaimer in relation to render testimony and attend court proceedings in relation to the contents of the Business Valuation Report, unless declared beforehand.
13.	Declaration that no part of the Business Valuation Report may be communicated to the public by any means unless there is written consent and approval by authoring organisation.
14.	Declaration providing the validity period (and date) of the Business Valuation Report.

is assumed to be complete and accurate. Table 11.2 provides a list of possible limiting conditions that may impact the Business Valuation Report .

Addendums

The addendums section is the final segment of the Business Valuation Report. This section consists of a statement of the Business Valuation Report appraiser credentials and certification; list of abbreviations; and appendices if applicable.

The Business Valuation Report appraiser credentials and certification provides the qualifications and competencies of the individual (or individuals) involved in the formulation of the Business Valuation Report. The following information is provided:

- Name and academic (and professional) qualifications;
- Position within the Business Valuation Report authoring organisation;
- Professional affiliations.

It is advisable to limit the use of abbreviations. However, a list of abbreviations must be included for any terms or formulae that may be used within the report. The list of abbreviations may be placed at the beginning of the report, after the contents page or alternatively at the end of the report before the appendices.

Appendices are placed at the end of the report. These provide supporting material, such as worksheets and other documentary evidence related to the subject business. It is best to have a cover page at the start of each appendix that clearly indicates the appendix title and general contents.

Business Valuation Report: covering letter

The Business Valuation Report is prepared on behalf of a client and as such must be submitted to the client for its consideration and any action it deems necessary. The submission of the Business Valuation Report to the client is carried out once the report has been completed and internally verified and approved by the authoring organisation management. Therefore, the Business Valuation Report covering letter is basically the formal submission of the report to the client.

The covering letter is addressed to the person who has engaged the authoring organisation to prepare the Business Valuation Report. It basically contains the following:

- Reference to the engagement letter and date of engagement;
- The purpose of the assignment (e.g. subject business for sale);
- Type of report prepared (e.g. restricted use limited appraisal report);
- Reference to the statement of limiting conditions;
- Reference to the definition of fair market value;
- Reference to the premise of standard and value;
- The estimated fair market business value;
- The basis of the estimated fair market business value (the assets included and excluded);
- The basic assumptions of the estimated fair market business value;
- Declaration of assignment conclusion;
- The appraisal standard applied in the preparation of the report;
- Signature of author.

From the above, it may be ascertained that the covering letter is basically informing the client that the Business Valuation Report assignment has been concluded according to the agreed assignment scope.

Conclusion

Businesses are being continually traded and therefore compiling a Business Valuation Report using best practice methods is essential for both the purchaser and seller of the business entity in question. Both desire the best deal in relation to the market conditions and their particular circumstances.

The consequence of this is that there are numerous situations when an objective and accurate assessment of a business's value is not only required but is essential to finalise a deal. This chapter has taken the topic of business valuation a step further. It has provided a detailed explanation of the format and content of the Business Valuation Report based on best practice criterion. Following the Business Valuation Report framework depicted in Figure 11.1 will provide the practitioner with the proper methodology to present a Business Valuation Report that is professional in both appearance and content.

References

Crumbley, D. Larry, Stevenson Smith, G., and Heitger, Lester E., 2003. *Forensic and Investigative Accounting*. Chicago, IL: CCH Tax and Accounting, pp. 5–35.

International Valuation Standards Council (IVSC), 2013. *International Valuation Standards 2013*. London: IVSC.

Reilly, Robert F., 2010. *The AICPA Professional Valuation Standards: Statement on Standards for Valuation Services*. Valuation Professional Standards Insights, pp. 91–94.

Reilly, Robert F., and Schweihs, Robert P., 1999. *The Handbook of Advanced Business Valuation*. New York: McGraw-Hill Professional, p. 100.

Sipes, Bill, 2006. *Business Valuation Sourcebook*. Chicago, IL: CCH Tax and Accounting, pp. 5011–5021.

PART 4

Money laundering: the curse of financial services

This concluding segment of the book deals with money laundering, which represents an important topic when discussing business entities and financial instruments. There is only one chapter, which provides an overview of the European Union Anti-Money Laundering (AML) directive and the various AML measures adopted in the United States of America. It also describes the measures and recommendations of the Financial Action Task Force (FATF) to counter the use of the financial system by criminals. FATF is an independent international policy-making body established during the 1989 G7 World Economic Summit.

FATF currently has 34 members that include the United States, United Kingdom, France, Italy, Germany, Russia, Brazil, China and Australia. FATF is funded by the Organisation for Economic Co-operation and Development (OECD) and is based in Paris at the OECD headquarters. Other issues that will be discussed include international cooperation in combating money laundering; the gatekeeper initiative; the risk-based approach; and how financial institutions, particularly banks and gambling establishments, manage money risk.

The chapter concludes with the regulatory issues stemming from the G20. Globalisation has meant that international collaboration becomes a central theme in the regulation process, through international protocols. These protocols are on the whole important for issues related to money laundering and the financing of terrorism; the environment; and other matters affecting economic growth. Furthermore, the seeds for the international protocols are normally the result of world leadership summits, particularly the G20. The G20 is composed of 19 countries, namely Argentina, Australia, Brazil, Canada, China, France, Germany, India, Indonesia, Italy, Japan, Mexico, Russia, Saudi Arabia, South Africa, South Korea, Turkey, United Kingdom and United States, and the European Union being the twentieth member. The G20 is particularly important because its leaders represent the world's economic powers, and their respective populations.

The aftermath of the Swiss Leaks and Panama Papers demonstrates that despite the efforts by the G7 and G20 to bring money laundering under control, there is still a long road ahead to achieve this objective.

12

ANTI-MONEY LAUNDERING REGULATORY ISSUES

> Dirty money has no place in our economy, whether it comes from drug deals, the illegal guns trade or trafficking in human beings. We must make sure that organised crime cannot launder its funds through the banking system or the gambling sector. Our banks should never function as Laundromats for mafia money, or enable the funding of terrorists.
>
> Cecilia Malmström,
> EU Home Affairs Commissioner

As a concluding chapter about the accounting fundamentals for financial services, it is appropriate to focus on the regulatory provisions when dealing with investments. In earlier chapters when discussing accounting practices, certain accounting standards regarding investments were addressed in some detail. The business community in recent years has had to face an increasing number of regulations that require a formalised process that spans a wide spectrum of activities. This chapter is related to the regulatory provisions when dealing with investments, specifically regarding anti-money laundering.

In this context, this chapter has two important implications. First, the impact of enforceable regulatory measures affects every enterprise, irrespective of size. Second, this chapter examines contemporary regulatory issues, some of which are still under discussion, and will have a significant impact on enterprises in the future, suggesting that the topics covered are relatively new and are still evolving.

Anti-money laundering (AML)

What exactly is money laundering? Laundering implies washing something to make it clean. Money laundering (ML) attempts to cover up the source and ownership of money that results from criminal activity. ML is directly linked to crime, such as drugs, human trafficking, prostitution, corruption, embezzlement and illegal arms trading. Criminals 'clean' their money by finding ways to wash their 'dirty money' and getting it into the financial system without detection or arousing suspicion.

A common method of cleaning money is often through the use of regulated mechanisms, such as, currency exchange and stock brokerage houses, gold dealers, casinos, automobile dealerships, insurance firms and trading companies. Often, private banking facilities, offshore banking, shell corporations, free trade zones and trade financing all can conceal illegal activities. Figure 12.1 illustrates that laundering money has become a very sophisticated process. Figure 12.1 demonstrates that the money laundering process consists of three stages.

Stage-1: Placement

The first stage of the process is 'Placement'. This involves camouflaging and moving the dirty money from its source of generation and placing or inserting it into circulation through legitimate means, such as financial institutions, currency exchange bureaus, casinos, commercial outlets and other commercial enterprises, both local and foreign. For instance, the Swiss-Leaks scandal involved thousands of secret accounts at HSBC's Swiss subsidiary HSBC Private Bank (Suisse), and the billions of euros held in them over a five-month period in 2006/2007. This scandal was

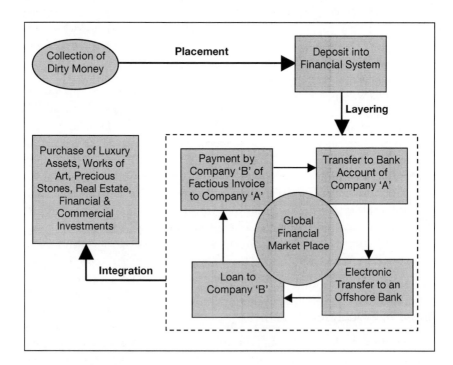

FIGURE 12.1 Stages in the money laundering process

exposed by the International Consortium of Investigative Journalists and news organisations that alleged that HSBC hid millions of dollars to help wealthy people dodge taxes. HSBC paid 40 million Swiss francs (€38 million) to settle a money laundering investigation by Geneva prosecutors into its Swiss subsidiary for suspected aggravated money laundering.

More recently (April 2016) the attorney general's office in Switzerland announced an investigation into the role Swiss banks may have played in potentially illicit financial transactions exposed by the Panama Papers. Swiss banks are reputed to be the world's biggest wealth managers, with an estimated $2 trillion of offshore wealth, and many have been the focus of international investigations and paid hefty fines for violations. Geneva Canton's chief prosecutor maintained that there is a risk that criminal offenses may have been committed. The leak of 11.5 million documents from the Panama law firm Mossack Fonseca, which allegedly helps clients hide financial assets, revealed that Switzerland's largest bank, UBS, created 1,100 offshore companies, and the second largest, Credit Suisse, set up 1,105.

The CEO of the Swiss government agency responsible for financial regulation contended that his organisation would launch its own investigation if there is any evidence that the country's institutions participated in money-laundering or other illegal schemes to hide their clients' wealth using Panamanian corporations. He also stated that the risk posed by money laundering is on the increase in Switzerland and banks need to do more to combat it. It is also noted that in 2009, UBS paid a $780 million penalty to settle US tax evasion charges and in 2014, Credit Suisse paid a $2.6 billion fine to settle similar charges. In 2015, the US fined UBS more than $500 million for its role in manipulating currency markets and in 2016 Belgium started the investigation of UBS on suspicion of money laundering.

Stage-2: Layering

Layering is the second stage in the money laundering process. This stage channels funds through different modes in an attempt to make it more difficult to detect and uncover a laundering activity. The diverse channels are used to make the audit trial of illegal proceeds more difficult to trace by the law enforcement agencies. For instance, cash deposited into financial institutions may be converted into financial instruments, such as bonds, money orders and bank drafts. Furthermore, material assets bought by illicit money, such as luxury cars, may be resold. The transaction may not result in a profit but the assets become more difficult to trace.

Stage-3: Integration

Integration is the final stage in the money laundering process. This stage involves transferring money that has been laundered back into the normal economic channels, such as the banking system. Hence, these funds appear to be part of the normal business proceeds. Unlike layering, the detection and identification of laundered monies are through disclosure by informants, for example the Swiss-

Leaks or the Panama Papers. Integration takes place through normal business dealings, such as complicity of banks; real estate transactions; having bogus import/export invoices; and establishing front companies or having bogus loans.

Anti-money laundering legislation

Table 12.1 provides a brief summary of AML legislation of various countries, including the regulatory body and parties affected. Costa (2008, p.3) argues that ML is an elusive concept in that 18 definitions have been detected in national or supranational legislations, depending on how the law considers the money laundered (stock or flow), the feeder activities (illegal or criminal), and the goal of money laundering (hiding the source of the money or making it appear legal). However, he maintains that there is wide consensus on the objective of ML, namely, that since the direct use of illegal proceeds would increase the probability of discovering the crime, the criminals need to conceal the illegal origin of that revenue before being able to spend it in a legal economy.

International criminals have fine-tuned their expertise at transferring assets from one country to another. These criminals take advantage of lenient laws and regulations in some countries that provide safe havens for those seeking to hide their assets. Note that the current financial system has the objective of providing a safer exchange structure for enterprises on a global basis and not to prevent ML. However, the financial system provides an audit trial of all generated transactions. The difficulty that arises is that not all countries apply the same level of surveillance, regulations and legislation. It is these inconsistencies that allow money launderers to exploit the financial system to transform their dirty money into clean money.

Effects of AML legislation on business enterprises

AML reforms support financial institutions through enhanced financial prudence. Some of the core AML policies have the aim of promoting overall good governance of financial institutions, and therefore have positive secondary effects on economic growth. According to Bartlett (2002, p.12) the Bank for International Settlements which fosters 'cooperation among Central Banks and other agencies in pursuit of monetary and financial stability' has endorsed key elements of the AML practices as explicitly supportive of sound banking practices that reduce financial risks for individual banks and, by extension, national and international financial systems as a whole.

There is no doubt that the requirements from AML laws have significant compliance costs for financial institutions and other organisations. These AML compliance costs will normally be passed on to the client, in terms of high transaction costs. However, AML legislation is likely to reinforce the integrity of financial institutions. For example, in the absence of AML legislation and due to the high integration of capital markets, ML can adversely affect currencies and interest rates. The reason for this is that launderers reinvest funds where their schemes are less

TABLE 12.1 AML legislation of various countries

Country	Regulatory body	AML/CTF legislations
Australia	Australian Transaction Reports and Analysis Centre (AUSTRAC)	Anti-Money Laundering and Counter-Terrorism Financing Act 2006 Anti-Money Laundering and Counter-Terrorism Financing Regulations 2008 No.2
China	China Anti-Money Laundering Monitoring & Analysis Centre Anti-Money Laundering Bureau (both of the above authorities are located within the People's Bank of China)	Anti-money Laundering Law of the People's Republic of China Anti-money Laundering Work Guideline for Members of the China Futures Association Anti-money Laundering Work Guideline for Members of the Securities Association of China Criminal Law, 2009
Hong Kong	Joint Financial Intelligence Unit	The Drug Trafficking (Recovery of Proceeds) Ordinance (Cap. 405) The Organised and Serious Crimes Ordinance (Cap. 455) The United Nations (Abti-Terrorism Measures) Ordinance (Cap. 575)
Malaysia	Unit Perisikan Kewangan, financial intelligence unit within the Central Bank, Bank Negara Malaysia	Anti-Money Laundering and Anti-Terrorism Financing Act (AMLATF) 2001
Singapore	The Financial Investigation Division, Commercial Affairs Department, of the Singapore Police Force	Corruption, Drug Trafficking and Other Serious Crimes (Confiscation of Benefits) Act Terrorism (suppression of Financing) Act
Thailand	The Anti-Money Laundering Office (AMLO)	Anti-Money Laundering Act B.E. 2542 of 1999
USA	US Department of the Treasury Financial Crimes Enforcement Network	Bank Secrecy Act USA Patriot Act
UK	Secretary of State Assets Recovery Agency	Proceeds Crime Act (POCA) Serious Organised Crime and Police Act 2005; and Serious Crime Act 2015

likely to be detected, rather than where rates of return are higher. In this scenario unfavourable currencies and interest rates will in time result in harming the operations of enterprises.

McDowell and Novis (2001, p.2) argue that ML undermines the lawful private sector. They posit that front companies have access to substantial illicit funds, allowing them to subsidise front company products and services at levels well below market rates. This situation can result in the crowding-out of private sector enterprise by criminal organisations. Note that criminal entities do not operate according to traditional free market principles of lawful business. In some cases, front companies are able to offer products at prices below what it costs the manufacturer to produce. Hence, front companies have a competitive advantage over genuine firms that draw capital funds from financial markets. This makes it difficult for genuine firms to compete against front companies with subsidised ML funding. Therefore, AML legislation protects and strengthens the free market principles of the private sector.

McDowell and Novis (2001, p.4) also claim that ML hinders government tax collection, thus reducing government tax revenue. This harms honest taxpayers, since loss of government revenue usually means higher tax rates than would be the case if the untaxed proceeds of crime were lawful. Another adverse effect of ML is higher insurance premiums for those who do not make false claims. IAIS (2004) provides many examples of ML and suspicious transactions involving insurance. Fraudulent claims, in the long-term, apply pressure on insurance companies to revise and raise insurance premiums, often escalating the operational costs of a business enterprise. AML legislation prevents this from taking place.

Overview of anti-money laundering measures in the EU (the 4th Directive)

The EU 4th Money Laundering Directive (the '4th Directive') is considered significant upgrade to the EU 3rd Directive 2005/60/EC. Similar to other national legislations, the 4th Directive is aligned with FATF proposals and promotes the creation of flexible requirements and facilitates a risk based application of the require-ments in a practical sense, which may vary according to the circumstances. This means that the rules and regulations should be balanced and flexible in a way that minimises the burden on market participants and facilitates delivery of regulatory goals, but does not place undue restraint on innovation nor disadvantage the enterprises concerned. However, the EU in its 4th Directive has made further measures from that of FATF, to seek to strengthen international co-operation and harmonise the approach to AML compliance across Europe.

The 4th Directive was approved in December 2014. The main aim is still related to align EEA regulatory regime applicable to tackling ML and terrorist financing. However, it should be noted that similar to the 3rd Directive, individual EU Member States are allowed certain derogations. Derogation is the non-application of a rule or reduction in its stringency, usually for a specific period and in specific cases. For instance, the 3rd Directive had affected a wide range of existing and new sectors of businesses in the UK, Northern Ireland and Gibraltar but does not apply to other UK Overseas Territories or to the Crown Dependencies for example the Channel Islands. Under the Directive, the following conduct, when committed intentionally, shall be regarded as ML:

1 'The conversion or transfer of property, knowing that such property is derived from criminal activity or from an act of participation in such activity, for the purpose of concealing or disguising the illicit origin of the property or of assisting any person who is involved in the commission of such activity to evade the legal consequences of his action';
2 'The concealment or disguise of the true nature, source, location, disposition, movement, rights with respect to, or ownership of property, knowing that such property is derived from criminal activity or from an act of participation in such activity';
3 'The acquisition, possession or use of property, knowing, at the time of receipt, that such property was derived from criminal activity or from participation in such activity';
4 'Participation in, association to commit, attempts to commit and aiding, abetting, facilitating and counselling the commission of any of the actions mentioned in the foregoing points.'

Furthermore, 'ML shall be regarded as such even where the activities which generated the property to be laundered were carried out in the territory of another Member State or in that of a third country.' The 4th Directive still maintains the wide scope of persons subject to regulation that includes credit and financial institutions, and legal or natural persons acting in the exercise of their professional activities, including:

1 'Auditors, external accountants and tax advisors';
2 'Notaries and other independent legal professionals, when they participate, whether by acting on behalf of and for their client in any financial or real estate transaction, even by assisting in the planning or execution of such transactions';
3 'Trust or company service providers, real estate agents, and casinos';
4 'Other natural or legal persons trading in goods with cash payments amounting to €15,000 or more, whether the transaction is executed in a single operation or in several operations which appear to be linked.'

The 3rd Directive had provided for detailed customer due-diligence requirements. It also provided a basis where simplified due diligence may be applied where the customer or product falls within certain categories, for example where the customer is a credit or financial institution or a company listed on a regulated market as defined in the Act. Hence, many Designated Persons have sought to rely automatically on this exemption, known as the 'Specified Customer' or 'Specified Product' exemption without sufficiently examining the appropriateness of applying the exemption. The 4th Directive requires Designated Persons to first determine the level of risk posed by a customer before applying the simplified procedure. The 4th Directive introduces a more measured application of this exemption by placing the onus on the Designated Person to carry out a risk assessment notwithstanding the customer would, on the face of it, fall within the scope of the simplified customer due diligence client category.

Furthermore, credit and financial institutions are prohibited from keeping anonymous accounts or passbooks. The institutions and persons covered by the Directive shall apply customer due diligence measures

> when starting a business relationship; when carrying out occasional transactions amounting to EUR 15 000 or more; when there is a suspicion of ML or terrorist financing, regardless of any derogation, exemption or threshold; and there are doubts about the veracity or adequacy of previously obtained customer identification data.

However, under the 4th Directive lower exemptions for one-off transactions and expansion of the perimeter have been included. Under the proposals, the numbers of transactions in which customer due diligence will be required will also be increased by the reduction of the threshold over which traders in high value goods must undertake customer due diligence when dealing with cash transactions, from €15,000 to €7,500. Customer due diligence requirements will also be extended from 'casinos' to other parts of the gambling sector.

Additionally, the 4th Directive has an extended definition of politically exposed persons. The new directive will clarify that enhanced due diligence will always be appropriate where transactions involve politically exposed persons ('PEPs'). The definition of PEPs has been widened to include domestic individuals occupying prominent public positions, in addition to those from abroad.

The 3rd Directive had allowed institutions to decide the 'extent of the due-diligence measures on a risk-sensitive basis', but institutions must be able to show that the measures are appropriate to the established risks. For instance, casino clients are to be identified and verified if they purchase/exchange gambling chips with a value of €2000 or more. Simplified customer due diligence may be applied for institutions representing a low risk. However, sufficient data to verify that the client qualifies for an exemption must still be gathered. The application of customer due diligence is exempt in respect of

> life insurance policies where the annual premium is no more than EUR 1000 or the single premium is no more than EUR 2500; insurance policies for pension schemes if there is no surrender clause and the policy cannot be used as collateral; a pension, superannuation or similar scheme that provides retirement benefits to employees, where contributions are made by way of

deduction from wages and the scheme rules do not permit the assignment of a member's interest under the scheme; and certain classes of electronic money as defined in Article 1(3)(b) of Directive 2000/46/EC.

The 4th Directive continues to stipulate that enhanced customer due diligence is applied on a risk-sensitive basis, in situations that present a higher risk. If a customer is not physically present for identification purposes, additional measures to compensate for the higher risk are to be applied. In respect of cross-frontier correspondent banking relationships with respondent institutions from third countries, Member States shall require their credit institutions to:

1   'Gather sufficient information about a respondent institution to understand fully the nature of the respondent's business and to determine from publicly available information the reputation of the institution and the quality of supervision';
2   'Assess the respondent institution's anti-money laundering and anti-terrorist financing controls';
3   'Obtain approval from senior management before establishing new correspondent banking relationships';
4   'Document the respective responsibilities of each institution';
5   'With respect to payable-through accounts, be satisfied that the respondent credit institution has verified the identity of and performed ongoing due diligence on the customers having direct access to accounts of the correspondent and that it is able to provide relevant customer due diligence data to the correspondent institution, upon request.'

Furthermore, the 4th Directive requires that

> in respect of transactions or business relationships with politically exposed persons residing in another Member State or in a third country, Member States shall require those institutions and persons covered by this Directive to have appropriate risk-based procedures to determine whether the customer is a politically exposed person; have senior management approval for establishing business relationships with such customers; take adequate measures to establish the source of wealth and source of funds that are involved in the business relationship or transaction; and conduct enhanced ongoing monitoring of the business relationship.

The 4th Directive will increase the emphasis on the risk based approach which has formed an integral part of the Member States AML regime for many years, and moves away from the current system of exemptions from customer due diligence requirements based on third country equivalence. It acknowledges that the levels and types of action required to be taken by member states, supervisors and firms will vary according to the nature and severity of risks in particular jurisdictions and sectors, and clarifies the types of situations in which simplified customer due diligence will be appropriate, as against those where it is necessary for firms to conduct enhanced checks.

Moreover, the 4th Directive will update the current list of circumstances when simplified customer due diligence will be appropriate by removing financial institutions which are themselves subject to AML/CTF regulation, listed companies and domestic public authorities from the categories of clients to be regarded as posing a lower risk. Instead, regulated firms will need to consider guidance issued by member states on lower risk categories and they will then have to decide whether each customer relationship or transaction presents a low risk. Under the 4th Directive, transactions including those involving public limited companies, public bodies, particular types of insurance, pensions and some other financial products and some defined jurisdictions will qualify for simplified due diligence. Conversely, examples of transactions where enhanced due diligence will be required include those involving asset holding vehicles and cash-intensive businesses, those where unusual or apparently unnecessarily complex ownership structures are in place and those associated with 'higher risk' jurisdictions such as countries subject to financial sanctions or identified as not having effective AML or CTF systems.

Likewise,

> Member States shall prohibit credit institutions from entering into or continuing a correspondent banking relationship with a shell bank and shall require that credit institutions take appropriate measures to ensure that they do not engage in or continue correspondent banking relationships with a bank that is known to permit its accounts to be used by a shell bank.

The 4th Directive will still allow regulated sector firms to rely on third parties for the purposes of undertaking customer due-diligence processes, provided that such firms are 'subject to mandatory professional registration', and in the case of third countries, equivalent regulation and supervision. However, ultimately firms have the responsibility for the proper systems and controls to ensure safe reliance (including in situations of intra-group reliance).

The 4th Directive still obliges third parties on whom reliance is placed for conducting customer due-diligence to provide on request 'copies of identification and verification', and other relevant data and records on the client or the beneficial owner. However, the 4th Directive introduces new requirements on beneficial ownership information. The 4th Directive aims to increase transparency by requiring companies and trusts to hold information on their beneficial ownership, and to make this information available to supervisors and parties conducting due diligence on them. The definition of a beneficial owner will remain unchanged, covering those who own or control 25 per cent or more of a business, but revised clarification is given as to how such persons are to be identified.

It is mandatory for Member States to establish a national 'Financial Intelligence Unit (FIU)' for the purpose of effectively combating 'ML and terrorist financing'.

The FIU is 'responsible for receiving, analysing and circulating to the competent authorities disclosures of information that concern potential ML and terrorist financing.' Furthermore, the FIU in each Member State has the authority to request information from institutions and request that institutions must promptly report cases or suspect cases where ML or terrorist financing is being or has been committed or attempted, and must refrain from conducting known or suspect ML or terrorist financing transactions until the FIU has been informed. The 4th Directive provides details of the documents and information that are to be kept by institutions or persons covered by the Directive for use in any investigation into, or analysis of, possible ML or terrorist financing by the FIU or by other competent authorities in accordance with national laws.

Similar to the 3rd Directive, the 4th Directive requires Member States to ensure that the competent authorities have adequate powers to compel the production of any information that is relevant to monitoring compliance and perform checks, and have adequate resources to perform their functions. In the case of credit and financial institutions and casinos, competent authorities have enhanced supervisory powers, notably the possibility to conduct on-site inspections. These measures are still required under the 4th Directive.

For example, in the UK, the Financial Services Authority (FSA), HM Revenue and Customs, and the Office of Fair Trading have exceptional levels of powers to request information; require persons in the regulated sector (or persons connected with them) to attend interviews; and enter and inspect premises with (subject to certain safeguards) or without a warrant. Moreover, the Proceeds of Crime Act is a key legislation in the UK related to anti-money laundering activities. This act provides power to the Secretary of State to establish an Assets Recovery Agency that has the authority to confiscate proceeds from crime. The EU enforcing authorities also have powers to impose civil penalties, for failures to comply with the AML regime, such as, failure to comply with the customer due diligence and the mandatory registration requirements. It should be noted that the above are the minimum measures that are to be adopted by Member States.

Other measures being introduced by the 4th Directive include the inclusion of tax crimes as predicate offences. Although tax crimes have long been predicate offences in the UK, this has not been the case in many other jurisdictions. The proposals add tax evasion and other serious fiscal offences to the list of predicate offences. The 4th Directive has reinforced the powers of sanctions and other requirements to coordinate cross-border action. These powers include a new set of minimum principles-based rules aims to strengthen administrative sanctions. Stronger and clearer requirements are imposed in relation to the collection and reporting of data by national authorities and in relation to the exchange of information and co-operation between them. Measures have also been introduced related to national and Europe-wide risk assessments. Each member state will be required to conduct a risk assessment at national level and to make the findings available to regulated firms to help them conduct their risk assessments. In addition, it is proposed that the European Supervisory Authorities will undertake an assessment, provide a joint opinion on the AML risks facing the EU and provide regulatory technical standards on specific issues.

Under the 4th Directive, additional information for funds transfers is required. The regulation on wire transfers tightens existing legislation and aims to increase the traceability of payments by requiring the inclusion of information on payees. It will introduce requirements on payment service providers to verify the identities of beneficiaries for payments originating outside the EU for amounts over EUR 1,000, to put in place risk based procedures to determine when to execute, reject or suspend transfers and to keep records for five years. It also clarifies that credit or debit cards and mobile phones and other electronic devices will be covered by the requirements if they are used to transfer funds. Generally, the 4th Directive provides a comprehensive basis to combat ML and the financing of terrorism within the European Union.

Overview of anti-money laundering measures in the United States of America

The United States of America (USA) Anti-Money Laundering measures are based on the FATF recommendations, similar to the EU 3rd Directive. The primary laws applicable in the USA regarding anti-money laundering are the Bank Secrecy Act of 1970 (BSA) and Patriot Act of 2001. The BSA being the first major act to regulate money laundering had the objective of preventing the use of secret foreign bank accounts and providing an audit trail for law enforcement by establishing regulatory reporting and recordkeeping requirements to help identify the source, magnitude and flow of cash and monetary instruments into or out of the USA or deposited in financial institutions.

The Patriot Act (or precisely the International Money Laundering Abatement and Anti-Terrorist Financing Act) was the consequence of the 11th September terrorist violation. It specifically deals with money laundering and terrorist financing. This Act considerably extended the scope of coverage by including non-banking financial institutions. Furthermore, it obliges financial institutions to establish AML programs that embrace policies, procedures and controls, designation of a compliance officer, training and independent review. Particular financial institutions (such as banks) are required to implement customer identification procedures for new accounts, including an enhanced due diligence (EDD) process for correspondent and private banking accounts maintained by non-USA individuals.

Apart from the Bank Secrecy Act and Patriot Act, the USA government has enacted other important legislation regarding anti-money laundering. These include:

1 Money Laundering Control Act of 1986 (MLCA);
2 Anti-Drug Abuse Act of 1988;
3 Annunzio-Wylie Anti-Money Laundering Act of 1992;
4 Money Laundering Suppression Act of 1994 (MLSA);

5   Money Laundering and Financial Crimes Strategy Act of 1998;
6   Intelligence Reform and Terrorism Prevention Act of 2004.

Money Laundering Control Act of 1986 (MLCA)

The MLCA was an important piece of legislation because it prohibits the structuring of currency transactions to avoid filing requirements and requires financial institutions to establish BSA compliance programmes. The MLCA was also the first time that money laundering became a criminal offence with fines of up to $500,000 and penalties of up to 20 years for each count.

Anti-Drug Abuse Act of 1988

The objective of the Anti-Drug Abuse Act was to provide financial support and technical assistance to State and Local government organisations to fight crime and drug abuse. Additionally, this Act recognised new BSA violations, such as, the forfeiture of property or assets involved in an illegal transaction related to money laundering. The Act also permitted the identification and recording of purchases of monetary instruments, including bank drafts, foreign drafts, cashier cheques, money orders or traveller's cheques in amounts between $3000 and $10,000 inclusive. The Act permitted authorities to designate specific geographic areas as showing signs of series drug trafficking concerns so as to combat drug abuse.

Annunzio-Wylie Anti-Money Laundering Act of 1992

The Annunzio-Wylie Anti-Money Laundering Act protects any financial institution and its employees (directors, officers or employees) from liability that may arise from lodging a Suspicious Activity Report (SAR) under any local, state or federal law.

Money Laundering Suppression Act of 1994 (MLSA)

The MLSA focuses on the money services businesses requiring each business to register and maintain a list of its agents. This act also encourages states to adopt uniform laws applicable to the money services businesses that permit them to exempt certain customers from filing a Currency Transaction Report.

Money Laundering and Financial Crimes Strategy Act of 1998

The Money Laundering and Financial Crimes Strategy Act specifically identified designated areas at high-risk for money laundering (and other related crimes) to be classified by geography, industry, sector or institution so that they may be targeted for participation in the High Risk Money Laundering and Related Financial Crimes areas programmes. The major aim of this Act is to fight against money laundering.

Intelligence Reform and Terrorism Prevention Act of 2004

This Act amended the BSA to oblige the USA Treasury Secretary to formulate regulations that compel particular financial institutions to report cross-border electronic transmittals of funds, if the Secretary ascertains that such reporting is 'reasonably necessary' to help in the fight against money laundering and terrorist financing.

United States of America anti-money laundering legal framework

The USA, similar to many other jurisdictions, is not fully compliant with the Financial Action Task Force (FATF) recommendations. The FATF recommendations will be addressed in the next section of the chapter. The aspects where the US requires improvement to be compliant with FATF include customer due diligence relating to beneficial owners, authorised signatories, legal persons and trusts; ongoing due diligence; and general requirements for designated non-financial businesses and professions, such as casinos, accountants, attorneys, dealers in precious metals and stones and real estate agents.

The US regulatory framework is fairly complex due to the wide jurisdiction that it represents. Figure 12.2 provides the US legal framework related to anti-money laundering. The Secretary of the Treasury has the political responsibility to assess civil penalties. However, this responsibility is delegated to the Financial Crimes Enforcement Network (FinCEN) and the primary federal banking regulators or self-regulatory organisations (SROs). A number of state regulatory agencies have their own mandate to assess civil penalties. However, criminal penalties are decided through the legal proceedings at both state and federal levels. Moreover, the Department of Justice can also bring criminal and civil actions, as well as forfeiture actions.

FinCEN is a bureau of the US Treasury Department with the specific mission to safeguard the financial system from abuses of financial crime. The bureau is the Financial Intelligence Unit (FIU) of the United States. One should note that under FATF, every affiliate country must establish an FIU to support law enforcement agencies to combat money laundering and terrorist financing and other financial crimes. The FIU analyses gathered data and shares information with law enforcement agencies at both domestic and international levels.

The operational mandate of the FinCEN is through the Bank Secrecy Act and the Patriot Act. However, FinCEN may issue regulations in conjunction with other federal regulators and the Internal Revenue Service (IRS) regarding the Bank Secrecy Act and specifically anti-money laundering. It may also issue enforcement actions for contraventions of Bank Secrecy Act and the Patriot Act through its Office of Enforcement jointly or unilaterally by assessing enforcement matters, including civil money penalties.

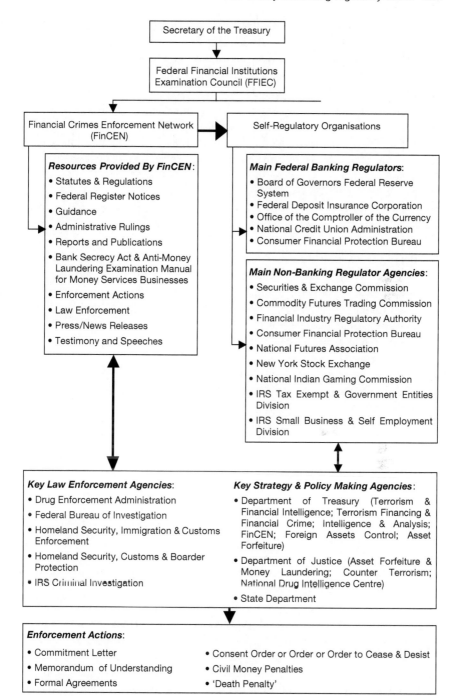

FIGURE 12.2 United States of America anti-money laundering legal framework

Figure 12.2 indicates that FinCEN is also a key strategy and policy making agency. For instance, it formed the Bank Secrecy Act Advisory Group to coordinate and inform the financial community about Bank Secrecy Act related issues. More recently, FinCEN established the Financial Fraud Enforcement Task Force. This brings together federal, state and local stakeholders to improve efforts to investigate and prosecute major financial crimes, recover proceeds for victims, and address financial discrimination in the lending and financial markets. Through its extensive resources, FinCEN has created a number of information communication systems to assist and simplify the information sharing process between domestic and international entities.

The self-regulatory organisations consist of two major groups, namely, the federal banking regulators and the non-banking regulatory agencies. The objectives of the key federal banking regulators are the following:

1   Board of Governors Federal Reserve System (FRS). This supervises the state-chartered banks and trust companies that are within the mandate of the Federal Reserve System; and financial, bank and thrift holding companies.
2   Federal Deposit Insurance Corporation (FDIC). The FDIC regulates state-chartered banks that are not under the supervisory mandate of the Federal Reserve System and all state-chartered thrifts.
3   Office of the Comptroller of the Currency (OCC). This also has a regulatory function, specifically for federal chartered banks that have 'National' as part of their company name or the letters 'N.A.' after their name. It also regulates federal thrifts.
4   National Credit Union Administration (NCUA). This is the regulatory authority for federally chartered credit unions.
5   Consumer Financial Protection Bureau (CFPB). This was constituted by the Dodd-Frank Wall Street Reform and Consumer Protection Act of 2010 to regulate consumer protection related to financial products and services.

There are numerous non-banking regulatory agencies that have a specific function. The major ones being the Securities and Exchange Commission (SEC), New York Stock Exchange (NYSE), and Internal Revenue Service (IRS) related to tax exempt and government entities (IRS-TEGE), and small business and self-employment (IRS-SBSE).

The SEC is the federal regulator of the securities markets. Its specific function is to administer a number of federal securities legislations, including: Securities Act of 1933; Securities Exchange Act of 1934; Investment Company Act of 1940; Investment Advisors Act of 1940; and the Trust Indenture Act of 1939. Moreover, the SEC has wide jurisdiction, with direct responsibility for the supervision and control of securities exchanges, securities brokers and dealers, investment advisors and investment companies, and the self-regulatory organisations. On the other hand, the jurisdiction of the NYSE is restricted to New York exchange member organisations.

The IRS-TEGE has the specific function of providing federal oversight to all US non-profit organisations including the determination as to whether a particular non-profit entity is facilitating terrorist financing. While the IRS-SBSE has the regulatory authority over all the financial institutions that do not have a federal functional regulator as defined in the Bank Secrecy Act, such as, insurance companies; credit card companies; businesses that cash cheques, exchange currency, issue money orders, traveller's cheques and currency transmitters; non-federal insured credit unions; casinos; and dealers in precious metals, stones and jewels.

As Figure 12.2 illustrates, FinCEN and the regulators have a close interaction with the law enforcement agencies and the strategic and policy making agencies. This permits these organisations, particularly the law enforcement agencies to take appropriate enforcement action to address anti-money laundering compliance program deficiencies and more specifically, anti-money laundering laws and regulations infringements. The enforcement actions permissible to US bank regulators include, among others:

1   Commitment Letter. This is a pledge between a bank's board of directors and a bank regulator, where the bank consents to take the necessary action to address certain concerns raised by the regulator.
2   Memorandum of Understanding (MOU). An MOU is an agreement between bank's board of directors and one or more regulatory agencies undertake certain corrective measures. MOUs are not available for public scrutiny and similar to Commitment Letter, they are not legally binding.
3   Formal Agreements. Are similar to MOUs but the infringement of a formal agreement may provide the legal basis for appraising civil money penalties against the signatories.
4   Consent Order or Order to Cease and Desist. These are similar to the formal agreements. The regulator's decision to issue a Consent Order or Order to Cease and Desist, rather than a formal agreement depends on the severity of the concerns related to the particular bank being investigated.
5   Civil Money Penalties. These are financial penalties that are imposed by the regulator for the contravention of the law or regulation or non-compliance with a formal enforcement action.
6   'Death Penalty'. The Annunzio-Wiley Act of 1992 provides the regulators with the option to take action for the revocation (annulment) of a license/charter (referred to as the 'Death Penalty') if a licence/charter of a depository institution is found guilty or pleads guilty to money laundering charges. This is the most severe action that may be taken against a financial institution.

The FinCEN has the authority to take enforcement action, which it often takes in conjuction with a financial institution's functional regulators. As previously stated, the US and many other countries are affiliated with Financial Action Task Force (FATF). The consequence of this affiliation is that many of the recommendations of FATF are the basis of the legislative system that has the primary objective of combating money laundering.

Recommendations of Financial Action Task Force (FATF)

The Financial Action Task Force (FATF) is an independent inter-governmental body that was established during the 1989 G-7 World Economic Summit. FATF develops and promotes policies to protect the global financial system against money laundering, terrorist financing and the financing of proliferation of weapons of mass destruction. Its purpose is to counter the use of the financial system by criminals and terrorists. The FATF Recommendations are recognised as the global anti-money laundering (AML) and counter-terrorist financing (CFT) standard.

Currently it has 34 members, including Australia, Brazil, China, France, Germany, Italy, Russia, United Kingdom and United States. FATF is funded by the Organisation for Economic Co-operation and Development (OECD) and is based in Paris. FATF member countries aim to base their AML and counter-terrorist financing (CFT) legislation on FATF proposals that have been endorsed by over 180 countries. The FATF Recommendations establish the key measures that countries should have in place to:

- Identify the risks, and develop policies and domestic coordination;
- Pursue money laundering, terrorist financing and the financing of proliferation;
- Apply preventive measures for the financial sector and other designated sectors;
- Establish powers and responsibilities for the competent authorities (e.g., investigative, law enforcement and supervisory authorities) and other institutional measures;
- Enhance the transparency and availability of beneficial ownership information of legal persons and arrangements;
- Facilitate international cooperation.

Note that FATF has no authority to impose laws on any jurisdiction. However, it exerts international political pressure on its member states to enact its AML/CFT proposals. Table 12.2 illustrates that FATF (2012) recommendations are broadly categorised into eight classes.

The key requirements regarding the FATF (2012) recommendations are the following:

1　AML/CFT policies and coordination;
2　money laundering and confiscation;
3　terrorist financing and financing of proliferation;
4　preventative measures;

5   transparency and beneficial ownership of legal persons and arrangements;
6   international cooperation.

AML/CFT policies and coordination

Two aspects are covered under this category. First, the need for countries to identify, assess, and understand the money laundering and terrorist financing risks for the country, and to take action, including designating an authority or mechanism to coordinate actions to assess risks, and apply resources, aimed at ensuring the risks are mitigated effectively. Therefore, countries should require financial institutions and designated non-financial businesses and professions to identify, assess and take effective action to mitigate their money laundering and terrorist financing risks.

Second, countries should have national AML/CFT policies, informed by the risks identified, which should be regularly reviewed, and should designate an authority or have a coordination or other mechanism that is responsible for such policies. Countries should ensure that policy-makers, the financial intelligence unit (FIU), law enforcement authorities, supervisors and other relevant competent authorities, at the policy-making and operational levels, have effective mechanisms in place which enable them to cooperate, and, where appropriate, coordinate domestically with each other concerning the development and implementation of policies and activities to combat money laundering, terrorist financing and the financing of proliferation of weapons of mass destruction.

Money laundering and confiscation

This recommendation also addresses two aspects. First, countries should criminalise money laundering on the basis of the Vienna Convention and the Palermo Convention. Countries should apply the crime of money laundering to all serious offences, with a view to including the widest range of predicate offences. Second, countries should adopt measures similar to those set forth in the Vienna Convention, the Palermo Convention and the Terrorist Financing Convention, including legislative measures, to enable their competent authorities to freeze or seize and confiscate the following, without prejudicing the rights of bona fide third parties: (a) property laundered, (b) proceeds from, or instrumentalities used in or intended for use in money laundering or predicate offences, (c) property that is the proceeds of, or used in, or intended or allocated for use in, the financing of terrorism, terrorist acts or terrorist organisations, or (d) property of corresponding value.

Such measures should include the authority to: (a) identify, trace and evaluate property that is subject to confiscation; (b) carry out provisional measures, such as freezing and seizing, to prevent any dealing, transfer or disposal of such property; (c) take steps that will prevent or void actions that prejudice the country's ability to freeze or seize or recover property that is subject to confiscation; and (d) take any appropriate investigative measures.

TABLE 12.2 Broad categorisation of the FATF (2012) recommendations

Ref. No.	Old Ref. No.	Recommendation
A		**AML/CFT POLICIES AND COORDINATION**
1	-	Assessing risks and applying a risk-based approach *
2	R.31	National cooperation and coordination
B		**MONEY LAUNDERING AND CONFISCATION**
3	R.1, R.2	Money laundering offence *
4	R.3	Confiscation and provisional measures *
C		**TERRORIST FINANCING AND FINANCING OF PROLIFERATION**
5	SRII	Terrorist financing offence *
6	SRIII	Targeted financial sanctions related to terrorism & terrorist financing *
7		Targeted financial sanctions related to proliferation *
8	SRVIII	Non-profit organisations *
D		**PREVENTIVE MEASURES**
9	R.4	Financial institution secrecy laws
		Customer Due Diligence and Record Keeping
10	R.5	Customer due diligence *
11	R.10	Record keeping
		Additional Measures for Specific Customers and Activities
12	R.6	Politically exposed persons *
13	R.7	Correspondent banking *
14	SRVI	Money or value transfer services *
15	R.8	New technologies
16	SRVII	Wire transfers *
		Reliance, Controls and Financial Groups
17	R.9	Reliance on third parties *
18	R15, R22	Internal controls and foreign branches and subsidiaries *
19	SRVI	Higher-risk countries *
		Reporting of Suspicious Transactions
20	R13, SRIV	New technologies
21	R.14	Tipping-off and confidentiality
		Designated Non-financial Businesses and Professions (DNFBPs)
22	R.12	DNFBPs: Customer due diligence *
23	R.16	DNFBPs: Other measures *
E		**TRANSPARENCY AND BENEFICIAL OWNERSHIP OF LEGAL PERSONS AND ARRANGEMENTS**
24	R.33	Transparency and beneficial ownership of legal persons *
25	R.34	Transparency and beneficial ownership of legal arrangements *
F		**POWERS AND RESPONSIBILITIES OF COMPETENT AUTHORITIES AND OTHER INSTITUTIONAL MEASURES**
		Regulation and Supervision
26	R.23	Regulation and supervision of financial institutions *
27	R.29	Powers of supervisors
28	R.24	Regulation and supervision of DNFBPs

TABLE 12.2 Broad categorisation of the FATF (2012) recommendations (continued)

Ref. No.	Old Ref. No.	Recommendation
F		**POWERS AND RESPONSIBILITIES OF COMPETENT AUTHORITIES AND OTHER INSTITUTIONAL MEASURES (continued)**
		Operational and Law Enforcement
29	R.26	Financial intelligence units *
30	R.27	Responsibilities of law enforcement and investigative authorities *
31	R.28	Powers of law enforcement and investigative authorities
32	SRIX	Cash couriers *
		General Requirements
33	R.32	Statistics
34	R.25	Guidance and feedback
		Sanctions
35	R.17	Sanctions
G		**INTERNATIONAL COOPERATION**
36	R.35, SRI	International instruments
37	R.36, SRV	Mutual legal assistance
38	R.38	Mutual legal assistance: freezing and confiscation *
39	R.39	Extradition
40	R.40	Other forms of international cooperation *

NOTES:

The 'Old Ref. No.' column refers to the corresponding 2003 FATF Recommendations.

Recommendations marked with an asterisk '*' have interpretive notes, which should be read in conjunction with the Recommendation.

Source: FATF (2012). International Standards on Combating Money Laundering and the Financing of Terrorism and Proliferation: The FATF Recommendations. Paris: FATF/OECD

Terrorist financing and financing of proliferation

This category covers four aspects. The first aspect is related to establishing terrorism financing as a criminal offence. Countries should criminalise terrorist financing on the basis of the Terrorist Financing Convention, and should criminalise not only the financing of terrorist acts but also the financing of terrorist organisations and individual terrorists even in the absence of a link to a specific terrorist act or acts. Countries should ensure that such offences are designated as money laundering predicate offences.

The second aspect is for countries to establish a mechanism for targeted financial sanctions related to terrorism and terrorist financing by implementing targeted financial sanctions regimes to comply with United Nations Security Council resolutions relating to the prevention and suppression of terrorism and terrorist financing. The resolutions require countries to freeze without delay the funds or other assets of, and to ensure that no funds or other assets are made available, directly or indirectly, to or for the benefit of, any person or entity either (i) designated by, or under the authority of, the United Nations Security Council under Chapter VII of the Charter of the United Nations, including in accordance with resolution 1267 (1999) and its successor resolutions; or (ii) designated by that country pursuant to resolution 1373 (2001).

The third aspect is regarding the targeted financial sanctions related to proliferation. Countries should implement targeted financial sanctions to comply with United Nations Security Council resolutions relating to the prevention, suppression and disruption of proliferation of weapons of mass destruction and its financing. These resolutions require countries to freeze without delay the funds or other assets of, and to ensure that no funds and other assets are made available, directly or indirectly, to or for the benefit of, any person or entity designated by, or under the authority of, the United Nations Security Council under Chapter VII of the Charter of the United Nations.

The fourth and final aspect under this category is in relation to non-profit organisations. Countries should review the adequacy of laws and regulations that relate to entities that can be abused for the financing of terrorism. Non-profit organisations are particularly vulnerable, and countries should ensure that they cannot be misused: (i) by terrorist organisations posing as legitimate entities; (ii) to exploit legitimate entities as conduits for terrorist financing, including for the purpose of escaping asset-freezing measures; and (iii) to conceal or obscure the clandestine diversion of funds intended for legitimate purposes to terrorist organisations.

Preventative measures

The preventative measures are divided into six categories. The first category is regarding the financial institution secrecy laws whereby countries should ensure that financial institution secrecy laws do not inhibit implementation of the FATF Recommendations. The other five categories address the following:

a   Customer due diligence (CDD) and record keeping. Financial institutions should be prohibited from keeping anonymous accounts or accounts in obviously fictitious names. The principle that financial institutions should conduct CDD should be set out in law. Each country may determine how it imposes specific CDD obligations, either through law or enforceable means. Moreover, financial institutions should be required to maintain, for at least five years, all necessary records on transactions, both domestic and international, to enable them to comply swiftly with information requests from the competent authorities. Such records must be sufficient to permit reconstruction of individual transactions (including the amounts and types of currency involved, if any) so as to provide, if necessary, evidence for prosecution of criminal activity.

b   Additional measures for specific customers and activities. The additional measures to be taken in specific circumstances address a number of situations related to politically exposed persons, correspondent banking, money or value transfer services, new technologies and wire transfers. Financial institutions are to have the necessary control mechanisms in place in addition to performing normal customer due diligence measures to ensure that politically exposed persons, including family members or close associates (domestic or foreign) are rigorously scrutinised. This principle should also be applicable to correspondent banking. Financial institutions should be prohibited from entering into, or continuing, a correspondent banking relationship with shell banks. Financial institutions should be required to satisfy themselves that respondent institutions do not permit their accounts to be used by shell banks. Money and value transfer services are a source of concern. Hence, countries should take measures to ensure that natural or legal persons that provide money or value transfer services (MVTS) are licensed or registered, and subject to effective systems for monitoring and ensuring compliance with the relevant measures called for in the FATF Recommendations. Countries should take action to identify natural or legal persons that carry out MVTS without a licence or registration, and to apply appropriate sanctions. Countries and financial institutions should identify and assess the money laundering or terrorist financing risks that may arise in relation to the development of new products and new business practices, including new delivery mechanisms; and the use of new or developing technologies for both new and pre-existing products. Regarding wire transfers, countries should ensure that financial institutions include required and accurate originator information, and required beneficiary information, on wire transfers and related messages, and that the information remains with the wire transfer or related message throughout the payment chain.

c Reliance, controls and financial groups. Financial institutions are to apply enhanced due diligence measures to business relationships and transactions with natural and legal persons, and financial institutions, from countries for which this is called for by the FATF. The type of enhanced due diligence measures applied should be effective and proportionate to the risks. Countries should be able to apply counter measures independently of any call by the FATF to do so. Such counter measures should be effective and proportionate to the risks.

d Reporting of suspicious transactions. If a financial institution suspects or has reasonable grounds to suspect that funds are the proceeds of a criminal activity, or are related to terrorist financing, it should be required, by law, to report promptly its suspicions to the financial intelligence unit (FIU). Hence, financial institutions, their directors, officers and employees should be protected by law from criminal and civil liability for breach of any restriction on disclosure of information imposed by contract or by any legislative, regulatory or administrative provision, if they report their suspicions in good faith to the FIU, even if they did not know precisely what the underlying criminal activity was, and regardless of whether illegal activity actually occurred; and prohibited by law from disclosing ('tipping-off') the fact that a suspicious transaction report (STR) or related information is being filed with the FIU.

e Designated non-financial businesses and professions. The customer due diligence and record-keeping requirements are also to apply to designated non-financial businesses and professions (DNFBPs), such as: (i) Casinos, when customers engage in financial transactions equal to or above the applicable designated threshold; (ii) Real estate agents, when they are involved in transactions for their client concerning the buying and selling of real estate; (iii) Dealers in precious metals and dealers in precious stones, when they engage in any cash transaction with a customer equal to or above the applicable designated threshold; (iv) Lawyers, notaries, other independent legal professionals and accountants, when they prepare for or carry out transactions for their client concerning a number of designated activities; and (v) Trust and company service providers, when they prepare for or carry out transactions for a client concerning a number of designated activities defined by the FATF.

Transparency and beneficial ownership of legal persons and arrangements

Countries are to take measures to prevent the misuse of legal persons for money laundering or terrorist financing. Countries should ensure that there is adequate, accurate and timely information on the beneficial ownership and control of legal persons that can be obtained or accessed in a timely fashion by competent authorities. Moreover, countries should take measures to prevent the misuse of legal arrangements for money laundering or terrorist financing. In particular, countries should ensure that there is adequate, accurate and timely information on express trusts, including information on the settler, trustee and beneficiaries that can be obtained or accessed in a timely fashion by competent authorities.

Powers and responsibilities of competent authorities and other institutional measures

This section covers four aspects related to regulation and supervision, operational and law enforcement, general requirements and sanctions. Countries are to ensure that financial institutions are subject to adequate regulation and supervision and are effectively implementing the FATF Recommendations. Moreover, supervisors are to have adequate powers to supervise or monitor, and ensure compliance by, financial institutions with requirements to combat money laundering and terrorist financing, including the authority to conduct inspections. Designated non-financial businesses and professions should be subject to regulatory and supervisory measures that have been specifically designed for them.

The second aspect is related to operational and law enforcement process. This specifically obliges countries to establish a Financial Intelligence Unit (FIU) that serves as a national centre for the receipt and analysis of suspicious transaction reports and other information relevant to money laundering, associated predicate offences and terrorist financing, and for the dissemination of the results of that analysis. Countries are to ensure that designated law enforcement authorities have responsibility for money laundering and terrorist financing investigations within the framework of national AML/CFT policies. When conducting investigations of money laundering, associated predicate offences and terrorist financing, competent authorities should be able to obtain access to all necessary documents and information for use in those investigations, and in prosecutions and related actions. In addition, countries should have measures in place to detect the physical cross-border transportation of currency and bearer negotiable instruments, including through a declaration system and/or disclosure system.

The third aspect specifies that countries should maintain comprehensive statistics on matters relevant to the effectiveness and efficiency of their AML/CFT systems. The competent authorities, supervisors and SRBs are to establish guidelines, and provide feedback, which will assist financial institutions and designated non-financial businesses and professions in applying national measures to combat money laundering and terrorist financing, and, in particular, in detecting and reporting suspicious transactions. The final aspect within this section is related to sanctions. Countries are to ensure that there is a range of effective, proportionate and dissuasive sanctions, whether criminal, civil or administrative, available to deal with natural or legal persons covered by the FATF recommendations, that fail to comply with AML/CFT requirements.

International cooperation

FATF requires that countries implement fully with urgency, the Vienna Convention, the Palermo Convention and the 1999 UN International Convention for the Suppression of the Financing of Terrorism. FATF encourages countries to ratify and implement other relevant international conventions, such as the 1990 Council of Europe Convention on Laundering, Search, Seizure and Confiscation of the Proceeds from Crime and the 2002 Inter-American Convention against Terrorism. These conventions all support the principle of international cooperation in dealing with AML/CFT related crimes.

Role of international cooperation

Collaboration is vital to the successful implementation of all FATF recommendations. At the domestic level, adequate coordination among customs, immigration and other authorities is needed and at the international level, countries must allow for the greatest possible measure of cooperation and assistance among competent authorities.

Figure 12.3 illustrates the five directions of ML flows with respect to cross-border global economies. These, flows are:

1   Domestic ML flows. These are flows in which illegal domestic funds are laundered within a country's economy and reinvested or spent within the same economy.

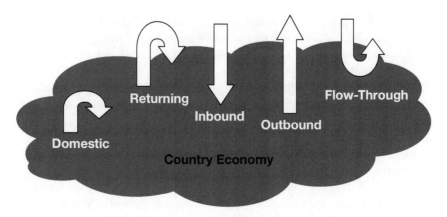

FIGURE 12.3 Money laundering flows through cross-border global economies

Source: Adapted from Bartlett, B.L. (2002). *The Negative Effects of Money Laundering on Economic Development*. International Economics Group, p.3.

2 Returning laundered funds. These originate in a country, are laundered (in part or in full) abroad, and returned for integration.

3 Inbound funds. With these funds, the predicate crime occurs abroad, or is initially laundered ('placed') abroad and ultimately is integrated into a country's economy.

4 Outbound funds. Typically these constitute illicit capital flight from a developing economy, where funds do not return for integration in the original economy.

5 Flow-through funds enter a country as part of the laundering process and largely depart for integration into another country.

Figure 12.3 shows that ML flows from one or several countries to another with the exception of the domestic flow. This illustrates that crime related to ML crosses international boundaries. Therefore, international cooperation and mutual legal aid is essential to ensure swift and effective AML/CFT related investigations and prosecutions.

FATF requires countries to provide the widest possible range of mutual legal assistance in relation to AML/CFT investigations, prosecutions and related proceedings by:

1 Not prohibiting or placing unreasonable or unduly restrictive conditions on the provision of mutual legal assistance and ensuring that clear and efficient processes for the execution of mutual legal assistance requests are in place;

2 Not refusing to execute a request for mutual legal support on the ground that the offence is not considered to involve fiscal matters or that laws require financial institutions to maintain secrecy or confidentiality.

To avoid conflicts of jurisdiction, FATF encourages countries to develop a mechanism that ascertains the best venue for prosecution of defendants, in cases that are subject to prosecution in more than one country. Moreover, mutual legal assistance should be rendered despite the absence of dual criminality. Where dual criminality is mandatory, particularly for extradition, the obligation should be satisfied regardless of whether both countries place the offence within the same category or denominate the offence by the same terminology, as long as both countries criminalise the conduct underlying the offence. FATF requires countries to take prompt action in response to requests by foreign countries to freeze and confiscate assets (or property of corresponding value) linked to AML/CFT crimes. FATF insists that ML should be an extraditable offence, and that countries cooperate with each other, in particular on procedural and evidentiary aspects, to ensure the efficiency of prosecutions. FATF suggests that the extradition process be shortened by allowing direct transmission of extradition requests between appropriate ministries, extraditing persons based only on warrants of arrests or judgements, and/or introducing a simplified extradition of consenting persons who waive formal extradition proceedings.

FATF requires countries to provide the widest possible range of international cooperation, by having clear and effective gateways to facilitate the prompt and constructive exchange between competent authorities and their foreign counterparts. FATF requires that authorities should be able to conduct inquiries and investigations on behalf of foreign counterparts. Where the ability to obtain information sought by a foreign competent authority is not within the mandate of its counterpart, countries are encouraged to permit a prompt and constructive exchange of information with non-counterparts. However, countries should establish controls and safeguards to ensure that information exchanged by authorities is used only in an authorised manner, consistent with the obligations concerning privacy and data protection.

FATF gatekeeper initiative

The term 'gatekeeper' was used at the 1999 G-8 justice ministers meeting in Moscow. The FATF gatekeeper initiative is an effort by government authorities to enrol the support of gatekeepers to defy money laundering and terrorist financing. Gatekeepers include lawyers, notaries, trust and company service providers, real estate agents, accountants, auditors and other designated non-financial businesses and professions who assist with transactions involving the transfer of money in domestic and international financial systems. Note that FATF has no authority to impose laws on any jurisdiction. However, it exerts international political pressure on its member states to enact its AML/CFT proposals.

The gatekeeper initiative has become a controversial issue because compliance is extended to professional advisers, including lawyers and accountants. Shepherd (2009, p612) argues that 'FATF's efforts have created unprecedented challenges to the sanctity of the attorney-client privilege, the duty of client confidentiality, and the general delivery of legal services in the American legal system.' The obligation of the gatekeeper initiative on lawyers to conduct customer due diligence, record keeping, and reporting 'suspicious transactions' of their clients is seen as ethically risky and highly improper to lawyers and bar associations around the globe. A major criticism is that 'when FATF decided to include gatekeepers, especially legal professionals, within the AML/CFT standards, it did so without empirical evidence that ML by gatekeepers and legal professionals was a major problem' (Shepherd, 2009, pp.622–623).

It must be recognised that criminals have historically used skilled professional advisers to conduct their ML process. In fact, professional advisers are viewed as being essential to the layering phase of ML. This phase is seen as a key stage of the process, since it is during this phase that the funds obtained from illicit activity are concealed and moved through seemingly lawful transactions and businesses to eventually become 'clean'. Professional advisers such as accountants, lawyers and auditors have (purposely or unintentionally) helped develop ever more sophisticated methods for ML. Lawyers and accountants, in particular, have specific skills and provide services needed by money launderers to create complex schemes designed to reduce the risk of detection, and protect the source of the illegal earnings. Moreover, the confidentiality requirement of lawyers appeals to those who take on ML activities.

To overcome this dispute, FATF developed a risk-based guidance for the legal profession, referred to as Lawyer Guidance. Shepherd (2009, p.670) argues that lawyers need to develop their own good practices to stave off federal intervention and intrusion. He posits that in doing so, lawyers are able to shape the good practices so that these practices conform to the general tenets of Lawyer Guidance, but at the same time are attuned to the unique nature of the attorney-client relationship and the business realities of a global economy. In the context of ML, lawyers, accountants and other professional advisers are viewed as 'gatekeepers' to the domestic and international monetary regime. Generally, the gatekeeper initiative forming part of FATF recommendations, defines the function and responsibilities of lawyers in resisting ML activities with the aim of monitoring and hindering the integration of illicit earnings into the financial system.

Anti-money laundering (AML) risk-based approach

The risk-based approach to AML is a methodology that is used by both the regulated and the regulator for managing an entity's business processes to combat ML. The basic principles for entities regarding risk management are:

1   Risk identification. This involves identifying the ML/TF risks faced by an entity, taking into account its clients, products and services, delivery outlets and geographical profile;

2   Risk assessment. This entails assessing the probability of the identified risks and the impact if they were to occur;

3   Risk mitigation. This is selecting and adopting measures to deal with the identified risks;

4   Risk monitoring. This entails having suitable systems that continually update data about changes to the firm's risk profile due to business transformation or to the threats;

5   Documenting and quality assurance of the AML process. This implies having AML policies and procedures that deliver effective accountability throughout the organisation, including processes that verify the effectiveness of the firm's risk management.

Robinson (2006, p.2) argues that a firm's risk-based needs will depend partly on the type of risks its employees are managing. For example, employees involved with taking on new clients will need to know more about recognising impersonation fraud than a senior manager who has overall responsibility for AML. In a risk-based approach an enterprise will adapt the content and frequency of its training to the risk that its employees face. Moreover, a business entity will seek out and respond to information about threats from law enforcement agencies, its own experience, and other sources. For instance, if authorities highlight a threat from certain ML methods, an entity will want to ensure that where feasible, the monitoring process caters for these identified threats. Why is the risk-based approach important?

A risk-based approach is important because it maximises the resources utility that entities apply to AML. The risk-based approach is based on the belief that entities are best placed for assessing risk because they know the finer points of their products and clients. The approach removes unnecessary costs, because it minimises the work effort needed to cover a risk. The risk-based approach is also dynamic because it allows an entity to modify its processes with a change in risk status. This is a key capability, because criminals are continually searching for weaknesses in AML systems. Robinson (2006, p.3) posits that to maximise the benefit from the risk-based approach, a number of key components need to be place by the authorities:

1   Providing tools that give firms a free hand as to the tool specification and application;

2   Providing industry guidelines on good AML practice, regarding ways to manage risk and that are designed to maximise their impact on crime;

3   Giving firms the necessary freedom to develop effective risk management arrangements that are appropriate to them and their circumstances;

4   Promoting awareness that the national regulator is committed to the risk-based approach;

5   Aiding firms in having effective risk assessment processes by circulating intelligence and information on crime and terrorist finance between firms, industry and law enforcement;

6   Ensuring firms deliver high levels of ML risk management, via effective AML practice;

7   Ensuring sensitive and well-informed supervision that focus on the firms' AML outputs, combined with the regulator being prepared to use appropriate sanctions against firms who are falling short of the required AML standards.

Auditing and testing AML programs

According to Sartip (2008, p.55) international standards including Basel Committee on Banking Supervision (BCBS), FATE recommendations, and the Wolfsberg AML principles require that all financial institutions have AML programs that are reviewed by the internal auditor or an independent audit firm. The BCBS provides a forum for regular cooperation on banking supervisory matters and develops guidelines and supervisory standards in areas where they are considered desirable.

In this regard, BCBS has promulgated three key documents since late 2001, namely, Customer Due Diligence for Banks; Sound Practices for the Management and Supervision of Operational Risk; and the Compliance Function of Banks. The Wolfsberg Group has a resilient link with the BCBS in that it consists of leading international banks that formulate AML guidelines, procedures and preventative measures. Khan (2007, pp.46–48) suggests that testing AML programs requires three major activities, namely, preparing an AML program testing strategy; developing an audit program for testing and validating AML/CTF activities; and reporting findings and follow up.

Prepare an AML program testing strategy

In preparing an AML program testing strategy, the audit team needs to understand the firm's products and delivery channels; types of clients and their geographic location; the company's organisational structure, infrastructure, policies, procedures and controls for mitigating ML/TF risks. As part of the audit strategy, auditors must list all regulatory requirements in the countries in which the organisation does business. These activities will permit the auditor to develop a risk profile to ascertain risk levels and enable the creation of an appropriate audit program, staffing and overall management of the audit assignment.

Audit program for testing and validation of AML/CTF activities

Separate audit programs should be developed for testing and validating activities associated with mitigating AML/CTF risks. Examples of key activities of AML/CTF programs include processes for identification of terrorist and drug trafficker activities; transaction monitoring and reporting of suspicious activities to government authorities; and staff training programs. The use of template audit programs should be avoided. Audit programs are to be efficient, precise and aligned with the specific nature of the area being audited. Selecting the proper sampling methodology for performing the required testing and validation is essential. Inappropriate sampling will lead to incorrect and unsupportable conclusions. Sampling criteria and attributes must be defined clearly and be consistent with the audit objectives.

The auditor needs to verify compliance with local regulations. Firms having high transaction volumes will likely have computerised transaction-based processes, hence, exception reports showing transactions that deviate from expected outcomes will be required. Furthermore, a useful reference for auditors are the FATF typologies that provide insights into emerging threats and may suggest new areas for auditors to test. FATF holds a global typologies exercise each year, which includes active participation by regional anti-money laundering bodies. The outcome of the typologies exercise is a yearly typologies report that addresses priority topics in detail, include selected case studies.

Report findings and follow-up

The auditor must compile a formal audit review report with the results being documented and rated. This report is to be distributed to the business owners, senior management, and depending on the severity of deficiencies, the board and audit committee. The highest level of severity would represent issues where there are no compensating controls in place for deficiencies that directly contravene local laws. Medium level of severity would encompass those issues that are material, but some compensating controls are in place. Low-level risks are minor control weaknesses where correction should be considered. The severity levels would be applied for giving an overall rating to an organisation's AML/CTF program.

Khan (2007, p.48) recommends that the auditor should develop guidelines for rating the overall quality of controls, since individual organisations may have their own criteria for determining the overall rating levels. He also suggests that a process should be instituted to ensure action plans are implemented in accordance with committed completion dates. In addition, the responsibility for ensuring that timely corrective actions are undertaken, resides with the business or process owner. However, the internal audit department may be assigned the responsibility for escalating unresolved issues to senior management using formal reporting protocols.

Financial institutions are the front-line in the fight against ML/TF. Therefore, it is important that they have the mechanisms to put into practice an effective independent audit plan of the AML/CTF program, to appraise the quality of controls in place. Khan (2007, p.48) argues that sound independent testing by auditors who have extensive knowledge of AML/CTF regulations, risks, controls and businesses, is considered a key control within an entity. Their audit work provides management with the vital intelligence for proactively managing deficiencies, and ensuring that a well-aligned top-down control setting with appropriate resources and infrastructure, is in place for mitigating AML/CTF risks.

Example: how not to conduct an independent audit of AML/CTF programs

Former Riggs Bank NA, based in Washington, DC, allegedly had total violations of law occurring within all principal compliance areas. The US Financial Crimes and Enforcement Network stated in its report:

> Riggs did not implement an adequate system for independent testing of Bank Secrecy Act (BSA) compliance. The independent testing for compliance with the BSA was neither timely nor effective for the level of risk within Riggs. The internal audit could not verify that management's corrective action for identified deficiencies was effective or timely. In addition, the scope of the audit failed to include an evaluation of the areas of ML vulnerabilities, BSA compliance, or the suspicious activity reporting process.
>
> (Khan, 2007, p.48)

The bank was fined US $25 million by the US Treasury for AML violations.

Impact of AML regulations on financial institutions

The focus of this section is the impact of AML regulations on financial institutions related to how they manage money risk, particularly, banks and gambling establishments. Casinos are a special case and differ from other financial institutions. Casinos are clearly involved in currency and other financial services, because their function is to make it convenient and easy to gamble, since the amount of gambling is directly correlated to revenue. In addition, the casino floor is where gaming activity takes place, but it is the 'casino cage' which conducts the casino's financial operations. The casino cage operates similar to a bank, offering services like those available at a teller window at a commercial bank. The client can deposit funds into a depository account and withdraw those funds; establish a line of credit and draw against that credit; can wire transfer money both into and out of the casino; and purchase or cash cheques. Moreover, casinos offer one service that is not available at a bank, that is, a client can redeem gaming chips and receive currency.

Most countries adopt the FATF Recommendations that require financial institutions to show that they have suitable processes in place to carry out their obligations. It is a well-known fact that institutions, such as banking, insurance and gambling, deal with very high volumes of transactions that make it extremely difficult to conduct proper surveillance, even when using the risk-based approach. For example, casinos unlike other financial institutions, do not exist solely for the purpose of facilitating financial transactions, but are primarily in the tourist and entertainment business. Therefore, apart from handling a great volume of transactions, they also handle a large number of clients that are in transit. This makes it difficult to comply with some AML/CFT legal provisions, particularly, client identification and client due diligence. According to Sartip (2008, p.56), financial institutions are exposed to four major ML risk categories, these are:

1   Compliance risk. The focus of institutions should be more on compliance program development and management, rather than on AML record-keeping and reporting rules.
2   Operational risk. Institutions should conduct a gap analysis that will map out, process by process, the inherent risks and the controls in place to manage those risks, and also identify control deficiencies requiring action or remediation.
3   Reputational risk. Two types of ML actions harm firms' reputation: a compliance failure or major control flaw, resulting in a bad review or an enforcement action by a regulator; and a direct ML/TF scandal, or merely an alleged link to an ML operation or transaction.
4   Strategic risk. As ML becomes more complicated and difficult to detect, the organisation will be less able to plan, implement and respond to challenges effectively, and may find it too risky to continue operations.

So how do these institutions carry out their regulatory obligations and manage money risk? In this context the management of money risk is related to having adequate procedures in place to ensure that money being handled through the institution is not being laundered. It is not uncommon for financial institutions to be confronted with high recurring numbers of false alerts when using their normal information systems, since these systems are typically not intelligent, but merely process transactions. This not only causes high administrative burdens and costs, but also creates risks as a result of untreated alerts or application of selection criteria on alerts.

The key to avoiding this is for institutions having large volume of clients and transactions to use intelligent technologies. Figure 12.4 shows how intelligent technologies are able to integrate an expert system using a neural network and rules-based strategies, to monitor and score all aspects of the AML/CFI process to help identify unusual financial activity and offer a fast track to compliance. An expert system is computer software that attempts to provide an answer to a specific problem, or clarify uncertainties where normally one or more human experts would need to be consulted. In this case the expert system would have the objective of identifying unusual financial activity, particularly, suspicious transactions.

Expert systems are able to transform data into useful knowledge and can automatically analyse and detect suspicious and unusual transactions, and assist with name matching abilities. These intelligent systems also provide automatic monitoring and detection by checking customer due diligence and know-your-customer when opening new accounts; provide integrated real-time and batch scanning; message filtering (SWIFT message filter); batch and manual AML scanning (TTR and SMR); automatic screening of bank's transactions; automatically providing reasons for suspecting ML activities; providing scrutiny of sanctions, politically exposed people, blacklisted people and firms, and high risk industries;

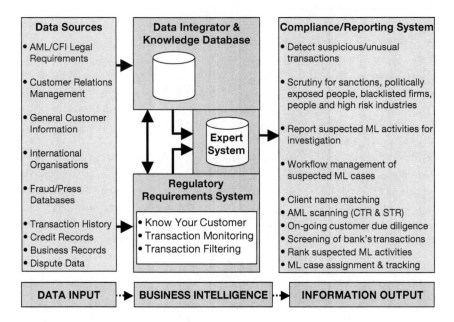

FIGURE 12.4 Expert system using neural network and rules-based strategies

Source: © Dr. Emanuel Camillieri

providing risk scores and ranks of suspected ML activities; and allow manual reporting of suspected ML activities for investigation. These systems also provide case work-flow management by prioritising suspected ML cases for inspection; providing workflow to manage investigation of suspected ML cases; providing assignment of a case to an officer most suited to handle a specific case; allows entries for recommendations and remarks; allows attachment of documents to cases; provides tracking of cases; and provides audit trial for traceability. Expert systems may be developed in-house, or purchased as proprietary software packages, or a mixture of both.

Regulatory issues stemming from the G20

Globalisation has meant that international collaboration becomes a central theme in the regulation process, through international protocols. These protocols are on the whole important for issues related to money laundering and the financing of terrorism; the environment; and other matters affecting economic growth. Furthermore, the seeds for the international protocols are normally the result of world leadership summits, particularly the G20. The G20 is composed of 19 countries, namely Argentina, Australia, Brazil, Canada, China, France, Germany, India, Indonesia, Italy, Japan, Mexico, Russia, Saudi Arabia, South Africa, South Korea, Turkey, United Kingdom and the United States, and the European Union being the twentieth member. The G20 is particularly important because its leaders represent the world's economic powers, and their respective populations.

In the recent past, the G20 has predominately focused on turning around the ailing world economy. Four basic issues where general consensus appears likely are related to injecting a big capital boost for the International Monetary Fund; the need to impose stricter global rules on banks and other financial actors; controlling GHG emissions; and applying further pressure on so-called tax havens. The disagreement within the G20 is likely to be more related to the approach and the extent of the regulatory measures that may be proposed.

More recently, the G20 are likely to turn their attention to four other issues, namely the reform of international organisations, further financial regulation, trade, accountability and anti-corruption.

Potential regulatory issues

Economic observers differentiate between reforms aimed at stabilising markets and those aimed at strengthening regulation. It is argued that improving market concerns requires urgent deliberation. However, regulatory reforms are more complex and require more foresight. Experts fear that political pressures may compel some leaders to try to tackle complex regulatory issues too hastily.

The Lowy Institute for International Policy (2014) highlights the role of the G20 in a number of areas: strengthening international institutions, introducing ex ante (before the event) regulatory impact statements when considering new financial regulations and trade liberalisation. Callaghan (2014, pp.7–17) from G20 Monitor (Lowy Institute for International Policy) argues that the G20 being the premier forum for international economic cooperation should focus on ensuring that the international economic institutions are effective, since this is viewed as a way of increasing global economic growth. He contends that effectiveness is attained by ensuring that the representation and governance arrangements of the institutions are appropriate and that their mandates adapt to meet the needs of an increasingly integrated global economy.

Callaghan (2014) identifies specific measures that the G20 should address regarding these international economic institutions, namely:

1   Their surveillance function;
2   Quota and governance reform;
3   Regulatory impact assessments by the Financial Stability Board (FSB);
4   Financial standard-setting bodies;
5   The tax agenda;
6   The future of the WTO;
7   International energy governance.

Callaghan (2014) contends that surveillance functions of the IMF, OECD and World Bank would be strengthened if the G20 encourage these institutions to actively participate in providing ongoing oversight of the development and implementation of growth strategies by G20 members. He posits that in particular, the G20 should ensure that the IMF is impartial in terms of access to its resources and its surveillance functions. Furthermore, measures should be implemented to improve the representation arrangements in the FSB in addition to reforming the way that the FSB, and the financial standard-setting bodies, approach their work. As an example, Callaghan (2014) cites the introduction of new international financial regulations that incorporate mandatory cost-benefit analysis, assessment of implementation difficulties, comprehensive consultation and an assessment of alternative approaches.

Joy (2014) argues that the G20 should commit to the use of ex ante regulatory impact assessments before introducing new financial regulations, along with considering the costs and benefits associated with any application of domestic financial regulation to non-domestic entities (that is, taking into account the extra-territorial impact of new regulations). He claims that neither the FSB nor the standard-setting bodies have consistently undertaken ex ante assessments of the costs and benefits of financial regulations before they have been introduced. In fact, the most commonly used assessment measure by the FSB has been public exposure of proposed standards through consultation processes.

Joy (2014) maintains that regulatory process would be improved by conducting an ex ante cost-benefit analysis as early as possible in the policy-making process and making the assessment available for public comment. He also proposes that the assessments should follow the OECD recommended approach. This includes undertaking a cost-benefit assessment that takes into account the welfare impacts of regulation, identifying the specific 'policy needs' being addressed by the regulation, considering alternative ways of meeting the policy objectives, assessing proposals including quantification of the costs, benefits, and risks wherever possible, and incorporating the analysis as part of the consultation arrangements.

These proposals are consistent with some of the recommendations on financial regulation made by the B20, which leads engagement with G20 governments on behalf of the international business community. In particular, the B20 has suggested that the G20 introduce high-level guiding principles for proposed new financial standards, including mandatory cost-benefit assessments and better approaches towards consultation.

Combating tax evasion and avoidance is viewed as a key G20 priority and the G20/OECD initiative on Base Erosion and Profit Shifting (BEPS) is an important aspect to achieve this objective. Therefore, the institutional framework for addressing international tax issues needs to be reinforced by having the mechanisms in place to directly involve developing countries in the negotiations. It is posited that global economic growth can only be attained through the liberalisation of trade. The accord reached by WTO ministers in Bali in December 2013, after 12 long years of negotiations, is seen as a resurgence of the WTO.

Oliveira (2014) argues that it is important for the G20 to strengthen the role and future of the WTO. He contends that this is particularly important in the wake of the recent stalemate in implementing the Bali Package and the consequential lowering of expectations about the prospects of concluding the Doha Round of trade talks. He notes that this stalemate is a result of actions by G20 members and that this brings into question the overall commitment to cooperation within the forum. Consequently, the next G20 summit must restore faith in the global trading system and in the future of the WTO, not only for the sake of the WTO but for the G20 itself. Oliveira (2014) suggests that the G20 members should making a definitive commitment to implement the Bali Package, defining an agenda for concluding the Doha Round, establishing a common approach to the role that the WTO can play in the global trading system in the future (particularly focused on advancing plurilateral trade agreements), and reinforcing the role of the WTO in monitoring the roll-back of protectionist measures by G20 members.

Callaghan (2014) notes that international energy governance has not kept pace with changes in the global economy and no international agency currently brings together all of the major players on an equal basis for the specific purpose of strengthening cooperation on energy. He contends that one outcome from the Brisbane Summit should be the explicit acknowledgement of the need for a global forum that focuses on global energy challenges and brings together all the major countries that will most heavily rely on global energy markets in the twenty-first century.

Conclusion

It is appropriate that this concluding chapter regarding accounting fundamentals related to financial services should focus on the regulatory provisions when dealing with investments, particularly anti-money laundering. Mandatory regulatory measures related to anti-money laundering affect every individual and enterprise. Furthermore, the anti-money laundering regulations are fairly new phenomena. Therefore they deal with contemporary regulatory issues, some of which are still under discussion, and will have a significant impact on enterprises in the future.

Globalisation has meant that international collaboration becomes a central theme in the regulation process, through international protocols. Furthermore, the seeds for the international protocols and the resulting regulatory regimes are normally the result of world leadership summits, particularly, the G20.

Basic issues where general consensus appears likely are related to injecting a big capital boost for the IMF; the need to impose stricter global rules on banks and other financial actors; and applying further pressure on so-called tax havens. The disagreement within the G20 is likely to be more related to the approach and the extent of the regulatory measures that may be proposed. Economic observers differentiate between reforms aimed at stabilising markets and those aimed at strengthening regulation. It is argued that improving market concerns requires urgent deliberation. However, regulatory reforms are more complex and require more foresight. Experts fear that political pressures may compel some leaders to try to tackle complex regulatory issues without proper deliberation.

References

Bartlett, B.L. (2002). *The Negative Effects of Money Laundering on Economic Development.* International Economics Group, Dewey Ballantine LLP, for the Asian Development Bank, Regional Technical Assistance Project No.5967, Countering Money Laundering in the Asian and Pacific Region.

Callaghan, Mike. (2014). G20 and Strengthening the International Economic Institutions. *G20 Monitor No. 13: G20 Studies Centre.* Sydney: Lowy Institute for International Policy, September.

Costa, S. (2008). *Implementing the New Anti-Money Laundering Directive in Europe: Legal and Enforcement Issues.* The Italian case. 'Paolo Baffi' Centre on Central Banking and Financial Regulation, 'Paolo Baffi' Centre Research Paper Series No. 2008–13.

Dewatripont, Mathias, Freixas, Xavier, and Portes, Richard (2009). *Macroeconomic Stability and Financial Regulation: Key Issues for the G20.* Centre for Economic Policy Research, London UK.

FATF, (2012). *International Standards on Combating Money Laundering and the Financing of Terrorism and Proliferation: FATF Recommendations.* Paris: FATF/OECD.

IAIS, (2004). *Examples of Money Laundering and Suspicious Transactions Involving Insurance.* International Association of Insurance Supervisors, October.

Joy, Martin. (2014). The G20, financial regulation, and regulatory impact assessments. *G20 Monitor No. 13: G20 Studies Centre.* Sydney: Lowy Institute for International Policy, September.

Khan, S.M. (2007). Tips for testing anti-money laundering programs. *Internal Auditor,* October, 45–48.

KPMG. (2014). *Brisbane G20 Summit: A New Agenda for Financial Services.* KPMG Global Financial Services.

McDowell, J. and Novis, G. (2001). *The Consequences of Money Laundering and Financial Crime.* Money Laundering – Economic Perspectives, May, Bureau of International Narcotics and Law Enforcement Affairs, US State Department.

Milliner, Robert. (2014). Unlocking Private Sector Led Growth and Investment. *G20 Monitor No. 9: G20 2014 – Perspectives from business, civil society, labour, think tanks and youth.* Sydney: Lowy Institute for International Policy.

Oliveira, Ivan. (2014). The Trade Agenda at the Brisbane Summit: A Crucial Moment. *G20 Monitor No. 13: G20 Studies Centre.* Sydney: Lowy Institute for International Policy, September.

Robinson, P. (2006). The risk-based approach to AML: an opportunity not to be missed. *Money Laundering Bulletin,* July/August, 1–3.

Sartip, A. (2008). Auditing the integrity of AML programs. *Internal Auditor,* February, 55–58.

Shepherd, K.L. (2009). Guardians at the gate: the gatekeeper initiative and the risk-based approach for transaction lawyers. *Real Property, Trust and Estate Law Journal,* 43, 606–671.

Wilkes, Karen L. and Lemmo, Kaitlin. (2012). *Guide to U.S. Anti-Money Laundering Requirements,* 5th edn. Protiviti.

INDEX